POSTMISSIONARY MESSIANIC JUDAISM

POSTMISSIONARY MESSIANIC JUDAISM

Redefining Christian Engagement with the Jewish People

MARK S. KINZER

Brazos Press

Grand Rapids, Michigan

Published by Brazos Press
a division of Baker Publishing Group
P.O. Box 6287, Grand Rapids, MI 49516-6287
www.brazospress.com

Printed in the United States of America

Library of Congress Cataloging-in-Publication Data

Kinzer, Mark.
    Postmissionary Messianic Judaism : redefining Christian engagement with the Jewish people
/ Mark S. Kinzer.
        p.   cm.
    Includes bibliographical references and index.
    ISBN 1-58743-152-1 (pbk.)
    1. Bible. N.T.—Criticism, interpretation, etc. 2. Israel (Christian theology)—Biblical teaching.
3. Election (Theology)—Biblical teaching. I. Title.
BS2417.J4K56 2005
289.9—dc22   2005012190

To the Memory of Haskell Stone
Mentor, Critic, Friend

"One does not live by bread alone,
but by every word that proceeds
from the mouth of God."
Deuteronomy 8:3; Matthew 4:4

Contents

PREFACE

In 1999 I wrote a short monograph entitled *The Nature of Messianic Judaism: Judaism as Genus, Messianic as Species*.[1] This extended essay, directed to the Messianic Jewish world, presented for the first time the bilateral ecclesiology that is central to the present volume. Published in the spring of 2000, *The Nature of Messianic Judaism* was introduced and discussed that summer at the theology forum of the national conference of the Union of Messianic Jewish Congregations (UMJC). Three responses to the book appeared in the Winter 2001 issue of *Kesher*, a journal published by the UMJC, followed by my reply in the Summer 2001 issue.[2]

The character of the discussion stimulated by the *The Nature of Messianic Judaism* convinced me that the book should be expanded and revised so as to be accessible to a wider audience. I completed this revision in the spring of 2003. The new book was still short and was still directed primarily to the Messianic Jewish world. However, an interested outside reader could now make better sense of its terminology and reasoning.

I sent a copy of the revised monograph to Douglas Harink, who encouraged me to pass it on to Rodney Clapp at Brazos Press. Rodney liked the book and wanted to publish it. However, he questioned whether it could attract a broad readership. Pondering his input, and considering the message I wanted to convey,

---

1. Mark Kinzer, *The Nature of Messianic Judaism* (West Hartford, CT: Hashivenu Archives, 2000).
2. "On Mark Kinzer's *The Nature of Messianic Judaism: Judaism as Genus, Messianic as Species*—A Response by Derek Leman, A Response by Jamie Cowen, A Response by Michael Rudolph and Ralph Finley," *Kesher*, no. 12 (Winter 2001): 98–127; Mark S. Kinzer, "On *The Nature of Messianic Judaism: Judaism as Genus, Messianic as Species*—Replying to My Respondents," *Kesher*, no. 13 (Summer 2001): 36–67.

I decided that I should write a completely new book, directed entirely to the Christian world. The new volume would retain much of the material found in *The Nature of Messianic Judaism*, but it would also include argumentation and conclusions suitable to a different audience. I began working on the new book in the spring of 2004, and at the end of December sent *Postmissionary Messianic Judaism* to Brazos Press.

Even more than most, this book is the product of a community discussion. The ideas it contains emerged from conversation with many friends and colleagues in the Messianic Jewish movement. Special thanks go to the members of the board of *Hashivenu*—Robert and Susan Chenoweth, Stuart Dauermann, Richard Nichol, Ellen Quarry, Paul Saal, and Michael Schiffman. I am also grateful to the members of the theology committee of the Union of Messianic Jewish Congregations, especially Daniel Juster, who has been a dedicated pioneer both institutionally and theologically. Of course, the book would be mere theory without the efforts of all the members of Congregation Zera Avraham in Ann Arbor, Michigan, to embody its vision in a living, dynamic community.

I would have never written this book were it not for the enthusiastic support of Douglas Harink and Rodney Clapp. Doug and Rodney also joined Mark Nanos, Daniel Keating, David Rudolph, and Carl Kinbar in reading and critiquing the first draft of the manuscript. I am deeply grateful for their wise and erudite comments, which have made this a far better book than it otherwise would have been. Whatever imperfections remain are to be laid at my door and not theirs.

Finally, I must express thanks to my family for patiently enduring my obsessive preoccupation with this book throughout the period of its composition and production. Above all, I am forever in debt to my beloved wife, whose kindness, humanity, and sense of humor give me the confidence and courage to think new thoughts and dream new dreams.

I dedicate this book to the memory of my first mentor, Haskell Stone, whose creative and incisive intelligence were rivaled only by his passionate devotion to the Jewish people and the Jewish Messiah. I know that he would have rejoiced with me at the publication of this book—and we would have both taken enormous pleasure in arguing its contents! That debate will now have to wait till I join him (God willing) in the heavenly academy.

INTRODUCTION

Religious etiquette in the mainline Christian churches—as in the Jewish world—prescribes that Messianic Judaism is not a suitable topic for serious conversation. This is as true for theologians and clergy as for those in the pews. Most presume that Christianity and Judaism are two separate religions, historically related but now independent and self-contained. Therefore, Messianic Judaism—the attempt of Jewish Yeshua-believers to sustain their Jewish identity and religious expression as intrinsic to and required by their faith in Yeshua[1]—can only be a syncretistic system that disrespects two great religious traditions.

If, instead of entering the Presbyterian or Methodist sanctuary, one crosses the street and visits the local Pentecostal or Baptist congregation, one discovers that Messianic Judaism is no longer a forbidden subject. Some will likely voice critical or wary opinions, but religious etiquette does not prohibit the view that Messianic Jews are (or can be) good "Christians" who are merely pioneering new methods of Jewish evangelism.[2]

As a Messianic Jewish leader, I address this book as a challenge to both the foes and friends of our movement. Mainline and evangelical Christians will likely find my thesis equally unsettling. I run the risk of provoking the one

1. This is an informal definition of Messianic Judaism that has the advantage of encompassing most of those who would identify themselves as participants within it. For reasons to be explained later in this introduction, I will refer to Jesus by his Hebrew name, Yeshua.

2. There are a few in both the mainline and evangelical churches who support Messianic Judaism because their reading of the New Testament has convinced them that Jewish Yeshua-believers should maintain their covenantal responsibilities as Jews. Messianic Jews are sincerely grateful for such visionary friends.

group and alienating the other. But I am convinced that the potential gain is worth the risk.

Postmissionary Messianic Judaism and Non-Supersessionist Ecclesiology

Despite its title, this is not mainly a book about Messianic Judaism. Instead, it is a book about the *ekklesia*—the community of those who believe in Yeshua the Messiah—and its relationship to the Jewish people. It is a book about supersessionism and the ecclesiological implications of its repudiation. Supersessionism teaches that the ekklesia replaces the Jewish people as the elect community in covenant with God, in whom the divine presence resides and through whom the divine purpose is realized in the world.[3] According to this traditional Christian view, the church is the new and spiritual Israel, fulfilling the role formerly occupied by "carnal" Israel. In the decades since the Holocaust, many Christians have repudiated this teaching. However, it would appear that few have learned to read the New Testament in a non-supersessionist manner. Even fewer seem to have considered the ecclesiological implications of their new stance.

Christian communal identity is founded on two critical convictions: (1) the mediation of Yeshua in all of God's creative, revelatory, reconciling, and redemptive activity, and (2) the church's participation through Yeshua in Israel's covenantal privileges. These two convictions are embodied in the church's twofold biblical canon. They constitute nonnegotiable beliefs located at the core of the church's existence. Nevertheless, the repudiation of supersessionism raises serious questions about these two convictions. If the Jewish people remain in covenant with God, with their own distinct calling and way of life intact despite their apparent communal rejection of Yeshua's divine mediation, how can the church convincingly hold either of these two critical convictions?

3. R. Kendall Soulen in *The God of Israel and Christian Theology* (Minneapolis: Fortress, 1996) distinguishes three types of supersessionism: (1) *punitive supersessionism* ("God abrogates God's covenant with Israel . . . on account of Israel's rejection of Christ"), p. 30; (2) *economic supersessionism* (as in punitive supersessionism, "everything that characterized the economy of salvation in its Israelite form becomes obsolete and is replaced by its ecclesial equivalent"; however, in contrast to punitive supersessionism, "Israel is transient not because it happens to be sinful but because Israel's essential role in the economy of redemption is to prepare for salvation in its spiritual and universal form"), p. 29; and (3) *structural supersessionism* (the deepest level of supersessionism, this form entails a way of construing the underlying narrative of Christian doctrine such that "God's history with Israel plays a role that is ultimately indecisive for shaping the . . . narrative's overarching plot"), p. 32. Soulen contends that many Christians have renounced economic and punitive supersessionism but have not yet grappled with the implications this must have for their overall theological framework.

It is difficult to squeeze these two convictions into a non-supersessionist ecclesiological framework. To alter the metaphor slightly, the church's two central convictions and the repudiation of supersessionism are like three puzzle pieces that do not fit together. In this book I contend that a fourth piece is required in order to complete the puzzle: a postmissionary form of Messianic Judaism. This is why I assert that this book is not mainly about Messianic Judaism. While I *am* arguing for the legitimacy and importance of Messianic Judaism, my thesis is that the church's own identity—and not just the identity of Messianic Jews—is at stake in the discussion.

In a later chapter I will recount the history of the Messianic Jewish movement and its origins in late nineteenth- and early twentieth-century Hebrew Christianity.[4] This movement displays enormous diversity. Most of those who would call themselves Messianic Jews participate in Messianic Jewish congregations, but one also finds them in the church world. Many Messianic Jews seek to observe the laws of the Torah (i.e., the Pentateuch), whereas others treat these laws as national customs that are valuable but optional. What do all those who call themselves Messianic Jews have in common? *All Messianic Jews believe that Yeshua of Nazareth is Israel's Messiah, and that faith in Yeshua establishes rather than undermines their Jewish identity.* However, no consensus exists as to what this "faith in Yeshua" means for their relationship to the church, or what this "Jewish identity" means for their relationship to the Jewish community and tradition.

In the present volume I am arguing for a particular form of Messianic Judaism that I call *postmissionary*. What do I mean by this term? The word "missionary" evokes negative reactions from many at the beginning of the twenty-first century. It is often associated with a colonial mentality, a condescending patriarchal orientation that evades the challenges inherent in any authentic encounter with the "other." However valid such concerns may be, this book is not an attack on the missionary endeavor in general and in every context. Instead, my argument that Messianic Judaism should assume a postmissionary form focuses on the specific and unique relationship between Yeshua (and his ekklesia), the Jewish people, and the Jewish way of life.

I employ the term *postmissionary* to capture at least three aspects of the type of Messianic Judaism that is needed for the emergence of an integrated, faithful, non-supersessionist ecclesiology. First, *postmissionary Messianic Judaism summons Messianic Jews to live an observant Jewish life as an act of covenant fidelity rather than missionary expediency.* In the early twentieth century Leopold Cohn, founder of the American Board of Missions to the Jews, was unconventional

4. See chapter 8.

among Hebrew Christian missionaries in his continued commitment to Jewish practice. According to his son, however, his motive for this commitment was purely evangelistic:

> He followed the method introduced by Paul, 'To the Jew I became as a Jew'. Pork he would not touch, and it was not allowed at any time in our home. . . . The Mosaic law was adhered to. . . . The reason for my father's dietetic asceticism was not that he felt himself under the law of Moses, but that by this method he was able to win Jews to Christ who could not have been won otherwise.[5]

A century later, some missionary-minded Messianic Jews approach Jewish practice in much the same way. If they could be convinced that Messianic Judaism was an ineffective evangelistic strategy, they would set it aside and search for something more effective. This is the type of Messianic Judaism which Jewish theologian Michael Wyschogrod chastises:

> What I find painful are messianic Jewish congregations which adopt Jewish symbols and practices to attract Jews but are not committed in principle to Torah observance. These groups use Jewish symbols and practices to make the transition of Jews to gentile Christianity easier. Their aim is Jewish integration into a Christianity that does not demand sustained Jewish Torah observance indefinitely.[6]

Postmissionary Messianic Jews agree with Wyschogrod. Their congregations are "committed in principle to Torah observance" and "demand [it] . . . indefinitely." The motivation is covenant fidelity, not missionary expediency.[7]

Second, *postmissionary Messianic Judaism embraces the Jewish people and its religious tradition, and discovers God and Messiah in the midst of Israel.* Messianic Jews with this orientation discern the hidden sanctifying reality of Yeshua already residing at the center of Jewish life and religious tradition. They understand their inner mission as the call to be a visible sign of this hidden messianic presence. Postmissionary Messianic Judaism does bear witness, but not to a reality external to Jewish communal life. It testifies to a reality already internal to Jewish life, existing independent of its witness, but manifested and

---

5. Dan Cohn-Sherbok, *Messianic Judaism* (New York: Cassell, 2000), 40–41.

6. Michael Wyschogrod, "Response to the Respondents," *Modern Theology* 11:2 (April 1995): 237.

7. This does not mean that pragmatic concerns play no role in determining the shape of postmissionary Messianic Jewish observance. All Jews take such concerns seriously in the ordering of their religious practice. It also does not mean that postmissionary Messianic Jews lack an appreciation for the practical benefits of Jewish observance. My point here deals solely with what is considered by practitioners to be the most important reason for adopting such practice.

confirmed through its witness. It believes that the mysterious messianic reality at the heart of Israel's life will one day be acknowledged by the community as a whole, and that this acknowledgement—set within the context of a national movement of revived fidelity to the ancestral covenant—will prepare the way for the final redemption. Because it discovers God and Yeshua within the Jewish people and its tradition, postmissionary Messianic Judaism feels at home in the Jewish world.

In contrast, many other Messianic Jews treat *postbiblical* Jewish history, customs, and institutions with wariness or even disdain. They see even devout Jews who do not believe in Yeshua as lacking a life-giving relationship with God; only by accepting Yeshua as Israel's Messiah can Jews draw near to God and experience God's saving power. These Messianic Jews never truly feel at home in the Jewish world, for they consider it a domain bereft of Yeshua's sanctifying presence.

Third, *postmissionary Messianic Judaism serves the (Gentile) Christian church by linking it to the physical descendants of Abraham, Isaac, and Jacob, thereby confirming its identity as a multinational extension of the people of Israel.*[8] While postmissionary Messianic Judaism's inner mission consists of bearing witness to Yeshua's presence within the Jewish people, its outer mission directs it to the church, before whom it testifies to God's enduring love for the family chosen in the beginning to be God's covenant partner. The church thereby participates in Israel's riches without displacing Israel. In the process the church setting can become a second home—a "home away from home"—for Messianic Jews.

In contrast, many Messianic Jews find their primary home in the Christian church—the only setting where they recognize the presence of Yeshua. They feel away from home when among the Jewish people who do not accept Yeshua. Therefore, their outer mission is to bring Jews to faith in Yeshua, so that the Jewish people can also become home. Whereas postmissionary Messianic Jews seek to represent the Jewish people to the church, Messianic Jews with a missionary focus make their primary concern representing the church's concerns and beliefs to the Jewish community. A missionary-oriented Messianic Judaism has been a significant obstacle in the relationship between the church and the Jewish people. Postmissionary Messianic Judaism can serve as the missing link that binds the church and the Jewish people, so that the Christian church

---

8. "If through Christianity hundreds of millions of people have entered into relationship with the God of Israel, Christianity must be, in some important sense, an extension of Judaism. . . . The God of Israel is not separable from the people of Israel. It follows that to be in relationship with the God of Israel is to be in relationship with the people of Israel." Richard John Neuhaus, "Salvation is from the Jews," in *Jews and Christians,* ed. Carl E. Braaten and Robert W. Jenson (Grand Rapids: Eerdmans, 2003), 68.

becomes a multinational extension of the Jewish people and its messianically renewed covenantal relationship with God.[9]

In summary, the form of Messianic Judaism required for an integrated, faithful, non-supersessionist ecclesiology is postmissionary in three senses: (1) it treats Jewish observance as a matter of covenant fidelity rather than missionary expediency; (2) it is at home in the Jewish world, and its inner mission consists of bearing witness to Yeshua's continued presence among his people; (3) its outer mission consists of linking the church of the nations to Israel, so that the church can become a multinational extension of Israel and its messianically renewed covenantal relationship with God. The third aspect of its postmissionary character is dependent on the first two. Messianic Judaism can perform its necessary ecclesiological role only if it is an embodiment of Jewish covenant fidelity at home in the Jewish world. The church of the nations can become an extension of Israel only if its Messianic Jewish partner is deeply rooted in Jewish soil.

Postmissionary Messianic Judaism is the missing piece that completes the puzzle. With such a piece in place, the Christian church can affirm Yeshua's universal mediation in a non-supersessionist manner, since its postmissionary Messianic Jewish partner enables it to recognize Yeshua's mysterious presence throughout Jewish history. Israel's covenant endures, the church draws nourishment from its Jewish root, yet Yeshua remains the Messiah and Lord for both Jews and Gentiles. The Christian church can now affirm its own identity as an extension of Israel in a non-supersessionist manner, since its connection to the Jewish heritage has become a concrete sociological reality rather than a spiritual abstraction. Postmissionary Messianic Judaism bears witness to the enduring importance of the Jewish people and its way of life for the identity of the Christian church, and likewise bears witness to the enduring importance of Yeshua's mediation for the identity of the Jewish people.

Mentors and Friends

I wrote this book quickly, easily, happily, passionately. At times the book seemed to write itself. Once I was seated with my laptop computer, a cup of

---

9. As noted above, the Messianic Jewish movement is very diverse. I do not mean to suggest in this introduction that the movement as a whole can be divided into two distinct parties, the missionaries and the postmissionaries. Instead, my intention is to describe clearly what I mean by postmissionary Messianic Judaism and to contrast it with some forms of Messianic Judaism that take a markedly different approach. Upon reading this section, it is possible that many Messianic Jews will not identify completely with either of the approaches I have described.

tea at my side, hours passed without notice. I eagerly looked forward to those hours, and ended each session with reluctance.

From another perspective, I have been laboring painfully over this book for fifty-three years. The vision expressed here has matured slowly through the twists and turns of my own personal history. *Postmissionary Messianic Judaism* sums up that history in theological form.

Readers might therefore gain insight into the book by learning something about the experiences that engendered it. Those experiences were all personal encounters, relationships with extraordinary human beings that left an indelible mark on my perception of the world. It is fitting to begin with my grandfather, of blessed memory, an eminent Talmudic authority who made his way from Austria-Hungary to Detroit early in the twentieth century. For a short time he lived with my immediate family, taking over my parents' bedroom, which was next to my own. He would rise at 4:00 A.M. or earlier, and the exotic tone of his Talmudic chant would waft through the thin wall and deprive me of sleep. He was a kindly man, gentle and generous, but he was utterly absorbed in a spiritual and intellectual world that I understood as poorly as the Yiddish he spoke.

My father adored and revered him. He did his best to honor the things my grandfather cherished, but he was not cut out to be a scholar. Instead, he employed his own gifts—which were political and practical—in the service of our small neighborhood Conservative synagogue. Like his father before him, he faithfully attended daily prayer services at the synagogue. This expressed his simple yet deep-seated faith, his loyalty to the Jewish people and tradition, and his commitment to congregational life. He served multiple terms as synagogue president and oversaw the construction of two different facilities in two different decades. He also emulated his father's generosity and kindness in personal relationships. Though an attorney, my father never made a great deal of money, as he preferred poor clients to wealthy ones and charged neither at the level his services deserved. This frustrated my mother no end, but he was constitutionally incapable of acting in any other way.

The examples of my grandfather and father made an impression, but they could not compete with the youth culture of the 1960s. The rich Jewish world they inhabited made no sense to me. The liturgical calendar I observed followed the seasonal rhythm of American athletics, and my weekend "worship" usually took place at a rock concert. My sacred texts were works of fiction, philosophy, psychology, and history—all reflecting the radical tastes of that peculiar era. Eventually, my countercultural journey brought me to faith in Yeshua the Messiah—and, ironically, back to the Judaism of my father and grandfather.

I have dedicated this book to the man who taught me that Yeshua-faith summons Jews to wholehearted solidarity with their people and tradition—my first mentor, Haskell Stone, of blessed memory. Haskell had been raised in an orthodox Jewish home in Detroit in the 1930s, and as a young man he had fallen in love with Yeshua. He participated in the Hebrew Christian movement of the 1950s and 60s and attended Fuller Theological Seminary in Pasadena. His study and experience led him to the conclusion that Jewish believers in Yeshua should not become members of Christian churches or serve in Christian organizations, but should make their home fully within the Jewish world. He criticized Jewish missions and mission culture, saying that Jews should not make their living representing the Gentile church to the Jewish people. His hero from the Hebrew Christian past was Isak Lichtenstein—the late nineteenth-century Hungarian rabbi who, while believing in Yeshua, refused to be baptized so he could continue to participate in the Jewish community and be buried in a Jewish cemetery.

I first met Haskell in the summer of 1971, within a week or two of my initial acceptance of Yeshua as the Messiah. He did not waste any time but addressed me bluntly and unequivocally: "You are a Jew. Your faith in Yeshua should strengthen rather than weaken your awareness of that fact. Do not join a Christian church, but live as a Jew, and marry a Jewish girl." The force of his personality, intellect, and way of life intensified the impact of these words. I sensed in his presence and his home the Jewish erudition, piety, and passion that my grandfather possessed, but translated into a language I could now understand and integrated with a keen devotion to Yeshua the Messiah. He became my respected mentor and trusted friend and likewise won the admiration and affection of my father. He presided at my wedding, and my father presided at his graveside funeral.

Upon returning to my undergraduate studies at the University of Michigan, I decided to join an ecumenical charismatic community that was then gaining international attention. One of the reasons I was attracted to this group was that its ecumenical composition meant that I could comply with Haskell's advice—I could participate fully without joining a church! At the same time, I was brought into close contact with people from both mainline and evangelical Christianity. The founders of the community were, in fact, Catholic charismatics, and, while the community was 35 percent Protestant, it was nevertheless a major center for the worldwide Catholic charismatic renewal.

My second mentor, Stephen Clark, was one of the community's two founders. His father was Jewish, but Steve had been raised without any religious affiliation. As a college student at Yale he converted to Roman Catholicism. He began his doctoral studies in philosophy at Notre Dame but left grad school before completing his dissertation in order to devote himself to "apostolic service." In the late 1960s he and his friends at Notre Dame, influenced by Pentecostalism, came to experience God in a new way. Together they pioneered a spiritual renewal movement—ecumenical in inspiration and effect—that has had a profound impact on the Catholic church throughout the world.

While Haskell insisted that I find my home in the Jewish world and alerted me to the history of Christian anti-Judaism, Steve—a true ecumenist—helped me to appreciate the riches of the Christian tradition as a whole, in all its diverse forms. He helped me to take a positive attitude toward the Christian churches, to see the distinctive gifts that each has received. He enabled me to escape from a narrow and naïve sectarian viewpoint and to perceive the necessary cultural component in every faith tradition.

At the same time, Steve actively encouraged me to pursue my way as a Jew. He esteemed rabbinic thought and introduced me to *Pirke Avot*, a tractate of the Mishnah that gathers the wise sayings of the sages of the early rabbinic period. He supported my decision in 1975 to begin attending Sabbath services at the local Conservative synagogue. He guided me through a year of study in 1977–78, at the conclusion of which I resolved to begin observing the Sabbath, the Jewish dietary laws, and the daily customs of Jewish prayer. With Steve's assistance, I came to see the importance of the Jewish tradition for the ecumenical healing of the entire "people of God."

It was at the local Conservative synagogue that I met my third mentor—Rabbi Allan Kensky. After attending several services, I asked to meet with the young rabbi, who was only a few years older than I. Sitting in his synagogue office, I informed him that I was a Messianic Jew and asked him if he objected to my coming to services. I assured him that I was there only to worship with other Jews and to grow in my Judaism, and had no evangelistic intentions. Rabbi Kensky warmly invited me to continue in my attendance, though he said that I could not become an official member of the congregation. He then asked if I would like to study regularly with him. Just as I had assured him that I had no intentions of attempting to persuade my fellow-worshipers that Yeshua was the Messiah, so he assured me that his purpose was not to dissuade me from my messianic convictions. He only wanted me to see the beauty of Judaism, and to love it.

I gladly took him up on his offer, and we began meeting to study *Genesis Rabbah*—one of the classic texts of rabbinic midrash (i.e., imaginative biblical commentary). In those sessions in Rabbi Kensky's home, I came to understand the delight Jews through the centuries have taken in the text of the Torah. I also came to see how Jewish study involves a communal conversation with the great commentators through the centuries. Rabbi Kensky would run his finger beneath the minute Hebrew print in the margins of those huge pages of text and would translate for me the insights of eminent scholars of the past. In this way he became a window for me into the Jewish exegetical tradition. He also welcomed my comments on parallels I saw between the rabbinic midrash and the New Testament, saying that he viewed the New Testament as itself an insightful midrash. As a result of Rabbi Kensky's patience, wisdom, and vast knowledge, our study accomplished its stated aim: I now knew the beauty of Judaism, and had come to love it.

Rabbi Kensky's success in my case was due not only to those study sessions in his home. It also derived from his skill as a worship leader in the synagogue. Beth Israel Congregation was small at the time and had no paid cantor. (It is larger today, but it still has no paid cantor!) Its rabbi was expected to do a creditable job of leading the worship service—a task not usually imposed upon rabbis. Rabbi Kensky went far beyond the minimum standard required of him. He had an attractive voice, and the congregation participated actively in the service, singing heartily. He prayed with evident intensity—with what Jewish tradition calls *kavannah*—and his spirit was contagious. Under his leadership, I found the weekly services to be more than exercises in formal worship; they were for me times of authentic encounter with the God of Israel.

In 1991 I began a new stage of my journey, enrolling in a doctoral program in biblical studies at the University of Michigan. I studied under two fine European scholars, Jarl Fossum and Gabriele Boccaccini, who practiced different historical methodologies yet shared the view that the early Yeshua movement was a thoroughly Jewish phenomenon that could only be understood in Jewish terms. In my years with them I learned how to read ancient Jewish texts—including the New Testament—as a historian and exegete.

Haskell Stone connected me to the best of the Hebrew Christian past. Stephen Clark connected me to the riches of the Christian churches. Rabbi Allan Kensky connected me to the wealth of the rabbinic tradition. Jarl Fossum and Gabriele Boccaccini connected me to the world of modern scholarship and to the critical study of ancient Jewish texts. All that remained was immersion in the Messianic Jewish movement. In 1993 my wife, Roslyn, and I, along with a small group of friends, founded a Messianic Jewish congregation in Ann Arbor. In that same year we attended the annual conference of the Union of Messianic Jewish Congregations (UMJC) and initiated the process that led to our congregation's joining the Union in 1996. In the years since, we have developed many friendships with other congregational leaders in the UMJC that have refined my thinking and helped me to synthesize the wisdom of my own past. This book is the fruit of that synthesis.

Terminology and Preview

In arguing that ecclesiology demands authentic engagement with the Jewish people and its religious tradition, I am urging that we rethink our presuppositions regarding the relationship between Christianity and Judaism, the church and Israel, Christians and Jews. The terms themselves express an underlying conceptual framework that envisions two separate religions, two separate communities practicing the two separate religions, and the members of those two separate communities. It is time to challenge the notion that Christianity and Judaism are two separate religions.[10] We should heed the advice offered by Karl Barth a half-century ago: "The Church must live with the Synagogue, not, as fools say in their hearts, as with another religion or confession, but as the root from which it has itself sprung."[11] Some Christian thinkers are beginning to catch up with Barth. Thus, Richard John Neuhaus writes, "It is misleading, I believe, to speak of two peoples of God, or of two covenants, never mind to speak of two religions."[12] In reality, we are dealing with one people and one religion, but it is

10. In his recent volume, *Border Lines: The Partition of Judaeo-Christianity* (Philadelphia: University of Pennsylvania Press, 2004), Daniel Boyarin argues that Christianity invented the category of religion, in part to clearly distinguish itself from the Jewish people and Judaism. While Christianity defined itself and Judaism as two rival religions, the Judaism that emerged from the Babylonian Talmud does not separate faith from "ethnicity, nationality, language, and shared history" (8). Boyarin contends that "the difference between Christianity and Judaism is not so much a difference between two religions as a difference between a religion and an entity that refuses to be one" (8; see also 214–20, 224–25). (Boyarin views early "Judeo-Christianity" as a seamless network of communities that was gradually carved into two rival blocks by Christian and rabbinic authorities. The invention of the category of religion was one of the tools used to do the carving.) In this book I will speak about the Jewish people as a religious community embodying a religious tradition. By the use of these terms I am not implying that Judaism is merely a religion, but instead recognizing that the beliefs and practices that we commonly associate with religion have shaped Jewish identity and communal life through the centuries.

11. Karl Barth, *Church Dogmatics* IV.3 (New York: T&T Clark, 1962), 878. Barth here uses the term *Synagogue* to refer to the Jewish people as an organized community with a distinct religious tradition. The term so used is problematic for many reasons and will not be employed in this sense in the current volume.

12. Neuhaus, "Salvation is from the Jews," 68. Robert W. Jenson writes in similar fashion: "The Church can regard neither the religion of old Israel nor Judaism as an 'other religion'; and that holds even if Judaism cannot return the recognition." "Toward a Christian Theology of Israel," *Pro Ecclesia* 9, no. 1 (Winter 2000): 43.

a people and a religion that is inherently twofold in nature. Sadly, what should have been an enriching differentiation became a bitter schism.

Because the terms themselves imply mutual exclusivity, in this book I will not use the words *Christianity, Christians,* and *church* in a conventional manner. I will employ them only to refer to the developed institutional reality that became overwhelmingly Gentile in composition and character.[13] In speaking of realities that should be conceived of as integrally bound to Judaism and the Jewish people, or even as situated within those spheres, I will speak of *Yeshua-faith* (rather than Christianity), *Yeshua-believers* (rather than Christians), and the ekklesia (rather than the church). These terms may detract from the literary quality of the text, but they are necessary to the book's thesis and the demonstration of that thesis.

The one known in the church as Jesus Christ will here be referred to as *Yeshua the Messiah.* As a matter of historical record, all scholars today recognize that the first-century figure Yeshua of Nazareth was a Jew. However, very few of those who believe that he was raised from the dead acknowledge that he remains a Jew today and will do so forever, or consider the implications of this fact. By using an alien, Jewish-sounding name to refer to the one who is so familiar to the church, I hope to suggest that Yeshua is still at home with those who are literally his family, and that the church must reckon with the subtle ways it has lost touch with its own identity as a messianic, multinational extension of the Jewish people.

In accordance with common usage, I will employ the term *Gentile* to refer to all non-Jews—including non-Jewish Christians. This usage conforms not only to scholarly norms and contemporary custom but also to the New Testament itself. Both Paul and the author of Acts speak of non-Jewish Yeshua-believers as Gentiles (and not merely as those "from the Gentiles").[14] At the same time, Paul and other New Testament authors occasionally use Gentile to mean "non-Jewish idolater," and in such contexts the non-Jewish Yeshua-believers are treated as former Gentiles.[15] It is crucial to recognize that the non-Jewish members of the ekklesia are not "goyim" in the pejorative sense of the word, but share in Israel's blessings and worship Israel's God. Nevertheless, Paul and his colleagues continue referring to these non-Jewish Yeshua-believers as Gentiles. In the new

13. "Christianity" here thus means Gentile Christianity as Boyarin defines the term: "I employ *Gentile Christianity* in a sort of subtechnical sense to refer to Christian converts from among non-Jews (and their descendants) who have neither a sense of genealogical attachment to the historical, physical people of Israel (Israel according to the flesh), nor an attachment (and frequently the exact opposite of one) to the fleshly practices of that historical community." *Border Lines*, 29.

14. See Romans 1:13; 9:30; 11:13–14; 15:9; 15:15–16; 15:25–27; Galatians 2:11–12; Ephesians 3:1; Acts 10:45–46; 11:1; 11:18; 14:27; 21:25.

15. 1 Corinthians 12:2; 1 Thessalonians 4:3–5; Ephesians 4:17; 1 Peter 2:12.

eschatological setting created by Yeshua's resurrection and Israel's multinational extension, the term loses its negative connotations of idolatry and alienation from the people of the covenant. The term can even take on a positive meaning, since it implies a relationship between the nations of the world and Israel, the elect community.[16]

The argument of *Postmissionary Messianic Judaism* proceeds in the following manner. Chapter 1, "Ecclesiology and Biblical Interpretation," prepares the ground for the exegetical conclusions reached in the subsequent chapters. Acknowledging that definitive interpretations rarely result from exegesis, I here argue that a variety of historical factors should incline the reader to accept my exegetical conclusions, so long as these conclusions are as plausible as rival readings of the text.

Chapter 2, "The New Testament and Jewish Practice," examines the major New Testament texts that bear upon the continuing validity of Jewish practice (i.e., circumcision, dietary restrictions, Sabbath and holiday observance) after the coming of Yeshua. Contrary to what is usually assumed, I conclude that the New Testament—read canonically and theologically—teaches that all Jews (including Yeshua-believers) are not only permitted but are obligated to follow basic Jewish practice.

Chapter 3, "The New Testament and the Jewish People," examines the major New Testament texts that bear upon the continuing validity of God's covenant with the Jewish people. I conclude that the New Testament—again read canonically and theologically—teaches that God's covenant with the Jewish people remains intact. As in previous eras, many of the leaders of Israel refuse to accept the divine messengers sent to them, and the community invites divine judgment. Nevertheless, God's love forever rests upon the Jewish people, sanctifying its life and in the end accomplishing its redemption.

Chapter 4, "Bilateral Ecclesiology in Solidarity With Israel," asserts that the conclusions of chapters 2 and 3 could only be lived viably in an ekklesia that consists of two distinct but united corporate bodies—a Jewish and a Gentile ekklesia. The Jewish ekklesia would live as part of the wider Jewish community, and the Gentile ekklesia would express its solidarity with the Jewish people through its loving bond with the Jewish ekklesia. I test this hypothesis by look-

16. Paraphrasing Karl Barth's theology of Israel and the nations, R. Kendall Soulen portrays Gentile identity as positive rather than negative, even though the term itself is defined in negative terms (i.e., non-Jew): "Creaturely identity as such does not imply actual participation in covenant history. In principle, God could have created the world without summoning it into covenant history (*CD* IV.1, 9). In contrast, the term *Gentile* implies actual participation in covenant history because it conceives of (non-Jewish) humanity within the horizon of Israel's particular election." Soulen, *God of Israel*, 88.

ing at New Testament ecclesiological practice and teaching and conclude that the biblical evidence supports such an ecclesiological model.

Chapter 5, "The Christian No to Israel—Christian Supersessionism and Jewish Practice," looks at the ascendancy of the Gentile ekklesia and the way its supersessionist convictions expressed themselves in the prohibition of Jewish practice for Jewish Yeshua-believers. Whereas Jewish practice was previously seen as normative, now it was considered mortal sin. Thus, a schism ruptured the messianic ekklesia and helped to produce the wider rupture between the ekklesia and the Jewish people as a whole. While this schism damages the church, it does not invalidate its vocation or tradition.

Chapter 6, "Jewish Tradition and the Christological Test," turns attention to the Jewish side of the schism. While the New Testament treats first-century Jewish leadership as culpable for its response to Yeshua, it also sees God's providential intervention at work in this response. Once the church had prohibited Jewish practice—as it did at a very early stage—the Jewish no to Yeshua actually expressed its yes to God and God's covenant. In this way the Jewish no to Yeshua paradoxically shared in Yeshua's own yes to God. I conclude that the risen Yeshua dwells in a hidden fashion among his own flesh-and-blood brothers and sisters and that the schism with the church, while damaging the Jewish people, does not invalidate its vocation or tradition.

Chapter 7, "Jewish Tradition and the Biblical Test," looks at rabbinic tradition from a biblical perspective. I argue that the Pentateuch confirms the need for both an oral tradition of legal interpretation and an institutional framework in which that tradition can be developed and practically applied. I argue further that later rabbinic tradition is compatible with—though not identical to—the teaching of the New Testament. This chapter supports the results of the previous chapter, affirming the value and importance of Jewish religious tradition in the post-Yeshua era.

Chapter 8, "From Missionary to Postmissionary Messianic Judaism," studies the emergence of Hebrew Christianity in the nineteenth century and Hebrew Catholicism and Messianic Judaism in the twentieth century, assessing them in relation to the conclusions reached in the previous seven chapters. Those conclusions are summarized as entailing a *bilateral ecclesiology in solidarity with Israel that affirms Israel's covenant, Torah, and religious tradition.* In this chapter we see how Hebrew Christianity and Messianic Judaism were missionary movements with a missionary orientation, nevertheless affirming principles that could eventually transform them into a postmissionary reality serving a bilateral ecclesiology in solidarity with Israel.

Chapter 9, "Healing the Schism," concludes the book by offering recommendations for how Christians can facilitate the healing of the schism.

As this chapter summary indicates, I am covering an enormous amount of territory in a relatively compact volume. As a result, I am unable to engage the full range of scholarship available on each biblical text and theological proposition. I will mainly cite authorities whose work supports my own. I do not seek to answer all possible objections or discuss every alternative theory. Instead, I intend to present a constructive proposal that covers the data and addresses the crucial questions, and does so in a creative, responsible, economical, and practically useful manner.

As stated above, a postmissionary Messianic Judaism finds its home in the wider Jewish world. In keeping with this orientation, I would have preferred to address this book to the Jewish community—explaining the new form of Messianic Judaism that is gradually emerging, and providing reasons for why we deserve a place within Jewish communal life. However, upon consideration I determined that the Jewish community needs to hear something else first: it needs to hear postmissionary Messianic Jews addressing the church and fulfilling the obligation they own to be theirs—of representing and defending the Jewish people and the Jewish tradition before the multinational ekklesia. The Jewish community needs to know that what postmissionary Messianic Jews say to them is borne out by what they say and do in their relationship with the Christian church.

Thus, while I have written this volume for Christians, I hope that many of my Jewish brothers and sisters will be listening in on the conversation. Of course, as a Messianic Jew I interpret Jewish history and tradition in ways that will sometimes differ from standard Jewish perspectives. Nevertheless, I take my stance as an advocate rather than a critic of my people and its tradition. Postmissionary Messianic Judaism may be written off as hopelessly quixotic, but its sincere solidarity with the Jewish people should not be doubted. Those who read this book—be they Jew or Gentile—can judge for themselves whether this solidarity is founded on mere wish fulfillment or on a previously unrecognized New Testament mandate.

In a sense this book is an apologia, addressed to Christians, for a particular form of Messianic Judaism. However, it is far more than that. It is an apologia for the Jewish people as a whole and for Judaism as an ongoing religious tradition. Moreover, it is an argument that the church's understanding of its own identity stands or falls on how it responds to this apologia. If the ekklesia is truly the earthly body—or part of the earthly body—of a resurrected Jew, it needs finally to come to terms with the people and tradition to which that Jew belongs. This book is intended to help the ekklesia realize and meet that need.

1

ECCLESIOLOGY AND
BIBLICAL INTERPRETATION

In the course of this book I will present a particular proposal for how to construe New Testament teaching concerning the Jewish people, the Jewish way of life, and the ekklesia, and how to apply that teaching to our circumstances in the twenty-first century. Since this proposal entails a substantial revision of traditional ecclesiology, I will need to offer persuasive arguments in its favor. In my estimation, the proposal has a sound exegetical basis. At the same time, I recognize that the exegetical arguments offered in support of my thesis—like all exegetical arguments—have their limits. Other reasonable interpretations exist. So why accept my proposal?

In this chapter I will present several nontextual factors that add considerable weight to my proposed reading of the New Testament and contemporary application of its teaching. Unless we attend to these factors at the outset, the argument contained in the chapters that follow may seem less compelling than it actually is.

Irreducible Ambiguity

Charles Cosgrove introduces his book *Elusive Israel* with the question: "What ought Christians do when faced with conflicting reasonable interpretations of scripture?" He then amplifies this question by explaining why it is so challenging, especially in the Protestant world:

> At the dawn of the historical-grammatical (philological) approach to biblical interpretation, there was optimism that adherence to the plain grammatical sense could deliver interpretation from interminable debate over the true meaning of the text. . . . One assumed that the true meaning of the text was the meaning originally intended by the author, and that this was the only valid meaning of the text as the church's scripture. Hence each new effort to clarify the original historical meaning of a difficult passage involved an at least implicit claim to represent the one, correct meaning of the text for the church. . . . But competing historical demonstrations of that meaning always existed. . . . This is not to deny that we have made progress in our historical understanding of the Bible. . . . But those advances include not only historical clarification of what the various biblical writings (and traditions) originally meant but also mounting evidence that many questions of exegesis cannot be historically resolved, because the texts themselves are irreducibly ambiguous.[1]

That biblical texts are "irreducibly ambiguous" does not mean that every interpretation of those texts has equal validity. Cosgrove thinks that biblical scholarship can "establish the limited range of interpretations" that the "text warrants."[2] Thus, certain readings can be ruled out. But no one reading may be enthroned as the definitive "meaning originally intended by the author."

If this is true for individual texts, how much more so is it the case with attempts at summarizing biblical teaching as a whole. Of course, those who treat the Bible as a mere collection of ancient near-eastern writings have no expectation that this collection will speak with one voice on any particular matter. But those who honor the Bible as a sacred text and treat its books as canonical expect—in the midst of its rich diversity—to find an underlying common vision. However, competing principles of coherence are often available and are sometimes equally plausible.

In deciding which principle of coherence deserves our allegiance, it is appropriate to give respectful consideration to ecclesial traditions of interpretation. Just as scripture was written, edited, collected, and canonized in the context of a community and its tradition, so it should be read and interpreted in such a context. The message contained in the sacred text should not be divorced from the sacred reality lived by the community that carries that text. At the same time, we cannot become so wedded to ecclesial traditions of interpretation that we

1. Charles H. Cosgrove, *Elusive Israel* (Louisville: Westminster John Knox, 1997), xi–xii.
2. Ibid., xii.

lose the capacity to hear God speak through scripture in a way that corrects, refines, and purifies those traditions.

These interpretive issues come to a head when we study New Testament teaching about the Jewish people and the Torah. The tensions within the New Testament on this topic are so severe that even Richard Hays—a scholar who regards the Bible as sacred and authoritative—thinks that no unifying vision can be discerned. Instead, he thinks that we are forced to choose between contrary voices:

> The issue of the relation between church and Israel brings sharply into focus a crucial issue of *method* in New Testament ethics: How do we deal with the diversity of the New Testament witnesses in a case where different texts stand fundamentally in tension with one another? . . . In the case of the church-Israel question, we find texts that take radically divergent paths. . . . Simple harmonization is impossible.[3]

> Given the variety of incompatible positions within the New Testament canon, I believe that we are forced in this case to make a clear choice among the possible options offered us. No thoroughgoing synthesis is possible.[4]

While I sympathize with Hays's despair at finding a coherent New Testament teaching on the "church-Israel question," I do not share it. Hays finds irresolvable tension only because he rejects supersessionism and anti-Judaism (and rightly finds a basis for doing so in the text), and at the same time accepts traditional Christian ways of reading Matthew, Luke, and John and their views on Judaism and the Jewish people. In this case, rather than providing a helpful principle of coherence, the interpretive tradition that Hays embraces leads him to deny that such a principle exists!

Is it not possible that in this case the interpretive tradition itself needs correction, refinement, and purification? If so, how can we hear the voice of scripture speak coherently to us in a way that differs from what the community of faith has heard before? Careful and insightful scholarly exegesis plays an essential role in such a process. But if the text is often "irreducibly ambiguous," then exegesis alone is insufficient for the task.

My contention in this chapter is that there are several crucial historical factors that must be considered before we even begin our detailed exegetical work. These factors can help us navigate as we interpret the New Testament texts dealing with

3. Richard B. Hays, *The Moral Vision of the New Testament* (San Francisco: HarperSanFrancisco, 1996), 408–9.
4. Ibid., 430.

the Jewish people and the ekklesia. While not predetermining our exegetical results, they will dispose us to go in certain directions, helping us discern our way when we face more than one plausible construal of the texts.

Sociology and History: The Identity of the Reading Community

All contemporary discussions of hermeneutics recognize the important role of a reader's social location in the interpretive process. Our communal identities and loyalties shape the expectations and the conceptual frameworks that we bring to any text. This is especially the case when the reader's community views itself as sacred and when that community regards the text as likewise sacred. The importance of the reader's social location reaches its apogee when the subject matter of the sacred text deals directly with the identity of that sacred community. This is the case when Christians study what the New Testament has to say about the church and the Jewish people.

As we noted above, reading the Bible in an ecclesial context is an essential part of receiving the text as authoritative scripture. The faith lived within the community provides a necessary interpretive key for understanding the text that witnesses to that faith. At the same time, defects in the community's life can also obstruct faithful reading of the text. For example, divisions among Christian churches make it difficult for Christians to understand the New Testament teaching about the unity of the ekklesia.

Most contemporary Christian readers of the New Testament practice a religion, Christianity, that they (and others generally) see as distinct from another religion, Judaism. They participate in church communities that consciously distinguish themselves from the Jewish community—and the Jewish community likewise consciously distinguishes itself from them. These church communities may include a small percentage of Jews, but these Jews are seen as converts to Christianity. Though some of them may continue to call themselves Jews, they no longer identify with the Jewish community and its tradition, and their children are unlikely even to use the name as an ethnic self-designation. They and their children are now "Christians of Jewish descent."

Christian readers in twenty-first century America may have Jewish neighbors or co-workers. Given the high rate of intermarriage, they may have family members who are married to Jews. They may have a high opinion of these Jews, and they may have great respect for the Jewish people as an ethnic community and for Judaism as a religious tradition. They may view Judaism as a sister-religion or even as the mother of Christianity. Nevertheless, they likely bring to their reading of the New Testament a clear conceptual framework in which Jew and

Christian, Judaism and Christianity, and the Jewish people and the church are mutually exclusive categories.

Reading the New Testament from this social location, many contemporary Christians are disposed to view Peter, Paul, and James in the way they view the Jews in their churches—as Jewish converts to Christianity, as Christians of Jewish descent. Their Jesus is the founder of a new religion, Christianity, and the basic division among human beings is Christian and non-Christian rather than Jew and non-Jew (Gentile). The latter distinction has now been nullified "for all who are in Christ Jesus." The law of Moses has significance only as a prophetic preparation for the coming of the Savior; it no longer serves as Israel's divinely authorized constitution. Whether or not these perspectives are grounded in the text, many contemporary Christian readers will be disposed by their social location to find them there.

In principle biblical scholars reject this way of viewing the New Testament. There is broad consensus that Peter, Paul, and James all saw themselves as disciples of the Jewish Messiah, not as the pioneers of a new religion. Most now concede that first-century Judaism was exceedingly diverse and that the early Yeshua-believers existed as a movement within that diverse Jewish world. Yet it is still common to use the terms "Christian" and "Christianity" when commenting on New Testament passages. Along with these terms comes the unspoken assumption that Christianity—while still in a sense a Jewish movement—had already broken away from the rest of the Jewish community when the New Testament documents were written. Warren Carter finds fault with Amy-Jill Levine's reading of Matthew because she employs this terminology and accepts the assumptions associated with it:

> Levine reveals this guiding assumption, that Christians and Jews were irrevocably separated from each other, in her comment that Christians "fought their battle for self-definition in the same neighborhood as the synagogue." She spends much energy establishing (rightly) that the terms "Jew," "Jewish," and "Judaism" are very difficult to define for this period. But equally problematic is the term "Christian," which she employs several times through this section without definition. Obviously, Matthew does not use the term "Christian" as a self-designation, and one should be careful about assuming or imposing it. In its absence, the Matthean community and its Gospel can be regarded, at least in a first-century context, as a (largely) Jewish group within the breadth of diverse, vibrant, first-century Judaism. It is not unfair to claim that such a historical location is by far the dominant view in contemporary Matthean scholarship.[5]

5. Warren Carter, "Response to Amy-Jill Levine," in *Anti-Judaism and the Gospels,* ed. William R. Farmer (Harrisburg, PA: Trinity Press International, 1999), 52.

While many scholars see Paul, Matthew, and even Luke as authors writing within a movement that is still in some sense identifiably Jewish, they nevertheless—like Levine—tend to employ the anachronistic terms "Christian" and "Christianity." Few scholars follow the approach articulated by John Gager:

> I will rigorously avoid the term *Christianity* when speaking of Jesus, his early followers and Paul. Instead I will employ the term *Jesus-movement*. . . . Behind this shift of terms, from Christian to Jesus-movement, lies a much broader contention, namely, that there was no Christianity at all until well after the time of Jesus, his earliest followers, and Paul. . . . To use the term Christian is anachronistic and misleading. The argument here is simple and convincing: the fact that his followers proclaimed Jesus the Messiah . . . does not place them outside the pale of Judaism. They become Christians only when they begin to view themselves, and are viewed by others, as standing outside, above, or even against Judaism.[6]

With these terms come mental associations, derived from the social location of contemporary Jews and Christians, that predispose readers to draw certain interpretive conclusions from the text.

My point here is not to argue about academic terminology. Instead, I see the consistent use of the terms "Christian" and "Christianity" by New Testament scholars to be symptomatic of the real problem: the challenge posed by our social location in Jewish and Christian communities whose identity has been defined over against one another for at least 1700 years. For those raised as Jews and Christians, who study, teach, serve, and worship in separate Jewish and Christian institutions, it takes a formidable act of historical imagination to consistently read the New Testament as a Jewish book. Therefore, if we are determined to read the text in this way, we must consciously labor to expose and reconsider ecclesiological assumptions that have shaped the entire history of interpretation. These must be reckoned with at the outset, before looking at particular texts. As with the other factors examined in this chapter, the issue of social location affects our judgment of where the burden of proof lies in dealing with conflicting interpretations that on purely exegetical grounds may be equally plausible.

6. John G. Gager, *Reinventing Paul* (Oxford: Oxford University Press, 2000), viii. The word *Christian* is found three times in the New Testament (Acts 11:26; 26:28; 1 Peter 4:16), but it does not become a common self-designation for Yeshua-believers until the second century, at which point it serves to distinguish Yeshua-believers from both pagans and members of the Jewish community. As Judith Lieu astutely notes, "The New Testament, notoriously, is far more sparing with the term than most of those who teach or write about it." *Neither Jew Nor Greek?* (London: T&T Clark, 2002), 226.

Ethics and History: "Hermeneutics of Ethical Accountability"

The first factor considered above dealt with the social location of biblical authors and readers. The insights that informed the discussion derived from the work of biblical scholars who examine the New Testament from a social historical perspective. Our second factor looks not at the history of the composition or canonization of the New Testament but at the history of its use. The perspective from which we will look at this history is not descriptive and academic but normative and ethical.

Those who treat the Bible as sacred and canonical believe that God speaks in and through the biblical text. Such a viewpoint presumes that we are dealing both with human authors and human intentionality and with a divine author and divine intentionality. To determine the divine intention, we must study these texts in a way that takes seriously their human authorship and intentionality. However, we must also allow for the possibility that the divine intention for the text may transcend the limited understanding of those who composed and edited it.

When attempting to determine what God desires to say through the Bible, we seek to understand individual texts in light of the overarching narrative that the Bible tells. That narrative speaks of a God who enters into a covenant with a people (Israel), delivers them from bondage, and gives them a way of life that manifests this God's character. The *theoretical* truths that the Bible conveys about this God are thus inextricably bound to the *practical* precepts whose purpose is to form the character of God in the people of God.

This has hermeneutical and theological implications that too few Christians recognize. If theoretical statements about God and God's purpose are true, then sincere commitment to the truths those statements affirm should support the practical expression of the divine character in the community that asserts those truths. In other words, we must not only employ abstract and theoretical criteria for evaluating theological claims; we must also have recourse to practical or functional criteria for determining theological truth.

Jewish theologians provide an example here worthy of imitation. The traditional Jewish focus on character and conduct leads most Jewish theologians to ascribe great weight to practical criteria in the assessing of theological claims. Eugene Borowitz states this explicitly:

> With Judaism centering itself on Torah, the classic criterion of the Jewish authenticity of beliefs was functional, not intellectual. That approach still commends itself. . . . To gauge the Jewishness of a new theological idea, then, we can inquire:

How would affirming this notion likely affect the behavior of the individual Jew and that of the community?[7]

David Novak advocates a similar approach:

> In deciding among theological views, one should be something of a consequential-ist: the choice of one theological position over another should be, if not actually determined, at least heavily conditioned by the fact that it implies a better ethi-cal outcome than the alternatives. By "ethics" I mean what the Jewish tradition teaches is to be done in relationships between humans. I derive this rule linking theology and ethics from the talmudic dialectic between the theoretical and the practical. All the questions discussed in the Talmud and related rabbinic litera-ture are normative questions: either they are questions of what one is to think or what one is to do. Every prescribed thought has some practical implication; every prescribed act has some theoretical implication.[8]

The inextricable bond between the theoretical and practical realms is fundamen-tal to Jewish thought. Recognition of this methodological insight has profound implications for the topic of this book.

Charles Cosgrove attempts to give a distinctive New Testament cast to this methodological approach. He begins by arguing that "canonical interpretation" of scripture implies that the "use" of scripture affects its interpretation:

> Canonical interpretation begins from the premise that scripture forms a literary-theological integrity in which different parts of the canon exist in a relationship of co-determination: one part affects the meaning of another part. But there is a further aspect of canon as genre. As Charles Wood observes, "A canon is a canon only in use." This suggests that the use or purpose of scripture ought to bear on the interpretation of scripture.[9]

Cosgrove then looks to the teaching of Yeshua for a formulation of the proper "use" or "purpose" of scripture. He finds in Matthew's version of the two great commandments—which concludes with the words, "On these two command-ments hang all the law and the prophets" (Matthew 22:40)—such a formulation. According to Cosgrove, this Matthean conclusion implies that Yeshua sees these two commandments as a guide for interpreting scripture as a whole.[10] Moreover,

7. Eugene B. Borowitz, *Renewing the Covenant* (Philadelphia: Jewish Publication Society, 1991), 57–58.

8. David Novak, "Arguing Israel and the Holocaust," *First Things* 109 (January 2001): 12–13.

9. Cosgrove, *Elusive Israel*, 42.

10. This was also the view of Augustine: "So what all that has been said amounts to . . . is that the fulfillment and the end of the law and of all the divine scriptures is love (Rom 13:8; 1 Tm 1:5). . . .

the second of the two great commandments—"You shall love your neighbor as yourself"—carries "hermeneutical priority" over the first:

> The fact that Jesus . . . goes on to add a second commandment suggests that the first commandment cannot function hermeneutically without the second. Moreover, in Matthew 7:12, Jesus says, "In everything do to others as you would have them do to you; for this is the law and the prophets." This suggests that the second commandment *can* stand on its own as a summary of scripture. While the first commandment may be greater in the hierarchy of obligations, the second commandment appears to include the first and to carry hermeneutical priority. The commandment to love one's neighbor gives decisive guidance for understanding the commandment to love God. For those who would be loyal to God in all things, including the interpretation of scripture, the second great commandment is the primary criterion for the adjudication of scripture.[11]

Yeshua thus provides an ethical criterion for the interpretation of scripture.

Cosgrove then applies this hermeneutical principle to the interpretation of Paul's teaching concerning Israel, which is the topic of his book. He examines Romans 9–11 and delineates the plausible interpretive options available to the exegete. Some of those options result in a negative or at least supersessionist portrayal of the Jewish people. Others yield a more hopeful picture. Applying the hermeneutical principle of the second commandment to this topic, he finds good grounds for affirming the latter rather than the former:

> These interpretive judgments, configured together, provide a basis in the canonical Paul for a more respectful and thus a more humane Christian attitude toward Jews and Judaism. In adjudicating the question of Israel in the canonical Romans, I opt to affirm this cluster of exegetical judgments. Among the various plausible interpretive possibilities, they form a synthetic construal that promotes the purpose of scripture, which requires making and keeping the church's life humane toward its Jewish neighbors.[12]

Cosgrove takes the "history of Christian anti-Semitism" as evidence for "moral reasons" to "opt to affirm" one "among the various plausible interpretive possibilities" in the reading of Romans 9–11.

So if it seems to you that you have understood the divine scriptures, or any part of them, in such a way that by this understanding you do not build up this twin love of God and neighbor, then you have not yet understood them." *Teaching Christianity,* trans. Edmund Hill, O.P. (Hyde Park, NY: New City, 1996), 123–24. I thank Daniel Keating for pointing out this patristic precedent for Cosgrove's ethical hermeneutics.

11. Ibid., 44.
12. Ibid., 74.

Cosgrove could have strengthened his case by stating explicitly that the alternative readings of Paul have been integral parts of the traditional Christian supersessionist theology of Israel and the church. These readings have been instrumental in cultivating a climate in which anti-Judaism and anti-Semitism thrived. If Christians believe that anti-Judaism and anti-Semitism are incompatible with the character of God, then they must question the theological assertions that have given these attitudes and actions such powerful impetus. Furthermore, when Christians seek to take responsibility for the sins of their forbears, they must also take responsibility for the interpretive judgments that made these sins possible.

Cosgrove applies this ethical criterion of theological truth to the writings of Paul. In the sordid history of Christian anti-Judaism, the use of other New Testament books has been even more problematic. Perhaps the most troubling book has been the Gospel of John. This Gospel consistently refers to the enemies of Yeshua as "the Jews." From context it is evident that this term in John generally means "the Jewish authorities." However, Christians have usually read it as referring literally to the Jewish people as a whole (minus Yeshua and his followers, who were "de-Judaized"). Thus, when Yeshua says to "the Jews," "You are of your father the devil, and your will is to do your father's desires" (John 8:44), many Christians understood this to mean that the Jewish people as a whole were the devil's children. This special connection between the Jewish people and Satan became a standard motif in the medieval imagination.

David Rensberger approaches the study of John in a manner that resembles Cosgrove's study of Paul.

> The recognition of historical realities, whatever they may be, is essential to exegesis, but historical exegesis alone cannot meet the responsibilities of those who interpret the Bible in this or any other age. . . . The gap between critical exegesis and theological and ethical interpretation, let alone the translation of these into responsible Christian preaching and teaching, is well known. . . . With regard to the Gospel of John and anti-Judaism, both Kelber and R. Alan Culpepper rightly assert that recognizing John's historical context without recognizing the later effect that John has had on Christian anti-Judaism and anti-Semitism cannot meet these contemporary needs. Culpepper proposes a "hermeneutics of ethical accountability," leading to interpretation that is both faithful to the text and ethically responsible, including a responsibility to those who have suffered as a result of oppressive elements in biblical texts. Not only theological and historical but also ethical concerns must inform interpretation.[13]

---

13. David Rensberger, "Anti-Judaism and the Gospel of John," in Farmer, *Anti-Judaism and the Gospels*, 137–38.

Like Cosgrove, Rensberger sees that "ethical interpretation" of the Bible must supplement "critical exegesis." Cosgrove's use of canonical interpretation situates this ethical criterion within the scope of the biblical text itself and thus provides a theological depth to "ethical interpretation" that is lacking in Rensberger (who finds "oppressive elements in biblical texts" themselves and not simply in their misuse). However, Rensberger adds a crucial element that Cosgrove glosses over too quickly: the need to give explicit attention to how Christian biblical interpretation has historically contributed to violent and oppressive conduct, and to acknowledge a special responsibility to those who have suffered as a result of such conduct. The Christian theologian and biblical scholar discharge this responsibility, not through breast-beating and reiterated apologies, but through practicing their craft in a way that takes account of and compensates for past wrongs.

A classic illustration of how this can be done is found in the Catholic Church's official treatment of Matthew 27:25. In this verse Matthew reports that a crowd of Jews ("all the people") gathered before Pilate and demanded that Barabbas be released and Yeshua executed, saying, "His blood be upon us and on our children." This verse permits a number of possible interpretations. Most past Christian commentators saw this crowd as representing the Jewish people as a whole, and as uttering an effective self-imposed curse that explained—and justi-fied—the history of Jewish exile and suffering. This verse was thus the linchpin in charging the Jewish people as a whole with the crime of "deicide"—the murder of God. Such an interpretation of Matthew 27:25 cannot be definitively refuted on exegetical grounds alone. However, other equally plausible readings exist. The verse could be understood to refer merely to the Jews of Jerusalem, and "our children" could be taken to mean only one generation, the generation that experienced the Roman destruction of Jerusalem in 70 CE. Or the crowd could be seen as intending a more global self-imprecation, but that intent could be seen as nullified by God's mercy. Or the words of the crowd could be seen not as an effective self-imposed curse but instead as a mere "formula for ratifying a judicial sentence" (see below).

This last reading of Matthew 27:25 is found in the *Catechism of the Catholic Church* in a section under the heading "Jews are not collectively responsible for Jesus' death" (597):

> The historical complexity of Jesus' trial is apparent in the Gospel accounts. The personal sin of the participants (Judas, the Sanhedrin, Pilate) is known to God alone. Hence we cannot lay responsibility for the trial on the Jews in Jerusalem as a whole, despite the outcry of a manipulated crowd and the global reproaches contained in the apostles' calls to conversion after Pentecost. Jesus himself, in

forgiving them on the cross, and Peter in following suit, both accept "the ignorance" of the Jews of Jerusalem and even of their leaders. Still less can we extend
responsibility to other Jews of different times and places, based merely on the
crowd's cry: "His blood be on us and on our children!" a formula for ratifying a
judicial sentence.[14]

The Catechism places this verse within a broader canonical context that includes
Yeshua's words of forgiveness on the cross. In the previous two units (595–596)
the Catechism emphasized that Jewish leaders were divided in their response
to Yeshua, with many showing him favor. The broader canonical context thus
justifies the rejection of the deicide charge.

The Catholic Catechism offers a coherent and plausible reading of the New
Testament teaching about Jewish responsibility for the death of Yeshua. However, what motivates this reading, and what makes it so persuasive to its late
twentieth- and early twenty-first-century audience, is not just the fact that it is
exegetically superior to the traditional interpretation. Living after the Holocaust,
we know more vividly than in any previous generation what the traditional
interpretation of Matthew 27:25 can lead to. Therefore, we know on ethical
grounds that it must be false.

Theology and History: Divine Action in Human History

We have now considered two nontextual factors that should influence our
interpretation of the biblical text: the difference in social location between
the New Testament authors and later readers, and the ethical consequences
of adopting certain theological positions and biblical interpretations. Both of
these factors involve historical analysis—from either a sociological or an ethical perspective. Our third nontextual factor involves a third way of analyzing
history: from an explicitly theological perspective.

The God revealed in the biblical witness is the Lord of history. According
to scripture, this God entered into a covenant with Abraham, Isaac, and Jacob;
delivered their descendants from bondage in Egypt; gave them the Torah at
Sinai; and led them into the land of promise. The God to whom scripture bears
witness chose David, David's progeny, and David's city; judged Israel and the
Davidic dynasty through foreign nations and sent them into exile in Babylon;
and restored a remnant of these exiles to their land and city. According to the
New Testament, this God is also the Father of Messiah Yeshua, David's heir,

---

14. *Catechism of the Catholic Church* (New York: Image, 1995), 168–69.

who was raised from the dead to be the firstfruits and instrumental agent of the final redemption. The God of Israel is thus revealed in history, through history, and for history.

The historical narrative embodied in scripture has a unique revelatory status. Nevertheless, its validity is called into question if the Lord of history to which it bears witness withdraws from history when that narrative ends. Wolfhart Pannenberg's argument is to the point:

> How can Christians talk of the God of Israel who acts in history if they are not ready to see God at work in their own history and also, like the OT prophets, in international history? It is hardly justifiable to speak in general terms about the global rule of the God of the Bible if the application of this thought to the concrete experience of history is at the same time said to be going too far. . . . In such matters we are as little protected against mistakes as in other spheres in which we form judgments, and we shall see the final meaning of the ways of God in history only in the light of the eschatological consummation of creation. Nevertheless, if we do not speak at all about the concrete acts of God in history in preservation and judgment, then it should be no surprise that people have a weaker sense of the reality of God in general.[15]

Paul van Buren takes a similar stance:

> If we dare to trust that God's hand is to be detected in Jesus Christ and so in the beginnings of our [i.e., Gentile Christians'] being in the Way, then we must dare also to trust that He has had much to do with the history which has come since. Certainly other hands, sometimes all too painfully evident, have also been at work in that history, but that is the price that God was willing to pay for calling actual people into cooperating with Him in completing His creation. It is a risky business to see history as the location of God's work, and both the Jewish people and the church have been hurt by false readings of its signs. Yet to reject this risk is to close ourselves to any living relationship to the God of this world. If God is a living God, then we must accept the risk of living with Him and under Him, *hic et nunc.*[16]

Both Pannenberg and van Buren recognize the dangers inherent in attempting to decipher "the signs of the times." Yet they argue persuasively that the cost of ignoring these signs and the potential benefits of recognizing them outweigh the risks of error.

---

15. Wolfhart Pannenberg, *Systematic Theology,* vol. 3 (Grand Rapids: Eerdmans, 1998), 497–98.

16. Paul M. van Buren, *A Theology of the Jewish-Christian Reality,* vol. 1, *Discerning the Way* (San Francisco: Harper & Row, 1980), 65.

Attention to God's action in history has played a pivotal role in Jewish thinking about Yeshua and the church. Maimonides, Yehuda Halevi, and Franz Rosenzweig all sought to give some account for the rise of Christianity as a historical force and its impact in spreading essential Jewish teaching to the nations of the earth.[17] They were impelled by theological convictions well stated by Fritz Rothschild:

> Judaism is a religion that finds God's revelation and manifestations in history as it unfolds from creation to its messianic fulfillment. . . . To assume that the transformation of the Greco-Roman world into Christendom . . . was a mere accident, and not part of God's redemptive plan, is difficult to believe for Jews who take history seriously as the arena in which God and man are engaged in the achievement of ultimate redemption.[18]

This willingness to "take history seriously" derives from a willingness to take scripture seriously. Though the historical narrative of scripture has a unique and determinative function in guiding our understanding of God and God's purposes, the God who spoke and acted in ancient times has not retired but is still in the business of speaking and acting in and through history. Traditional Jewish thinkers have recognized this fact and have based their views of Christianity on it. A Christian appraisal of Judaism should do the same.

Theological reflection on the events of history has special relevance to the topic of ecclesiology. The object of ecclesiological study is the community that is in covenant with God. The ekklesia is more than a natural human community making its way through history, but it is not less or other than such a body! Certainly, its founding events and the vision of its founding figures are crucial for understanding its character, structure, and purpose. But these events and this vision, and the canonical texts that describe them, do not present a complete or comprehensive picture of the community's character, structure, and purpose. For the full picture, one must study the canonical text in light of the living and breathing community itself, as it has developed on its historical journey.

We should be clear on what we are looking for in our theological reflection on the history of the covenant community. There are Jewish and Christian thinkers who suggest that some of the events of the past nineteen centuries—and especially of the last century—have a revelatory status comparable to the revelatory

---

17. See David Novak, *Jewish-Christian Dialogue* (Oxford: Oxford University Press, 1989). A readiness to see God's hand at work in Christian history is also found in many twentieth-century Jewish thinkers such as Will Herberg, Abraham Joshua Heschel, and Irving Greenberg.

18. Fritz A. Rothschild, "General Introduction," in *Jewish Perspectives on Christianity*, ed. Fritz A. Rothschild (New York: Continuum, 1996), 6–7.

events recorded in scripture. Thus, Irving Greenberg states that "the Holocaust and the rebirth of the State of Israel as revelatory events in Judaism are the key to a new relationship [between Judaism and Christianity]."[19] Paul van Buren, a friend of Greenberg, is more tentative, but he nevertheless shows his openness to the possibility that Greenberg is right:

> The pattern of revelation which shaped the Scriptures and the church's beginning has once again reasserted itself. Events in Jewish history, perhaps the most staggering and unexpected events in its history since the church split off from the Jewish people, have worked a reorientation in the mind of many responsible Christians which has led to that new interpretation of the tradition of which we have spoken. If there follows eventually a reorientation of the community of the church, then it will be appropriate to speak of these events as revelatory.[20]

This way of looking at history and revelation fails to acknowledge the unique position of the central revelatory events recounted in the biblical narrative. It thereby threatens to relativize these central events and make them subject to forms of reinterpretation that distort rather than enrich their meaning.

In arguing for the need to reflect theologically on the history of the covenant community, I am not suggesting that we should be looking to that history for fresh revelation. Instead, I am proposing that God's actions in history may offer us guidance as we seek to interpret canonical texts that are at times "irreducibly ambiguous." If the God who is acting in history is the same God who inspired and speaks through the biblical text, then the merit of this proposal should be self-evident. Rather than endorsing the views of Greenberg and van Buren, I would affirm instead the more modest approach of Robert Louis Wilken:

> Interpretation has always been a matter of relating what is said in one part of the Bible to what one finds in other parts of the Bible, and relating that in turn to the faith of the community that lives out of the Bible, the Church. The Bible is not primarily a book from the past. . . . What any given passage or book meant in its original setting is not the goal of interpretation. The historical task is only one aspect of the work of exegesis, and not the most important. It is introductory, propaedeutic, and must be completed by relating the text to the rest of the Bible, to the Church's faith and life, and to what has taken place since the Bible was written.[21]

19. Irving Greenberg, "Judaism, Christianity, and Partnership after the Twentieth Century," in *Christianity in Jewish Terms,* ed. T. Frymer-Kensky, D. Novak, P. Ochs, D. F. Sandmel, and M. A. Signer (Boulder: Westview, 2000), 33.

20. Van Buren, *Jewish-Christian Reality,* 1:176.

21. Robert Louis Wilken, "The Jews as the Christians Saw Them," *First Things* 73 (May 1997): 32.

The point is not that "our own cultural setting" should determine the meaning of the Scripture, but that Christian engagement with the Jewish people in the twentieth century has helped us to see dimensions of the Holy Scriptures that were not apparent to earlier generations. Of course the interpretation of the Bible must be related to what we take to be the original sense, but if the interpretation is to be "organic" . . . then it must grow out of the Church's history and experience, and the experience with the Jews in the twentieth century has been unprecedented.[22]

Wilken's concern, like mine, is with interpreting and applying scripture. However, he recognizes that the process of interpretation and application involves more than historical exegesis. The goal of interpretation—or, as Cosgrove puts it, the "use" or "purpose" of scripture—can only be attained "by relating the text to the rest of the Bible, to the church's faith and life, and to what has taken place since the Bible was written."

What historical developments of the past two millennia require theological assessment if we are to properly gauge the New Testament teaching on the Jewish people, the Jewish way of life, and the church? At this point in our discussion we will simply list some of the key developments, adding only a brief commentary on them. Reflecting on this list, even without an in-depth analysis, will influence our interpretive judgments when we study the relevant biblical texts. In later chapters we will look more closely at some of these historical developments and seek to understand them in theological terms.

The first historical development that demands attention is the loss of a visible Jewish presence in the ekklesia. What began as a movement among Jews soon became a movement led by Jews but populated substantially by Gentiles, and then a movement led and populated by Gentiles. Few biblical scholars or theologians even note, much less reckon with, the significance of this development. Paul van Buren is among those few:

> Staggering and unexpected events have occurred since the Apostolic Writings. Not least of these is the historical fact that the early church of Jews and Gentiles soon became an overwhelmingly Gentile enterprise.[23]

Peter von der Osten-Sacken is another:

> For the apostle [Paul], therefore, a purely gentile church, existing for itself and out of itself, without a Jewish Christian section, would quite simply be not conceivable, let alone theologically tenable.[24]

22. Robert Louis Wilken, "Correspondence," *First Things* 76 (October 1997): 6.
23. Van Buren, *Jewish-Christian Reality,* 1:128.
24. Peter von der Osten-Sacken, *Christian-Jewish Dialogue* (Philadelphia: Fortress, 1986), 108.

When the ekklesia contained a visible Jewish nucleus, its right to claim continuity with Israel was reasonable and not necessarily supersessionist. When that nucleus disappeared, the claim to direct continuity *with* Israel became spiritual and abstract, and easily morphed into a claim to be a replacement *for* Israel.

The second historical development that demands attention is the survival and flourishing of the Jewish people and Judaism. If the first development ran contrary to the expectations of the Jewish founders of the apostolic community, then this development ran contrary to the expectations of their Gentile heirs. Gentile Christians of the second and third centuries made their own theological reading of the "signs of the times" and drew conclusions that turned out to be erroneous. Wilken points this out and notes its significance.

> The destruction of the city of Jerusalem in A.D. 70, the end of temple worship and the demise of the priesthood, the subjugation of the Land of Israel to the Romans, all of which seemed permanent, led Christians to think that the Jewish way of life had been replaced by Christianity and that the Jews would no longer continue to exist as a distinct people. . . . To the outsider it appeared that the Jewish way of life was in decline and destined for extinction. . . .
>
> Contrary to the expectations of Christians in antiquity, the Jewish way of life did not come to an end, and today, two thousand years after the coming of Christ, there exist Jewish communities that observe the ancient laws of Moses concerning the Sabbath, circumcision, diet, Passover, etc., in much the same way they were observed before the beginning of Christianity. Recognition of this historical *and* spiritual fact sets us apart from earlier generations of Christians.[25]

By the time of Augustine it was clear that the Jewish people were not departing from the historical stage. Thus Augustine offered a theological explanation of their survival, asserting that they must continue to exist as a witness to God's judgment on sin. This explanation carried weight as long as one could view Jewish life as weak, impoverished, and spiritually bankrupt. However, it loses credibility once the depth, richness, and enduring vitality of Jewish life become inescapably evident. As van Buren notes,

> It is a matter of historical fact . . . that the Christians saw the prospering of the Gentile church as the work of God, but not the prospering of the Jewish people. The question which confronts us now is whether we shall continue to see the one and not the other and thus continue to give our traditional answer that the church has displaced the people of Israel as God's people and we alone

---

25. Wilken, "The Jews as the Christians Saw Them," 28–29.

are those whose manner of walking is the only one in which God's Way can be walked.[26]

> What is clearly revealed to the mind of the church in the events of modern Jewish history is obviously the continued existence of God's people. The people of God's covenant are still here, still very much alive, and the faithful among them are still devoted to the life of that covenant. This surely implies that God continues to concern Himself with the history of His people.[27]

We cannot ignore the fact that Judaism has flourished through the centuries and continues to possess spiritual vitality in our own day. This is a historical reality that demands theological assessment.

A third historical development requiring our attention is the emergence of virulent and violent anti-Judaism in the Christian tradition. We have already noted this development in our discussion of the ethical criteria of interpretation. But here our perspective is different. We are not asking about the ethical consequences of certain ways of understanding the biblical text, but instead are inquiring into the inherent theological significance of Christians persecuting Jews for ostensibly Christian reasons. How do we explain theologically the following scenario: During holy week Christians hear the passion story read or watch it reenacted, with Jews cast as the deicidal villains. They then reenact it themselves by storming Jewish neighborhoods, destroying Jewish property, and beating and killing Jewish people. Ironically, in their participative reenactment the Christians imitate the Jerusalem mob and their Jewish victims are compelled to play the role of the suffering Messiah. Does this phenomenon say anything to us about the ongoing, mysterious relationship between the Jewish people and their unrecognized Messiah?[28]

A fourth historical development has already made its mark on Christian theology. I am speaking of the Holocaust. This event has so shaken the Christian theological world that it is often used as a fundamental chronological divider, marking off pre-Holocaust from post-Holocaust Christian theology. Christian theologians justifiably see here the ultimate outcome of Christian supersessionism and anti-Judaism that reveals the full evil of this sinful posture.[29] In this way the Holocaust underlines the importance of "the hermeneutics of ethical

---

26. Van Buren, *Jewish-Christian Reality,* 1:61.

27. Ibid., 179–80.

28. This topic will be discussed at greater length in chapter 6.

29. Of course, Nazi anti-Semitism was a racial rather than a religious ideology. Nevertheless, grassroots Nazi anti-Semitism fed on the fuel of the anti-Judaism endemic to European Christian culture.

accountability." At the same time, the Nazis did not exterminate Jews in the name of Christ or the Christian church. In fact, their hatred of Jews was linked to their hatred of all forms of traditional Christianity—and of Western civilization as a whole. Does this diabolical attack on the Jewish people, now evidently associated not with Christ but with anti-Christ, reveal something significant about the true relationship between the Jewish people, the Christian church, and Yeshua the Messiah?

A fifth historical development—one that, like the Holocaust, has already made its mark on Christian theology—is the return of the Jewish people to the land of Israel. If the destruction of Jewish Jerusalem and its temple in 70 CE had a profound impact on Christian thought, the rebuilding of Jewish Jerusalem in the twentieth century has likewise left an indelible impression. For dispensationalists and avowed Christian Zionists, the implications of this development seem clear. But even Christians of a more traditional cast of mind have been deeply affected. As stated by Wilken, a Roman Catholic historian,

> For two generations Christian theology has been engaged in a fundamental re-thinking of Christianity's relation to Judaism and to the Jewish people.... We must not forget, however, that this new movement of the Spirit was born out of Jewish suffering and of the struggles of the Jewish people. The occasion for the Church's reconsideration of her relation to the Jews was the Holocaust.... The other factor that awakened Christian thinking was the establishment of the state of Israel. For the first time since antiquity the Jews were able to reestablish Jewish life and institutions under Jewish rule in the Land of Israel. . . . Christians began to look at the Jewish people, as well as the Bible and Christian theology, with fresh eyes.[30]

Political realities in the Middle East have kept the State of Israel—and the Jewish people—at the center of world attention. While these realities have not always cast a favorable light on the Jewish people and have even alienated some Christian observers, they nonetheless confirm—for those who think theologically about history—the significance of the Jewish people in the divine purpose.

The sixth and final historical development brings us back to the first. If the loss of a visible Jewish presence in the ekklesia should strike us as significant, then the reappearance of such a presence should be even more noteworthy. The emergence of the Messianic Jewish movement in the second half of the twentieth century constitutes just such a reappearance. Remarkably, the his-

---

30. Wilken, "The Jews as the Christians Saw Them," 28.

tory of this movement parallels that of the return of the Jewish people to the land of Israel. Just as Jewish immigration to the land and thinking about a Jewish state originated in the mid-nineteenth century, so the first "Hebrew Christian" institutions took root at the same time. The shift toward a more explicitly Jewish expression within this movement coincided with the reunification of Jerusalem in 1967. The enterprise itself—seeking to resurrect a form of life that had died in the Greco-Roman era—has much in common with the effort to reforge a Jewish national existence in the land promised to Abraham, Isaac, and Jacob.

This last historical development is, of course, the subject of the present book. It is clear that our interpretation of the New Testament teaching regarding the church and the Jewish people will shape what we make of the Messianic Jewish movement. At this stage of our argument, I would propose something that is less clear, namely, that the reverse should also be true: what we make of this movement—especially in light of the other historical developments mentioned previously—should exert some influence on our interpretation of the New Testament teaching.

All of these historical developments deserve serious theological reflection. As already noted, I will say more about some of them later, after first examining the biblical texts. However, it is important to mention them at the outset, since they provide an essential twenty-first-century context for reading and interpreting the New Testament teaching dealing with the Jewish people and the church.

Conclusion

In this chapter I have argued that the biblical text contains a measure of ambiguity that cannot be eliminated simply by historical exegesis. This is especially the case when attempting a synthetic treatment of a topic, and even more the case when that topic is the Jewish people, the Jewish way of life, and the church. Therefore we need guidance in making interpretive decisions among the various plausible views propounded. In other matters, ecclesial tradition can provide some of that guidance. In this case, however, ecclesial tradition is itself part of the problem.

I have argued that decisions among competing interpretive schemes should be influenced—but not determined—by three important historical factors: (1) recognition that the social location of the authors and initial readers of the text (all part of a Jewish movement) was dramatically different from our own (boxed into mutually exclusive Jewish and Christian categories and social worlds); (2) examination of the ethical implications of each interpretive scheme, as seen in the histories of those who have adopted them; (3) reflection on the theological implications of important historical developments in the life of the Jewish people in relation to the church.

With this preparatory work completed, we can now turn our attention to the main task at hand: studying the New Testament teaching on the Jewish people, the Jewish way of life, and the church, as the basis for an ecclesiology in which the Messianic Jewish movement plays a central role.

2

THE NEW TESTAMENT
AND JEWISH PRACTICE

To emphasize the radical diversity of Jewish religious life in antiquity, Jacob Neusner speaks of multiple "Judaisms," each with its own distinctive way of defining Jewish identity, worldview, and way of life. Most historians have accepted Neusner's basic contention without adopting his terminology. Whether we speak of diverse Judaisms (plural) or diverse forms of Judaism (singular), we must eschew any notion of a single, universal, and uniform Jewish religion in the world of the first century CE.

At the same time, even Neusner recognizes some commonality among these diverse expressions of religious life—otherwise he would not be able to designate each of them as a Judaism. What did all forms of first-century Judaism have in common, so that one can justly call them Judaism(s)?

Neusner himself offers this definition of Judaism:

Judaism is a religion that has three components: (1) It takes as its Scripture the Torah revealed by God to Moses at Mount Sinai . . . ; (2) it believes that its adherents through all times and places form part of that extended family, or "Israel," the singular or holy people of whom the Pentateuch speaks; and (3) it requires "Israel" to live in accord with the teachings of the Torah.[1]

Thus, to qualify as a Judaism or a form of Judaism, a religion must have adherents whose worldview, identity, and way of life are all rooted in the Torah (i.e.,

1. Jacob Neusner, *A Short History of Judaism* (Minneapolis: Augsburg, 1992), 3.

the Pentateuch).[2] In accordance with such a definition, historians generally see Judaism as beginning with the period of Ezra, since only with Ezra do we find the Pentateuch functioning as an authoritative constitution for Jewish life.

One of the central themes of the books of Ezra and Nehemiah is Jewish distinctiveness. While Israel may have constructive relations with its neighbors (Ezra and Nehemiah are both Persian civil servants), it may not compromise its holy (i.e., separate) identity and way of life. This theme grew in importance as a result of the Maccabean crisis of the second century BCE, in which elements within the Jewish world and beyond sought to weaken or destroy Jewish distinctiveness and to facilitate full integration with the surrounding Hellenistic culture. The radical Hellenizers waged a fierce campaign against the major pillars of Jewish distinctiveness: they burned Torah scrolls (1 Maccabees 1:56–57); prohibited circumcision (1 Maccabees 1:15, 48, 60–61); and encouraged violation of the Sabbath, holiday (1 Maccabees 1:45; 2 Maccabees 6:5), and dietary laws (1 Maccabees 1:47, 62–63). As a result, the Jewish way of life rooted in the Torah became closely associated in the minds of most first-century Jews with those practices which "reinforced the sense of distinctive identity and marked Israel off most clearly from other nations."[3]

Defining the Question

Yeshua and his followers were born and reared within a Jewish world where such practices (i.e., circumcision, Sabbath and holiday observance, and dietary laws), commanded in the Torah, were presumed rather than disputed. Fierce disputes arose over *how* these commandments were to be interpreted and applied—but not over *whether* they were to be interpreted and applied. Nevertheless, according to conventional Christian readings of the New Testament, Yeshua and his followers ultimately rejected or transcended these basic Jewish practices. The purpose of this chapter is to examine this conventional assumption in order to determine if the evidence warrants it. We will find that it does not.

It is crucial that we be explicit and precise in formulating the questions we are asking—and the questions we are not asking. Many Christian thinkers approach this subject by studying the New Testament teaching about the Torah. They ask: What are the various meanings of the Greek word for Torah (*nomos*)

---

2. Speaking of first-century Judaism, James Dunn remarks that "the degree to which Torah was bound up with Jewish self-understanding and identity can hardly be over-emphasized for our period." *The Partings of the Ways* (Philadelphia: Trinity Press International, 1991), 31.

3. Ibid., 28. Dunn singles out circumcision, Sabbath, and food laws as particularly important elements of first-century Jewish practice (28–31).

in the New Testament? Is the Torah still valid in the New Covenant? What does Paul mean by "dying to the Torah" and being "free from the Torah"? What is the relationship between the Sinai covenant and the Abrahamic covenant? After answering these theological questions to their satisfaction, such interpreters then proceed to draw conclusions about the New Testament's view of Jewish practice. This procedure fits the traditional Christian priority placed on doctrine and theology, with matters of practice seen as secondary and derivative.

Our inquiry will proceed in a different way. Our basic question is this: What do the New Testament authors (and, when discernable, the sources they draw upon and the audiences they address) think about distinctive Jewish practices honored and followed by virtually all Jews of the first-century world, practices such as circumcision, Sabbath and holiday observance, and dietary restrictions? To be more specific, did these authors assume that these practices retained their validity after the coming of Yeshua? Did they expect Jewish members of the Yeshua-movement to observe these practices? If so, did they consider such observance obligatory or optional? If they considered these practices obligatory for Jews, did they consider this obligation universal and enduring, or temporary, transitional, and circumstantially contingent? We will thus begin, in traditional Jewish fashion, with questions about actual practice and its basis, and then move to questions of theological explanation.

There are other notable questions we are not asking. We are not asking about Jewish practices that were observed or observable only in Jerusalem or the temple precincts. In other words, we are not asking about the New Testament teaching regarding the temple, its sacrificial rites, and its purity requirements. While these questions are important, they are not as important as the ones we are asking. The temple and its rites affected only those Jews who were in Jerusalem. They also affected only those living while the temple was standing. On the other hand, circumcision, Sabbath and holiday observance, and dietary customs affected and affect all Jews, everywhere, at all times.[4] Inquiry concerning the status of the temple and its rites can also lead to unjustified conclusions about the more universal forms of Jewish practice. There were Jews in the first century who opposed the temple administration and boycotted its liturgy—and

---

4. The laws of ritual purity and the dietary laws should not be confused. "There are decisive differences between food and purity laws which many exegetes ignore. The inherent 'uncleanness' of forbidden meats differs in character from the transferable ritual impurity emanating from a corpse, a leprous body or bodily excretion. . . . In post-biblical times the respective laws developed into two completely separate halakhic sub-systems. Food laws . . . remained static for a long time and were accepted as basic. In contrast the laws of Levitical purity . . . expanded greatly and were the subject of continuous controversy." Peter Tomson, *Paul and the Jewish Law* (Minneapolis: Fortress, 1990), 240. See also Jonathan Klawans, *Impurity and Sin in Ancient Judaism* (Oxford: Oxford University Press, 2000), 31–32.

who nevertheless scrupulously observed the elements of Jewish practice we are examining. There also have been Jews since the first century who have thought that the temple system was temporary and transitional, while holding no such view of circumcision, Sabbath observance, etc.

We are also not asking about the controversial issue that is at the forefront of New Testament discussions of Jewish practice: Is Jewish practice incumbent upon non-Jewish Yeshua-believers? We are not asking this question because we regard its answer as obvious. The Acts of the Apostles and Paul's letter to the Galatians provide an authoritative ruling on this matter that is central to the New Testament canon. Instead, we are asking a question that is not explicitly addressed in the New Testament because its answer was at the time presumed and uncontroversial: is Jewish practice incumbent upon *Jews* (and, in particular, Jewish Yeshua-believers)? At a later time and place, with almost exclusively non-Jewish readers and interpreters, the answer to this question was also largely presumed and uncontroversial. The thesis of this chapter is that the presumed answer of these later readers and the presumed answer of the New Testament authors are diametrically opposed.

Mark

We will begin our discussion with what is generally considered the earliest of the synoptic Gospels, the Gospel of Mark. It is surprising how little Mark has to say about Yeshua and Jewish practice.[5] In all likelihood, this lack of attention to issues of Jewish practice derives from Mark's intended audience, which was non-Jewish in composition.[6] While showing slight interest in distinctive Jewish practice, Mark does present Yeshua as following the norms accepted by all Jews of his day. He attends the synagogue on the Sabbath (Mark 1:21; 3:1–2). He wears fringes (*tzitzit*) on his garments as commanded by Numbers 15:37–41 (Mark 6:56). He directs a healed leper to go to a priest to be pronounced clean and, presumably, to offer the sacrifices prescribed for the occasion in the Torah (Mark 1:44; Leviticus 14:1–32).

At the same time, some of Yeshua's actions (healing and plucking grain on the Sabbath, eating with sinners, eating with unwashed hands) provoke controversy.

---

5. "In surveying the final text of Mark, in contrast to the other Gospels, surprisingly enough Judaism and the Jewish law hardly appear to constitute a theme." Peter J. Tomson, *"If this be from Heaven"* (Sheffield: Sheffield Academic, 2001), 258.

6. The non-Jewish character of his intended readers may be inferred from the frequent explanation of Aramaic terms (Mark 3:17; 5:41; 7:11, 34; 14:36; 15:22, 34), the parenthetical explanation of Jewish purity customs (Mark 7:3–4), and the Markan version of Yeshua's teaching on divorce (Mark 10:12) that presumes a non-Jewish juridical situation. On the Markan divorce pericope, see Tomson, *Heaven*, 258–59.

While these actions involve no explicit rejection or violation of common first-century Jewish practice, they do ignore traditions of practice that existed among certain groups of pious Jews (e.g., Essenes, Pharisees). The fact that controversy erupted at all on these matters points to the expectation that as a respected teacher, miracle worker, and holy man, Yeshua would conform to the standards upheld by the most pious parties of his day. Thus these conflicts actually confirm Yeshua's position as a practicing Jew while also demonstrating that he did not fit neatly and comfortably into any existing group.

Only one Markan text—as commonly read—challenges this view of Yeshua and Jewish practice. In defense of his disciples (who ate with unwashed hands, contrary to Pharisaic practice), Yeshua teaches a "parable" (v. 17):

> There is nothing outside a person that by going in can defile,
> but the things that come out are what defile. (Mark 7:15)

Yeshua proceeds to explain to his disciples the meaning of the "parable":

> Do you not see that whatever goes into a person from outside cannot defile, since it enters, not the heart but the stomach, and goes out into the sewer? . . . For it is from within, from the human heart, that evil intentions come: fornication, theft, murder, adultery, avarice, wickedness, deceit, licentiousness, envy, slander, pride, folly. All these evil things come from within, and they defile a person. (Mark 7:18–19a, 21–23)

While this saying of Yeshua appears to contradict the Torah's laws of purity, most commentators today recognize that this need not be the case. E. P. Sanders notes that the "not . . . but" contrast should not be taken literally:

> Its meaning could be understood to be, "What matters morally is what comes out" or "What comes out is much more important." The "not . . . but" contrast can mean "not this only, but much more that." . . . "*Not* what goes in *but* what comes out" in Mark 7:15, then, could well mean, "What comes out—the wickedness of a person's heart—is what really matters," leaving the food laws as such untouched. In this case there is no conflict with the law.[7]

This saying is quite similar in form and substance to the quotation from Hosea 6:6 cited by Yeshua in Matthew 9:13 and 12:7: "I desire mercy, not sacrifice."

---

7. E. P. Sanders, *Jewish Law From Jesus to the Mishnah* (Philadelphia: Trinity Press International,, 1990), 28. James Dunn makes the same point in *Jesus, Paul and the Law* (Louisville: Westminster John Knox, 1990), 51, in regard to the parallel verse in Matthew 15:11. Dunn sees Mark 7:15 as more radical than Matthew 15:11.

In the two Matthean texts, "sacrifice" is associated with restrictions on eating with sinners (9:13) and plucking and eating grain on the Sabbath (12:7). The quotation thus means, "Mercy is more important than ritual restrictions." Yeshua does not thereby annul all ritual restrictions. If the parallel holds, in Mark 7:15, 18–19a, 21–23 Yeshua emphasizes the "weightier matters of the Torah," but does not annul all purity restrictions.

This reading of Mark 7:15 fits well with the narrative context. Yeshua responds to Pharisaic criticism of his disciples' conduct by attacking the Pharisees for giving greater weight to their oral tradition than to the written Torah (Mark 7:9–13). In doing so, they "make void the word of God" (i.e., the written Torah). If Yeshua now proceeds to teach that the laws of purity are nullified, he is guilty of the same crime that he just charged others with committing!

The real problem lies with words we have not yet examined. In what is generally considered a parenthetical comment by the author, Mark writes (as translated by the NRSV): "Thus he declared all foods clean" (Mark 7:19b). The Greek text for this verse fragment is in dispute. Some manuscripts (though not the most ancient and reliable) have one different letter (an omicron rather than an omega), "that amounts to the rendering that the natural process of digestion 'makes all foods clean.'"[8] This alternate textual tradition fits better with the overall context of Mark 7. However, the weak manuscript support for this reading compels us to try to make sense of the more dominant textual tradition.

According to almost all commentators, the dominant text of Mark 7:19b constitutes an explicit abrogation of the biblical dietary laws.[9] It goes beyond the "not . . . but" of Mark 7:15. As we have seen, those words may be taken to involve a prioritization of categories of impurity rather than a denial of all physical impurity. The parenthesis, on the other hand, shifts the focus from the impurity of hands to the impurity of food, and asserts that all foods are inherently pure.[10] Is there any way to understand this assertion that leaves the dietary laws intact?

---

8. Tomson, *Heaven,* 260. See the KJV and NKJV.

9. For example, Dunn states that if Mark 7:19b accurately represents the meaning of Yeshua's teaching, "the conclusion is unavoidable that Jesus denied the necessity of treating some foods as 'unclean' and so in effect called for the abolition of the important sequence of laws dealing with unclean foods (Lev. 11; Deut. 14)." *Jesus, Paul and the Law,* 38.

10. As noted above, the categories of ritual purity (i.e., handwashing) and nonkosher meat should not be confused. However, the dominant text of Mark 7:19b appears to draw a conclusion about the latter from a saying about the former. This is explicable by the loose connection that exists between the two categories. The same Hebrew word (*tamey*) is used in the Pentateuch to refer to both types of impurity. It is also worth noting that the main reason the Pharisees showed

A story from rabbinic literature will help to answer this question. It has often been cited in discussions of Mark 7, but its significance is rarely noted.[11] The story speaks of an encounter between a Gentile and Rabban Yohannan ben Zakkai, the central figure in the rabbinic reconstitution of Jewish life in the immediate aftermath of the destruction of the temple in 70 CE. The Gentile asks about the Torah's method of dealing with the most serious form of ritual impurity, namely, that derived from contact with a corpse.

> A gentile asked Rabban Yohanan ben Zakkai, saying to him, "These rites that you carry out look like witchcraft. You bring a cow and slaughter it, burn it, crush the remains, take the dust, and if one of you contracts corpse uncleanness, you sprinkle on him two or three times and say to him, 'You are clean.'"
>
> He said to him, "Has a wandering spirit never entered you?"
>
> He said to him, "No."
>
> He said to him, "And have you ever seen someone into whom a wandering spirit entered?"
>
> He said to him, "Yes."
>
> He said to him, "And what do you do?"
>
> He said to him, "People bring roots and smoke them under him and sprinkle water on the spirit and it flees."
>
> He said to him, "And should your ears not hear what your mouth speaks? So this spirit is the spirit of uncleanness, as it is written, *I will cause prophets as well as the spirit of uncleanness to flee from the land* (Zech. 13:2)."
>
> After the man had gone his way, his disciples said to him, "My lord, this one you have pushed off with a mere reed. To us what will you reply?"
>
> He said to him, "By your lives! It is not the corpse that imparts uncleanness nor the water that effects cleanness. But it is a decree of the Holy One, blessed be He. Said the Holy One, blessed be He, 'A statute have I enacted, a decree have I made, and you are not at liberty to transgress my decree: *This is the* statute *of the Torah* (Num. 19:1).'"[12]

---

such great concern for the laws of ritual purity was their commitment to eating normal meals as though they were sacrificial banquets. Thus in Mark 7 the issue of handwashing (ritual purity) arises in connection with eating. Therefore our discussion of this text must address ritual purity and dietary laws together. Nevertheless, the distinction should not be lost.

11. David Daube, *The New Testament and Rabbinic Judaism* (Peabody, MA: Hendrickson, 1956), 141–43; Joachim Jeremias, *New Testament Theology* (New York: Charles Scribner's Sons, 1971), 210–11; Samuel Tobias Lachs, *A Rabbinic Commentary on the New Testament* (Hoboken: Ktav, 1987), 247; Dunn, *Jesus, Paul and the Law*, 58, n. 75. Peter Tomson is one of the few scholars to recognize the potential import of the parallel, though he focuses on Romans 14:14, 20 rather than Mark 7; see *Paul*, 248–49.

12. *Pesiqta deRab Kahana* 4:7, trans. Jacob Neusner, *Pesiqta deRab Kahana*, vol. 1 (Atlanta: Scholars, 1987), 65. Strack and Stemberger trace this midrashic collection to the land of Israel in the fifth century. H. L. Strack and G. Stemberger, *Introduction to the Talmud and Midrash* (Min-

In his response to his disciples, Rabban Yohannan ben Zakkai drives a wedge between the laws that define impurity and the means of removing it, on the one hand, and the objective ontological status of ritual impurity, on the other. Yohannan implies that ritual purity as a quality in human beings comes, not from the external conditions or acts ordained by the Torah *in themselves*, but instead from Israel's decision to obey the *mitzvoth* (commandments). Thus, observance of the *mitzvoth* of ritual purity (or, by implication, the dietary laws) is not contingent upon a worldview in which ritual impurity has an objective external reality.[13]

I am not arguing that the meaning of Mark 7:19b and of this saying attributed to Yohannan ben Zakkai are the same. Nor am I arguing that this rabbinic story is typical of the rabbinic view of ritual impurity. I am only arguing that a rejection of the objective ontological status of ritual impurity does not necessarily imply a rejection by Jews of the practices ordained by the Torah that relate to ritual impurity. The saying attributed to Yohannan ben Zakkai demonstrates that it is possible to reject one without rejecting the other.

How might we read the dominant text of Mark 7:19b in light of this possibility? It is reasonable to understand Mark 7:19b as "designed to point out or serve as a reassurance to Gentile believers that the Jewish food laws were not obligatory

---

neapolis: Fortress, 1992), 321. Though the story is attributed to the first century, rabbinic attribution cannot be taken at face value. While a first-century dating of this tradition would strengthen my case, the argument here is not founded on such early dating. Regardless of its chronological origins, the story demonstrates that a denial of ontological impurity is compatible with adherence to the biblical laws dealing with impurity. If the story itself, or even the ideology of impurity that it embodies, could be traced back to the end of the first century, all the better.

13. Jacob Neusner has argued that the rabbinic approach to impurity and holiness shifts the focus from external objects to the intentionality of human agents: "He [the human being] is not a passive object of an independent process of material sanctification, begun and elected by heaven working solely through nature, but the principal subject in the contingent process of relative and circumstantial sanctification. . . . By an act of will, a human being possesses the power of sanctification." *Purity in Rabbinic Judaism* (Atlanta: Scholars, 1994), 48–49. Jacob Milgrom contends that this view of impurity and holiness is not a rabbinic innovation but is rooted in the priestly tradition of the Torah. *Leviticus 1–16*, The Anchor Bible, vol. 3 (New York: Doubleday, 1991), 485–87. Milgrom contrasts the approach to impurity taken by Leviticus with that found in ancient pagan religions, where impurity is associated with the demonic realm. According to Milgrom, the priestly authors of Leviticus accomplished a "thoroughgoing evisceration of the demonic," which "transformed the concept of impurity" (43). Whether or not Milgrom's view of Leviticus is correct, it is evident that some Second Temple Jews (e.g., those who wrote and revered the Enochic literature) did associate impurity with demonic forces and thus did see impurity (and holiness) as external and ontological in character; see Gabriele Boccaccini, *Beyond the Essene Hypothesis* (Grand Rapids: Eerdmans, 1998), 64–66, 94–95. Therefore the Pharisaic approach to impurity and holiness—if indeed later rabbinic tradition derives its own view of impurity and holiness from the Pharisees, or from a particular school of Pharisees—did not represent the Jewish consensus of the period.

for them."[14] As noted above, Mark is directed to a non-Jewish audience. If the Jewish dietary laws are based on an objective distinction between certain meats that are inherently impure and others that are pure, then one cannot hold that non-Jewish Yeshua-believers are permitted to eat what is impure unless one considers those non-Jews to be consigned to a lower level of purity. As we will soon see, this issue of Gentile purity and impurity is of major concern in the Acts of the Apostles. If Gentile Yeshua-believers are purified through Yeshua, then they, just like the Jews, should refrain from eating what is inherently impure. In order to maintain equality of status between Jewish and Gentile Yeshua-believers, either those foods permitted to Gentiles but prohibited to Jews must be recognized as inherently pure, or Gentiles must be required to observe the same food laws as the Jews. If the former position is held, however, it need not imply that Jewish Yeshua-believers are now free to eat what is permitted to non-Jews. There may be other considerations besides inherent impurity (such as a commandment from God) that would dictate distinct dietary regimens for Jews and Gentiles.

I am not proposing that Yeshua himself denied the objective ontological status of ritual impurity, nor am I proposing that the gospel tradition transmitted in Mark 7 and Matthew 15 expresses such a position. I am suggesting that the author of the final version of the Gospel of Mark (in Mark 7:19b) interprets the tradition in this manner in order to support the view that (1) Gentile Yeshua-believers were exempt from the Jewish dietary laws and (2) this exemption did not relegate them to a secondary status of purity in relation to Jewish Yeshua-believers.[15] As we will soon see, in Romans 14 Paul appears to make a similar interpretive move.[16]

Christian readers generally never even consider such an interpretation of Mark 7:19b. It is taken for granted that Yeshua (or at least the Gospel of Mark) abolishes Jewish food laws. But there are strong reasons that favor this understanding of Mark 7:19b. First, it is more in keeping with the rest of the book than is the abolitionist view. As seen above, the Gospel of Mark as a whole presents Yeshua as an observant Jew who never undercuts accepted Jewish practice. Does

14. Dunn, *Jesus, Paul and the Law*, 45. Dunn does not seem to recognize the discrepancy between this statement and his earlier assertion that Mark 7:19b "called for the abolition of the important sequence of laws dealing with unclean foods" (38).

15. "The motivation behind Mark's editorial comment in verse 19b is not stated. However, in light of the historical context and given the Gentile Christian audience of the gospel, the plausibility exists that Mark was attempting to construct a theological basis for the Acts 15 food law exemption in the teachings of Yeshua." David J. Rudolph, "Yeshua and the Dietary Laws: A Reassessment of Mark 7:19b," *Kesher* 16 (Fall 2003): 111.

16. Rudolph makes a reasonable case for the hypothesis that Mark knew of Paul's interpretation and was influenced by it (ibid., 111–12).

it make sense to describe Yeshua in this way and then state parenthetically that he actually abolished a fundamental element of Jewish life? Second, it is more in keeping with the other synoptic Gospels. As we will soon see, Matthew and Luke give no support to the view that Yeshua abolished the Jewish food laws. This is especially clear in Matthew's version of the same incident described in Mark 7 (which, according to the theory of Markan priority, is actually a redaction and interpretation of Mark 7). Third, it is more in keeping with the Acts of the Apostles and the writings of Paul, which show that eating with Gentiles was a major hurdle for Jewish Yeshua-believers—even apart from the issue of nonkosher food. If Yeshua abolished the Jewish dietary laws, then why did his Jewish followers (such as Peter in Acts 10) require special divine intervention before they would even sit at table with non-Jews? Fourth, in light of the hermeneutical factors considered in the previous chapter, we should favor plausible readings of the New Testament that support the ongoing validity and spiritual significance of the Jewish people and its distinctive way of life. *The abolition of the dietary laws is in effect an abolition of the Jewish people itself.* Like circumcision and Sabbath and holiday observance, the Torah's dietary regimen serves as a fundamental sign of the particular vocation and identity of the Jewish people. This provides strong theological grounds for a nonabolitionist reading of Mark 7:19b.

I am not concerned here solely with the intention of the human author of Mark 7:19b. This parenthetical statement could be an addition to the original text of the Gospel made by an early editor.[17] If so, the human author of those words might have had a different intent from that of the original author of the book. Regardless, those words are now part of the canonical text. They must be interpreted in light of that text as a whole, not in isolation. Thus the question before us is not primarily historical. It is theological. We are reading the New Testament as sacred scripture. What is the divine intention behind Mark 7:19b? Those who assume that the intent must be abolitionist should pause and consider whether the alternative proposed here provides grounds for challenging that assumption.

Matthew

Whereas the Gospel of Mark appears to be written for a non-Jewish audience, the Gospel of Matthew is composed within and for a Jewish context. This becomes especially evident if we accept the dominant scholarly view that Matthew knows and uses the Gospel of Mark as a source. We can then compare

17. Tomson, *Heaven*, 260–63.

Matthew with Mark, note the changes Matthew makes, and ask about the reasons for those changes. We can also examine the material that Matthew and Luke share in common but that is not found in Mark, noting the distinctive features of Matthew's version.[18] Whenever Matthew has unique characteristics, those characteristics call out for explanation.

The Gospel of Matthew presents Yeshua as the definitive teacher of the Torah.[19] At the beginning of the Sermon on the Mount, in a passage unique to Matthew and programmatic for the book as a whole, Yeshua speaks about his mission in relation to the Torah:

> "Do not think that I have come to abolish the law or the prophets;
>   I have come not to abolish but to fulfill.
>   For truly I tell you, until heaven and earth pass away, not one letter,
>   not one stroke of a letter, will pass from the law until all is accomplished.
>   Therefore, whoever breaks one of the least of these commandments,
> and teaches others to do the same, will be called least in the kingdom of heaven;
>   but whoever does them and teaches them will be called great in the kingdom of heaven." (Matthew 5:17–19)

The implicit distinction made here between "lesser" and "greater" commandments is echoed later in the book (Matthew 23:23), where Yeshua speaks of the "weightier matters of the Torah." In that context the weightier/greater commandments are what are often called "moral" or "relational": "justice and mercy and faith." The lighter/lesser commandments are what is often called "ritual": in this case, scrupulous tithing. This fits a major theme of Matthew, in which Yeshua emphasizes that where there is a conflict between these two types of commandments, the weightier/greater take precedence.[20] What is most remarkable

18. Most New Testament scholars believe that Matthew and Luke are independent sources. The material they share in common that is not found in Mark is attributed to a hypothetical source that they both know and use. This hypothetical source is called Q, after the German word for "source."

19. When Matthew's Yeshua articulates the golden rule (7:12), he adds, "for this is the law and the prophets" (not found in the parallel verse in Luke 6:31). When Matthew's Yeshua states the two greatest commandments in the Torah (22:40), he adds, "on these two commandments depend the law and the prophets" (not found in the parallel verse in Mark 12:31). Matthew thereby emphasizes that Yeshua's teaching offers the key for rightly interpreting and living the Torah.

20. In Matthew Yeshua makes this point through citing Hosea 6:6: "I desire mercy and not sacrifice" (9:13; 12:7). As noted above, "sacrifice" in the two Matthean texts is associated with restrictions on eating with sinners (9:13) and plucking and eating grain on the Sabbath (12:7). The quotation means that mercy is more important than ritual restrictions. On the use of Hosea 6:6 in Matthew, the Qumran writings, and rabbinic literature, see Anthony J. Saldarini, *Matthew's Christian-Jewish Community* (Chicago: University of Chicago Press, 1994), 130–31.

about Matthew 5:19 and 23:23, however, is that both texts affirm that attentive obedience to the weightier/greater commandments should not lead to violation or neglect of the lighter/lesser commandments.[21]

For Matthew, Jewish practice constitutes an integral part of the lighter/lesser commandments of the Torah. The book gives no grounds for concluding that Yeshua has abrogated Jewish practice for Jews. To the contrary, Matthew underlines the importance of such practice and its status as a divine commandment. This becomes clear when we compare parallel texts in Matthew and Mark that deal in some way with Sabbath and dietary laws.

In recounting the Sabbath controversies between Yeshua and the Pharisees, Matthew seeks to make clear that Yeshua's teaching and practice uphold the validity and the importance of the Sabbath commandment. This is evident in the case of the healing of the man with the withered hand.

Matthew 12:9–13	Mark 3:1–5
[9]He left that place and entered their synagogue;	[1]Again he entered the synagogue, and a man was there who had a withered hand.
[10]a man was there with a withered hand, and they asked him, "Is it lawful to cure on the sabbath?" so that they might accuse him.	[2]They watched him to see whether he would cure him on the sabbath, so that they might accuse him.
[11]He said to them, "Suppose one of you has only one sheep and it falls into a pit on the sabbath; will you not lay hold of it and lift it out?	[3]And he said to the man who had the withered hand, "Come forward."
[12]How much more valuable is a human being than a sheep! *So it is lawful to do good on the sabbath.*"	[4]Then he said to them, "Is it lawful to do good or to do harm on the sabbath, to save life or to kill?" But they were silent.
[13]Then he said to the man, "Stretch out your hand." He stretched it out, and it was restored, as sound as the other.	[5]He looked around at them with anger; he was grieved at their hardness of heart and said to the man, "Stretch out your hand." He stretched it out, and his hand was restored.

In Mark Yeshua asks his critics, "Is it lawful to do good or to do harm on the sabbath?" They do not answer, and he does not return to the question. In Matthew Yeshua's critics ask *him* the question, "Is it lawful to cure on the sabbath?' The scene now turns into a legal discussion, with Yeshua employing a technical *kal vachomer* ("from lesser to greater") argument to explicitly assert that "it *is* lawful to do good on the sabbath." Rather than employing a rhetorical question to silence his critics (as in Mark), Matthew's Yeshua engages in a legal discussion in which he argues that healing is permitted on the Sabbath. Matthew has not altered the substance of Mark's narrative. But Matthew's version highlights

---

21. "For Jesus, the 'weighty' matters of the Torah do not suspend the other commandments." Markus Bockmuehl, *Jewish Law in Gentile Churches* (Edinburgh: T&T Clark, 2000), 8.

Yeshua's argument and its conclusion, "So it is lawful to do good on the sabbath."[22] In this way Matthew emphasizes that Yeshua's teaching and practice uphold Jewish Sabbath observance.

More telling is a phrase Matthew adds to Mark's eschatological discourse. Yeshua warns his followers to flee Jerusalem when they see "the desolating sacrilege standing in the holy place" (Matthew 24:15; see Mark 13:14). He then mentions conditions that could make this flight difficult or impossible.

Matthew 24:19–20	Mark 13:18
Woe to those who are pregnant and to those who are nursing infants in those days!	Woe to those who are pregnant and to those who are nursing infants in those days!
Pray that your flight may not be in winter or on a sabbath.	Pray that it may not be in winter.

This reference to the Sabbath would only carry weight with an audience that took Sabbath observance seriously. Anthony Saldarini has this to say about Matthew 24:20:

> Some Christian commentators on Matthew 12 . . . argue that Matthew is rejecting a "legalistic" or "ritualistic" observance of the Sabbath. However, Matthew has no such problem because his group observes the Sabbath seriously. Their understanding of Sabbath observance does not allow them to flee the dangers and horrors of the end of the world because journeys are not allowed on the Sabbath. Thus the author has Jesus hope that these events do not occur on a Sabbath (24:20).[23]

Matthew 24:20 implies that Matthew and his audience viewed Sabbath observance as obligatory for all Jews.

We reach the same conclusion when we examine Matthew's view of the Jewish dietary laws. Matthew's version of the dispute with the Pharisees over handwashing differs in significant ways from that in Mark.

---

22. On Matthew 12:9–13, see Saldarini, *Matthew's Christian-Jewish Community,* 131–34; Lachs, *Rabbinic Commentary,* 199–200; J. Andrew Overman, *Church and Community in Crisis* (Valley Forge: Trinity Press International, 1996), 177–78; William Loader, *Jesus' Attitude towards the Law* (Grand Rapids: Eerdmans, 2002), 205.

23. Saldarini, *Matthew's Christian-Jewish Community,* 126. For similar comments, see Tomson, *Heaven,* 287–88; David C. Sim, *The Gospel of Matthew and Christian Judaism* (Edinburgh: T&T Clark, 1998), 138; James D. G. Dunn, *Unity and Diversity in the New Testament,* 2nd ed. (Harrisburg, PA: Trinity Press International, 1990), 127. For a contrary opinion, see Graham N. Stanton, *A Gospel for a New People* (Louisville: Westminster/John Knox, 1992), 192–206.

Matthew 15	Mark 7
[10]Then he called the crowd to him and said to them, "Listen and understand:	[14]Then he called the crowd again and said to them, "Listen to me, all of you, and understand
[11]it is not what goes into the mouth that defiles a person, but it is what comes out of the mouth that defiles."	[15]there is nothing outside a person that by going in can defile, but the things that come out are what defile."
[15]But Peter said to him, "Explain this parable to us."	[17]When he had left the crowd and entered the house, his disciples asked him about the parable.
[16]Then he said, "Are you also still without understanding?	[18]He said to them, "Then do you also fail to understand? Do you not see that whatever goes into a person from outside cannot defile,
[17]Do you not see that whatever goes into the mouth enters the stomach, and goes out into the sewer?	[19]since it enters, not the heart but the stomach, and goes out into the sewer?" (Thus he declared all foods clean.)
[18]But what comes out of the mouth proceeds from the heart, and this is what defiles.	[20]And he said, "It is what comes out of a person that defiles.
[19]For out of the heart come evil intentions, murder, adultery, fornication, theft, false witness, slander.	[21]For it is from within, from the human heart, that evil intentions come: fornication, theft, murder,
[20]These are what defile a person, but to eat with unwashed hands does not defile."	[22]adultery, avarice, wickedness, deceit, licentiousness, envy, slander, pride, folly
	[23]All these evil things come from within, and they defile a person."

First, as James Dunn notes, Matthew "softens Mark's version" of the parable itself (Mark 7:15; Matthew 15:11).[24] In Mark, Yeshua's statement is apparently universal in scope: "There is nothing outside a person that by going in can defile." In Matthew the statement is more readily recognized as a form of "dialectical negation," in which the "not . . . but" is understood to mean "more important than."[25] Second, Matthew omits Mark's parenthetical comment, "Thus he declared all foods clean." Matthew wants to keep the focus on the topic of handwashing and ritual purity. He probably sees Mark's inference regarding the dietary laws as tangential and potentially misleading (at least for a Jewish audience like his own). Third, Yeshua's final words in Matthew bring the reader's attention back to the issue that initially provoked the discussion: "But to eat with unwashed hands does not defile." The addition of these words, combined with the omission of Mark's parenthesis, shows that Matthew wants the reader to see this as a controversy over Pharisaic custom rather than over basic biblical commandments.[26] Fourth, in Matthew the list of

24. Dunn, *Unity and Diversity*, 247.
25. Dunn, *Jesus, Paul and the Law*, 51.
26. "When Jesus says . . . that it is not 'what goes into the mouth that defiles a man, but what comes out of the mouth, this defiles a man" (11), he is not deprecating the laws of kashruth

what defiles is reorganized to conform to the Decalogue: murder ("You shall not murder"), adultery and fornication ("You shall not commit adultery"), theft ("You shall not steal"), and false witness and slander ("You shall not bear false witness"). In this way Yeshua's teaching on impurity is connected to his earlier rebuke of his interlocutors for their willingness to compromise basic biblical commandments such as "Honor your father and mother" (also from the Decalogue) for the sake of Pharisaic tradition. Thus the entire passage becomes a unified admonition regarding true Torah observance.[27]

The evidence strongly supports the view that the author and intended audience of Matthew would have seen distinctive Jewish practice, such as the Sabbath and dietary laws, as an obligation imposed by the Torah upon all Jews, and most especially upon those who adhered to Yeshua the Messiah and his teaching.

Luke-Acts

Since the Gospel of Luke and the Acts of the Apostles have the same author and reflect the same viewpoint on Jewish practice, we will treat the two books together.

Even more than Matthew, Luke-Acts displays an unambiguously positive perspective on Jewish practice. For Matthew, Yeshua is the ultimate Torah teacher, and the Torah itself (as interpreted and lived by Yeshua) is the universal blueprint for life. Distinctive Jewish practice is affirmed within this context (as the "lighter/lesser" *mitzvoth*), but such practice is not the primary focus of attention. For Luke-Acts, on the other hand, the Torah is God's particular gift to the Jewish people, and the distinctive Jewish way of life is the fitting response

---

and abrogating them but resisting the halakhic innovations of the Pharisees, which these wish to impose as traditions of the elders. With respect to the handwashing ritual before eating, the Evangelist surely has the upper hand historically. Rabbinic literature is still at some pains hundreds of years later to justify this relatively new (and apparently sectarian) practice. . . . The battle of Jesus with the Pharisees over this issue was apparently still being fought *within* 'Jewish' circles nearly half a millennium later." Boyarin, *Border Lines*, 251–52, n. 125 (emphasis original).

27. This way of reading Matthew 15 in relation to Mark 7 is common among exegetes. See Dunn, *Unity and Diversity*, 247–48; Tomson, *Heaven*, 288; Saldarini, *Matthew's Christian-Jewish Community*, 134–39; Sim, *Matthew and Christian Judaism*, 132–35; Overman, *Crisis*, 222–27; Loader, *Jesus' Attitude*, 213–16; W. D. Davies and Dale C. Allison, Jr., *A Critical and Exegetical Commentary on the Gospel According to Saint Matthew*, vol. 2 (Edinburgh: T&T Clark, 1991), 516–40; Daniel J. Harrington, S.J., *The Gospel of Matthew* (Collegeville, MN: Liturgical Press, 1991), 228–34; Amy-Jill Levine, *The Social and Ethnic Dimensions of Matthean Salvation History* (Lewiston, NY: Edwin Mellen, 1988), 160–61.

to this gift. In an insightful chapter on "The Law in Luke-Acts," Jacob Jervell sees this clearly:

> For Luke, the law remains the law given to Israel on Sinai, in the strict meaning of the word, the law of Israel. And Luke is concerned about the law because it is Israel's law. . . . It is significant that Luke is most concerned about the ritual and ceremonial aspects of the law. The law is to him not essentially the moral law, but the mark of distinction between Jews and non-Jews. The law is the sign of Israel as the people of God.[28]

Luke actually has a term that expresses much of what we mean by Jewish practice. He speaks of the "customs" (*ethe*)—the distinctive national practices of the Jewish people that have their roots in the teaching of Moses.[29] Luke knows that some among the early Yeshua-believers (e.g., Stephen, Paul) are suspected of undermining these national practices (Acts 6:14; 21:21), but Luke insistently denies that this is the case (Acts 21:24; 28:17).

The Gospel of Luke

Luke begins his Gospel with an infancy narrative that highlights the faithful Jewish practice of the families of John and Yeshua. The infancy narrative as a whole begins and ends by commenting on this fidelity.

> Both of them [i.e., Zechariah and Elizabeth] were righteous before God, living blamelessly according to all the commandments and regulations of the Lord. (Luke 1:6)

> When they [i.e., Joseph and Mary] had finished everything required by the law of the Lord, they returned to Galilee, to their own town of Nazareth. (Luke 2:39)

What sort of "regulations of the Lord" does Luke have in mind? The narrative itself provides the answer. Luke gives special prominence to the circumcision of both John and Yeshua (Luke 1:59; 2:21). He also speaks of the redemption of the first-born (*pidyon haben*), a practice still observed by religious Jews (Luke 2:22–23). In a supplement to the infancy narrative dealing with Yeshua's early adolescence, Luke also refers to Joseph and Mary's annual pilgrimage to Jerusalem to observe the Passover (Luke 2:41). Thus these families observe the basic life-cycle and holiday practices incumbent upon faithful Jews. And Luke treats this fact as a point to be noted.

---

28. Jacob Jervell, *Luke and the People of God* (Minneapolis: Augsburg, 1972), 137.

29. See Luke 1:9; Acts 6:14, 15:1, 21:21, 26:3, 28:17. In Acts 16:21 and 25:16 the word is used for Roman custom. On Luke's view of customs as national practices, see Daniel Schwartz, "God, Gentiles, and Jewish Law," in *Geschichte—Tradition—Reflection, Band I,* ed. Hubert Cancik, Hermann Lichtenberger, and Peter Schafer (Tübingen: J. C. B. Mohr/Paul Siebeck, 1996), 263–64.

In his description of Yeshua's life and teaching, Luke adheres to the pattern found in both Mark and Matthew. As we have seen above, Matthew edits the only Markan text that could be understood as undermining Jewish practice so as to eliminate that potential misunderstanding. Luke simply omits that incident from his story.[30] Then, near the end of his book, while describing Yeshua's death and burial, Luke adds a significant comment unique to his Gospel:

> It was the day of Preparation, and the sabbath was beginning. The women who had come with him from Galilee followed, and they saw the tomb and how his body was laid. Then they returned, and prepared spices and ointments. On the sabbath they rested according to the commandment. (Luke 23:54–56)

Just as his family conformed scrupulously to Jewish practice in their care for Yeshua at the beginning of his life, so these women behave with similar piety in their care for Yeshua as his life reaches its apparent conclusion.

Acts of the Apostles

This evident Lukan regard for Jewish practice could be interpreted as his respect for the Jewish way of life that Yeshua fulfills—and renders obsolete—in his death and resurrection. It could be interpreted in this manner, however, only by ignoring the Acts of the Apostles. This second Lukan volume presents the Jewish Yeshua-movement of the pre–70 CE era in the same light as the first volume presents Zechariah, Elizabeth, Joseph, Mary, and the women at the tomb. The death and resurrection of Yeshua have not diminished this movement's commitment to faithful Jewish practice. This is true not only at the beginning of the book but also at the end. This is true not only for Peter and James but even for Paul! We can discern no trajectory in the book that would point to a time when Jewish practice would cease to be obligatory for Jewish people.

In Acts Luke presents the Sabbath and holidays as unquestioned components of the Jewish way of life. In his account of Yeshua's ascension, Luke mentions in passing that the Mount of Olives is "a sabbath day's journey" from the city of Jerusalem (Acts 1:12). One would normally describe a distance in this way only if one observes the Sabbath and recognizes that Sabbath observance imposes defined limits on distances that may be traveled.[31] The eschatologi-

---

30. Jervell, 139–40.

31. "A Sabbath-day's journey" was probably a normal expression among first-century Jews as a measurement of distance; see F. F. Bruce, *The Book of the Acts* (Grand Rapids: Eerdmans, 1988), 39. Nevertheless, its use by the author of Acts is striking. Given the book's frequent reference to Jewish holidays and the fact that a description of the distance covered was unnecessary to the narrative, we are justified in seeing more to Acts 1:12 than a neutral term of measurement.

cal gift of the Holy Spirit is received on the Jewish holiday of Shavuot (Pentecost): "When the day of Pentecost had come, they were all together in one place" (Acts 2:1). Why were they "all together in one place"? From historical and narrative context, one reasonably assumes that they had assembled to celebrate the Jewish holiday. Later in the book we find Paul traveling to the land of Israel because "he was eager to be in Jerusalem, if possible, on the day of Pentecost" (Acts 20:16). Why? For the same reason that Joseph and Mary journeyed to Jerusalem every Passover—because it is a *mitzvah* (a sacred privilege and obligation) for a Jew to be in Jerusalem for the three pilgrimage holidays of Passover, Pentecost, and Booths. Similarly, Luke mentions in passing the feast of Unleavened Bread (Acts 20:6) and the Day of Atonement (Acts 27:9), not to focus attention on them, but to show his readers that the characters in his narrative are faithful Jews whose lives are ordered according to the Jewish calendar.

Luke's expectation that Jewish Yeshua-believers will live according to Jewish practice receives further support from the event that is the centerpiece of the book of Acts—the apostolic meeting in Jerusalem (Acts 15). At this meeting the leadership of the new movement debates and resolves the question of the status of Gentiles in the movement. Luke introduces the controversy in this way:

> Then certain individuals came down from Judea [to Antioch] and were teaching the brothers, "Unless you are circumcised according to the custom of Moses, you cannot be saved." And after Paul and Barnabas had no small dissension and debate with them, Paul and Barnabas and some of the others were appointed to go up to Jerusalem to discuss this question with the apostles and the elders. When they came to Jerusalem . . . some believers who belonged to the sect of the Pharisees stood up and said, "It is necessary for them to be circumcised and ordered to keep the law of Moses." (Acts 15:1–4)

The issue before the apostles and elders is whether non-Jewish Yeshua-believers are obligated to be circumcised and to live as Jews ("to keep the law of Moses"). For our purpose in this chapter, the most noteworthy feature of this narrative lies not in what is recorded about the discussion or its final outcome. What is most important is that the Jerusalem leadership treats this as a legitimate halakhic question meriting careful reflection, communal discussion, and authoritative response. They do not dismiss the question as absurd or excommunicate as heretics those who raised it. As Michael Wyschogrod has argued, the fact that the case is debated at all reveals that both sides accepted as a given the obligation of *Jewish* Yeshua-believers to live as Jews, in conformity with Jewish national custom as codified in the Torah:

It is clear that both parties agreed that circumcision and Torah obedience remained obligatory for Jewish Jesus believers since, if this were not the case, one could hardly debate whether circumcision and Torah obedience were obligatory for gentiles. Such a debate could only arise if both parties agreed on the lasting significance of the Mosaic Law for Jews. Where they differed was its applicability to gentiles.[32]

Once recognized, this conclusion appears self-evident. At least from the perspective of the book's author, the entire leadership in the early Yeshua movement shared this conviction. There was controversy over Gentiles and Jewish practice but no controversy over Jews and Jewish practice. And the shared conviction involved more than freedom to maintain Jewish practice. If one was a Jew, one was not just free to live as a Jew, one was obligated to do so. Otherwise, the issue of Gentile obligation to live as a Jew would have been nonsensical.

This conclusion contradicts what most readers assume to be Pauline teaching. In our next section we will examine the Pauline letters to see if this is actually the case. At this point it is sufficient to note that Luke presents Paul as being in full agreement with this shared conviction. Paul fights vigorously in Acts against the imposition of Jewish practice on non-Jews, and Luke himself realizes that this combative stance led many to believe that Paul was opposed to Jewish practice in general. But according to Luke, this was a misunderstanding of Paul's position. Luke makes this clear in his description of Paul's meeting with James and the Jerusalem leadership in Acts 21:

> Then they [i.e., James and the Jerusalem leaders] said to him [i.e., Paul], "You see, brother, how many thousands of believers there are among the Jews, and they are all zealous for the law. They have been told about you that you teach all the Jews living among the Gentiles to forsake Moses, and that you tell them not to circumcise their children or observe the customs. What then is to be done? They will certainly hear that you have come. So do what we tell you. We have four men who are under a vow. Join these men, go through the rite of purification with them, and pay for the shaving of their heads. Thus all will know that there is nothing in

32. Michael Wyschogrod, "Letter to a Friend," *Modern Theology* 11, no. 2 (April 1995): 170. This piece is included in the recent collection of Wyschogrod essays, *Abraham's Promise* (Grand Rapids: Eerdmans, 2004), 202–10. A similar view was presented two decades earlier by the National Council of Catholic Bishops in a 1975 statement on Catholic-Jewish relations: "How Jewish the Church was toward the midpoint of the first century is dramatically reflected in the description of the 'Council of Jerusalem' (Acts 15). The question at issue was whether Gentile converts to the Church had to be circumcised and observe the Mosaic Law. The obligation to obey the Law was held so firmly by the Jewish Christians of that time that miraculous visions accorded to Peter and Cornelius (Acts 10) were needed to vindicate the contrary contention that Gentile Christians were not so obliged." *The Bible, the Jews, and the Death of Jesus* (Washington, DC: United States Conference of Catholic Bishops, 2004), 63.

what they have been told about you, but that you yourself observe and guard the law. But as for the Gentiles who have become believers, we have sent a letter with our judgment that they should abstain from what has been sacrificed to idols and from blood and from what is strangled and from fornication." Then Paul took the men, and the next day, having purified himself, he entered the temple with them, making public the completion of the days of purification when the sacrifice would be made for each of them. (Acts 21:20–26)

In order to make this text fit with the presumed anti-Torah teaching of Paul in his letters, many exegetes over the centuries have attempted to avoid the obvious intent of these verses.[33] Nevertheless, a straightforward reading of this text on its own terms can lead to only one reasonable conclusion: according to Luke, Paul does not teach Jews to forsake Moses, circumcision, and the customs, nor does he live in a way that would imply that such defection from Jewish practice is acceptable.[34] In the final chapter of Acts, we hear this from Paul's own mouth:

Three days later he [i.e., Paul] called together the local leaders of the Jews. When they had assembled, he said to them, "Brothers, though I had done nothing against our people or the customs of our ancestors, yet I was arrested in Jerusalem and handed over to the Romans." (Acts 28:17)

Luke wants to leave us with this image of Paul: speaking to his fellow Jews, arguing that Yeshua is the Messiah, and asserting that he has never done anything against his people or violated its way of life.

Peter's Vision

There is only one text in the entire Luke-Acts corpus that at first glance seems to run counter to this unambiguously positive affirmation of Jewish practice. Peter's vision in Acts 10 has often been interpreted as an authoritative abolition of the dietary laws.[35] In this vision, Peter sees a multitude of nonkosher animals and is told by a voice, "Get up, Peter, kill and eat" (Acts 10:9–13). As a practicing Jew, Peter is appalled and rejects the command—even though he realizes it

33. For a recent example, see David Trobisch, *The First Edition of the New Testament* (Oxford: Oxford University Press, 2000), 83: "The two apostles [James and Paul] devise a plan to fool the naïve Jewish converts. . . . In order to create the impression that Paul lives in strict observance of the law, James advises Paul to participate in the private ritual of Nazirite purification." What basis is there in Acts for thinking that this "impression" of Paul is false, as Trobisch implies?

34. Luke probably includes the story of Paul's circumcising Timothy (Acts 16:1–3) in order to reinforce this point.

35. For example, see F. F. Bruce, *The Book of Acts* (Grand Rapids: Eerdmans, 1988), 206; I. Howard Marshall, *Acts* (Grand Rapids: Eerdmans, 1980), 185–86.

comes from heaven: "By no means, Lord; for I have never eaten anything that is profane or unclean" (Acts 10:14). Perhaps Peter thinks his fidelity to the Torah is being tested.[36] His response demonstrates how all the early Jewish Yeshuabelievers must have looked at basic Jewish practice such as the dietary laws. The heavenly voice answers Peter with these important words: "What God has made clean, you must not call profane." Does Luke narrate this vision in order to justify the abolition of the Jewish dietary laws? Does the vision entail a positive command that Jews now eat nonkosher meat? Does this author, who elsewhere unconditionally affirms distinctive Jewish practice, here side with Antiochus Ephiphanes and the Hellenizers of the Maccabean period?

Such a conclusion seems inherently unlikely—and a careful reading of the story of Peter's vision in its interpretive context (Acts 10–11) demonstrates that it is unwarranted. We should first notice Peter's response to the vision: "Now . . . Peter was greatly puzzled about what to make of the vision that he had seen" (Acts 10:17). Like the seer of the book of Daniel, Peter realizes he has received a symbolic vision that requires interpretation. As a practicing Jew and a knowledgeable reader of scripture, Peter presumes that the vision is not to be taken at face value. But what does it mean?

As he ponders this question, messengers from a Gentile soldier (Cornelius) arrive at the house where Peter is staying. At this moment, Peter receives an initial prophetic interpretation of the meaning of the vision:

> While Peter was still thinking about the vision, the Spirit said to him, "Look, three men are searching for you. Now get up, go down, and go with them without hesitation; for I have sent them." (Acts 10:19–20)

On two occasions in the next two chapters Peter will link this prophetic directive to the meaning of the vision itself. He does so first in speaking to Cornelius and his household:

> And he said to them, "You yourselves know that it is unlawful for a Jew to associate with or to visit a Gentile; but God has shown me that I should not call anyone profane or unclean. So when I was sent for, I came without objection." (Acts 10:28–29)

The vision spoke of clean and unclean animals. But Peter interprets these animals as symbolizing Jews and Gentiles.[37] Thus he sees the vision as requiring that he

---

36. Witherington, *The Acts of the Apostles* (Grand Rapids: Eerdmans, 1998), 350.

37. The use of animal symbols to represent categories of human beings is common in apocalyptic literature. Outside the biblical canon, the most striking example is found in Enoch's Book of Dream Visions (Enoch 83–90).

"associate with," "visit," and eat with those he formerly considered impure, not that he eat impure food.[38] According to the NRSV, Peter describes this act of associating with Gentiles as "unlawful (*athemiton*) for a Jew." As Ben Witherington notes, the word *athemiton* "could be translated 'unlawful,' but it probably has its weaker sense of 'taboo' or 'strongly fowned upon.' There was no formal law that strictly forbade Jews from associating with Gentiles, it was just that they had to be prepared to pay a price for doing so, the price being becoming ritually unclean."[39] Thus, the vision directed Peter to break with an apparently common custom, but it did not command him to violate basic Jewish pratices (such as the dietary laws) ordained by the Torah.

Similarly, in the following chapter Peter must defend his actions to the Yeshua-movement leadership in Jerusalem, who criticize him, not for eating nonkosher food, which was unthinkable, but for visiting "uncircumcised men" and eating with them (Acts 11:2–3). He answers their criticism by recounting the vision with its core message, "What God has made clean, you must not call profane" (Acts 11:9). He then tells of the arrival of the messengers and the prophetic interpretation of the vision:

> At that very moment three men, sent to me from Caesarea, arrived at the house where we were. The Spirit told me to go with them and not to make a distinction between them and us. (Acts 11:11–12)

Peter does not here use the terms "profane or unclean" as he does in his explanation of the prophetic word to Cornelius. But the wording in Acts 11:12 clearly has the same meaning. The voice in the vision commanded Peter to eat clean and unclean animals without distinguishing between them. Now "the Spirit" tells Peter to go with these Gentiles and to make no distinction between them and Jews in his willingness to associate with them. To remove all doubt, Luke describes a third speech of Peter in which he tells of the Cornelius episode—and this time the imagery of purity/impurity and of "distinction" are brought together:

> And God, who knows the human heart, testified to them by giving them the Holy Spirit, just as he did to us; and in cleansing their hearts by faith he has made no distinction between them and us. (Acts 15:8–9)

---

38. Luke takes pains to depict Cornelius as a scrupulous and pious Godfearer (Acts 10:1–4), a non-Jew who himself observed much of Jewish practice. It is unlikely that such a man would have nonkosher foods in his house—and far more unlikely that he would insult a Jewish guest by serving him pork or shellfish.

39. Witherington, *Acts,* 353.

Peter's vision calls for radical rethinking of the relationship between Jews and Gentiles. But according to the interpretation found within the Lukan text itself, the vision does not call for an abolition of the dietary laws for Jews.[40]

If we read Acts 10–11 theologically and canonically in light of our discussion of Mark 7:19, it is reasonable to hold that accepting the purity of Gentiles (who are free to eat nonkosher food) itself implies that nonkosher food is not inherently impure—and yet we could continue to assert that Jews are obliged to maintain the dietary laws. Thus the traditional reading of Acts 10 would be partly justified. The "impure" animals are not possessors and conveyors of an ontologically objective property called "impurity." Yet the command to Peter—"get up, kill and eat"—would apply only to Jewish association with Gentiles and not to Jewish eating of nonkosher food. This is a reading of Acts 10 that renders it consistent with Mark 7, with the rest of the Lukan corpus, and with the theological implications of its own core principles (e.g., Gentile purity).

Conclusion

In summary, Luke-Acts provides the strongest evidence in the New Testament for the validity and importance of Jewish practice for Jews. From the beginning of the Gospel of Luke to the end of the Acts of the Apostles, we find no deviation from this orientation. Whether Luke is describing Yeshua himself or his family or followers, whether he is describing the devout Torah-observant Jerusalem community or the preeminent Jewish apostle to the Gentiles, we find a universal assumption—that the message and power of the Messiah leads Jews to more rather than less fervent Jewish practice. It also leads Jews into new relationships of love, friendship, and partnership with non-Jews. But these new relationships do not violate the ancestral commitment of Jews to their people and their distinctive way of life.

Paul

The Pauline Syllogism

The Lukan portrait of Paul has posed a problem for New Testament scholars. The standard reading of the Pauline letters has assumed that Paul treated Jewish practice (for Jews) as at best a matter of indifference. In contrast, the Lukan Paul is himself an observant Jew who approaches Jewish practice (for Jews) as obligatory. As seen above, some scholars reconcile this conflict by refusing

---

40. For similar readings of Peter's vision, see Tomson, *Heaven,* 99, 231–32; Robert C. Tannehill, *The Narrative Unity of Luke-Acts,* vol. 2 (Minneapolis: Fortress, 1990), 134–36; Jervell, *Luke,* 149, n. 24; Loader, *Jesus' Attitude,* 368–71.

to take the Lukan portrait at face value. In this reading, Luke does not really consider Paul an observant Jew. Luke expects us to understand that Paul's actions and statements that show him in this light are merely tactical maneuvers. Yet this reading so violates both the overall perspective of Luke-Acts and the plain-sense representation of Paul found there that it is losing contemporary adherents. More common among critical scholars is the dismissal of Acts as a historical source. Luke does present Paul as an observant Jew, but this portrayal is pure fiction. The historical Paul as discerned in his undisputed letters treats distinctive Jewish practices such as circumcision, the dietary laws, and the Sabbath as at best optional (but of no value) for Jews.

Despite the dominant view of Paul as hostile or neutral toward Jewish practice, a growing minority of scholars—most of whom are critical historians, with no prior theological commitment to biblical harmonization—are concluding that on this matter Luke largely had it right.[41] Paul taught that Gentile Yeshua-believers should not become Jews or take on distinctive Jewish practices. However, he expected Jewish Yeshua-believers to live a faithful and observant Jewish life, and his own practice conformed to this expectation.

The positive case for this position rests primarily on the following three texts:

> However that may be, let each of you lead the life that the Lord has assigned, to which God called you. This is my rule in all the churches. Was anyone at the time of his call already circumcised? Let him not seek to remove the marks of circumcision. Was anyone at the time of his call uncircumcised? Let him not seek circumcision. Circumcision is nothing, and uncircumcision is nothing; but obeying the commandments of God is everything. Let each of you remain in the condition in which you were called. (1 Corinthians 7:17–20)

> Once again I testify to every man who lets himself be circumcised that he is obliged to obey the entire law.[42] (Galatians 5:3)

41. In the first half of the twentieth century such scholarly luminaries as Adolf von Harnack, Albert Schweitzer, and W. D. Davies endorsed a view much like this. In the second half of the century it has received support from Krister Stendahl, Markus Barth, George Howard, Jacob Jervell, John Howard Yoder, Peter Tomson, Michael Wyschogrod, Stanley Stowers, Mark Nanos, Terence Donaldson, Markus Bockmuehl, Donald Harmon Akenson, John Gager, Oskar Skarsaune, Douglas Harink, and John McRay, among others. Not all of these scholars would see Paul's practice and teaching as presented in this chapter, but they have all reckoned with Paul's genuine respect for Jewish observance.

42. This verse refers, not merely to an obligation to keep particular commandments, but to living an integrated Jewish life. "The mistake, once again, has been to individualize the teaching, as though Paul had in mind simply a sequence of individuals confronting each other, Jews and Gentiles, without any sense of the corporate dimensions of a tradition which saw salvation in terms

But my friends, why am I still being persecuted if I am still preaching circumcision? In that case the offense of the cross has been removed. (Galatians 5:11)

When linked together, the first two texts form a striking syllogism.

Major premise: All those who are circumcised should remain circumcised (i.e., should accept and affirm their circumcision and its consequences).

Minor premise: All who are circumcised are obligated to observe the Torah (i.e., live according to distinctive Jewish practice).

Necessary conclusion: All those who are born as Jews are obligated to live as Jews.

With this conclusion established, the third text makes sense. "Paul was accused by . . . other missionaries of being inconsistent: that although he preached a circumcision-free gospel to the Galatians, he continued to 'preach circumcision' among Jews."[43] In other words, Paul urged Jewish Yeshua-believers to live as faithful Jews and Gentile Yeshua-believers to remain as non-Jews.[44] His early Jewish opponents found this twofold message inconsistent and untenable. His later Christian adherents found it incomprehensible.

1 Corinthians 7:19

For traditional Pauline exegetes, this syllogism is contradicted by 1 Corinthians 7 itself—in particular, by verse 19:

Circumcision is nothing, and uncircumcision [foreskin] is nothing; but obeying the commandments of God is everything.

Such commentators read this verse as revealing two Pauline conclusions: (1) Circumcision has no spiritual significance. Whether one is circumcised or uncir-

---

of membership in a people. . . . 'To do the whole law' was . . . (in Paul's perspective not least) to adopt a Jewish way of life. . . . No Jew that we know of thought of the Jewish way of life as a *perfect* life, that is, without any sin or failure. Rather, it was a *total* way of life. . . . It is this total way of life to which Paul refers here. He reminds his would-be Gentile judaizers that what was being demanded of them was not simply a matter of a single act of circumcision, but a whole way of life, a complete assimilation and absorption of any distinctively Gentile identity into the status of Jewish proselyte." James D. G. Dunn, *The Epistle to the Galatians* (Peabody, MA: Hendrickson, 1993), 266–67.

43. Dunn, *Galatians*, 278–79.

44. The above three Pauline texts were already combined in this way by Adolf von Harnack; see Tomson, *Paul*, 9.

cumcised is irrelevant to one's relationship with God. (2) Circumcision (for Jews) is no longer among "the commandments of God." If this is true, then Paul sees Jewish identity as having no spiritual significance and believes there is no need for Jewish parents to transmit this identity to their children. Yet these conclusions are contradicted by other Pauline texts (Romans 3:1–2; 9:4–5; 11:1–2, 28–29). If circumcision has no spiritual significance, then why is Paul so concerned to prevent Gentile Yeshua-believers from being circumcised? And how can he state that one who is circumcised is "obliged to obey the entire law"?

Peter Tomson offers a more compelling interpretation that brings 1 Corinthians 7:19 into harmony with Paul's overall teaching:

> Paul can only mean that gentiles should obey commandments also, although evidently not the same ones as Jews. He views gentiles as included in the perspective of the Creator which involves commandments for all. In other words: he envisages what elsewhere are called Noachian commandments. . . . The saying would then imply that whether or not one is a Jew does not matter before God, but whether one performs the commandments incumbent upon one does: Jews the Jewish Law, and gentiles the Noachian code—in the version to be propagated by Paul.[45]

> I conclude that the observance of distinct sets of commandments by Jewish and gentile Christians was the basic principle of Paul's missionary work, and he laid it down in the rule, "circumcision is nothing and the foreskin is nothing, but keeping God's commandments."[46]

When Paul states that "circumcision is nothing and uncircumcision (the foreskin) is nothing," he does not mean that one's identity, whether Jewish or Gentile, is thus irrelevant to one's relationship with God. If there are different commandments for Jews and Gentiles, different roles and responsibilities assigned by God, then circumcision or uncircumcision make a great difference in one's relationship with God. What Paul means is that circumcision and Jewish identity do not elevate the Jew above the Gentile before God. There is a difference in role, but no hierarchy of status.[47]

If we accept Tomson's reading of 1 Corinthians 7:19, then the Pauline letters reveal a figure much like the one seen in Luke's account. Paul himself lives according

---

45. Tomson, *Paul*, 271–72.

46. "Paul's Jewish Background in View of His Law Teaching in 1 Cor 7," in *Paul and the Mosaic Law,* ed. James D. G. Dunn (Grand Rapids: Eerdmans, 2001), 268.

47. Tomson rightly sees Galatians 3:28 ("there is neither Jew nor Greek") as a parallel to 1 Corinthians 7:19 (Tomson, *Paul*, 271). In both texts "Paul's 'egalitarianism' did not mean an eradication of all distinctions" (273). Mark Nanos points out the theological weakness of the traditional reading of Galatians 3:28, which sees it as Paul's nullification of all distinctions between Jews and Gentiles: "In effect, this position maintains that when Paul argued that there was neither Jew nor

to the commandments of the Torah applicable specifically to Jews, teaches other Jews to do likewise, and sees this practice as a sacred obligation. At the same time, he strongly discourages Gentiles from seeking to become Jews—since they have already been joined to the people of God through their union with Yeshua and share equal status with Jews in that now-expanded multinational community.

Romans 14–15

There are several other Pauline texts that have usually been interpreted in a manner incompatible with the Corinthians-Galatians syllogism. We must examine these texts to see if the Pauline syllogism sheds any light on them. We will begin with Romans 14–15.[48] In these chapters Paul refers to two groups, the "weak" and the "strong." He directs his instructions primarily to the "strong," with whom he appears to identify (Romans 15:1). Most commentators understand the "weak" to be Torah-observant Jewish Yeshua-believers (along with some Gentile supporters), and the "strong" to be Torah-free Gentile Yeshua-believers (along with some enlightened Jews, such as Paul). While he urges the "strong" to tolerate and respect the "weak," the fact that Paul identifies with the "strong" and sees the Torah-observant party as "weak in faith" (Romans 14:1) are generally taken to mean that Jewish Torah-observance is permissible but not obligatory.

Mark Nanos has offered a fresh reading of Romans 14–15 that challenges the traditional interpretation and calls into question the dominant view of Paul's relationship to Judaism and the Jewish community.[49] According to Nanos, the "weak" of Romans 14–15 are Jews outside of the Yeshua-movement, and their weakness consists not in their Jewish practice but in their lack of Yeshua-faith. Among the arguments marshaled by Nanos, three are especially weighty. First, he points to the message of Romans as a whole, which deals not with the relationship between Jewish and Gentile Yeshua-believers but with the relationship between Yeshua-faith and non-Yeshua-believing Judaism.[50] Second, he points to Romans 9–11, and in particular to the admonition Paul delivers in Romans

---

gentile in Christ he actually meant that there was no Jew in Christ, for they became gentiles, as it were, in that they disregarded Torah and lived and even ate *as* gentiles." Mark D. Nanos, *The Mystery of Romans* (Minneapolis: Fortress, 1996), 345.

48. For a summary of the main lines of interpretation of this passage in the scholarly literature, see Mark Reasoner, *The Strong and the Weak* (Cambridge: Cambridge University Press, 1999), 5–22.

49. Nanos, *The Mystery of Romans*, 85–165. For a critique of Nanos, see Robert A. J. Gagnon, "Why the 'Weak' at Rome Cannot Be Non-Christian Jews," *Catholic Biblical Quarterly* 62, no. 1 (January 2000): 64–82. For the response of Nanos to Gagnon, see Nanos's Web site (http://mywebpages.comcast.net/nanosmd/index.html).

50. "It can safely be said that no one has yet provided a comprehensive solution that successfully harmonizes the audience addressed in the theological concerns of the first eleven chapters with those addressed in the behavioral instructions of the final five." Nanos, *The Mystery of Romans*, 90.

11 to Gentile Yeshua-believers who are tempted to "boast" of their superior position vis-à-vis the Jewish people (11:18–25).[51] This admonition has much in common with Paul's exhortation addressed in Romans 14–15 to the "strong." Third, the Septuagint frequently uses the Greek word for "weak" to translate the Hebrew word "stumbling."[52] In Romans 9:30–33 Paul refers to non-Yeshua-believing Jews as "stumbling," and he employs the same terminology for the "weak" in Romans 14:21.

While many Pauline scholars have found this thesis creative and intriguing, few have adopted it. In part, resistance springs from a deeply rooted traditional model of understanding Paul and Yeshua-faith in general. This model presents Paul as a Torah-free Jew, and the consensus reading of Romans 14–15 fits this picture well. The traditional model also presents Paul as alienated from the Jewish community and as forming Gentile Yeshua-believing cells that are independent of the synagogue. This Paul would never assume that Gentile Yeshua-believers participate in the wider Jewish community and would never urge them to relate to Jews outside the Yeshua-movement as "brothers and sisters." Nanos has challenged this traditional way of understanding Paul, and the scholarly world has found it difficult to digest his insights.

The reading of Romans 14–15 championed by Mark Nanos conforms to the Pauline syllogism presented in this chapter. While I find his interpretation persuasive, it is not the only way to bring these chapters into line with the syllogism. Let us now look at Romans 14–15, assuming—contrary to Nanos but in accord with the scholarly consensus—that the "weak" are Yeshua-believers. How can we best understand Paul's apparent identification with the "strong"?

In these chapters Paul describes a conflict among his hearers and exhorts the disputing parties to a particular course of action. Apparently the conflict arises in the setting of community meals.[53] In direct and indirect statements, Paul portrays two extreme and irreconcilable positions. On one side, as we have

51. "Is the attitude that Paul confronts in chapters 9–11 not the same kind of boastful arrogance that characterizes the 'strong' in Rome? Are they not clearly the aggressor Paul confronts throughout this letter?" Ibid., 102.

52. Ibid., 120–24.

53. "Paul is discussing here not the general practices of the Christians concerned but their specific behaviour when they meet and eat together. The disputes arise when they do (or do not) welcome one another to meals (14:1–3), and their debates are given urgency not as general discussions of lifestyle but as specific arguments about the food set before them on such occasions. It is hard to see why the strong should despise the weak or the weak judge the strong with such strength of feeling unless their different behaviour made immediate impact on their lives, and this would occur, of course, when they attempted to share common meals." John M. G. Barclay, "'Do we undermine the Law,'" in *Paul and the Mosaic Law*, 291.

seen, we have those he calls "the weak" (Romans 14:1–2; 15:1). These people consider the meat and wine served at the community meals to be "intrinsically impure" (Romans 14:13) and on such occasions will consume only vegetables. They also view certain days—probably the Sabbath and Jewish holidays—as (intrinsically) more sacred than other days, though this does not appear to be the main point of dispute. In the context of Romans, it is reasonable to assume that this group consists of scrupulous, Torah-observant Jews (along, perhaps, with some Gentile supporters), who see impurity (of food) and holiness (of days) as objective ontological categories.[54]

On the other side, we have those Paul calls "the strong" (Romans 15:1). These people consider all food to be pure, and, acting on this conviction, they publicly consume meat and wine that the "weak" view as impure (Romans 14:2–4). In like fashion, they treat all days as sacred and refuse to show greater honor to one day than to another (Romans 14:5–6). In the wider context of Romans, it is reasonable to assume that this group consists mainly of Gentiles—though some Jews, such as Paul, share their perspective in part—who take a rationalist philosophical approach to both impurity (of food) and holiness (of days).[55]

This description of the two extreme positions would be incomplete without noting their attitudes toward one another. From Paul's exhortations to the parties, it is evident that each side adopts the position of judge in regard to the other and finds the other guilty.[56] In addition, the "strong" despise the "weak" (Romans 14:3, 10). As the exhortations indicate, these attitudes and the actions they engender are what truly concern Paul.

As noted above, most interpreters have concluded that Paul agrees with the "strong" on every point except their attitude toward the "weak." While this is a reasonable reading of Romans 14–15, it is not the only reasonable reading. Paul does not tell us in this passage all that we would like to know about his views regarding Jewish practice. At one point (Romans 15:1) he identifies with the "strong" ("we who are strong"), but this need not imply agreement with

54. Some interpreters have questioned the dominant thesis that the dispute concerns matters of Jewish practice; see Reasoner, *Strong*, 16–17. Nevertheless, the overall argument of the letter appears to support the dominant thesis. "It is now generally recognized that the theme of Romans is the 'righteousness of God' with specific reference to 'both the Jew, first, and the Greek' (1:16). . . . It is therefore natural to interpret the paranesis as related to such ethnic and cultural issues, which were indeed central to Paul's mission. . . . The fact that 15:7–13 returns to the topic of Jew and Gentile united in Christ gives further support to our position." Barclay, "Undermine," 290.

55. On the Hellenstic philosophical background to this text, see Tomson, *Paul and the Jewish Law,* 245–54.

56. Romans 14 employs the verb "to judge" (*krino*) in numerous verses (3, 4, 5, 10, 13, 22, 23). It is a key word in the chapter, signaling one of its major themes.

them in every respect. In fact, he has good rhetorical reasons for emphasizing this identification: since he directs his exhortation primarily to the "strong," the effectiveness of the exhortation is heightened by his willingness to place himself among them.

It is actually unlikely that Paul agrees with the "strong" in every respect. The two sides of this dispute, as characterized by Paul, occupy extreme ends of a spectrum of possible positions (see chart). Thus, the "weak" refuse to drink wine at the community meals. There are no prescriptions in the Torah prohibiting wine consumption for nonpriests (or for priests outside the temple precincts). Pious Jews at this time would sometimes refrain from drinking wine produced or owned by Gentiles because of the possibility that the wine had been consecrated to a foreign deity.[57] Later rabbinic legislation imposed severe restrictions on the use of such wine for this very reason.[58] However, if the Gentiles in question had renounced idolatry and embraced Yeshua-faith, Jewish Yeshua-believers could reasonably assume that their wine was untainted. Therefore refraining from wine at the community meal was not required by the dietary laws or universal Jewish practice. It was instead an example of scrupulous devotion to custom that implicitly called into question the monotheistic commitment of Gentile members of the community.[59]

**Chart: Key Reference Points in the Spectrum of Opinion
in the Early Yeshua-Movement[60]**

The "Weak"	James and The Jerusalem Council	Paul	The "Strong"
Gentiles must become Jews to be pure/holy	Gentile Yeshua-believers are purified and sanctified through Yeshua-faith	Gentile Yeshua-believers are purified and sanctified through Yeshua-faith	The only purification and sanctification of any value is that which comes through Yeshua-faith

57. "Finally, some Jews were *generally* unwilling to eat pagan food, even when there might be no legal objection to it. Some, if they had to eat Gentile food, would eat only vegetables and drink only water; some would eat nothing cooked at all. That is, some Diaspora Jews responded to their pagan environment, full of idolatry and sexual immorality (from their perspective), by cutting themselves off from too much contact with Gentiles. . . . Other Jews, it must be emphasized, participated in numerous aspects of pagan culture, such as the theatre and games, quite cheerfully. . . . These people may have felt less queasy about Gentile food." E. P. Sanders, *Judaism: Practice and Belief, 63 BCE–66 CE* (Philadelphia: Trinity Press International, 1992), 216.

58. See Tomson, *Paul*, 168–77; Gary G. Porton, *Goyim: Gentiles and Israelites in Mishnah-Tosefta* (Atlanta: Scholars, 1988), 251–58.

59. "Apparently as long as the gentiles did not abstain from meat and wine, these Jews [in Rome] were unable to accept that idolatry was really excluded." Tomson, *Paul*, 244.

60. I do not discuss or defend all of the contents of this chart in the body of this chapter. The purpose of the chart is to suggest the range of opinion that existed in the early Yeshua-movement

The "Weak"	James and The Jerusalem Council	Paul	The "Strong"
	Jews are obligated to observe the Torah	Jews should continue to live as Jews	Yeshua-faith abolishes and invalidates Jewish practice for Jews
All Gentile wine is forbidden to Jews	The only food restrictions for Gentile Yeshua-believers are blood, meat derived from animals slaughtered through strangling, and food clearly offered to idols		
Purity/impurity of food and holiness of days are intrinsic rather than imputed		Purity/impurity of food and holiness of days are imputed rather than intrinsic	Purity/impurity of food and holiness of days are non-existent

Therefore we should not consider the views and practices of the "weak" as representative of all Jewish Yeshua-believers at Rome who continued to observe the Jewish way of life. This conclusion draws further support from Paul's exhortation to the "weak." They judge the "strong" for eating certain types of meat and drinking wine at the community meal. They also apparently judge them for not honoring Jewish holy days. If we assume that the party of the "strong" consists mainly of Gentiles, this condemnation implies that the "weak" believe that Gentile Yeshua-believers should be required to live in full compliance with Jewish law and custom.[61] Therefore, they reject the decisions reached in Jerusalem by James, Peter, and John. This confirms our contention that the views of the "weak" occupy an extreme end of the spectrum and do not represent all those who see Jewish practice as obligatory for Jewish Yeshua-believers.

The views and practices of the "strong" stand at the extreme opposite end of the spectrum. In accordance with the Jerusalem decisions, the "strong" insist that they (as Gentiles) have no obligation to keep the Jewish dietary laws or holy days. In agreement with Paul, they reject ritual impurity (and perhaps ritual holiness) as an objective ontological status. However, their beliefs and actions take them far beyond James, Peter, John, and Paul. Just as the Gentiles addressed by Paul in Romans 11:13–24 appear to have adopted an early form

---

on these matters and to show that Paul could have differed dramatically from the "weak" in his views without adopting the extreme positions advocated by the "strong."

61. "If those who ate only vegetables *judged* (i.e. condemned) the meat-eaters (14:2), they must have considered their abstinence a universal requirement: for them, to eat the meat constituted a serious Christian sin." Barclay, "Undermine," 292.

of supersessionism in relation to Israel's election, so the "strong" addressed in Romans 14 show historical precocity in regard to Jewish observance by Jewish Yeshua-believers. They "despise" their Jewish associates because these associates hold outmoded beliefs and practice an invalid way of life. If we may enlist their second-century theological heirs to fill in the gaps, we may presume that the "strong" believe that Yeshua came to liberate the Jewish people from their ancestral customs and to create a new community in which the distinction between Jew and Gentile is entirely eliminated.

Paul may identify with the "strong" in some respects, but he clearly does not share their perspective *in toto*.

In Romans 14:14 and 14:20 Paul tells us what he has in common with the strong: the view that "everything is indeed clean" and "nothing is unclean in itself." As we saw above, these statements resemble Mark's interpretation of Yeshua's teaching on impurity (Mark 7:19b). Some scholars see these two comments by Paul as his interpretation of that dominical teaching.[62] In our study of Mark 7:19b we cited a rabbinic story about Yohannan ben Zakkai to demonstrate that the denial of an ontologically objective ritual impurity could coexist with the affirmation of the laws of ritual impurity. In similar fashion, Mark Nanos argues that Paul's denial of intrinsic impurity does not nullify the laws of impurity but instead grounds them in the divine word rather than in the cosmic order:

> Paul's declaration of the purity of all things should not be taken out of its contextual argument . . . Paul is really just appealing to the inherent truth of the purity laws; they exist because the holy God declared them so (e.g., Lev. 11:41–45; 19:2; 20:25–26). God has chosen what is pure to eat and what is impure, both for the Jew and for the gentile who worships him. Everything was created good, yet God declared to Adam, to Noah, and to Moses what was and was not to be eaten. Purity is not intrinsic; it is imputed. God has spoken and it is so.[63]

We may assume that first-century Jews had various opinions on this topic. The position advanced by Paul and Mark resembles that represented by Yohannan ben Zakkai and was well within the accepted boundaries of Jewish thought—as long as it did not undermine Jewish observance of the Torah.

Peter Tomson sees a connection between this approach to ritual impurity and Paul's remark in Romans 14:5 about holy days: "Some judge one day to be better

---

62. W. D. Davies, *Paul and Rabbinic Judaism* (Philadelphia: Fortress, 1948), 138; Barclay, "Undermine," 300.

63. Nanos, *The Mystery of Romans*, 199–200.

than another, while others judge all days to be alike."[64] Citing several striking parallels to these words in Jewish sources from the Greco-Roman era, Tomson concludes: "Thus Paul's sympathetic statement that 'some distinguish every day' appears to relate to the universal atmosphere found in the Hillel traditions and in Philo, associated with biblical wisdom and expressed in the vocabulary of popular Cynico-Stoicism."[65] The material he cites from rabbinic literature and from Philo combines the exalting of "every day" with the literal observance of Shabbat and holidays, just as the story of Yohannan ben Zakkai combines the denial of ritual purity with the laws of ritual purity. The parallels cited by Tomson do not demonstrate that Paul observed the dietary laws and the Sabbath or considered them authoritative for all Jews. However, they do demonstrate that Paul's affirmations in Romans 14 do not exclude such a proposition.

Paul identifies with the "strong" in Romans 15:1 because he shares with them their view of ritual purity and ritual holiness, because he is the apostle to the Gentiles and zealously defends their status and rights within the ekklesia, and because his main purpose is to persuade them to modify their attitudes and behavior. The fact that he seeks a change in their conduct itself indicates that he does not identify with every aspect of their approach. Therefore, while he defends their right to eat anything (Romans 14:2), we need not conclude that he likewise eats anything.

Paul's main contention in Romans 14–15 is the primacy of "righteousness and peace and joy in the Holy Spirit" (14:17), of "walking in love" (14:15), of pursuing "what makes for peace and for mutual upbuilding" (14:19), and of "building up the neighbor" (15:2). In comparison with these things, matters of "food and drink" are of secondary concern (14:17). This emphasis echoes the teaching of Yeshua, who likewise presented the love of God and love of neighbor as the "weightier matters of the Torah" (Matthew 23:23). When one approaches Jewish dietary practice as did the "weak," food and drink place a wall between

---

64. In an earlier footnote (note 13) we pointed to the Enochic approach to impurity and the demonic realm as evidence for the thesis that not all first-century Jews shared the later rabbinic perspective on the ontological status of impurity. We may likewise contrast the approach to holy days found in the Enochic tradition (as expressed, for example, in *Jubilees* and *The Temple Scroll*) with that expressed in rabbinic literature. According to *Jubilees*, "The Jewish feasts are written in the heavenly tablets and are celebrated in heaven before being performed on earth (cf. 6:18). The 364-day solar calendar is the heavenly calendar that regulates the heavenly liturgy by establishing a series of holy and profane days. No one is allowed to change the appointed times (6:32–35)" (Boccaccini, *Beyond the Essene Hypothesis*, 95–96). Rabbinic tradition takes a radically different approach, emphasizing the role of human authorities in administering the calendar and determining the dates of holy days, ordering obedience to the decisions of those authorities even if their calculations are in error; see *m. Rosh Hashanah* 2:8–9.

65. Tomson, *Paul*, 247.

neighbor and neighbor and impede mutual respect and love. When one asserts the objective ontological status of ritual impurity and food impurity, one cannot treat as equally pure the Gentile Yeshua-believer who follows a Gentile rather than a Jewish dietary regimen. Thus the approach to Jewish practice advocated by the "weak" is defective in Paul's eyes.

By the standards upheld by Paul in Romans 14–15, the approach to Jewish practice adopted by the "strong" is just as defective as that of the "weak." This is obvious in the text, since the "strong" are Paul's primary audience, the Gentiles he seeks to correct. In despising their Jewish partners in Messiah and their way of life, they are not walking in love. Furthermore, even if one does not accept the thesis of Nanos that the "weak" are Jews outside the Yeshua-movement, do Paul's exhortations in Romans 14–15 not apply also to them? Do the "strong" have no obligations to the Jewish people as a whole? In Romans 11 Paul urges his Gentile audience to "not boast over the branches" that have been (temporarily) cut off (Romans 11:18). He is there speaking of Jews outside the Yeshua-movement. Would not a concern for walking in love, building up the neighbor, and pursuing "what makes for peace" apply also to relationships with them?

Finally, would not the overwhelming imperatives of love and peace, stressed by Yeshua and reiterated by Paul, lead Jewish Yeshua-believers, and all Jews, to faithfully observe Jewish customs of "food and drink" *for the sake of* the "righteousness and peace and joy" of Jewish covenantal existence? The kingdom of God does not consist in food and drink, but the "rejoicing" of that kingdom makes use of food and drink, and Israel's *shalom* may be advanced by its common way of life that includes customs of food and drink. If Paul concerns himself only with relations *within* the Yeshua-movement, then why devote so much attention to the Jewish people as a whole in Romans 9–11? Once we are open to a broader context for Paul's exhortations in Romans 14–15, these chapters may be read as providing a positive basis for Jewish observance rather than its abolition.

Whether we adopt the thesis of Mark Nanos or read these chapters in the alternative mode I have proposed, we find that Romans 14–15 are not incompatible with the Pauline syllogism concerning Jewish practice.

Galatians 2:11–14

The second text requiring examination is Galatians 2:11–14:

But when Cephas [Peter] came to Antioch, I opposed him to his face, because he stood self-condemned; for until certain people came from James, he used to eat with the Gentiles. But after they came, he drew back and kept himself separate for fear of the circumcision faction. And the other Jews joined him in this hypocrisy, so that even Barnabas was led astray by their hypocrisy. But when I saw that they were not acting consistently with the truth of the gospel, I said to Cephas before them all, "If you, though a Jew, live like a Gentile and not like a Jew, how can you compel the Gentiles to live like Jews?"

There are two issues in the above verses relevant to our discussion: (1) What was it about Peter's conduct that drew criticism from the people who "came from James"? (2) What is the meaning of Paul's rebuke of Peter in verse 14?

As to the first question, it has usually been assumed that Peter was eating nonkosher food with the Gentile Yeshua-believers in Antioch. Since Paul commends Peter's actions *before* the people came from James, this would imply that Paul saw the dietary laws as no longer authoritative for Jewish Yeshua-believers. Yet several telling objections may be raised to this understanding of the situation depicted in Galatians 2. First, the text nowhere speaks of *what* Peter eats. Instead, it focuses on those *with whom* he eats. The people from James criticize Peter for eating with Gentile Yeshua-believers—not for eating nonkosher food.[66] He pacifies these critics not by passing up the pork ribs and shrimp but by withdrawing from the table. Second, the criticism here of Peter by the people from James is strikingly similar to the criticism (reported by Luke) of Peter's interaction with the household of Cornelius (Acts 11:1–3). There Peter is taken to task by Jerusalem leaders for visiting "uncircumcised men" and eating with them. In both cases the issue is Peter's company, not his food. Third, in the dominant reading of Romans 14–15 Paul urges Gentile Yeshua-believers to be sensitive to the dietary concerns of Jewish Yeshua-believers and to avoid setting any obstacles in the way of their sharing common meals in peace.[67] Thus Paul would apparently urge all Gentile Yeshua-believers to honor Jewish food customs when eating with Jewish Yeshua-believers.[68] In accordance with this teaching,

66. In his article "What Was at Stake in Peter's 'Eating with Gentiles' at Antioch?" (in *The Galatians Debate,* ed. Mark Nanos [Peabody, MA: Hendrickson, 2002], 282–318), Mark Nanos proposes that at issue in the Antioch incident was not the fact that Jews were eating with Gentiles, but instead the way that Jews were eating with Gentiles (i.e., the meals were conducted in a manner that expressed Gentile equality with Jews). In either case, there is no evidence that the controversy involved Jews eating nonkosher food.

67. As previously discussed, Mark Nanos argues that Paul in Romans 14–15 is urging Gentile sensitivity to non-Yeshua-believing Jews. If Nanos is followed, then all the more should Gentile Yeshua-believers show sensitivity to Yeshua-believing Jews!

68. "Another problem with the traditional interpretation of Paul's convictions as revealed in his retelling of the Antioch incident is that it positions Paul in a contradiction of the traditional reading of Romans 14, not to mention the interpretation I have suggested. . . . Isn't Peter in Antioch adopting precisely the behavior that Paul some ten or more years later outlined as proper in Romans, namely, to accommodate Jewish opinions of proper behavior when in the company of Jews who believed such behavior appropriate so as not to cause them to 'stumble'?" Nanos, *The Mystery of Romans,* 345–46.

we should assume that the common meals in Antioch—as in the household of Cornelius—were conducted in a way that allowed the Jewish participants to minimally comply with the basic dietary restrictions of the Torah. If this was the case, then the issue in Galatians 2 was not biblical dietary laws but the relationship between Jewish and Gentile Yeshua-believers and their relative status within the early Yeshua-movement.

The second issue in Galatians 2 is Paul's rebuke of Peter in verse 14: "If you, though a Jew, live like a Gentile and not like a Jew, how can you compel the Gentiles to live like Jews?" At face value, these words imply that though they are Jews by birth, Peter and Paul no longer order their lives according to Jewish practice. Of course, this would contravene the Pauline syllogism. Two insightful interpretations of this verse have been offered that both avoid such a conclusion. Dunn has presented the first interpretation:

> For one Jew to accuse another Jew of "living like a Gentile" was wholly of a piece with the language of intra-Jewish sectarian polemic. . . . Here then we should probably recognize that Paul was using not his own language (by that time Peter had ceased "living like a Gentile"), but the language used against Peter earlier by the "individuals from James." That is to say, Paul was probably echoing the accusation made by those from James against the practice of "eating with the Gentiles.". . . For the James group, what Peter was doing when they arrived was "living like a Gentile and not like a Jew."[69]

In this reading, the phrase "live like a Gentile" is used ironically. Paul himself does not think that he and Peter live *like* Gentiles when they eat with Gentile Yeshua-believers. This is the language of their critics. Yet Paul and Peter do live *with* Gentiles, in partnership and close association with them, without any intention of altering the distinct non-Jewish identity of these partners and associates. Paul is therefore willing to adopt the language of their critics in order to shame Peter into the recognition that his withdrawing from the common table will send a message that he does not want to send—that Gentile Yeshua-believers must convert to Judaism in order to have equal status in the Yeshua-movement.

Mark Nanos accepts Dunn's proposal that Paul borrows the phrase "live like a Gentile" from the charges leveled by the "people from James."[70] However, Nanos thinks that in borrowing the term Paul also deliberately changes its meaning.

---

69. Dunn, *Galatians*, 127–28. See also James D. G. Dunn, "Echoes of Intra-Jewish Polemic in Paul's Letter to the Galatians," *Journal of Biblical Literature* 112, no. 3 (Fall 1993): 468–69. Bockmuehl, *Jewish Law*, 81 follows Dunn.

70. Nanos, *The Mystery of Romans*, 351 (in nn. 28 and 29 Nanos cites Dunn).

The "people from James" used the word to refer to one's *ethos*—one's national custom, or concrete way of life. In contrast, Paul uses the term in reference to the foretaste of the life of the world to come that Yeshua-believers receive through the Holy Spirit. This interpretation receives support from Paul's use of the word later in the same chapter (Galatians 2:19–20), where "life" is virtually equivalent to "justification," and from the central role of Habbakuk 2:4 in his argument ("the one who is righteous will live by faith" [Galatians 3:11]). Thus, when Paul says to Peter that he lives like a Gentile, he means that he has received life in the same way as the Gentile Yeshua-believers—through faith in the faithfulness of Yeshua the Messiah.

> To paraphrase this extremely compact argument, Paul was saying to Peter that if he lived (justified) as (an equal, that is, justified in the same manner as) a gentile (through faith in Christ) and not like (those) Jews (who still relied on the works [status] of the Law for their justification), then why would he now withdraw in such a way as to compel the gentiles (also justified by faith in Christ) to believe that they are not equals unless they also live (justified) as Jews (by the works [status] of the Law).[71]

Thus, the issue is not Peter's Jewish "life" or practice, but the eschatological gift of "life" that he has received in the same way as the Gentile Yeshua-believers (see Acts 10:47; 11:17; 15:8–9). As with Dunn's reading, so with that of Nanos: there is no conflict between Galatians 2:14 and the Pauline syllogism.[72]

1 Corinthians 9:19–23

The third Pauline text that we must examine is 1 Corinthians 9:19–23:

> For though I am free with respect to all, I have made myself a slave to all, so that I might win more of them. To the Jews I became as a Jew, in order to win Jews; to those under the Torah as one under the Torah (though I myself am not under the Torah) so that I might win those under the Torah; to those outside the Torah as one outside the Torah (though I am not outside the Torah of God but am within

---

71. Ibid., 355. See also Nanos, "What Was at Stake," 311–14. Markus Barth offered the same interpretation of Galatians 2:14 in "Jews and Gentiles: The Social Character of Justification in Paul," *Journal of Ecumenical Studies* (June 1968): 246, 250.

72. The interpretations of Dunn and Nanos both build on the surprising use of the present tense of the verb ("you live like a Gentile") employed by Paul in addressing Peter *after* Peter has withdrawn from eating with the Gentile Yeshua-believers. Dunn explains it as an ironic allusion to a charge made by others (i.e., the people from James). Nanos (and Barth) explain it as an affirmation of an unchangeable truth that Peter must acknowledge—that he has received eschatological life from God along with and in the same way as the Gentile Yeshua-believers.

the Torah of Messiah) so that I might win those outside the Torah. To the weak I became weak, so that I might win the weak. I have become all things to all people, that I might by all means save some. I do it all for the sake of the good news, so that I may share in its blessings. (Translation mine, based on the NRSV)

Commentators have traditionally understood this text to be Paul's missionary principle of accommodation that justified his living as a practicing Jew when around Jews and as a nonpracticing Jew when around Gentiles. If this interpretation is correct, Paul did not view Jewish practice as obligatory for all Jews, since he was sometimes exempt.

Much hinges here on the meaning of the expression "under the Torah." Though it is difficult to know precisely what Paul intended by this phrase, it evidently refers to a relationship to the Torah that exists legitimately for a Jew before the death and resurrection of Yeshua and that is supposed to change after those events (see Galatians 3:23–26; 4:4–5).[73] The term has more to do with status than with observing particular behavioral norms. Thus it is compared to the status of a child who has not yet reached the age of maturity (Galatians 4:1–2) and is contrasted with the full realization of adult "sonship." It is a status that the Gentile Yeshua-believers in Galatia mistakenly seek (Galatians 4:21), thinking that it provides something beyond what they currently enjoy through faith in Messiah's faithfulness.

Being "*under* the Torah" (*hupo nomon*) is contrasted here with being "*outside* the Torah" (*anomos*). If the former refers to the status of *Jews* apart from the death and resurrection of Yeshua, the latter refers to the status of *Gentiles*, who, apart from those events, are entirely outside the framework of the divine covenants established with the people of Israel. Whereas *hupo nomon* is negative only in relation to the greater status offered through Messiah's death and resur-

---

73. Lloyd Gaston, *Paul and the Torah* (Vancouver: University of British Columbia Press, 1987), 29–30, and John Gager, *Reinventing Paul* (Oxford: Oxford University Press, 2000), 91–92, argue that the Pauline phrase "under the law" refers only to Gentiles. Gaston thus asserts that Paul in 1 Corinthians 9:19–23 speaks of four distinct groups: (1) Jews; (2) those under the law (i.e., Gentiles); (3) the lawless (i.e., the Corinthian antinomians); (4) the weak (i.e., those under discussion in 1 Corinthians 8–10). Gager explains Galatians 4:4 ("God sent his Son, born of a woman, born under the law") as meaning that Yeshua identified with the condition of the Gentiles and suffered vicariously on their behalf—not as meaning "Yeshua was born a Jew." However, Paul's reference to Yeshua's birth (*genomenos*, the same term used in Romans 1:3, "*descended* from David according to the flesh") does indeed appear to point to his natural condition as a human being ("born of a woman") and as a Jew ("born under the law"). According to C. E. B. Cranfield, *The Epistle to the Romans* (Edinburgh: T&T Clark, 1975), 320, the Pauline phrase "under the law" can mean either "under the law's condemnation of sinners" or "under a legalistic misunderstanding of the law's purposes" (my paraphrases). The former meaning would work for Galatians 4:4, but not the latter; neither seems to suit 1 Corinthians 9:20.

rection, *anomos* is an entirely negative term. Both are contrasted with a third unambiguously positive term—"*within* the Torah" (*ennomos*). This compound word refers to the new relationship to the Torah established for both Jews and Gentiles through faith in Yeshua's faithfulness.

To be "under the Torah" and to enjoy the relatively positive status that it confers, one must live in strict separation from those "outside the Torah." However, once both Jew and Gentile receive the foretaste of eschatological life in Messiah Yeshua, they are together brought "within the Torah" and are summoned to a life of partnership. That partnership does not eliminate all distinctions between Jews and Gentiles, but it does forge a new positive relationship between the two, one that must be embodied in a genuine communal commitment. Thus the new status of life "within the Torah" brings changes in the relationship between Jews and Gentiles.

Paul states that when relating to non-Yeshua-believing Jews he lives as though he were "under the Torah"—though he is in fact not "under the Torah" but "within the Torah." This probably means that he treats these Jews as his genuine covenant siblings rather than adopting a position of superiority and separation in relation to them. He identifies with them and builds upon what they truly share in common. He seeks to "win them" to Messiah Yeshua and to a life "within the Torah," but he does it not by speaking down to them but by addressing them as his covenant partners. The phrase may also imply that he is willing to adopt a level of halakhic stringency when operating within a strictly Jewish environment that would be inappropriate in the new intercommunal Jewish-Gentile setting established "within the Torah." However, as one who is in fact "within the Torah" and not "under the Torah," Paul would never so identify with his siblings "under the Torah" as to act in a way that implied the inferior status of Yeshua-believing Gentiles. According to Paul, this was Peter's mistake in Antioch (Galatians 2:11–14).

Paul also states that when relating to those "outside the Torah" (i.e., Gentiles who are not Yeshua-believers), he identifies with *them*—even though he is not "outside the Torah," but "within the Torah." As one who now eats, travels, works, and resides with non-Jewish Yeshua-believers and who recognizes them as his covenant partners in the expanded multinational people of God, Paul has the capacity to understand and empathize with Gentiles who are not yet Yeshua-believers. He does all that he can to meet them on their own level.[74] At

---

74. "What I mean to suggest is that those in positions of power or social status are faced with a choice when in the company of those not similarly distinguished: they may 'pull rank' so to speak or they may choose to relate on an 'equal' basis. . . . In this sense Paul speaks of how he relates to Jews as Jews and gentiles as gentiles (1 Corinthians 9:19–23). He need not cease Jewish behavior when in the company of gentiles, but he does not make any more of it than necessary so as to minimize the distinction." Nanos, *The Mystery of Romans*, 368, n. 60.

the same time, we have no reason to think that Paul put aside Jewish practice when among such Gentiles. Just as his willingness to operate as though "under the Torah" with those in a similar condition did not mean that he would ever speak or act in a way that undermined the full spiritual equality of Yeshua-believing Gentiles, so his willingness to operate as though "without the Torah" did not mean that he would ever speak or act in way that violated basic Jewish practice "within the Torah."

Looking at 1 Corinthians 9:19–23 within the wider context of 1 Corinthians 8–10, Markus Bockmuehl contends that the issue may be Paul's readiness to give Gentiles the benefit of the doubt when determining whether they were to be considered idolaters:

> Quite possibly, the passage means no more than what 1 Corinthians 8 and 10 also say: Paul has come to follow a lenient halakhah on the Gentiles' supposedly idolatrous intention, and therefore to give them the benefit of the doubt as far as that more liberal tradition allows. When he eats with conservative Jews, on the other hand, he is prepared to accommodate himself to their stricter parameters of observance. Thus, "not being under the law" means that while Paul himself does not affirm the narrowly ethnic type of halakhah, he can happily adapt to it and operate within it, if thereby he can win some of his stricter compatriots.[75]

Thus Paul had a certain amount of halakhic flexibility—but not a complete freedom from halakhah. He varied in his Jewish practice depending on his circumstances, but this text gives us no grounds for thinking that he ever actually violated basic Jewish practice (i.e, by eating nonkosher food or by profaning the Sabbath or holidays).

Conclusion

In conclusion, Romans 14–15, Galatians 2, and 1 Corinthians 9 need pose no obstacles to the Pauline syllogism. While the interpretations we have offered are not the only plausible possibilities, they have the advantage of bringing coherence to Pauline teaching and practice. They also present us with a Paul closely resembling the figure seen in the Lukan history. Finally, they have the support of the hermeneutical factors enunciated in the previous chapter: (1) they show us an authentically Jewish Paul; (2) they support the ongoing validity of Jewish practice and identity and thus counter historically anti-Jewish theological tendencies in Christian exegesis; and (3) they enable Christians to see the continuity of Jewish practice through the past two millennia as providentially guided and protected.

75. Bockmuehl, *Jewish Law*, 170–71. See also Tomson, *Paul*, 276–81.

John and Hebrews

The only remaining books of the New Testament that require special attention are the Gospel of John and the letter to the Hebrews. Readers often see these books as abolishing Jewish practice. However, on closer inspection we find that neither book has much to say on the topic, whether positive or negative.

The Gospel of John

The narrative structure of the first half of the Gospel of John is ordered in relation to the Jewish holidays.[76] John's purpose in so arranging the book is evident: in keeping with the christological focus of this Gospel, John presents Yeshua as the realization and embodiment of the worship institutions ordained in the Torah. Thus Yeshua is the definitive temple (John 2:19–22) and Passover lamb (John 19:36), and the water-drawing ceremony of the feast of Booths points to the gift of the Spirit that he imparts (John 7:37–39). This is what is meant in John when Yeshua asserts, "If you believed Moses, you would believe me, for he wrote about me" (John 5:46). This does not refer to Messianic prophecies in the Torah (which are not prominent in John) but to the events described and institutions ordained in the Torah.[77]

Interpreters sometimes infer from John's typological reading of Torah institutions that the book sees Yeshua as the replacement for these institutions. However, without explicit support from the text, such an inference is unwarranted.[78] Why would the recognition that Yeshua perfectly realizes the intent of an institution necessarily lead to the abolition of that institution rather than to its revitalized practice? Second-century Christian controversy actually provides support for the latter rather than the former, at least in regard to one particular practice—the sanctifying of the day of Passover. Disagreement arose between the congregations of the province of Asia (in Asia Minor, which is roughly equivalent to modern Turkey) and the congregations outside that province regarding the proper dates for celebrating the death and resurrection of Yeshua.[79] The con-

76. John 2:13, 23 (Passover); 5:1 ("a Jewish feast"); 5:9 (the Sabbath); 6:4 (Passover); 7:2 (Booths); 7:37 ("the last day of the feast [of Booths], the great day"); 9:14 (the Sabbath); 10:22 (Dedication—Hanukkah); 11:55; 12:1,12, 20; 13:1 (Passover).

77. For an event from the Torah that is applied in John to Yeshua, see John 6:31–35 and its treatment of the manna in the wilderness.

78. Daniel Boyarin argues that John presents Yeshua "as a supplement to the Torah" rather than its replacement: "For John, as for that other most 'Jewish' of Gospels, Matthew—but in a very different manner—Jesus comes to fulfill the mission of Moses, not to displace it. The Torah simply needed a better exegete, the Logos Ensarkos, a fitting teacher for flesh and blood." *Border Lines* (Philadelphia: University of Pennsylvania Press, 2004), 104.

79. For more on this controversy, see chapter 5.

gregations elsewhere claimed that the resurrection could only be celebrated on a Sunday. Those in the province of Asia Minor, on the other hand, claimed that the Messiah's death and resurrection should be honored on the day of Passover as determined by the Jewish calendar. To support their practice, they cited the authority of the apostle John, the author of the fourth Gospel! Thus, while no longer living according to Jewish practice as a whole, these Christians preserved one particular custom in which typological fulfillment and traditional Jewish practice were mutually reinforcing—and they traced this custom to the author of the fourth Gospel. Is it not reasonable to think that this pattern of mutual reinforcement might have existed for other Jewish customs among Jews in the early Johannine community?

We find one text in John that points in such a direction. It deals with the only area in which Yeshua's Jewish observance is criticized in John—his healing on the Sabbath.

> "Didn't Moshe give you the *Torah*? Yet not one of you obeys the *Torah!* Why are you out to kill me? . . . I did one thing, and because of this, all of you are amazed. Moshe gave you *b'rit-milah* [circumicision]—not that it came from Moshe but from the Patriarchs—and you do a boy's *b'rit-milah* on *Shabbat*. If a boy is circumcised on *Shabbat* so that the *Torah* of Moshe will not be broken, why are you angry with me because I made a man's whole body well on *Shabbat*? Stop judging by surface appearances, and judge the right way!" (John 7:19, 21–24, *Jewish New Testament*)

There are several noteworthy features of this passage. First, Yeshua rebukes his opponents for not obeying the Torah. While this refers primarily to their lack of receptivity to the man in their midst who embodies the Torah, in the current context it also has implications for the proper observance of the Sabbath (as is clear in John 7:23, with its concern that "the *Torah* of Moshe . . . not be broken"). Second, the point of Yeshua's rabbinic-style argument is that his work of healing on the Sabbath does not violate the Sabbath any more than does the work of circumcision. Thus, as in the synoptic Gospels, we have here a halakhic dispute over what activities are permitted on the Sabbath rather than a rejection on Yeshua's part of the continuing validity of the Sabbath commandment. Third, Yeshua bases his argument on the practice of circumcision, which he presents as a "healing" of one part of the child's body. Yeshua thus endorses the fundamental Jewish practice of circumcision. It is highly unlikely that Jewish members of the community that initially read and revered this text would have done otherwise.

As noted above, Sabbath observance is the only issue in which Jewish practice arises as a point of controversy in John. The issue appears in two healing narratives—the paralytic (John 5) and the man born blind (John 9).[80] In the latter incident Yeshua makes a mud compound and applies it to the eyes of the blind man. His opponents take this as evidence that Yeshua "does not observe the Sabbath" (John 9:16) and is thus "a sinner" (John 9:16, 24). However, the point of the narrative is to reveal the absurdity of viewing Yeshua as "a sinner" (John 9:31). Therefore it is likely that John does not view Yeshua's action as a violation of the Sabbath.

In the first incident Yeshua directs the healed paralytic to carry his mat on the Sabbath (John 5:8–9)—perhaps to demonstrate and celebrate his healing. Yeshua's critics see this as a violation of the Sabbath (John 5:10). Yeshua does not respond to this charge but instead defends his healing on the Sabbath: "My Father is still working, and I also am working" (John 5:17). Raymond Brown explains the background of this saying and Yeshua's elaboration of it in John 5:19–30:

> The theologians of Israel realized that God did not really cease to work on the Sabbath. There are a whole series of rabbinic statements . . . to the effect that Divine Providence remained active on the Sabbath, for otherwise, the rabbis reasoned, all nature and life would cease to exist.
>
> In particular, as regards men, divine activity was visible in two ways: men were born and men died on the Sabbath. Since only God could give life . . . and only God could deal with the fate of the dead in judgment, this meant that God was active on the Sabbath. . . .
>
> . . . In the rest of vs. 20 he [Yeshua] begins to expound the nature of the works that he has seen the Father do and which he is imitating. They are the same works that according to Jewish theology it was proper for the Father to do on the Sabbath. In vs. 21 the *first* of these works is mentioned: Jesus grants life. . . . In vv. 22–23 the *second* of the works is mentioned: Jesus is the judge, for the Father has turned over the power of judgment to the Son.[81]

The issue thus quickly shifts from Sabbath observance to Christology. This is evident in John 5:18, which tells us that Yeshua's opponents sought to destroy him "because he was not only breaking the Sabbath, but was also calling God his own Father, thereby making himself equal to God."

What are we to make of this statement? Does John agree that Yeshua was breaking the Sabbath? In John 7:21–24 Yeshua argues that his healing

---

80. The two narratives are parallel in structure. On the relationship between the two, see Craig S. Keener, *The Gospel of John,* vol. 1 (Peabody, MA: Hendrickson, 2003), 639–40.

81. Raymond E. Brown, *The Gospel according to John I-XII,* The Anchor Bible, vol. 29 (New York: Doubleday, 1966), 217–19.

did not violate the Sabbath. Can John 5 be seen as a similar argument? The argument in John 5 hinges on Yeshua's claim to be God's Son. God obviously does not violate the Sabbath when he gives life and judges. He is not subject to the commandment in the same way that Israel is subject to the commandment. If Yeshua is who he claims to be, he is also not breaking the Sabbath when he gives life through healing. Therefore, it is likely that John's reference to Yeshua's breaking the Sabbath is ironic. He is merely reporting the charge leveled by Yeshua's opponents—not affirming it. This conclusion is supported by the second part of the statement: "making himself equal to God." While John presents Yeshua as saying, "I and the Father are one" (John 10:30), he also records the words, "the Father is greater than I" (John 14:28). At the very least, John would have cringed at the notion that Yeshua "*made himself* equal to God." This is in effect a charge of blasphemy. John would never describe Yeshua's divinity as a matter of his own independent actions or arrogant claims. Therefore, it is best to see John 5:18 as a charge that John himself rejects.[82]

Even if we were to adopt the unlikely view that John saw Yeshua as in some sense breaking the Sabbath, the defense he gives for his action—his authority as the unique divine Son—hardly provides a basis for his followers to imitate his actions. The book gives no rationale for Jews to cease observing the Sabbath—or any other distinctive Jewish practice enjoined by the Torah. Therefore, as with the other New Testament books we have examined, the Gospel of John provides no support for the view that Jewish practice ceases to be obligatory for Jews after the coming of Yeshua.

The Letter to the Hebrews

Unlike the Gospel of John, the letter to the Hebrews does appear to propose a change in the observance of the Torah.[83] The book's central thesis is that Yeshua is the new high priest, who offers a better sacrifice than could be offered by the Aaronic priests in the wilderness tabernacle or in the Jerusalem temple. Since Yeshua is not of Aaronic descent, the law has obviously been changed:

82. For a more detailed argument for our thesis, see Keener, *John,* vol. 1, 645–48.

83. Tomson argues that this is not the case: "While the author is clear on the superbness of the worship of the 'new' covenant, he speaks of the 'old' as something that still continues and that is symbolized in the temple service in the present time. The work of Christ consists, then, not so much in disbanding the worship prescribed by the old covenant, but in fulfilling its true significance while 'the first tent still stands.' . . . The implementation of the law and the temple worship continue unimpeded, even after its real purpose had been fulfilled in Christ." *Heaven,* 361–62. While Tomson's view is intriguing, it will not persuade many. Our argument here will depart less radically from the consensus reading of the text.

> For when there is a change in the priesthood, there is necessarily a change in the law as well. Now the one of whom these things are spoken belonged to another tribe, from which no one has ever served at the altar. For it is evident that our Lord was descended from Judah, and in connection with that tribe Moses said nothing about priests. (Hebrews 7:12–14)

This change in the law involves the abrogation of a commandment establishing the Levitical priesthood as Israel's primary representative before God (Hebrews 7:18) and the abolition of the Levitical sacrificial system (Hebrews 10:8–9). It also entails a change in Israel's covenant with God, which is mediated by the priesthood and its sacrifices (Hebrews 8:6, 13).

Christian readers have almost universally understood these statements in Hebrews as a blanket abolition of the distinctive Jewish or "ritual" component of the Torah. The change in the Torah effected through Yeshua's sacrificial death thus nullifies circumcision, the Sabbath and holidays, and the dietary laws as divine ordinances for Jews. Such a reading of Hebrews makes sense to Christian readers who bring with them the assumption that Yeshua (in Mark 7 and John 5), Peter (in Acts 10), and Paul (in Galatians and Romans) all teach that such a change has occurred. However, in light of the exegesis of these texts presented above, we can no longer take for granted that Yeshua, Peter, and Paul annulled distinctive Jewish practice or saw it as merely optional. Given this fact, does the letter to the Hebrews *on its own* support the view that Yeshua's death and resurrection have rendered Jewish practice obsolete?

Once we have dropped the *presupposition* that Jewish practice is annulled, we find that Hebrews provides absolutely no evidence that this is the case. When speaking of changes in the Torah, the author deals exclusively with the tabernacle/temple and its associated institutions (the priesthood and the sacrifices). As Jewish history has shown, these elements of the Torah—while important—could be eliminated from Jewish life without the loss of the Torah or of the distinctive Jewish existence ordained in the Torah. The centralized worship institutions of Israel constituted a self-contained component of the Torah that was not required for the continuance of Jewish life. The destruction of the temple in 70 CE did not prevent Jews from circumcising their sons, resting on the Sabbath, or eating kosher food. And not one word in Hebrews implies that the author thought Yeshua's fulfillment of the temple institutions should lead to the cessation of those Jewish practices that were separable from the temple.[84]

---

84. Charles P. Anderson is one of the few writers on Hebrews who has noted this important feature of the book: "With the one fundamental exception relating to the cult, the Torah is

Only two texts in Hebrews could possibly be construed as pointing to a nullification of Jewish practice. The first is Hebrews 9:6–10:

> Such preparations having been made, the priests go continually into the first tent to carry out their ritual duties; but only the high priest goes into the second, and he but once a year, and not without taking the blood that he offers for himself and for the sins committed unintentionally by the people. By this the Holy Spirit indicates that the way into the sanctuary has not yet been disclosed as long as the first tent is still standing. This is a symbol of the present time, during which gifts and sacrifices are offered that cannot perfect the conscience of the worshiper, but deal only with food and drink and various baptisms, regulations for the body imposed until the time comes to set things right.

Verse 10 is sometimes construed as pointing to the abrogation of the dietary laws.[85] However, the context makes such a reading unlikely. Hebrews 9:6–9 deals with the ritual washings and sacrificial offerings of the Aaronic priesthood, arguing that they were unable to bring inner purification and access to God. What bearing does this have on the Jewish dietary laws? As noted above, the Jewish food laws have no connection to the temple sacrifices. Jews who never participated in the worship of the Jerusalem temple observed these restrictions in the first-century Diaspora, and over the past nineteen centuries since that temple was destroyed, Jews have continued to maintain them. Moreover, the dietary laws have nothing to do with providing purification or access to God. Instead, their essential function is to distinguish the Jewish people from the other nations of the earth.

The second text is also often read as an exhortation to forsake traditional Jewish food restrictions. The NRSV renders Hebrews 13:9 as follows:

> Do not be carried away by all kinds of strange teachings; for it is well for the heart to be strengthened by grace, not by regulations about food, which have not benefited those who observe them.

---

still valid for those to whom it was given by Moses. No break with Jewish tradition apart from priesthood, sacrifice, and temple is assumed in Hebrews. Discontinuity centers upon cult, not Torah. Of course, cult implicates Torah. But Torah is a larger category, and apart from priesthood and other cultic aspects, is left untouched by the critique of Hebrews. The new covenant does not imply a new Torah, but a 'changed' Torah in which earlier cultic legislation is replaced. . . . Judaism was more than the temple cult, as it demonstrated following the destruction of the temple and the cessation of its services." "Who are the Heirs of the New Age in the Epistle to the Hebrews?" in *Apocalyptic and the New Testament,* ed. J. Marcus and M.L. Soards (Sheffield: JSOT, 1989), 273–74.

85. Harold W. Attridge, *The Epistle to the Hebrews* (Philadelphia: Fortress, 1989), 243, n. 158.

In this translation, the author appears to be speaking pejoratively of the Jewish dietary laws ("regulations about food").[86] However, the Greek text contains no mention of regulations. It merely states that it is better for the heart to be strengthened by grace than by food. According to Harold Attridge, this could not refer to the Jewish dietary laws, since these rules prohibit certain foods but do not make the food that is eaten a source of spiritual sustenance.[87] The author more likely deals here with sacrificial food (see Hebrews 13:10) or with some sacramental practice known to the writer and his audience but hidden from us.

Of course, it is possible that the author of Hebrews saw all Jewish practice as superseded in Yeshua. Nothing in the letter is incompatible with such a view—which is why readers steeped in a supersessionist perspective have always assumed its presence. However, there is also nothing in the letter that points implicitly or explicitly to such a view. The fact is that, like the Gospel of John, the letter to the Hebrews has little or nothing to say on the question that is occupying us in this chapter.

Conclusion

Our survey of the New Testament teaching on Jewish practice (for Jews) has produced a surprising result. We have good grounds for upholding the view that the New Testament as a whole treats Jewish practice as obligatory for Jews.

The Gospels of Matthew and Luke portray Yeshua and his followers as Torah-observant Jews. Mark as a whole paints a similar picture, with one difficult text that could, but need not, be understood in a contrary manner. The Acts of the Apostles describes the postresurrection Jewish Yeshua-movement as maintaining scrupulous Jewish practice and as viewing such practice as a sacred obligation for all Jews—whether in the land of Israel or in the Diaspora. Jewish observance is as much a theme at the end of the book as at the beginning, indicating that the author saw no trajectory pointing to an ultimate negation of Jewish observance. Acts even presents the Apostle Paul as a Torah-observant Jew. And, in fact, our study of the Pauline letters showed that there is nothing in those letters that contradicts this picture and much that supports it. While the Gospel of John

---

86. TEV: "not by obeying rules about foods"; JB: "than on dietary laws"; NEB: "not from scruples about what we eat."

87. "The opposition between the 'eating' of the 'tabernacle servers' and the mode in which Christians participate in the sacrifice of their altar suggests that the verse objects not to abstention from or restrictions on consuming something, but to some act of eating." Attridge, *Epistle to the Hebrews*, 394.

and the letter to the Hebrews have little to contribute to the discussion, neither book offers a contrary perspective.

This conclusion has profound theological implications. In many ways, the remainder of this book is an attempt to reflect on those implications and on their significance for the church and for the Jewish people.

3

THE NEW TESTAMENT
AND THE JEWISH PEOPLE

We concluded in our previous chapter that the New Testament considers Jewish practice normative for Jews who believe in Yeshua, though not for Yeshua-believing Gentiles. We also noted the intimate connection between such practice and Jewish national identity. Given this connection, the obligation of Jewish practice for Jews (and not for Gentiles) implies that the New Testament regards the Jewish people as recipients of a particular calling and as servants with a distinctive role and mission in the divine purpose. They are not elevated above Gentile Yeshua-believers, but they are distinguished from them. Whatever the distinctive calling, role, and mission of the Jewish people may be, it is not transmitted to or absorbed by the multinational ekklesia as a whole.

This conclusion in itself undermines the traditional supersessionist premise. According to the New Testament teaching regarding Jewish practice that we have already examined, the church as a whole does not and cannot replace the Jewish people. However, our conclusion could still be interpreted in a revised supersessionist manner. In this modified supersessionism, the Yeshua-believing Jews who continue to live as Jews constitute the authentic heirs of the Jewish spiritual tradition, while the Jews who do not believe in Yeshua have forfeited their standing as part of the people of Israel. We know of at least one sectarian Jewish movement that adopted such a position (i.e., the Qumran community);[1] did the early Jewish Yeshua-movement as a whole believe likewise?

1. See Daniel Boyarin, *Border Lines* (Philadelphia: University of Pennsylvania Press, 2004), 49–50.

Such a modified supersessionist reading of the New Testament is a reasonable historical hypothesis worth testing. However, even antecedent to such a test, we should note the formidable theological problems raised by this hypothesis. Since a body of Yeshua-believing Jews faithfully devoted to Jewish practice ceased to exist at some point in the first millennium, this hypothesis leads to the disturbing conclusion that the Jewish people as a whole expired at that point. Is this theologically tenable? If Jewish practice is important to God, then the Jewish people are important to God. Did he permit this people to perish?

From a theological perspective, it is more reasonable to assume that God's commitment to the Jewish people and its distinctive way of life has been sustained throughout the past two millennia. This leads to rejection rather than revision of traditional supersessionism. Jews who have not believed in Yeshua but who have loyally sustained a continual Jewish communal presence in the world through hours of deepest darkness are heirs of God's covenant with Israel. This view is consistent with the conclusions reached in the last chapter regarding New Testament teaching on Jewish practice, and it is also consistent with the realities of the last two thousand years of history. But is it consistent with the explicit teaching of the New Testament regarding the Jewish people? This is the question we must ask in the present chapter.

We are concerned at this point with the spiritual status of *the Jewish people*. How do we initially assess the historical reality of Jewish existence these past two millennia in the light of the New Testament, and (just as important) how do we read the New Testament in the light of that historical reality? We are not at this point examining the spiritual status of *Judaism as a religious tradition*. We will take up that crucial question at a later point of our discussion.

Mark

The Gospel of Mark paints a strikingly positive picture of the Jewish people as a whole and a strikingly negative picture of its leaders. Emblematic of this dual characterization is Mark 6:34:

> As he went ashore, he [Yeshua] saw a great crowd; and he had compassion for them, because they were like sheep without a shepherd; and he began to teach them many things.

Israel's "sheep" are drawn to Yeshua. In contrast, Israel's supposed "shepherds" see him as menacing and demon-possessed.

According to Mark, the popular response to John the Baptist and Yeshua is overwhelming. The "whole Judean countryside and all the people of Jerusalem" come to John to be baptized (Mark 1:5). The "whole city" of Capernaum gathers outside the house where Yeshua is staying to hear him and be healed by him (Mark 1:32–33). Mark tells us that Yeshua's "fame began to spread throughout the surrounding region of Galilee" (Mark 1:28), so that he could no longer enter a town openly, but needed to remain in the countryside; even so, "people came to him from every quarter" (Mark 1:45). Yeshua's fame quickly spreads beyond Galilee, so that people come to him even from Jerusalem and the towns of Judea (Mark 3:8). This response to Yeshua never fades in the Gospel of Mark but continues to the end (see Mark 5:24; 6:56; 7:37; 10:1). Even in Jerusalem the crowds welcome his arrival at Passover (Mark 11:8–10), and the "chief priests and scribes" fear to arrest him openly lest there be "a riot among the people" (Mark 14:1–2).

Does Mark view this popular response as a superficial fascination or as a genuine response of sincere and earnest faith? The answer to this question is provided by the one episode in which Yeshua fails to receive popular approbation:

> He left that place and came to his hometown, and his disciples followed him. On the sabbath he began to teach in the synagogue, and many who heard him were astounded. They said, "Where did this man get all this? What is this wisdom that has been given to him? What deeds of power are being done by his hands! Is not this the carpenter, the son of Mary and brother of James and Joses and Judas and Simon, and are not his sisters here with us?" And they took offense at him. Then Jesus said to them, "Prophets are not without honor, except in their hometown, and among their own kin, and in their own house." And he could do no deed of power there, except that he laid his hands on a few sick people and cured them. And he was amazed at their unbelief. (Mark 6:1–6)

In Nazareth the unbelief of the people limits his capacity to heal the sick. Whereas elsewhere the people are amazed at Yeshua's teaching and deeds of power (Mark 5:20; 6:51; 12:17), here Yeshua is amazed at Nazareth's incapacity to believe. This contrast indicates that, in Mark's estimation, Yeshua's wonder working is dependent in part upon the openness of those to whom he comes. His success in the towns of Galilee and among the crowds in Jerusalem thus testifies not only to his divine authority but also to the people's genuine faith.

Of course, the people as a whole do not fully grasp Yeshua's identity. This becomes evident in Yeshua's dialogue with his disciples at Caesarea Philippi:

> Jesus went on with his disciples to the villages of Caesarea Philippi; and on the
> way he asked his disciples, "Who do people say that I am?" And they answered
> him, "John the Baptist; and others, Elijah; and still others, one of the prophets."
> (Mark 8:27–28)

In the light of Yeshua's resurrection and the completion of the New Testament
canon, these opinions are certainly inadequate. Nevertheless we should not
miss the positive assessment they express. The people recognize Yeshua as a
messenger from God, a prophetic voice speaking with divine authority.

In contrast, Mark portrays the leaders of the people as suspicious and hostile.[2] In Galilee these leaders—identified variously as scribes (Mark 2:6; 3:22)
or Pharisees (Mark 3:6; 8:11), or with both terms paired in a way that appears
to mean Pharisaic scribes (Mark 2:16; 7:1; 7:5)—raise concerns about Yeshua's
healing on the Sabbath, eating with tax collectors and sinners, and forgiving sins.
They dismiss his power over the demonic realm, seeing it as attained through
magic arts (Mark 3:22). According to Mark, these influential figures seek to
undermine Yeshua's mission (Mark 3:6).

However, Mark does not see the Pharisaic scribes, with their religious objections to Yeshua's conduct, as his main antagonists. The true villains of the story
are the temple authorities in Jerusalem, the chief priests along with their council
(Mark 8:31; 10:33; 11:18; 11:27; 14:1; 14:43; 14:53; 14:55; 15:1; 15:31). Led by
the high priest (Mark 14:53; 14:61; 14:63), these officials reject Yeshua out of
envy (Mark 15:10). Unlike the Pharisaic scribes, their hostility to Yeshua comes
not from misguided religious principle but from a concern to protect their own
position and authority, which Yeshua challenges (Mark 11:15–18; 11:27–33).
They are the ones who arrest Yeshua, convict him of blasphemy, and turn him
over to the Romans for execution. Their treatment of Yeshua reveals their failure
as stewards of God's vineyard (Mark 12:1–11). They are unworthy to lead the
people of Israel, whose devotion to Yeshua contrasts so starkly with their own
self-aggrandizing hatred (Mark 11:18; 11:32; 12:12; 12:37; 14:1–2).

There is nothing in the Gospel of Mark that would lead one to conclude
that the covenant with the Jewish people as a whole has been annulled. Yeshua
prophesies the destruction of the temple (Mark 13:1–2), but he does so in words
that allude to apocalyptic texts from Daniel (Mark13:14; Daniel 11:31; 12:11). His
words of judgment thus point to the eschatological fulfillment of Israel's hope

---

2. There are exceptions to this picture. A synagogue authority falls at Yeshua's feet and begs
his help (Mark 5:22–23). A scribe admires Yeshua's teaching and is told, "You are not far from the
kingdom of God" (Mark 12:28–34). Joseph of Arimathea, "a respected member of the Council,"
asks permission to bury the body of Yeshua (Mark 15:43). Not all of Israel's leaders are seen as
misguided or corrupt.

rather than to Israel's disinheritance. This hope of eschatological fulfillment is expressed positively in Yeshua's selection of the twelve apostles (Mark 3:13–19). As E. P. Sanders has argued, the selection of the twelve (corresponding to the twelve tribes of Israel) points to Yeshua's commitment to the restoration of "all Israel."[3] Furthermore, Mark portrays Yeshua as vividly conscious of Israel's special privileges. In his encounter with the Gentile woman in the region of Tyre, Yeshua refers to the Jewish people as "the children [of God]," fed by God at his table, while comparing Gentiles to "dogs" waiting under the table for scraps to fall. This insult to the woman is a test, which she passes by disregarding the rebuff and persevering in her request. Nevertheless, it also reveals Yeshua's sense of Israel's unique relationship with God.

Nothing demonstrates Mark's validation of the Jewish people and its future more clearly than the mocking charge under which Yeshua is executed by the Romans. Pilate asks Yeshua, "Are you the King of the Jews?" (Mark 15:2). He then asks the crowd, "What do you wish me to do with the man you call the King of the Jews?" (Mark 15:12). The Roman soldiers continue the mockery, clothing Yeshua in a purple cloak, placing a crown of thorns on his head, and saluting him as "King of the Jews" (Mark 15:17–19). Often the point of this ridicule is missed. Pilate and the Roman soldiers are not so much taunting Yeshua as ridiculing the people of Israel. They are saying to their Jewish subjects, "This poor, ill-clothed, uncouth carpenter, whom we are humiliating and torturing, is just the sort of king that you Jews deserve." Mark ironically agrees! The entire scene should be viewed in light of Mark 10:35–45, where Yeshua contrasts the way Gentile rulers "lord it over" their subjects with how the King of Israel governs as a humble servant, giving his life "as a ransom for many." Thus Yeshua shows himself to be Israel's true king at the very moment he is taunted with this title. In Mark's eyes, the Jewish people are ennobled rather than degraded by having such a humble servant-king.

In conclusion, the Gospel of Mark supports the hypothesis offered at the beginning of this chapter: the Jewish people as a whole remain "the children" to whom God shows special regard.

Matthew

For the most part, Matthew's view of the Jewish people is like that of Mark. The people respond enthusiastically to Yeshua, whereas the leaders are his bitter enemies. Denunciations of the latter in Matthew are more vehement than

3. E. P. Sanders, *Jesus and Judaism* (Philadelphia: Fortress, 1985), 95–106.

in Mark. Nevertheless, the Jewish people as a whole—even those not yet part of the Messianic vanguard—never forfeit their unique character as "lost sheep of the house of Israel" (Matthew 10:6; 15:24).

The Gentiles

Matthew's infancy narrative anticipates the future turning of Gentiles to the God of Israel. However, this conversion of the Gentiles is represented also as a turning to the Israel of God. The converted Gentiles do not replace Israel but are joined to her. Thus Matthew's genealogy of Yeshua mentions four Gentile women: Tamar, Rahab, Ruth, and Bathsheba (Matthew 1:3, 5–6). Two of them, Rahab and Ruth, have been treated consistently in Jewish tradition as model proselytes. They become ancestors of the Messiah through being joined to the people of Israel. In the same way, Matthew intimates, the Gentiles who believe in Yeshua are to be joined to the people of Israel. The story of the wise men carries an identical message. They come to Jerusalem in search of "the king of the Jews" (Matthew 2:2). The gifts they lay at his feet recall, not only a Psalm that speaks of the homage of Gentile kings to Israel's Messiah (Psalm 72:10–11, 15), but also a prophecy that foresees nations coming with reverence to Jerusalem and paying homage to the people of Israel (Isaiah 60:6, 12, 14–16). As the Catholic Catechism states, the wise men's "coming means that pagans can discover Jesus and worship him as Son of God and Savior of the world only by turning toward the Jews and receiving from them the messianic promise" (paragraph 528).[4]

While Matthew includes a story of a Gentile whose faith exceeded that of his Jewish neighbors (Matthew 8:10), the book does not idealize Gentiles at the expense of Jews.[5] In fact, Matthew's Yeshua often speaks of Gentile mores with disdain. Thus, when teaching about love of enemies, Matthew's Yeshua sets the *right* way over against the *Gentile* way:

> For if you love those who love you, what reward do you have? Do not even the
> tax collectors do the same? And if you greet only your brothers and sisters, what

---

4. Reflecting on this paragraph in the Catechism, Cardinal Ratzinger (now Pope Benedict XVI) remarks, "All nations, without the abolishment of the special mission of Israel, become brothers and receivers of the promises of the Chosen People; they become People of God with Israel through adherence to the will of God and through acceptance of the Davidic kingdom." Joseph Cardinal Ratzinger, *Many Religions—One Covenant* (San Francisco: Ignatius, 1999), 27–28. One should note the care taken by Ratzinger to avoid a supersessionist reading of Matthew 2 and its interpretation in the Catechism.

5. The story of the centurion (Matthew 8:5–13) is found also in Luke 7:1–10, though not in Mark. Therefore, according to the two-source hypothesis, the text derives from Q and is not original to Matthew.

more are you doing than others? Do not even the Gentiles do the same?[6] (Matthew 5:46–47)

Again, when teaching about prayer, Matthew's Yeshua draws the same contrast:

When you are praying, do not heap up empty phrases as the Gentiles do; for they think that they will be heard because of their many words. (Matthew 6:7)

In Matthew's account of Yeshua's teaching about faith and material needs, we find the same motif:

Therefore do not worry, saying, "What will we eat?" or "What will we drink?" or "What will we wear?" For it is the Gentiles who strive for all these things; and indeed your heavenly Father knows that you need all these things.[7] (Matthew 6:31–32)

Yeshua's instructions regarding the treatment of a recalcitrant member of the ekklesia presume the type of Jew-Gentile distinction seen above:

If the offender refuses to listen even to the church, let such a one be to you as a Gentile and a tax collector. (Matthew 18:17)

In all of these specifically Matthean texts, the term "Gentile" has a pejorative connotation. Matthew is not anti-Gentile. As the infancy narrative and other similar passages demonstrate, he welcomes the conversion of the Gentiles to the God of Israel. At the same time, the above texts suggest that Matthew drew a sharp distinction between Jews and Gentiles and between the Jewish and Gentile ways of life, and found in Yeshua the perfect embodiment of authentic Judaism.

"Lost Sheep of the House of Israel"

Matthew's view of those Jews who had not yet responded in faith to Yeshua is captured in the phrase found only in his Gospel: "the lost sheep of the house

---

6. Luke 5:32–34 employs the word "sinners" where Matthew has "tax collectors" and "Gentiles."

7. Luke 12:30 states that "all the nations of the world seek these things." The addition of the word "all" and the phrase "of the world" puts the focus on how people in general act. The Lukan expression could even include Jews within its scope. Matthew's wording ("the Gentiles"—*ta ethne*), on the other hand, leaves no doubt that those in mind are the "non-Jews."

of Israel." This phrase is found initially in Yeshua's instructions to the twelve before sending them out on their own for the first time:

> These twelve Jesus sent out with the following instructions: "Go nowhere among the Gentiles, and enter no town of the Samaritans, but go rather to the lost sheep of the house of Israel. (Matthew 10:5–6)

Matthew introduces this section by drawing upon Mark 6:34 (discussed above). In Mark the verse introduces Yeshua's multiplication of the loaves and fish. Matthew places it in a completely different context:

> When he saw the crowds, he had compassion for them, because they were harassed and helpless, like sheep without a shepherd. (Matthew 9:26)

The Markan phrase, "like sheep without a shepherd," alludes to several biblical texts (Numbers 27:17; 1 Kings 22:17; Ezekiel 34:5), all of which portray Israel as a flock that will languish without a true shepherd. By introducing this discourse with the Markan phrase, Matthew prepares us for the summons to the twelve to go only "to the lost sheep of the house of Israel." They are "lost" because they are "without a shepherd." The work of the twelve is to let them know that their true shepherd has come.

The phrase is found again in Matthew's version of Yeshua's dialogue with the Gentile woman. Before speaking of the children and the dogs, Yeshua first says: "I was sent only to the lost sheep of the house of Israel" (Matthew 15:24). Just as he sends the twelve only to the lost sheep, so Yeshua himself goes only to the lost sheep. This focused commitment to help his own people expresses Yeshua's compassion (Matthew 9:26) and appreciation for their status as God's scattered flock. While Matthew 28:19 extends the commission of the twelve to cover all the nations of the earth, there is no indication in the text that the risen Yeshua or the twelve ever give up on their own people, "the lost sheep of the house of Israel."[8]

---

8. As Craig S. Keener writes, "What is important to remember is that the Gentile mission extends the Jewish mission—not replaces it; Jesus nowhere revokes the mission to Israel (10:6), but merely adds a new mission revoking a previous prohibition (10:5)." *A Commentary on the Gospel of Matthew* (Grand Rapids: Eerdmans, 1999), 719. See also J. Andrew Overman, *Church and Community in Crisis* (Valley Forge: Trinity Press International, 1996), 404–8; W. D. Davies and Dale C. Allison, Jr., *A Critical and Exegetical Commentary on the Gospel According to Saint Matthew,* vol. 3 (Edinburgh: T&T Clark, 1997), 684; David C. Sim, *The Gospel of Matthew and Christian Judaism* (Edinburgh: T&T Clark, 1998), 242–43.

The Holy City

Though Matthew engages in virulent polemics against the Jerusalem temple authorities, he does not follow the Qumran sectarians in their view that the temple and the city are defiled. According to Matthew, Jerusalem is "the holy city" (Matthew 4:5; 27:53) and the temple is "the holy place" (Matthew 24:15).[9] Matthew's Yeshua calls Jerusalem "the city of the great King" (Matthew 5:35; see Psalm 48:3) and states that Israel's God dwells in the Jerusalem temple (Matthew 23:21) and sanctifies offerings through its altar (Matthew 23:20). Matthew's convictions about the holy city and holy temple confirm our conclusion that he has not given up on the people of Israel and its appointed destiny, nor does he see the small community of Yeshua-believing Jews as replacing all Israel.

Matthew also includes prophecies of judgment on Jerusalem. In a text found in both Matthew and Luke, Yeshua addresses the holy city in which he will soon die:

> Jerusalem, Jerusalem, the city that kills the prophets and stones those who are sent to it! How often have I desired to gather your children together as a hen gathers her brood under her wings, and you were not willing! See, your house is left to you, desolate. For I tell you, you will not see me again until you say, "Blessed is the one who comes in the name of the Lord." (Matthew 23:37–39)

Luke situates these words in Galilee, as Yeshua travels to Jerusalem (Luke 13:34–35). In Matthew Yeshua says these things in Jerusalem itself, after confronting Israel's leaders (Matthew 21–23) and before teaching on the events that will occur at the end of the age. The Matthean context, along with the addition of the word "again" (v. 39), makes clear that Matthew sees these words both as a prophecy of Jerusalem's coming destruction and as a definitive proclamation that Jerusalem's future redemption is contingent on its acceptance of Yeshua as the one "who comes in the name of the Lord."[10] We may infer from this that Matthew assumes (1) that Jerusalem will be standing as a Jewish city before the return of Yeshua, (2) that its inhabitants (and all Jews) are still the beloved lost sheep of Israel, whose response to God is crucial for the final redemption of the world, and (3) that the conduct rather than the legitimacy of its leaders is rejected, since the response demanded in Matthew 23:39 is not just popular but also official. This last point receives surprising support from the opening

---

9. Compare Matthew 4:5 with its parallel in Luke 4:9, and Matthew 24:15 with its parallel in Mark 13:14. In these texts only Matthew uses the term "holy" in reference to the city and the temple.

10. See Davies and Allison, *Matthew*, vol. 3, 322–24; Keener, *Commentary on the Gospel of Matthew*, 558–59; Daniel J. Harrington, *The Gospel of Matthew* (Collegeville, MN: Liturgical Press, 1991), 329–30.

words of this chapter, in which Matthew's Yeshua actually affirms the authority
of the Pharisaic scribes that he denounces (Matthew 23:1–3).[11]

Israel Rejected?

Thus, evidence from Matthew firmly upholds the hypothesis that the New
Testament recognizes the covenantal status of the Jewish people as a whole,
whether Yeshua-believers or non-Yeshua-believers. Before leaving our study of
Matthew, we must look at two texts that traditionally have been read to deny this
proposition. The first is Matthew's version of the parable of the wicked tenants
(Matthew 21:33–46). The tenants of the vineyard reject the owner's claims and
seek to possess the vineyard for themselves. Matthew leaves no doubt as to the
identity of these tenants:

> When the chief priests and the Pharisees heard his parables, they realized that he
> was speaking about them. (Matthew 21:45)

As in Isaiah's parable of the vineyard, "the vineyard of the LORD of hosts is the
house of Israel" (Isaiah 5:7). The parable represents Yeshua's prophetic denun-
ciation of the temple authorities who rule over Israel and a prediction of their
coming judgment. However, Matthew adds to Mark's account a final statement
that has been seen as going much further in its application:

> Therefore I tell you, the kingdom of God will be taken away from you and given
> to a people that produces the fruits of the kingdom. (Matthew 21:43)

In the traditional interpretation of this verse, the kingdom is now taken away, not
only from the chief priests and Pharisees, but also from the Jewish people, and
is given to another people, the church. As Graham Stanton states, "This verse
is probably the clearest indication in the gospel that the Matthean community
saw itself as a separate and quite distinct entity over against Judaism."[12]

However, as many recent commentators have noted, this reading of Matthew
21:43 does violence to its context.[13] The vineyard of the parable is, as in Isaiah,

---

11. We will look at these verses in detail in chapter 7.

12. Graham N. Stanton, *A Gospel for a New People* (Louisville: Westminster John Knox, 1993),
151. In similar vein, R. T. France calls this verse "the most explicit statement in Matthew of the
view that there is a new people of God in place of Old Testament Israel." R. T. France, *Matthew*
(Grand Rapids: Eerdmans, 1985), 310.

13. An influential and convincing refutation of the traditional reading of Matthew 21:43 is
offered by Anthony J. Saldarini, *Matthew's Christian-Jewish Community* (Chicago: University of
Chicago Press, 1994), 58–63. Saldarini's argument and conclusion are accepted by Overman (*Crisis,*

the people of Israel. The kingdom that is taken from the tenants is the adminis-tration of God's rule over Israel. Yeshua says that the "kingdom of God will be taken away from *you*," and the "you" of this verse is identified in Matthew 21:45 not as Israel or the Jewish people but as "the chief priests and the Pharisees," the temple authorities who confronted Yeshua in Matthew 21:23–27. They are "the builders" who have rejected the cornerstone (Matthew 21:42). The "people" referred to in Matthew 21:43 is not the church in contrast to the Jewish people, but a new leadership group that will replace the old.[14]

The second text to be considered has a more tragic history. It contains the words of the Jerusalem crowd after calling for Yeshua's execution: "His blood be upon us and our children" (Matthew 27:25). As we noted in chapter 1, most past Christian commentators saw this crowd, representing the Jewish people as a whole, as uttering an effective self-imposed curse that explained—and justified—the history of Jewish exile and suffering. This verse was thus the linchpin in charging the Jewish people as a whole with the crime of deicide—the murder of God. If this interpretation is accepted, then our hypothesis regarding Matthew's view of the Jewish people as a whole is refuted. God may still take special concern for the Jewish people, but only for the purpose of meting out special punishment for their uniquely abhorrent crime.

However, most contemporary exegetes rightly dismiss this traditional anti-Jewish reading of Matthew 27:25. They recognize that the crowd that utters these words represents, not all Jews everywhere, but only the Jews of Jerusalem or of the land of Israel; and that "our children" refers, not to all their descendants forever, but only to the next generation, which would experience the catastrophe of the war with Rome in 66–70 CE.[15] Matthew and his initial audience were Jews, and they still identified with the Jewish people as a whole. However, like Jeremiah and Ezekiel in their own time, they also believed that the suffering of Jerusalem was divine judgment, related to Jerusalem's failure to respond properly to God's appointed messengers.

Thus these two troubling texts fail to undermine the thesis that Matthew, like the New Testament in general, recognizes the covenantal status of the Jewish people as a whole, whether Yeshua-believers or non-Yeshua-believers. Rather

---

302–4), Sim (*Matthew and Christian Judaism*, 148–49), Harrington (*Gospel of Matthew*, 303–5), and Keener (*Commentary on the Gospel of Matthew*, 515–16; see nn. 171 and 172).

14. Describing the prayer of the high priest on the Day of Atonement, *m. Yoma* 4:2 refers to the priests as "the children of Aaron Your holy people (*'am*)." The same phrase is used in the introduction to the Aaronic benediction in the Jewish liturgy. See *Daily Prayer Book*, trans. Philip Birnbaum (New York: Hebrew Publishing Company, 1977), 358.

15. See Saldarini, *Matthew's Christian-Jewish Community*, 32–34; Davies and Allison, *Matthew*, vol. 3, 591–92; Harrington, *Gospel of Matthew*, 390–93; Keener, *Commentary on the Gospel of Matthew*, 662–63; Overman, *Crisis*, 381–84.

than proving an embarrassment to be avoided, the Gospel of Matthew actually provides strong support for this theological proposition.

Luke-Acts

In our previous chapter we found Luke-Acts to be pivotal for understanding New Testament teaching regarding Jewish practice. Unsurprisingly, these two volumes play the same crucial role in conveying the New Testament message concerning the Jewish people.

Judgment and Redemption

One of the central themes of Luke-Acts is the future redemption of the people of Israel and their capital city, Jerusalem. This theme is especially prominent in the Lukan infancy narrative. The angel Gabriel tells Miriam that her son "will reign over the house of Jacob forever" (Luke 1:33). Miriam responds with a song of praise in which she acknowledges that God "has helped his servant Israel, in remembrance of his mercy, according to the promise he made to our ancestors, to Abraham and to his descendants forever" (Luke 1:54–55). Zechariah, father of John the Baptist, praises God for the coming Messiah by reciting a blessing (in traditional Jewish form), "Blessed be the Lord God of Israel, for he has looked favorably on his people and redeemed them" (Luke 1:68). The remainder of his blessing deals exclusively with the fulfillment of God's redemptive promises to the people of Israel (Luke 1:70–77). The prophet Simeon is described as one "looking forward to the consolation of Israel" (Luke 2:25). Similarly, the prophetess Anna, who "never left the temple but worshiped there with fasting and prayer night and day" (Luke 2:37), speaks about Yeshua "to all who were looking for the redemption of Jerusalem" (Luke 2:38).

One might think that Luke intends these statements about the people of Israel to be understood in a metaphorical (and supersessionist) manner, with "the people of Israel" understood to be the church (consisting mainly of Gentiles). However, Simeon's prayer does not permit such a reading.

> Simeon took him in his arms and praised God, saying, "Master, now you are dismissing your servant in peace, according to your word; for my eyes have seen your salvation, which you have prepared in the presence of all peoples, a light for revelation to the Gentiles and for glory to your people Israel." (Luke 2:28–32)

It is certain here that "Israel" means the Jewish people, since the term is paired with "Gentiles" and the two terms together are equivalent to "all peoples." If

"Israel" here means the Jewish people, then we have good grounds for assuming that this is also its meaning throughout the Lukan infancy narrative.

One might think that the Lukan infancy narrative is unique within the wider narrative, a deliberately archaic-sounding prologue that emphasizes continuity between God's past dealings with the Jewish people and God's new work in Yeshua but that does not represent the overall worldview of Luke-Acts. However, we find that the data fail to support such a hypothesis. Just as Luke begins with an emphasis on Israel, so also it ends. It is surely significant that the friends who encounter the risen Yeshua on the road to Emmaus say that they "had hoped that he [Yeshua] was the one to redeem Israel" (Luke 24:21). The language recalls the infancy narrative and forms an inclusion bracketing the beginning and ending of the book.

Encounters with the risen Messiah do not change the perspective of Yeshua's followers. The book of Acts begins the way the Gospel of Luke ends.

> So when they had come together, they asked him, "Lord, is this the time when you will restore the kingdom to Israel?" He replied, "It is not for you to know the times or periods that the Father has set by his own authority. But you will receive power when the Holy Spirit has come upon you; and you will be my witnesses in Jerusalem, in all Judea and Samaria, and to the ends of the earth." (Acts 1:6–8)

While Yeshua refuses to answer their question, he does not correct them for asking it.[16] He does not suggest that they have misunderstood the purpose of the coming of the Messiah and that God has no concern to "restore the kingdom to Israel." Instead he points them to their immediate task and away from eschatological clock-watching.

The sermons in Acts addressed to Jewish audiences indicate that the assumptions underlying the disciples' question about Israel's restoration were entirely warranted. Peter assures his hearers that "the promise is for you, for your children, and for all who are far away" (Acts 2:39). The nature of this promise is made clear in Peter's next sermon:

> Repent therefore, and turn to God so that your sins may be wiped out, so that times of refreshing may come from the presence of the Lord, and that he may send the Messiah appointed for you, that is, Jesus, who must remain in heaven

16. "Luke has the disciples ask, 'Lord, is this the time when you restore the kingdom to Israel?' Jesus avoids the question, and we should note that this is *all* he does." Robert W. Jenson, "Toward a Christian Theology of Israel," *Pro Ecclesia* 9, no. 1 (Winter 2000): 49. See also Abraham Joshua Heschel, *Israel: An Echo of Eternity* (New York: Farrar, Straus and Giroux, 1967), 163–67.

until the time of universal restoration that God announced long ago through his
holy prophets. (Acts 3:19–21)

Robert Tannehill sees the connection between these words of Peter, the question in Acts 1:6 concerning the restoration of Israel's kingdom, and the Lukan
infancy narrative:

> Peter still hopes, and encourages the people of Jerusalem to hope, that they will
> share in the "times of restoration of all that God spoke" through the prophets.
> This will include a further sending of their Messiah to them, provided they re-
> pent (3:19–21). Peter's hope includes the hope expressed by Jesus' followers in
> 1:6, as the shared wording indicates. That is, it includes the restoration of Israel's
> national life through the reigning Messiah. The prophetic words of Zechariah in
> Luke 1:69–75 have not been forgotten.[17]

In Acts, the apostles address their Jewish audiences as "descendants of Abraham"
and heirs to the promises made by God through the prophets (Acts 3:25–26;
13:26). While it is clear that the prophetic promises also point to the redemption
of Gentiles (Acts 3:25–26), a distinct and primary concern for Israel's redemption is never lost.

This redemption is "the hope of Israel," and it presumes Israel's resurrection
from the dead, as Paul emphasizes:

> And now I stand here on trial on account of my hope in the promise made by
> God to our ancestors, a promise that our twelve tribes hope to attain, as they
> earnestly worship day and night. It is for this hope, your Excellency, that I am
> accused by Jews! Why is it thought incredible by any of you that God raises the
> dead? (Acts 26:6–8)

> It is for the sake of the hope of Israel that I am bound with this chain." (Acts
> 28:20)

Tannehill pays close attention to Paul's general reference to resurrection and its
relationship to Israel's hope and Yeshua's resurrection.

> The impression that Acts is making much of a minor matter in early Judaism,
> may be the result of ignoring the full range of meaning of hope and promise in
> Luke-Acts, under the assumption that resurrection of the dead simply means life

---

17. Robert C. Tannehill, *The Narrative Unity of Luke-Acts*, vol. 2 (Minneapolis: Fortress,
1990), 55.

after death for individuals. Klaus Haacker argues that the theme of resurrection, whether understood metaphorically or realistically, is closely connected in Old Testament–Jewish tradition with the hopes of Israel as a people. This communal hope is preserved in Luke-Acts, where hope and resurrection are linked with the reign of the Davidic Messiah, who brings salvation to the Jewish people. . . . Thus, the hope and promise of which Paul speaks in 26:6-7 is not merely a hope for individual life after death but a hope for the Jewish people, to be realized through resurrection.[18]

From beginning to end, Luke-Acts never loses sight of the importance of Israel's coming national redemption.

At the same time, Luke-Acts also announces a more sobering prophetic message for Israel's national life: the redemption of Jerusalem and Israel will be preceded by a time of judgment. While somewhat muted in the infancy narrative with its hopeful and joyful tone, this second prophetic theme nevertheless finds its place even there:

> Then Simeon blessed them and said to his mother Mary, "This child is destined for the falling and the rising of many in Israel, and to be a sign that will be opposed so that the inner thoughts of many will be revealed—and a sword will pierce your own soul too." (Luke 2:34–35)

Many commentators see this text as pointing to the division in Israel that will occur in response to the Messiah's words and actions. However, David Tiede argues that "the falling and rising of many in Israel" should be taken as a prophetic temporal sequence, with at first "many in Israel" falling and experiencing judgment, and afterward "many in Israel" rising to receive redemption.

> The sequence of words is significant. This is not a prediction of the rise and fall of the Roman Empire, the Third Reich, or the kingdom of Herod. This is a prophetic oracle disclosing the fall which will come before the rising of many in Israel, and the passive voice alerts the reader once again that it is God who has set this child for such falling and rising and for being a controverted sign.[19]

The sequence of judgment-redemption is common in the biblical prophets. It is also attested explicitly in a prophetic pronouncement of Yeshua recorded only in Luke:

18. Ibid., 319–20.
19. David L. Tiede, "'Glory to Thy People Israel: Luke-Acts and the Jews," in *Luke-Acts and the Jewish People*, ed. Joseph B. Tyson (Minneapolis: Augsburg, 1988), 28.

> When you see Jerusalem surrounded by armies, then know that its desolation
> has come near. Then those in Judea must flee to the mountains, and those inside
> the city must leave it, and those out in the country must not enter it; for these
> are days of vengeance, as a fulfillment of all that is written. Woe to those who
> are pregnant and to those who are nursing infants in those days! For there will
> be great distress on the earth and wrath against this people; they will fall by the
> edge of the sword and be taken away as captives among all nations; and Jerusalem
> will be trampled on by the Gentiles, until the times of the Gentiles are fulfilled.[20]
> (Luke 21:20–24)

Yeshua speaks with pathos of Jerusalem's suffering in the coming judgment, to
be experienced in 70 CE. He also speaks of the aftermath of this judgment: Jerusalem will be taken from Jewish hands by the Gentiles—but only for a limited
period. When read in the context of Luke-Acts as a whole, the implications are
clear. After the period of judgment has ended, the promise of redemption for
Jerusalem heralded in the infancy narrative will be realized.[21]

Sympathetic Portrayal

Though Luke believes that Jerusalem and Israel must face judgment before
receiving national redemption, and though he sees this judgment as related to
the inadequate national response to Yeshua, he does not portray non-Yeshua-
believing Jews simplistically and unsympathetically. Among the Gospels, only
Luke describes the people of Jerusalem as grieving while Yeshua is being tor-
tured and killed:

> A great number of the people followed him [as he was led to execution], and
> among them were women who were beating their breasts and wailing for him.
> (Luke 23:27)

20. A version of this teaching is found also in Mark 13:14–20 and Matthew 24:15–22, but
there Yeshua speaks not of the coming destruction of Jerusalem but of the suffering at the end of
the age that will immediately precede the return of the Messiah. Thus, where Mark and Matthew
refer to the "desolating sacrilege" set up in the temple as the warning to flee, Luke's Yeshua speaks
of "Jerusalem surrounded by armies" and the *city's* imminent desolation.

21. Robert Brawley states this forcefully: "Although the fall of Jerusalem is an unmitigated
disaster, the judgment upon Jerusalem is not definitive. In the first place, there is a temporal limit
implied by Luke 21:24: 'Jerusalem will be trodden down by the gentiles until the times of the
gentiles are fulfilled.' This is Luke's own interpretation of the destruction of Jerusalem in which he
sets forth a brief outline of future salvation history. The gentiles are the agents of the destruction
of Jerusalem, and their ascendancy has a purpose for their own fulfillment. But the end of the time
of the gentiles also anticipates the restoration of God's mercy to Jerusalem." Robert L. Brawley,
Luke-Acts and the Jews (Atlanta: Scholars, 1987), 125.

And when all the crowds who had gathered there for this spectacle saw what had taken place, they returned home, beating their breasts. (Luke 23:48)

In the same way, Luke describes how "devout men buried Stephen and made loud lamentation over him" (Acts 8:2)—and these devout men are almost certainly Jews who are not part of the Yeshua-movement.[22] Moreover, Luke sees even those directly involved in Yeshua's execution as acting without full knowledge of what they are doing. Thus while dying, Yeshua asks God to forgive his killers, "for they do not know what they are doing" (Luke 23:34). The apostles are blunt in telling the temple authorities and the people of Jerusalem that they bear responsibility for Yeshua's death (Acts 2:23; 2:36; 3:13–15; 4:10; 5:30; 7:52), yet they also acknowledge the same mitigating factor: "I know that you acted in ignorance, as did also your rulers" (Acts 3:17). Furthermore, though Jerusalem is seen as responsible (albeit ignorantly) for Yeshua's death, the Jews in the Diaspora are not held accountable for the actions of their compatriots. This is evident from Paul's first recorded synagogue sermon.

> Because the residents of Jerusalem and their leaders did not recognize him or understand the words of the prophets that are read every sabbath, they fulfilled those words by condemning him. Even though they found no cause for a sentence of death, they asked Pilate to have him killed. When they had carried out everything that was written about him, they took him down from the tree and laid him in a tomb. (Acts 13:27–29)

The Jerusalem sermons in Acts consistently employ second-person pronouns and verb forms when speaking of Yeshua's death. In contrast, this Diaspora sermon uses third-person pronouns and verb forms.[23]

There are also leaders in Jerusalem who seek to restrain official opposition to the early Yeshua movement. Thus, with the council on the brink of killing the apostles (Acts 5:33), Gamaliel, a Pharisaic "teacher of the law, respected by all the people" (Acts 5:34), stands up and persuades his fellow council members to let the apostles go (Acts 5:35–39). When Paul is in a similar situation, Pharisees again come to his defense (Acts 23:6–9). In this way Luke shows that hatred for the Yeshua movement was not universal among the Jerusalem elite.

---

22. Tannehill, *Narrative Unity*, vol. 2, 100–101.

23. On this topic, see Jon A. Weatherly, *Jewish Responsibility for the Death of Jesus in Luke-Acts* (Sheffield: Sheffield Academic, 1994).

Solidarity

The leaders of the Yeshua movement speak to their fellow Jews in ways that express solidarity and identification. They call their fellow Jews *adelphoi*—brothers (Acts 2:29; 3:17; 7:2; 22:1; 23:5; 28:17), a term of covenantal intimacy. They speak of God as "the God of our ancestors" (Acts 3:13; 22:14; 24:14), indicating that their fellow Jews are along with them descendants of the patriarchs and matriarchs and heirs of the covenant. Paul defends himself against charges that he taught "everyone everywhere against our people, our law, and this place" (Acts 21:28), stating that "after some years I came to bring alms to my nation and to offer sacrifices" (Acts 24:17). The Jewish people are *his* people (see also Acts 26:23; 28:17; 18:19).

There are no grounds for assuming that the Jewish leaders of the early Yeshua movement employed such terminology purely for rhetorical effect. The covenantal solidarity underlying this usage is revealed most strikingly when Paul appears before the high priest:

> While Paul was looking intently at the council he said, "Brothers, up to this day I have lived my life with a clear conscience before God." Then the high priest Ananias ordered those standing near him to strike him on the mouth. At this Paul said to him, "God will strike you, you whitewashed wall! Are you sitting there to judge me according to the law, and yet in violation of the law you order me to be struck?" Those standing nearby said, "Do you dare to insult God's high priest?" And Paul said, "I did not realize, brothers, that he was high priest; for it is written, 'You shall not speak evil of a leader of your people.'" (Acts 23:1–5)

Paul acknowledges that it is improper to speak to the high priest disrespectfully, even when that figure acts wrongly. This is because the high priest is a leader of Paul's people, the people to whom the commandment he cites from the Torah is addressed (Exodus 22:27). Paul thereby affirms Israel's ongoing covenantal status and takes his place as part of its communal life.

One might think that Luke expected only the Jewish members of the Yeshua movement to maintain a sense of solidarity and identification with the Jewish people. Gentile Yeshua-believers would have no special affinity for Israel. Luke certainly sees a difference between the way Jewish and Gentile Yeshua-believers participate in the life of the wider Jewish community. Nevertheless, the evidence suggests that he also expected Gentile Yeshua-believers to maintain a special love for the people of Israel. We may infer this from his version of the story of the Capernaum centurion:

After Jesus had finished all his sayings in the hearing of the people, he entered Capernaum. A centurion there had a slave whom he valued highly, and who was ill and close to death. When he heard about Jesus, he sent some Jewish elders to him, asking him to come and heal his slave. When they came to Jesus, they appealed to him earnestly, saying, "He is worthy of having you do this for him, for he loves our people, and it is he who built our synagogue for us." (Luke 7:1–5)

In Matthew's version of this story, the centurion himself comes to Yeshua (Matthew 8:5–13). In Luke the centurion asks leaders of the local Jewish community to present his petition to Yeshua. He does this because he considers himself unworthy to make such a request or to have a Jewish holy man enter his non-Jewish house (Luke 7:6–7). In acting as his agent, the delegation of Jewish leaders argues that in fact this Gentile *is* worthy to receive Yeshua's help, "for he loves our people" and "built our synagogue for us." The initial sign of the centurion's worthy faith is his commitment to the welfare of the Jewish people.

Luke presents this centurion as a paradigmatic Gentile convert to the Yeshua movement, whose love for the God of Israel is expressed both in concern for the people of Israel and in ready acceptance of the Messiah of Israel. Luke underlines the paradigmatic significance of the centurion of Capernaum by telling another story of a centurion—Cornelius of Caesarea.[24] In Acts the reception of Cornelius represents the opening of the door of Yeshua-faith to the Gentiles. Cornelius resembles closely the centurion of Capernaum:

> In Caesarea there was a man named Cornelius, a centurion of the Italian Cohort, as it was called. He was a devout man who feared God with all his household; he gave alms generously to the people and prayed constantly to God. (Acts 10:1–2)

It is clear that "the people" to whom Cornelius gives alms are the Jewish people. This Gentile fears the God of Israel, observes the times of prayer customary among devout Jews, and provides financial assistance to needy Jews. Like his comrade in Capernaum, he demonstrates his worth in part through his evident concern for the welfare of the Jewish people. Together, these two centurions function as model Gentile converts, illustrating the attitude Gentile Yeshua-believers should adopt toward the people of Israel.

---

24. Ben Witherington III is among many who comment on the correspondence between these two figures: "Theophilus [to whom Luke and Acts are addressed] would perhaps be reminded [in the story of Cornelius] of the somewhat similar story involving a centurion who sends messengers to Jesus to come heal his slave, and as the story unfolds we discover he also loves God's people and had built the local synagogue in Capernaum (cf. Luke 7:1–10)." Ben Witherington III, *The Acts of the Apostles* (Grand Rapids: Eerdmans, 1998), 347.

Turning Away From "the Jews"

There are three interrelated features of the Acts of the Apostles that call into question Luke's solidarity with the Jewish people. First, Acts includes many references to "the Jews" opposing the early Yeshua movement and its leaders (Acts 9:23; 12:3; 13:45; 13:50; 14:4; 17:5; 18:5–6; 18:12; 18:28; 20:3; 22:30; 23:12; 23:20; 24:9; 26:2; 28:19). One could read these texts as evidence that Luke distinguishes unambiguously between Jews and Yeshua-believers, with the former treated as evil and the latter as good. Second, in three of the above texts a pattern emerges in which Paul argues before a Jewish audience that Yeshua is the Messiah, receives a negative response, and then concludes that he will now go to the Gentiles (Acts 13:44–47; 18:1–6; 28:16–31). One could infer that this threefold turning from the unbelieving Jews to the receptive Gentiles expresses Luke's conviction that Jews are stonehearted enemies who have been set aside by God and replaced by Gentiles. Third, the last of these three texts serves as the conclusion of Acts and thus of Luke's two-volume opus. Paul is in Rome, the capital of the empire, and there meets with "the local leaders of the Jews" (Acts 28:17). As a result of their unwillingness to accept his message, he cites a prophetic text against them and announces, "Let it be known to you then that this salvation of God has been sent to the Gentiles; they will listen" (Acts 28:28). This conclusion is seen by many as the realization of the geographical mandate of Acts 1:8 ("You will be my witnesses in Jerusalem, in all Judea and Samaria, and to the ends of the earth") and as an implicit assertion that God's love and election have shifted from Jerusalem to Rome, from Israel to the Gentiles.[25]

However we deal with these three features of Acts, at the outset we must recognize that Luke emphatically rejects a hard distinction between Jews and Yeshua-believers. While he does speak of "the Jews" as a group hostile to the Yeshua movement, he also sees this movement as a Jewish reality, led by Jews and adhered to by many Jews. When Luke first introduces Aquila, he identifies him not as a Yeshua-believer but as "a Jew named Aquila" (Acts 18:2). The narrator introduces Apollos in the same way (Acts 18:24). Paul identifies himself as "a Jew" (Acts 21:39; 22:3). Pagan critics of Paul and Silas in Philippi bring them before the Roman magistrates of the city and accuse them of wrongdoing by stating, "These men are disturbing our city; they are Jews and are advocating [Jewish] customs that are not lawful for us as Romans to adopt or observe" (Acts 16:20–21). Speaking of the city of Jerusalem, James tells Paul, "You see, brother, how many thousands of believers there are among the Jews, and they are all zeal-

---

25. See, for example, Jack T. Sanders, *The Jews in Luke-Acts* (Philadelphia: Fortress, 1987), 296–99.

ous for the law" (Acts 21:20). When Jewish leaders attack Paul before the Roman authorities, they portray him as "an agitator among all the Jews throughout the world, and a ringleader of the sect of the Nazarenes" (Acts 24:5). They see Paul as a Jew who has a prominent position within a Jewish sect or party. Undoubtedly Luke recognizes the Jewish character of the Yeshua-movement and the Jewish identity of its leaders and its pioneering core membership.

The threefold turning to the Gentiles and the many negative references to "the Jews" in Acts are best explained by seeing the difference between the message issued to Jews and to Gentiles by Peter, Paul, and their associates. When Peter or Paul address a Jewish audience, they are speaking to an organized community—their own community—that is the rightful recipient of the blessings brought by the Messiah. Yeshua has been raised from the dead, not just to "save" individual Jews, but to accomplish "the redemption of Jerusalem." On the other hand, when Peter addresses Cornelius and his household, or when Paul speaks to a Gentile crowd, the aim is merely to win as many Gentiles as possible to Yeshua-faith. No corporate Gentile response is required or sought.

When Luke refers to the Jews, he is speaking of the communal body of Jews ordered under its leaders and acting in an official or semiofficial manner. One of the central themes of Acts is that a large number of Jews respond with faith to the message of the risen Messiah (Acts 2:41; 4:4; 5:14–16; 6:7; 21:20). At the same time, the Jewish community as a whole, as embodied in its leadership and its official communal institutions, does not respond with faith but instead often seeks to thwart the efforts of the new movement. This communal failure to receive the national redemption offered in Messiah Yeshua is also a central theme of Acts.

Robert Tannehill has perceptively interpreted the threefold turning to the Gentiles in light of this communal dimension:

> Paul's announcement that he is going to the Gentiles indicates a shift from a synagogue-based mission, addressed to Jews and to those Gentiles attracted to Judaism, to a mission in the city at large, where the population is predominantly Gentile. . . . Paul . . . has fulfilled his obligation to speak God's word to God's people. They are now responsible for their own fate. The pattern of speaking first to Jews and only later turning to the Gentiles testifies to Paul's sense of prophetic obligation to his own people. He is released from this obligation only when he meets strong public resistance within the Jewish community. Then he can begin the second phase of his mission within a city, a phase in which the conversion of individual Jews is still possible, although Paul is no longer preaching in the synagogue nor addressing Jews as a community.[26]

26. Tannehill, *Narrative Unity*, vol. 2, 222–23.

Tannehill notes that the last of these three texts actually describes the Jewish leadership as divided in its response, with some accepting Paul's message and others rejecting it (Acts 28:24–25). Nevertheless Paul understands this divided response as equivalent to communal rejection, since a majority of the leaders would need to respond favorably in order for his work to continue as a publicly sanctioned activity.

> The presence of disagreement among the Jews is enough to show that Paul has not achieved what he sought. He was seeking a communal decision, a recognition by the Jewish community as a whole that Jesus is the fulfillment of the Jewish hope. The presence of significant opposition shows that this is not going to happen.[27]

By ending his two-volume opus with this communal rejection in Rome, Luke appears to reluctantly accept the fact that for the immediate future the Jewish community as a whole would not officially affirm that Yeshua was the one sent to be "the consolation of Israel." This does not, however, imply a definitive divorce of the Yeshua movement from identification with that community, nor does it imply a surrendering of hope for an eschatological reversal of that official communal response.[28]

An Unfinished Work

The ending of Acts is a mystery for many reasons. After narrating the dramatic arrest of Paul in Jerusalem, his many court hearings, and his perilous journey to Rome, the book ends inconclusively with Paul under house arrest for two years. The book is certainly written after Paul's death, yet his death is not recounted. It is almost certainly written after the destruction of Jerusalem, yet that seismic event is also beyond the book's chronological scope. The final chapter of Acts presents a puzzling and unsatisfying ending to an otherwise well-crafted two-volume work. How could such a talented and skillful writer produce such a frustrating finale?

To answer this question, we must examine the geographic structure of the two books. Unlike any of the other Gospels, Luke begins in Jerusalem—in the

---

27. Ibid., 347.

28. This is the view of Tannehill. Joseph Tyson endorses Tannehill's insight into the communal dimension of Paul's efforts among the Jewish people, but he disagrees with Tannehill's suggestion that Israel's future is still open. Tyson thinks that Luke sees Israel as "a people without hope." As my entire argument shows, I find Tyson's contention totally unconvincing. See Joseph B. Tyson, "The Problem of Jewish Rejection in Acts," in *Luke-Acts and the Jewish People* (ed. Joseph B. Tyson), 126–27, and *Luke, Judaism, and the Scholars* (Columbia: University of South Carolina Press, 1999), 142–45.

temple, with Zechariah offering incense and receiving an angelic visitation. The events of the infancy narrative revolve around Jerusalem and its sanctuary. After a Galilean pause, constructed largely on materials taken from Mark, Luke orders the main part of his Gospel, beginning in Luke 9:51, around a lengthy journey to Jerusalem. After recounting the death of Yeshua, Luke describes resurrection appearances only in Jerusalem and its vicinity. The book tells us nothing about the Galilean encounters with the risen Messiah depicted or alluded to in Mark 16:7, Matthew 28:16–20, and John 21:1–23. In fact, Luke's Yeshua explicitly commands his followers to remain in Jerusalem (Luke 24:49). The Gospel ends as it began—in the Jerusalem temple, with a community of Jews worshipping the God of Israel (Luke 24:53).

Acts likewise begins in Jerusalem, with a community centered on the temple (Acts 2:46; 3:1–10; 4:1–2; 5:12; 5:20–21; 5:42). The story develops geographically, with the message of Yeshua radiating outward—first to the towns of Judea and Samaria (Acts 8:1, 4–25), then with reference to Yeshua-believers in Damascus (Acts 9:1–2, 10, 19). In Acts 10 Peter brings Yeshua-faith to Cornelius and his household in Caesarea. Then in Acts 13 Paul begins his travels, eventually finding his way through Asia Minor and finally to Greece and Rome. Thus Acts, like Luke, begins in Jerusalem and in relationship to its temple, but unlike Luke, it ends not in Jerusalem but in Rome.

In reality, the geographic structure of Acts is more complicated than the above summary suggests. It does not begin in Jerusalem and then progressively and steadily radiate outward. Instead, the story continually reverts back to Jerusalem. Paul encounters Yeshua on the road to Damascus but then returns to Jerusalem (Acts 9:26–29). Peter proclaims Yeshua to Cornelius in Caesarea but then returns to Jerusalem (Acts 11:2). A congregation arises in Antioch, but it sends aid to Jerusalem in a time of famine (Acts 11:27–30). Paul and Barnabas journey from Antioch to Asia Minor, but they return afterward to Jerusalem for the central event in the book of Acts—the Jerusalem council (Acts 15:2). From Jerusalem Paul travels with Silas to Greece, but he then returns again to Jerusalem (Acts 18:22).[29] Paul takes his final journey as a free man but then returns to Jerusalem, where he is arrested (Acts 21:17–23:11). As Robert Brawley rightly notes, "Acts does not delineate a movement away from Jerusalem, but a constant return to Jerusalem."[30]

---

29. "When he goes on to say that *Paul went up and greeted the church*, this is usually understood as a reference to going up to Jerusalem and seeing the church there. . . . If this is a correct assumption, it means that each of Paul's missionary campaigns concluded with a visit to Jerusalem, so that Paul's work began from and ended in Jerusalem in each case." I. Howard Marshall, *Acts* (Grand Rapids: Eerdmans, 1980), 301–2.

30. Brawley, *Luke-Acts and the Jews*, 35–36.

This complex geographic structure may explain the unsatisfying ending of Acts. If Luke took the redemption of Jerusalem as seriously as we have proposed, then he would realize that his story was unfinished. The drama would not reach its satisfying conclusion until the arc was again completed and the narrative returned to Jerusalem. Thus Luke deliberately composed an unsatisfying ending so that we would know *it was not really the ending!*

This hypothesis is supported by an intertextual analysis of Acts 1:6–12. The apostles ask Yeshua, "Lord, is this the time when you will restore the kingdom to Israel?" (Acts 1:6). He does not answer the question but instead urges them to devote themselves to the task of being his "witnesses in Jerusalem, in all Judea and Samaria, and to the ends of the earth" (Acts 1:8). This verse has often been read as an anticipation of the geographic structure of the book of Acts. In the next verse Yeshua is "lifted up," and he ascends to heaven in a cloud (Acts 1:9). While the apostles stare into the sky, two angelic figures appear and assure the astonished onlookers that their Messiah, "who has been taken up from you into heaven, will come in the same way as you saw him go into heaven" (Acts 1:10–11). The unit concludes by informing us that this all took place on the Mount of Olives (Acts 1:12).

What is the meaning of the angelic prophecy? What is intended by the words "in the same way"? Verse 12 likely offers the key to answering these questions. It points us to Zechariah 14:

> For I will gather all the nations against Jerusalem to battle. . . . Then the LORD will go forth and fight against those nations as when he fights on a day of battle. On that day his feet shall stand on the Mount of Olives, which lies before Jerusalem on the east; and the Mount of Olives shall be split in two from east to west by a very wide valley. . . . Then the LORD my God will come, and all the holy ones with him. (Zechariah 14:2–5)

Just as Yeshua ascends now *from* the Mount of Olives, so he will descend at the end *to* the Mount of Olives. Just as he ascends now *from* Jerusalem, so he will descend at the end *to* Jerusalem. Jerusalem will suffer many things, just as Zechariah 12–14 foretells. But she will be consoled when her Lord comes to defend her at the end, his feet standing on the Mount of Olives.

This intertextual reading of Acts 1:6–12 confirms the hypothesis that Luke in Acts deliberately tells an unfinished story. The story reaches its end only when the people of Israel as a whole responds to Yeshua with words of welcome, saying, "Blessed is he who comes in the name of the Lord."[31] Then the Messiah

---

31. It is surely significant that the preliminary enactment of this Messianic reception occurs at the Mount of Olives (Luke 19:37–38).

will return to Jerusalem, restore his people, and consummate all things. In the meantime, the geographic arc remains incomplete.

We may tentatively go even further. Might Luke think of what is yet to occur, not as a completion of his second book, but as a new and unwritten third book? This notion arises through recognizing the relationship between Luke-Acts and the first two of Israel's pilgrim feasts—Passover and Pentecost. Early in Luke we read of Yeshua and his family journeying to Jerusalem to celebrate the Passover (Luke 2:41). As we already noted, the central narrative of Luke is then structured around Yeshua's journey to Jerusalem, again in order to celebrate the Passover (Luke 22:1, 7–8, 11, 13, 15). The book of Acts has a similar relationship to the second pilgrim festival, Pentecost. The book begins with the giving of the Spirit on this day (Acts 2:1). Later the book describes Paul's final journey to Jerusalem in a way that makes it resemble Yeshua's pilgrimage before his death.[32] But whereas Yeshua went to Jerusalem to celebrate Passover, Paul goes for Pentecost (Acts 20:16). If this relationship between Luke-Acts and Passover-Pentecost is deliberate rather than accidental, we are justified in asking, What about the third pilgrim festival—the Feast of Booths? The festival year is incomplete without this crucial feast, which anticipates the final harvest and Israel's redeemed life (with the nations) in the world to come. Are we facing another mere coincidence in the fact that a key reading for this holiday is Zechariah 14?

> And the LORD will become king over all the earth; on that day the LORD will be one and his name one. . . . Then all who survive of the nations that have come against Jerusalem shall go up year after year to worship the King, the LORD of hosts, and to keep the festival of booths. (Zechariah 14:9, 16)

If the Gospel of Luke is related to Passover, and the Acts of the Apostles to Pentecost, then the as-yet-unwritten conclusion to this trilogy will be related to Booths—as Acts 1:6–12 intimates.

Luke thus has a firm hope for Israel's future. While he treats the negative Jewish communal response to Yeshua as a tragic feature of Israel's ongoing history, he does not sever the tie that binds the Yeshua movement to its Jewish communal matrix. Perhaps the best expression of Luke's attitude toward the wider Jewish community is found in the parable of the two sons (Luke 15:11–32). The opening verse of the chapter sets this parable in the context of the criticisms offered of Yeshua by the Pharisees and scribes for his eating with "sinners." Luke's immediate readers would undoubtedly see the prodigal son as representing the

---

32. "The parallels with Jesus' final journey to Jerusalem have often been noted and are considerable" (Witherington, *Acts of the Apostles,* 627–28).

early Yeshua movement as a whole. The context makes the connection between the older son and the Pharisees and scribes obvious. For Luke's first readers, the Pharisees and scribes would themselves represent the official leadership of the Jewish community. Operating with this interpretative framework, three elements of the second part of the parable are especially noteworthy. First, the father in the parable leaves the banquet hall and goes to the older son, who sullenly refuses to join the celebration. The father does not wait for the older son but actively seeks him out. Second, the father does not rebuke or threaten his son. Instead, he reassures and appeals to him:

> Then the father said to him, "Son, you are always with me, and all that is mine is yours. But we had to celebrate and rejoice, because this brother of yours was dead and has come to life; he was lost and has been found." (Luke 15:31–32)

Third, the parable ends with the father appealing to the older son. It does not tell us whether the son eventually accompanies his father into the banquet hall or remains outside on his own. Like Luke-Acts itself, the parable is unfinished. It will be finished only when the "older brother" hears the parable, realizes that it is addressed to him, and makes the appropriate response. In the meantime, through the figure of the parable's father, Luke's Yeshua conveys his vision of how God relates to the Jewish community and its leaders. He would presumably expect Yeshua-believers—especially those who are Jewish themselves—to behave likewise.

Paul

Of all New Testament authors, the apostle Paul offers the most explicit and concentrated treatment of the topic we are considering in this chapter. He does so at the heart of his most celebrated letter: Romans 9–11.

Solidarity

Paul begins this section of Romans by expressing his deep sorrow at the spiritual condition of his people:

> I am speaking the truth in Christ—I am not lying; my conscience confirms it by the Holy Spirit—I have great sorrow and unceasing anguish in my heart. For I could wish that I myself were accursed and cut off from Christ for the sake of my own people, my kindred [*adelphoi*] according to the flesh. (Romans 9:1–3)

Like the apostolic speeches addressed to Jewish audiences in the Acts of the Apostles, Paul speaks of the Jewish people in terms that reflect his solidarity with them, calling them "my own people" and "my kindred" (or "brothers"). Moreover, his solidarity goes beyond expressions of kinship. As virtually all commentators recognize, Paul here alludes to the intercession of Moses after the sin of the golden calf. God had said to Moses, "Now let me alone, so that my wrath may burn hot against them and I may consume them; and of you I will make a great nation" (Exodus 32:10). Moses responded first by appealing to God's promise to Abraham, Isaac, and Jacob (a theme also prominent in Romans 9–11) and then by refusing to live if his people must die: "But now, if you will only forgive their sin—but if not, blot me out of the book that you have written" (Exodus 32:32). In Romans 9:3, Paul wishes that he were in a position to put his life on the line for Israel, just as Moses did. Perhaps implicit in this verse is Paul's awareness that this is exactly what the Messiah himself has already done.

At Sinai Moses stood with and on behalf of Israel. Later in this unit of Romans, Paul recalls another great prophet who also appeared before God at Sinai during a time of spiritual crisis in Israel's national life:

> Do you not know what the scripture says of Elijah, how he pleads with God against Israel? "Lord, they have killed your prophets, they have demolished your altars; I alone am left, and they are seeking my life." But what is the divine reply to him? "I have kept for myself seven thousand who have not bowed the knee to Baal." (Romans 11:2–4)

Most commentators assume that Paul cites Elijah as a positive model—like Moses—for his current situation. Reading these verses in the light of later rabbinic texts, Peter Tomson reaches a different conclusion:

> It is, then, not surprising that a bit further on Moses' counterpart appears on stage: Elijah.... The story of this prophet, who in his righteous zeal assumes exactly the opposite position to Moses, contains undeniable irony (1 Kings 19.9–19). ... Confronted with Israel's failure, Paul does not choose a position *opposite to* the people as Elijah did: like Moses, he *vouches* for the people, prepared to offer himself. This obvious contrast between the "righteous" Elijah and an ideal prophet like Moses occurs also in rabbinic literature (*Mek. Bo* p. 4).[33]

33. Peter Tomson, *"If this be from Heaven . . ."* (Sheffield: Sheffield Academic Press, 2001), 210. On the contrast between Moses and Elijah in rabbinic literature, see Avivah Gottlieb Zornberg, *The Particulars of Rapture* (New York: Doubleday Image, 2001), 432–35.

Johannes Munck made the same point several decades earlier, without the aid of rabbinic parallels:

> It is important that, unlike Elijah, Paul does not appear before God against Israel, but that his heart's desire and concern before God is the salvation of the Jews (10:1). It is Moses, not Elijah, whom Paul resembles.[34]

The issue is one of identification and solidarity. Will Paul distance himself from Israel like Elijah and stand as Israel's accuser, or will he imitate Moses and take his stand with, among, and for his people? From the outset of these pivotal chapters, Paul signals that he will follow the way of Moses—for it is also the way of the Messiah.

The Remnant

Paul's passionate commitment to Israel derives from a source far deeper than ethnic sentiment. It is rooted in his consciousness of Israel's continued dignity as God's chosen covenant partner:

> They are Israelites, and to them belong the adoption, the glory, the covenants, the giving of the law, the worship, and the promises; to them belong the patriarchs, and from them, according to the flesh, comes the Messiah, who is over all, God blessed forever. Amen. (Romans 9:4–5)

He speaks of Israel's spiritual privileges in the present tense, and the antecedent of the pronoun "They" is unquestionably the same people over whom he grieved in Romans 9:2. Israel may be in crisis, but she is still Israel.[35]

Yet in Romans 9:6 Paul takes a new turn in his argument:

> It is not as though the word of God had failed. For not all Israelites truly belong to Israel.

While Paul identifies with Israel as a whole and acknowledges her national privileges, he also faces honestly his people's spiritual limitations. He combines these two convictions by speaking of an Israel *within* Israel, an elect core *within* the elect nation. To characterize the latter, he employs the biblical term "the

---

34. Johannes Munck, *Paul and the Salvation of Mankind* (Richmond: John Knox, 1959), 308.

35. Karl Barth, *Church Dogmatics* II.2 (Edinburgh: T&T Clark, 1957), 203; H. L. Ellison, *The Mystery of Israel* (Exeter: Paternoster, 1966), 47; Franz Mussner, *Tractate on the Jews* (Philadelphia: Fortress, 1984), 24; Daniel J. Harrington, *Paul on the Mystery of Israel* (Collegeville, MN: Liturgical Press, 1992), 49.

remnant": "So too at the present time there is a remnant, chosen by grace" (Romans 11:5).[36]

Whereas the prophetic text he cites implies that only the remnant is saved while the rest of Israel is lost (Romans 9:27), Paul develops his teaching of the remnant in a different direction. His thinking becomes clear in Romans 11:16:

> If the part of the dough offered as first fruits is holy, then the whole batch is holy; and if the root is holy, then the branches also are holy.

The "first fruits" mentioned here are probably to be equated with the remnant.[37] The "whole batch" and the "branches" refer to "all Israel," that is, the nation as a whole. Therefore, Paul sees the Jewish remnant as contributing to the sanctification (and salvation) of all Israel, so that it is now truly holy—despite its serious spiritual limitations. Douglas Harink articulates well this distinctive Pauline use of the remnant motif:

> The chosen remnant is not to be understood as the "saved" minority portion of Israel over against the "lost" majority. The remnant is rather the representative part of the whole, the very means by which the whole of Israel (including the hardened portion) is already made holy. "If the . . . first fruits [are] holy, then the whole batch is holy; and if the root is holy, then the branches also are holy" (11:16).[38]

In Paul's view the remnant does not replace Israel but instead represents and sanctifies Israel. It serves a priestly function on behalf of the entire nation. This representative and priestly dimension of the remnant fits well with Paul's allusions to the intercessory role of Moses at the beginning of Romans 9.

A Partial Hardening

Paul speaks of nonremnant Israel as having been "hardened":

> What then? Israel failed to obtain what it was seeking. The elect obtained it, but the rest were hardened. (Romans 11:7)

36. "Paul does make a distinction among Jews between the 'remnant' and the 'part hardened' so that he can say 'they are not all Israel who are descended from Israel.'" Mark Nanos, *The Mystery of Romans* (Minneapolis: Fortress, 1996), 276.

37. See F. F. Bruce, *Romans* (Grand Rapids: Eerdmans, 1985), 206; C. E. B. Cranfield, *The Epistle to the Romans,* vol. 2 (Edinburgh: T&T Clark, 1979), 563–65; Harrington, *Paul on the Mystery,* 54; Nanos, *The Mystery of Romans,* 252, n. 31; Terence Donaldson, *Paul and the Gentiles* (Minneapolis: Fortress, 1997), 159, 239, 346 (n. 42).

38. Douglas Harink, *Paul among the Postliberals* (Grand Rapids: Brazos, 2003), 174.

So that you may not claim to be wiser than you are, brothers and sisters, I want you to understand this mystery: a hardening has come upon part of Israel, until the full number of the Gentiles has come in. (Romans 11:25)

This NRSV rendering speaks of "a hardening" that has come upon "part of Israel." However, Charles Cosgrove argues that this translation misses Paul's main point:

> The expression *apo merous* ("in part") is perhaps most naturally taken adverbially: "A hardening has come in part on Israel." The alternative is to construe it as an adjectival phrase modifying "Israel": "A hardening has come on Israel in part." If we adopt the adverbial interpretation, it seems most reasonable to conclude that the partial hardening pertains to Jewish response to the Christian gospel about Jesus, not to a general blindness toward righteousness and the meaning of the scriptures.
>
> The "hardening" of Israel means not that Israel is, on the whole, blind but that God has given Israel a limited blind spot toward Christ.[39]

Moreover, this partial hardening is a divine action. While Paul speaks of Israel's accountability in Romans 10, his main emphasis in Romans 9 and 11 is on God's initiative and purpose. Harink states this point emphatically:

> Paul insists that the current condition of Israel's "hardening" is entirely God's doing. Israel's actions and moral condition . . . do not enter the picture at all. If Israel "remains bound" in a condition, it is because God has bound it there (11:32). Indeed, that is precisely the point of Paul noting, with reference to Jacob and Esau, that God's purpose was declared to Rebecca "before they had been born or had done anything good *or bad* . . ." (9:11). God's choosing "the younger," Jacob, is not injustice on God's part precisely because the issue is not about moral success or failure but about God's mercy and hardening, enacted not with respect to moral condition, but strictly with respect to a divine purpose that must be accomplished.[40]

Thus God has caused a partial hardening to come upon nonremnant Israel so that he might accomplish his purpose for Israel and the nations.

---

39. Charles H. Cosgrove, *Elusive Israel* (Louisville: Westminster John Knox Press, 1997), 16–17, 74. See the KJV ("blindness in part is happened to Israel"), the NIV ("Israel has experienced a hardening in part"), and most explicitly the NEB ("this partial blindness has come upon Israel").

40. Harink, *Paul among the Postliberals,* 170.

What is that purpose? Why does it require God's partial hardening of Israel? Paul hints at his answer to these questions in Romans 11:

> So I ask, have they stumbled so as to fall? By no means! But through their stumbling salvation has come to the Gentiles, so as to make Israel jealous. Now if their stumbling means riches for the world, and if their defeat means riches for Gentiles, how much more will their full inclusion mean! . . . For if their rejection is the reconciliation of the world, what will their acceptance be but life from the dead! (Romans 11:11–12, 15)

Israel's "stumbling," "defeat," and "rejection" lead to "salvation" and "riches" for the Gentiles and "the reconciliation of the world." Similarly, in developing his figure of the olive tree, Paul has an imagined Gentile listener saying, "[Jewish] branches were broken off so that I might be grafted in" (Romans 11:19). Thus for some reason the ingathering of the Gentiles requires a partial hardening of Israel. But why is this the case? Paul does not say. Of the various possible reasons that have been suggested, two fit especially well with the literary context of the letter and the social and religious context of the first-century Jewish world. Terence Donaldson offers the first:

> If Israel's acceptance of Christ will accompany—indeed, precipitate—the parousia, and if the parousia represents the termination of the Gentiles' opportunity for salvation, then Israel's immediate acceptance of the gospel would have meant the closing of the door to the Gentiles.[41]

Donaldson's view builds upon numerous New Testament texts that imply a close connection between Israel's future acceptance of Yeshua and his return, as well as upon a well-attested rabbinic tradition that Israel's repentance triggers the eschaton.

Charles Cosgrove presents a plausible alternative:

> Branches were broken off *in order that* the nations might be grafted in. This implies . . . that the pruning of some Jewish branches removes an impediment

---

41. Donaldson, *Paul and the Gentiles*, 222. Elizabeth Johnson offers the same explanation: "Paul shares with several of his Jewish and Christian contemporaries a conviction that Israel's repentance and faithfulness to God will inaugurate the eschaton. From that vantage point, Israel's immediate positive response to the gospel would have initiated the judgment and left the Gentile world under a death sentence. Only by God's gracious restraint of Israel are the Gentiles successfully evangelized." E. Elizabeth Johnson, "Romans 9–11: The Faithfulness and Impartiality of God," in *Pauline Theology*, vol. 3, ed. David M. Hay and E. Elizabeth Johnson (Atlanta: Society of Biblical Literature, 2002), 232.

to the inclusion of the nations. . . . In order that Jews will not dominate gentile Christians and require them to Judaize, God has temporarily pruned the vast majority of Israelites to make what we might call "political space" for those of other nations.[42]

Cosgrove's view builds upon the challenges that Paul faced in places such as Galatia. Whatever answer we give to this question, we know that Paul was convinced that God partially hardened Israel so that blessing might come to the nations of the world.

Israel's hardening is partial in several senses. As we have already seen, it applies only to its response to Yeshua, and not to all spiritual realities. It also affects only part of Israel. But Paul waits till the climax of Romans 11 to reveal the most dramatic sense in which Israel's hardening is partial:

> So that you may not claim to be wiser than you are, brothers and sisters, I want you to understand this mystery: a hardening has come upon part of Israel, until the full number of the Gentiles has come in. And so all Israel will be saved; as it is written, "Out of Zion will come the Deliverer; he will banish ungodliness from Jacob." "And this is my covenant with them, when I take away their sins." As regards the gospel they are enemies of God for your sake; but as regards election they are beloved, for the sake of their ancestors; for the gifts and the calling of God are irrevocable. (Romans 11:25–29)

Who is "all Israel"? We should certainly follow the majority of recent commentators in seeing here a reference to the Jewish people as a whole—Israel as an ordered community. How else can their salvation be a sign that God's love for the patriarchs and matriarchs is faithful and that his choice is irrevocable? It is those who are temporarily enemies (of the good news, not "of God," as in the NRSV) who are nevertheless beloved, and who will receive mercy (Romans 11:30–32).

This third sense in which Israel's hardening was partial would have been especially comforting to Paul and would have had enormous implications for the way he related to non-Yeshua-believing Jews. This is so because Paul firmly expected the return of Yeshua in his own lifetime or soon thereafter.[43] Thus,

---

42. Cosgrove, *Elusive Israel,* 87. See also Ellison, *Mystery of Israel,* 81–82.

43. In Romans itself he writes, "Salvation is nearer to us now than when we first believed; the night is far gone, the day is at hand" (Romans 13:11–12). Only a few years earlier he had written to another congregation in even clearer terms: "We who are alive, who are left until the coming of the Lord, shall not precede those who have fallen asleep" (1 Thessalonians 4:15). He wrote these words to people who were concerned by the fact that some of their congregational friends were dying before the coming of Yeshua. This was a development they had not expected (based on the

when Paul wrote of Israel's future acceptance, he was thinking, not of future generations participating in a remote eschatological scenario, but of his own generation and an imminent, dramatic change in the world. This means that he must have expected many of the very Jews who opposed him and his work and were now "broken off" to be among those who would once again be "grafted in"! We must take account of this fact when we seek to develop a theological perspective on the status of the Jewish people twenty centuries later.

Christomorphic Suffering

Whereas a traditional reading of Romans 9–11 has seen the hardening of nonremnant Israel as exclusively punitive in nature, the texts we have been exploring point in another direction. They depict Israel's partial hardening as a form of suffering imposed by God so that God's redemptive purpose for the world might be realized. When considered in the broader context of the letter to the Romans, this perspective on Israel's partial hardening reveals startling verbal associations with extraordinary theological implications.

Before the modern era, few interpreters understood Romans 9–11 to be dealing primarily with Israel as a nation. Fewer still saw these chapters as pivotal to the entire message of the letter. This situation has changed dramatically. It is now a consensus position among exegetes that these chapters are central to Romans and speak about the Jewish people. However, it is still common to view Romans 9–11 as a self-contained unit, sealed off from what comes before and after. The undisputed literary unity of these three chapters and the change in tone between chapters 8 and 9 have obscured the crucial connections binding Romans 9–11 to the rest of the letter.[44] Happily, some New Testament scholars are now beginning to correct this deficiency as well—with striking results.[45]

---

teaching Paul had previously given them)! In 1 Corinthians 7 Paul gives practical instructions based on his conviction that a cosmic crisis is imminent (v. 26), "the appointed time has grown short" (v. 29), and "the present form of this world is passing away" (v. 31).

44. Elizabeth Johnson underlines the literary integrity of Romans 9–11: "The literary unity of the passage . . . is marked first by the opening oath (9:1–6) and closing hymn (11:33–36) which begin and end the passage with the praise of God who is . . . 'above all' . . . and from whom, through whom, and to whom are . . . 'all things'" (Johnson, "Romans 9–11," 216). However, Johnson is among those who also recognizes the important continuities: "The supreme confidence in the trustworthiness of God's love which Paul expresses in 8:31–39 is followed by a remarkable shift in tone in 9:1 that has tended to suggest more of a break than is there" (222–23).

45. See Johnson, "Romans 9–11," 215, 222–23; Hays, *Echoes of Scripture,* 57–63; Harink, *Paul among the Postliberals,* 178–79, and "The Christ-Apocalypse and Israel's Election: A Pauline Contribution to a Christian Theology of Judaism," a paper delivered to the Duodecim Theological Society, Princeton, NJ, May 1, 2004. Mark Nanos lays out in a chart the parallels between terms Paul applies to the Jewish people, especially in Romans 9–11, and the terms he applies to Yeshua-believers elsewhere in the letter. *The Mystery of Romans,* 112.

Paul begins Romans 8 with a discussion of the gift of the Spirit and the imperative to live according to the Spirit. Referring to the Spirit as "a spirit of adoption"
(*huiothesia*), he proceeds to stress the filial relationship with God now available
to the ekklesia and the hope of a future inheritance that this filial relationship
ensures (Romans 8:14–17a). That inheritance involves the consummation of
adoption through the "redemption of our bodies" (Romans 8:23). Paul also
speaks of this bodily transformation, presumably through resurrection, as the
receiving of "glory" (*doxa*; Romans 8:17, 18, 19, 21, 30; see also 3:23; 5:2). However, in the period between Yeshua's resurrection and return, the ekklesia must
share in Yeshua's sufferings before entering into his glory (Romans 8:17b–18).
While Paul does not say so explicitly, it is likely that he sees this "co-suffering"
as an essential component in the eschatological redemption of creation (Romans
8:19–23). It is part of the living sacrifice that Yeshua-believers offer when they
present their bodies to God (Romans 12:1).

Unless the ekklesia views matters in this way, the suffering it experiences
may cause it to question its own convictions. "If we belong to God and are
favored by God, why is our life so difficult?" Paul seeks to assure his readers that their hardships confirm rather than undermine their status as God's
children. All things in their life, including their sufferings, will work together
for good, because God "foreknew" (*proegno*) them (Romans 8:29) and "called"
(*ekalesen*) them according to his purpose (Romans 8:28, 30). They are God's
elect (*eklecton*; Romans 8:33), and nothing can separate them from God's love
(*agapes tou Theou*; Romans 8:39). Because they share the sufferings of God's
Son now, they are predestined to be conformed to the image of his Son in the
world to come (Romans 8:29).

The distinctive language of Romans 8 recurs in Romans 9 and 11, but now it
is applied to Israel as a whole—the remnant *and* the rest. Just as the sufferings
of the ekklesia raise questions about its claims and hopes, so the "unbelief"
(i.e., lack of Yeshua-faith) of non-remnant Israel raises questions about Israel's
status and hopes.[46] Paul begins the discussion by asserting unequivocally, "They
are Israelites, and to them belong the adoption [*huiothesia*], the glory [*doxa*],
the covenants, the giving of the law, the worship [*latreia*], and the promises"
(Romans 9:4). The use of the terms "adoption" and "glory" bind this affirmation
of Israel's enduring status to Paul's treatment of the ekklesia in Romans 8, suffering in anticipation of the eschaton. The term "worship" (*latreia*) will be picked

---

46. Mark Nanos reads Romans 8:28 in this context: "Their [i.e., nonremnant Israel's] current
enmity is but temporal and does not bring harm as it appears; rather, it brings good, for 'we know
that God causes all things to work together for good to those who love God, to those who are
called according to His purpose' (8:28)." *The Mystery of Romans*, 285.

up again in Romans 12:1, where Paul's readers are summoned: "Present your bodies as a living sacrifice, holy and acceptable to God, which is your spiritual worship" (*ten logiken latreian*). Thus this solemn initial affirmation of Israel's enduring status binds Romans 9–11 to Paul's teaching in both the preceding and subsequent chapters.

The language of election, so plentifully displayed in Romans 8, also recurs in Romans 9 and 11.[47] Israel's remnant—the Jewish Yeshua-believers—is now seen as the "elect" (Romans 9:11; 11:5, 7). However, their election does not replace the election of the people as whole, but instead anchors it. They are the elect within the elect. Thus, Paul asserts at the beginning of Romans 11, "God has not rejected his people whom he foreknew" (*proegno*; Romans 11:2; see 8:29). And, at the climax of the chapter, he states: "As regards the gospel they are enemies (see Romans 5:10) for your sake; but as regards election (*eklogen*) they are beloved (*agapetoi*), for the sake of their ancestors; for the gifts and the calling (*klesis*) of God are irrevocable" (Romans 11:28–29). Like the ekklesia in Romans 8, the people of Israel are elect, foreknown, called, and beloved.

The linguistic and conceptual parallels between Romans 8 and 9–11, reflecting a parallel assurance of the status and future hope of the ekklesia and Israel, suggest that we should view Israel's partial hardening in relation to the ekklesia's eschatological participation in the sufferings of Yeshua. Richard Hays has argued persuasively for this position. He begins by examining Paul's citation of Psalm 44:22 in Romans 8:36:

> Who will separate us from the love of Christ? Will hardship, or distress, or persecution, or famine, or nakedness, or peril, or sword? As it is written, "For your sake we are being killed all day long; we are accounted as sheep to be slaughtered." No, in all these things we are more than conquerors through him who loved us. (Romans 8:35–37)

While Hays recognizes that Paul's main point in these verses "is that Scripture prophesies suffering as the lot of those (i.e., himself and his readers) who live in the eschatological interval between Christ's resurrection and the ultimate redemption of the world," he also probes more deeply into the significance of the citation from Psalm 44:[48]

> Other echoes, however, cluster about the quotation, echoes sympathetic with the central themes of Romans. Consider the source of the quotation: Psalm 44 is a

---

47. Harink points to these parallels and provides illuminating commentary on their significance. See *Paul among the Postliberals*, 178–79.

48. Hays, *Echoes*, 58.

complaint psalm, raising agonized doubts about God's justice and faithfulness to his covenant with Israel. . . . This psalm raises plaintively the issue that we have already seen to be the central theological problem of Romans: the question of God's integrity in upholding his promises to Israel. . . . The psalmist raises a question precisely analogous to the one that Paul is seeking to answer: does the community's experience of suffering indicate that God has abandoned them?[49]

Hays considers Psalm 44 an exilic text, but unlike Deuteronomy, Jeremiah, or Ezekiel, which focus on Israel's sin and God's punishment, this Psalm contends that Israel suffers innocently:

> All this has come upon us,
>> yet we have not forgotten you,
>> or been false to your covenant.
> Our heart has not turned back,
>> Nor have our steps departed from your way. (Psalm 44:17–18)

In the verse that Paul cites, the psalmist goes further: not only does Israel suffer despite its fidelity to the covenant—it actually suffers because of its fidelity to the covenant:

> As it is written, "For your sake we are being killed all day long; we are accounted as sheep to be slaughtered." (See Psalm 44:22)

As Hays remarks, "Heavy emphasis falls on the *heneka sou* in verse 22: 'for *your* sake' we are being put to death."[50]

Psalm 44 thus fits perfectly into the flow of Paul's thinking in Romans 8 as he urges his Yeshua-believing readers to view their afflictions as participation in Yeshua's vicarious, redemptive suffering. However, applied to the Jewish people as a whole, the Psalm also fits perfectly into the flow of Paul's thinking in Romans 11:

> Paul's extraordinary interpretation of the "stumbling" of his Jewish contemporaries as divinely ordained becomes less dissonant when read against the choral background of Psalm 44. If exilic Israel's suffering is interpreted by the psalmist not as punishment but as suffering for the sake of God's name, then perhaps even the temporary unbelief of Israel can be understood as part of God's design to encompass Jews and Gentiles alike with his mercy. And indeed, so Paul argues in Romans 11:11–32.[51]

49. Ibid., 58–59.
50. Ibid., 60.
51. Ibid., 61.

Just as the theme of confident hope in the midst of suffering, and the language of adoption, glory, and election, bind Romans 8 to Romans 9–11, so does the citation of Psalm 44—especially if one accepts Hays' hermeneutical principle that Paul expects his readers to reflect on the biblical context from which he draws his citations.

Is it possible that Paul is hinting through these striking parallels between Romans 8 and Romans 9–11 that Israel's temporary unbelief in Yeshua is itself, paradoxically, a participation in Yeshua's vicarious, redemptive suffering? Hays finds strong support for this extraordinary thesis in another verbal parallel between Romans 8 and Romans 11. In the verses immediately preceding the citation from Psalm 44, Paul writes:

> What then are we to say about these things? If God is for us, who is against us? He who did not withhold [*ouk epheisato*] his own Son, but gave him up for all of us, will he not with him also give us everything else? Who will bring any charge against God's elect [*eklekton*]? (Romans 8:31–33)

Along with most commentators, Hays sees the phrase "did not withhold his own Son" as an allusion to the binding of Isaac in Genesis 22:

> He [i.e., the angel of the Lord] said, "Do not lay your hand on the boy or do anything to him; for now I know that you fear God, since you have not withheld [*ouk epheiso*] your son, your only son from me." . . . The angel of the Lord called to Abraham a second time from heaven, and said, "By myself I have sworn, says the LORD: Because you have done this, and have not withheld [*ouk epheiso*] your son, your only son, I will indeed bless you, and I will make your offspring as numerous as the stars of heaven and as the sand on the seashore. And your offspring shall possess the gates of their enemies, and by your offspring shall all the nations of the earth gain blessing for themselves, because you have obeyed my voice." (Genesis 22:12, 15–18)[52]

God responds to Abraham's offering of Isaac by swearing a solemn oath that confirms the covenantal promises. Paul implies in Romans 8:32 that God has actualized these promises by imitating Abraham's offering of his "only son," thereby providing definitive assurance of the reliability of the promises. More-over, the eschatological suffering of Yeshua-believers is a privileged participation in that offering.

---

52. "It is difficult to avoid seeing in the first clause [of Romans 8:32] an allusion to Gen 22:16." James D. G. Dunn, *Romans 1–8*, Word Biblical Commentary, ed. Bruce M. Metzger, vol. 38A (Waco, TX: Word, 1988), 501.

Once again, we find Paul returning to this language and theme in Romans 11, as he speaks about non-remnant Israel's "unbelief" in Yeshua:

> They were broken off because of their unbelief, but you stand only through faith. So do not become proud, but stand in awe. For if God did not spare [*ouk epheisato*] the natural branches, perhaps he will not spare you. (Romans 11:20–21)

Hays now draws the conclusion that the citation of Psalm 44 had already implied:

> This language of "not sparing" should trigger a chain of reminiscences for Paul's readers. . . . By describing the fate of unbelieving Israel in the same language that he had used to describe Jesus' death, Paul hints at a daring trope whose full implications subsequent Christian theology has usually declined to pursue. What Paul has done, in a word, is to interpret the fate of Israel christologically. If Paul can write in Galatians that Jesus "became a curse . . . in order that in Christ Jesus the blessing of Abraham might come upon the Gentiles" (Galatians 3:13), he can say in Romans 11 something very similar about Israel's role in the drama of salvation. Israel undergoes rejection for the sake of the world, bearing suffering vicariously.[53]

The context in which these words are found in Genesis 22 supports this reading. Abraham's "not withholding his son" evokes a divine oath assuring God's enduring fidelity to the covenant with Abraham and his descendants. It is this covenant that is actualized in Yeshua's death and resurrection (Romans 8:32), it is this covenant that guarantees the election of all Israel as God's beloved (Romans 11:28–29), it is this covenant that brings mercy to the entire world, Jew and Gentile (Romans 11:30–32). That eschatological mercy is realized as the ekklesia and Israel participate in Yeshua's sacrificial offering to God (Romans 12:1).[54]

---

53. Hays, *Echoes*, 61. See also his *The Moral Vision of the New Testament* (San Francisco: Harper, 1996), 433. This exegetical insight of Hays has influenced many Pauline scholars, including Donaldson, *Paul and the Gentiles*, 223; Nanos, *The Mystery of Romans*, 253, n. 33; A. Katherine Grieb, *The Story of Romans* (Louisville: Westminster John Knox, 2002), 109. Also building upon Hays, Harink makes the theological implication thoroughly explicit: "Is it not possible to see Israel's present hardening as its unique (but unknowing) participation in the crucifixion of Jesus Christ, not as culpable 'failure,' but as its own share in suffering, waiting, and groaning with the church and the whole creation, as it too awaits the final redemption of all things?" (Harink, *Paul among the Postliberals*, 180).

54. "This quotation [from Psalm 44 in Romans 8] prepares the way for his direct exhortation in Romans 12:1: 'I beseech you then, brothers, through the mercies of God to present your bodies as a living sacrifice.' That is what is required of the eschatological people of God; God's elect must suffer and groan along with—and even on behalf of—the unredeemed creation (cf. Romans 8:18–25)." Hays, *Echoes*, 62.

To further confirm this inference from the numerous verbal and thematic correspondences binding Romans 8 and Romans 9–11, we may cite another related parallel. The initial text is from Romans 5 rather than Romans 8. However, as A. Katherine Grieb notes, Romans 5:1–11 should be seen in relation to Romans 8:31–39:

> Moreover, the unit 5:1–11 also forms an *inclusio* with 8:31–39, the unit at the end of Paul's larger section, Romans 5–8. A major theme in both sections is the powerful love of God in Christ our Lord. In both sections also, Paul deals with the issues of suffering and hope. Furthermore, Paul uses the same literary style of argument in each place.[55]

Near the end of this unit that introduces Romans 5–8, Paul assures his readers that their present experience of reconciliation through Messiah's death should give them confidence in their future salvation "by his [resurrection] life":

> For if while we were enemies, we were reconciled [*katellagemen*] to God through the death of his Son, much more surely, having been reconciled [*katallagentes*], will we be saved by his life [*zoe*]. (Romans 5:10)

In Romans 11:15 this language recurs, but in a startling new context:

> For if their rejection is the reconciliation [*katallage*] of the world, what will their acceptance be but life from the dead [*zoe ek nekron*]!

Reconciliation and resurrection life are here tied to Israel's rejection and acceptance, just as in Romans 5:10 they are tied to Yeshua's death and life.[56] Given the dense network of interconnections linking Romans 8 and 9–11, we are justified in inferring that this verse points to Paul's implicit conviction that nonremnant Israel's "temporary and partial hardening" is a participation in Yeshua's suffering and death, and that Israel's future acceptance will be both a participation in his resurrection and a catalyst for the general resurrection at the end of the age.

Hays completes his treatment of Romans 8 by pointing to another biblical text that may underlie both Romans 8 and 11, namely, Isaiah 53:

---

55. Grieb, *Story of Romans,* 61.

56. The relationship between Romans 5:10 and 11:15 is noted by Thomas Torrance, "The Divine Vocation and Destiny of Israel in World History," in *The Witness of the Jews to God,* ed. David W. Torrance (Edinburgh: Handsel, 1982), 91, and Philip Esler, *Conflict and Identity in Romans* (Minneapolis: Fortress, 2003), 297–98.

When Paul uses the psalmist's language to describe the people of God as "sheep to be slaughtered" [*probata sphages*], he can hardly fail to hear, sounding in sympathetic harmony, Isaiah's moving account of the fate of the servant of the Lord:

> He was oppressed, and he was afflicted,
> yet he opened not his mouth;
> like a lamb that is led to the slaughter,
>   [*probaton epi sphagen echthe*]
> and like a sheep that before its shearers is dumb,
> so he opened not his mouth. (Isaiah 53:7)[57]

No biblical text articulates the message of vicarious suffering more clearly or eloquently than Isaiah 53. It is a passage that can be taken either as a prophecy about a particular individual or as a revelation of Israel's national vocation in history (or at a specific juncture in history). Paul may well be combining these two readings, seeing the afflictions of both the ekklesia and Israel as participation in the affliction of that faithful representative Israelite, whose person and work constitute the substance of Paul's "good news."[58]

In Romans 11:25–29, Paul unveils—at least in part—a "mystery" (i.e., a feature of God's eschatological purpose that has formerly been hidden but is now revealed):

> I want you to understand this mystery: a hardening has come upon part of Israel, until the full number of the Gentiles has come in. And so all Israel will be saved. . . . As regards the gospel they are enemies for your sake; but as regards election they are beloved, for the sake of their ancestors; for the gifts and the calling of God are irrevocable. (Romans 11:25–29)

What is the mystery to which Paul refers? That "all Israel will be saved"? That is certainly part of the mystery. However, given the network of associations between Romans 8 and 9–11 that we have been exploring, the mystery may lie deeper than the surface of the text. Is it not possible that for Paul the divine mystery at least includes non-remnant Israel's present participation in the Messiah whom she does not yet consciously acknowledge? Mark Nanos suggests that Paul's "mystery" refers, not only to Israel's future salvation, but also to the meaning of her present partial hardening: "So the 'mystery' is not so much *that* Israel is 'stumbling' or will be saved, although it may be in part the reminder of these

---

57. Hays, *Echoes*, 62–63.
58. "Those who have ears to hear will hear and understand that the people of God, reckoned as sheep to be slaughtered, are suffering with Christ (Romans 8:17: *sympaschomen*) and thus living out the vocation prophesied for them according to the Scriptures. Upon them is the chastisement that makes others whole, and with their stripes is creation healed." Hays, *Echoes*, 63.

truths, but rather it is *why* Israel is stumbling and *how* Israel will be saved."[59]
Why is Israel stumbling? She is stumbling "for your sake" (i.e., on behalf of the
Gentile recipients of the good news).[60] In doing so, Paul implies, Israel shares
in the suffering of the Messiah. Paul only hints at this part of the mystery—but
his hints are extensive and mutually reinforcing. Perhaps he considered such
intimations the proper way to unveil such a profound and paradoxical truth.

Israel, First and Last

Paul discloses his radical solidarity with Israel even when he speaks of his
calling as a servant to the Gentiles. In Romans 11:13–15 Paul writes:

> Now I am speaking to you Gentiles. Inasmuch then as I am an apostle to the
> Gentiles, I glorify my ministry in order to make my own people jealous, and thus
> save some of them. For if their rejection is the reconciliation of the world, what
> will their acceptance be but life from the dead!

Johannes Munck was one of the first to take these verses seriously. According
to Munck, Paul's primary concern was the destiny of Israel, his own people.[61]
His zeal for work among the Gentiles derived from his conviction that the success of his efforts would "make [his] own people jealous, and thus save some of
them." Philip Esler has recently supported Munck's conclusion:

> Paul may not be declaring in these verses that the whole thrust of his ministry
> to the non-Israelites is to save Israel, but he is not far off it. How would his non-
> Israelite audience listening to these words in Rome have felt about these words,
> given their implication that Paul's work to non-Israelites is an instrument for the
> salvation of Israelites, who will in due course obtain what rightfully belongs to
> them? His heart really lies with Israel and not with foreigners.[62]

Paul began Romans 9 by expressing his willingness to offer his life for his people,
even as did Moses. His vocation consists of being an apostle to the Gentiles—but
even in this task his own people are never far from his thoughts.

---

59. Nanos, *The Mystery of Romans*, 260.

60. As for the second part of the mystery—"*how* Israel will be saved"—Nanos sees the faith
of the Gentile Yeshua-believers, when practiced in a way that honors Israel and her religious
tradition, as testifying to Jews that the Messianic promises are being realized. See *The Mystery of
Romans*, 274–79.

61. Munck, *Salvation of Mankind*, 62, 305.

62. Esler, *Conflict and Identity*, 297. See also Nanos (*The Mystery of Romans*, 274): "Now they
can see that even Paul's very apostleship to the gentiles is intended for the salvation of Israel
(11:13–14)."

Paul drew the imagery of Israel's jealousy from an important text in the Torah—Deuteronomy 32, the second song of Moses. This passage appears at the end of Moses's farewell address and contains a prophetic summary of Israel's future. It begins by recounting God's election of Israel, in the context of God's providential concern for the nations:

> When the Most High apportioned the nations,
>   When he divided humankind,
> he fixed the boundaries of the peoples
>   according to the number of the gods;
> the LORD's own portion was his people,
>   Jacob his allotted share. (Deuteronomy 32:8–9)

While exercising sovereignty over all the nations, God chooses Israel to be "the LORD's own portion." The song then tells of how Israel will violate this special relationship by worshiping other gods, thus making the Lord jealous (Deuteronomy 32:16). In response, God disciplines Israel by showing favor to other nations (i.e., granting them victory over Israel), so as to make *Israel* jealous:

> They made me jealous with what is no god,
>   Provoked me with their idols.
> So I will make them jealous with what is no people,
>   Provoke them with a foolish nation. (Deuteronomy 32:21)

As the song draws to a conclusion, God again turns to Israel with compassion (Deuteronomy 32:36) and judges the nations who abused Israel. In the Septuagint, the song ends with a summons to the nations: "Rejoice, O nations [i.e., Gentiles], with his people" (Deuteronomy 32:43).

The second song of Moses thus both begins and ends with God's love for Israel. The other nations provide the context for Israel's election and serve as God's instruments in restoring Israel to her proper place.

While Paul alludes in Romans 11 to the second song of Moses, he explicitly cites it in Romans 10 and 15. Commenting on nonremnant Israel's unbelief in Yeshua and the success of his apostolic efforts among the Gentiles, Paul refers to Deuteronomy 32:21:

> Again I ask, did Israel not understand? First Moses says: "I will make you jealous of those who are not a nation; with a foolish nation I will make you angry." (Romans 10:19)

Philip Esler stresses how these words would deflate the pride of Paul's Gentile audience:

> The picture of those who have succeeded to it is most unflattering—they are not a nation, and even though Paul could have omitted this clause, he chose not to: they are a senseless nation. Thus he describes non-Israelite Christ-followers.[63]

Furthermore, Esler suggests that Paul intended his readers to reflect on the second song of Moses in its entirety, including its final vindication of Israel.

> Moreover, if Paul's addressees had in mind the course of Deuteronomy 32 after Romans 10:21 they would have known that the final result of Israel's being provoked to jealousy was that her enemies, who for a time were aided by God, were eventually subjected to his vengeance, whereas Israel was restored to God's favor. Thus, in a verse where Paul is in one respect castigating Israel for her obstinacy, he is, by one of the passages from scripture he selects to make this point, also indicating that Israel will finally be vindicated and her enemies defeated. This theme will be powerfully developed in Romans 11.[64]

Esler's suggestion draws support from Romans 15:7–13, where Paul brings the major discourse of the letter to a solemn conclusion. He first speaks of Yeshua's mission in relation to both Jews and Gentiles:

> For I tell you that Christ has become a servant of the circumcised on behalf of the truth of God in order that he might confirm the promises given to the patriarchs, and in order that the Gentiles might glorify God for his mercy. (Romans 15:8–9a)

Because of the divine promises to the patriarchs, Yeshua's service to Israel demonstrates the faithfulness of God. Israel thus has a rightful claim upon the Messiah. In contrast, Yeshua's service to the Gentiles displays the overflowing, unexpected, and completely gracious character of God's mercy. Paul then cites four biblical texts—one from the Torah, one from the Prophets, and two from the Writings—all of which speak of the Gentiles' praise of God. The second of these texts is Deuteronomy 32:43: "And again he says, 'Rejoice, O Gentiles, with his people'" (Romans 15:10).

As Richard Hays notes, "The Gentiles do not stand alone around Christ; they are being summoned to join *with* Israel in rejoicing."[65] The Messiah cannot

---

63. Esler, *Conflict and Identity,* 293.
64. Ibid., 293.
65. Hays, *Echoes,* 72.

fulfill the "promises given to the patriarchs" merely by bringing the nations to the God of Israel. He must also bring those nations to the Israel of God.

The many allusions to and citations from Deuteronomy 32—including the important jealousy motif—indicate the importance and centrality of Israel for Paul. Just as the second song of Moses begins with Israel's election and ends with Israel's vindication, so Paul defends both the temporal priority of the Jewish people ("to the Jew first, and also to the Greek"—Romans 1:16; 2:9) and their decisive role at the end of the age. In the meantime, the remnant sanctifies the whole nation and sustains the Gentile mission (Romans 11:18), while nonremnant Israel suffers on behalf of those same Gentiles. In turn, the Gentile Yeshua-believers are entrusted with the mission of stirring Israel to jealousy. To do this, they must treat Israel with respect and recognize that their praise of God is complete only when it is offered "with his people."

Conclusion

This brief look at Romans 9–11 confirms the picture of Paul presented in the Acts of the Apostles and has much in common with the overall vision of Luke-Acts. Paul sees the community of Israel, even in its state of unbelief (in Yeshua), as a holy people, a nation in covenant with God. He identifies with Israel as his people and maintains solidarity with them

He embraces his vocation as the apostle to the Gentiles, but he also sees his mission to the Gentiles as instrumental in hastening Israel's redeemed future. He believes that the Jewish people retain their position as the heirs of God's promises and is certain that those promises will ultimately be realized in their national life.[66]

Excursus: "Unbelievers" in Paul

While Paul employs many metaphors in Romans 9–11 to characterize the spiritual condition of nonremnant Israel (e.g., "partial hardening," "stumbling,"

---

66. Ephesians 2:11–3:6 presents a similarly positive view of the Jewish people. The Gentile recipients are addressed as those who were formerly without the Messiah, "being aliens from the commonwealth of Israel, and strangers to the covenants of promise, having no hope and without God in the world" (Ephesians 2:12). They were formerly "far off," but they have now been "brought near" (Ephesians 2:13). Israel had already been near (Ephesians 2:17), but now, together with Yeshua-believing Gentiles, Israel is brought nearer still (Ephesians 2:18). The great prophetic mystery now revealed is that they as Gentiles now share in Israel's Messianic blessings (Ephesians 3:5–6). As Markus Barth concludes, "It is the distinctive message of Ephesians that no Gentile can have communion with Christ or with God unless he also has communion with Israel." *Ephesians 1–3*, The Anchor Bible, vol. 34 (Garden City, NY: Doubleday, 1974), 337. See also Mussner, *Tractate on the Jews*, 25.

"defeat," "rejection," "broken off"), he also uses a simple descriptive word: "unbelief" (*apistia*—Romans 11:20, 23; see also 3:3). The unbelief in question, of course, is the absence of Yeshua-faith. However, it is noteworthy that Paul does *not* speak of non-Yeshua-believing Jews as unbelievers. This is a certainty for Romans, but it is likely for his other writings as well. In 1 Corinthians 10:27, the unbelievers in question are Gentiles who could be suspected of idolatry. In 1 Corinthians 6:6, the unbelievers are Roman magistrates (whom he contrasts with the "holy ones" in 1 Corinthians 6:1–2). In 2 Corinthians 6:14–15, the unbelievers are associated with idolatry and impurity, and a summons to avoid inappropriate intimacy with them is conveyed through an exhortation to holiness (2 Corinthians 7:1). In 1 Corinthians 7:12–15, the identity of the unbeliever is not as obvious as in the above texts, but Paul shows the same concern for purity and holiness (1 Corinthians 7:14) when he assures the believer that a marriage with an unbeliever will sanctify the unbeliever and will produce holy offspring. 1 Corinthians 14:20–25 is a notoriously confusing text whose interpretation is uncertain, but the pairing of *unbeliever* with *outsider* suggests that Paul may be looking for a way to speak of both Gentile non-Yeshua-believers (unbelievers) and Jewish non-Yeshua-believers (outsiders).

In many of the above texts, the unbeliever is associated with impurity and the believer with holiness. In Romans 11:16, Paul asserts that all Israel is holy. If Romans 11:16 expresses a deeply held conviction that shaped Paul's general discourse, we would expect him to use the term *unbeliever* only in reference to pagan Gentiles. The nonremnant Jewish community may be caught in unbelief, but this condition is not so fundamental to its identity that its members should be called unbelievers.

There is only one Pauline text that calls this conclusion into question.[67] In 2 Corinthians Paul writes about non-Yeshua-believing Jews whose minds are hardened (2 Corinthians 3:14). Drawing upon Exodus 34:33-35, he speaks about a veil that covers their minds when they read the Torah (2 Corinthians 3:14–15). Paul then proceeds to contrast himself with Moses, saying that his practice has always been to speak God's word clearly and plainly (2 Corinthians 4:1-2). If his message is veiled, this is the case only for "those who are perishing" (2 Corinthians 4:3).

---

67. Many scholars note that 2 Corinthians 4:4 is the only text in which Paul *might* refer to Jews as "unbelievers," e.g., Peter Tomson, *Paul and the Jewish Law* (Minneapolis: Fortress, 1990), 118, n. 122; Victor Paul Furnish, *II Corinthians,* The Anchor Bible, vol. 32A (Garden City, NY: Doubleday, 1984), 221; Paul Barnett, *The Second Epistle to the Corinthians* (Grand Rapids: Eerdmans, 1997), 220, n. 49.

In their case the god of this world has blinded the minds of the unbelievers, to keep them from seeing the light of the gospel of the glory of Christ, who is the image of God. (2 Corinthians 4:4)

Paul uses some of the same language ("veil" and "minds") as in the previous chapter, and so many interpreters assume that the unbelievers mentioned here are Jews. However, this conclusion seems unlikely for several reasons. First, Paul is now speaking about the veiling of his gospel, not the veiling of the Torah. The metaphor remains from the previous chapter, but the application has changed. Second, these minds are blinded, not hardened. Paul nowhere uses the imagery of blindness to refer to his fellow Jews. Third, the agent who causes the blindness is "the god of this world," i.e., Satan. He is the one associated in Paul's mind with idolatry and Gentile religion (2 Corinthians 6:14–16; 1 Corinthians 10:20–21). But there is no indication in 2 Corinthians 3 that Paul sees Satan as the one who hardens Israel. The use of the passive in 2 Corinthians 3:14 ("their minds were hardened") actually implies the same agent as in Romans 9–11—the God of Abraham, Isaac, and Jacob. Thus Paul draws imagery from 2 Corinthians 3 but uses it in a different way in 2 Corinthians 4. The unbelievers of 2 Corinthians 4:4 are Gentiles, as elsewhere in his letters. The Jewish people are in a condition of unbelief (in regard to Yeshua), but they are still holy. Paul did not refer to them as unbelievers.

John

We have saved the most difficult and troubling book for last—the Gospel of John. Many exegetes and theologians consider John to go beyond supersessionism into the realm of flagrant anti-Judaism.[68] We must first examine why this is the case. We can then proceed to look at John theologically in light of the overall argument of the present chapter.

A Canonical, Theological Approach

In some ways the situation depicted in John is not so different from that seen in the synoptic Gospels. Yeshua enjoys widespread support from the people as a whole (John 2:23; 4:1; 4:39–42; 4:45; 6:2; 6:15; 7:31; 7:40; 10:40–42; 11:48; 12:9–19). In contrast, he elicits heated opposition from the Jerusalem authorities

68. For a thorough and up-to-date summary of scholarly views on John and Judaism, see Reimund Bieringer, Didier Pollefeyt, and Frederique Vandecasteele-Vanneuville, eds., *Anti-Judaism and the Fourth Gospel* (Louisville: Westminster John Knox, 2001).

(John 5:16–18; 7:32; 9:24; 11:47–53). The latter determine to have him executed, and they deliver him to Pilate for that purpose.[69]

However, John differs from the synoptic Gospels on one crucial point. In Matthew, Mark, and Luke, the authorities hostile to Yeshua are called "the chief priests," or "the chief priests, scribes, and elders," or "the scribes and Pharisees." In John these authorities are often called simply "the Jews" (John 1:19, 24; 2:18–20; 5:10, 15–16, 18; 7:1; 7:13; 11:8; 18:14; 18:31; 18:36; 19:31; 19:38; 20:19). This leads to some rather odd-sounding statements in which (Jewish) Yeshua-believers are constrained by their "fear of the Jews" (John 7:13; 19:38; 20:19), or where Yeshua tells Pilate why his (Jewish) followers do not fight to prevent his being "handed over to the Jews" (John 18:36). The impression conveyed to the reader by such usage is that Yeshua and his followers are not themselves Jews, and that those who are rightly called Jews are Yeshua's enemies. For this reason, some accuse John of being anti-Jewish.

John's use of the term "the Jews" shows far more complexity than the above would suggest. On one occasion Yeshua is addressed (by a Samaritan) as a Jew (John 4:9). In the same chapter Yeshua speaks of himself as a Jew ("we worship what we know") in contrast to the Samaritans ("you [plural] worship what you do not know") and proclaims, "Salvation is from the Jews" (John 4:22). John also tells us that the resurrection of Lazarus led many of the Jews to believe in Yeshua (John 12:11). John often uses the term in ways that are neutral or even positive.[70]

Nevertheless, we cannot avoid the overall negative connotation carried by the phrase "the Jews" in the Gospel of John. We also cannot avoid the terrible consequences that ensued in later centuries when Gentile Christians read this text and had their attitudes toward Jews shaped by it. Our immediate task, however, is to discover what John *teaches* about the Jewish people. Moreover, as those engaged in an explicitly theological (rather than a merely historical) inquiry, our determination of John's authoritative teaching must be shaped by the wider canonical context of the New Testament and the experience of the

69. John differs somewhat from the synoptic Gospels in the way he highlights divisions among the people and among the leaders in their response to Yeshua. He notes that some among the people do not believe (John 7:12; 7:40–43). He also describes division among the leaders (John 3:1–2; 7:45–52; 9:16). Whereas in the synoptic Gospels division arises *between* the people and their leaders, in John division exists also within each of the two bodies. Nevertheless, the emphasis of the synoptic Gospels is not lost in John: the people overall are supportive of Yeshua (especially in Galilee), while their leaders are opposed to him.

70. John uses the term to describe Jewish customs rooted in scripture (John 2:6; 2:13; 5:1; 6:4; 7:2; 11:55; 19:40; 19:42). He also uses the term to describe the sympathetic friends of Mary and Martha (John 11:19, 31, 33, 36, 45).

Yeshua-believing community who have carried and read the book over the last two thousand years of history.

Our task differs from that taken up by most New Testament scholars as they study John and the Jewish people. Such commentators usually seek to reconstruct John's personal biography or the social context in which he wrote, in order to explain why he chose the term "the Jews" to identify the Jewish leaders in Jerusalem.[71] They attempt to understand the author's relationship to the Jewish people of his own day so as to shed light on his attitudes and literary intentions. Sometimes such historical efforts conclude that John should be seen as engaged in a bitter intra-Jewish dispute.[72] More often they conclude that John and his community have definitively parted ways with Judaism and are looking at the Jewish people from outside.[73]

In contrast to this method of historical reconstruction, our canonical-theological approach will begin with the text as it is. We do not know for certain why John chose to call the Jewish leaders opposed to Yeshua "the Jews." We do know that these hostile figures in John's narrative are in fact Jerusalem authorities rather than the Jewish contemporaries of Yeshua in general. As we have already noted, John portrays a division among the people in regard to Yeshua that is similar to that seen in the synoptic Gospels. The people are in general favorable to Yeshua. The leaders are in general hostile to him.

Recently many New Testament scholars, having shifted their attention from historical to literary questions, have focused on the literary effect of John's usage and the various ways of reading the book in the twenty-first century.[74] Their purpose is to understand the way the text functions in relation to readers, independent of the author's attitudes or intentions. When read by Christians

71. The two classic examples of this way of studying John are Raymond E. Brown, *The Community of the Beloved Disciple* (New York: Paulist Press, 1979), and J. Louis Martyn, *History and Theology in the Fourth Gospel,* 3rd ed. (Louisville: Westminster John Knox, 2003).

72. For example, see James D. G. Dunn, *The Partings of the Ways* (Philadelphia: Trinity Press International, 1991), 143–46, 156–60; "The Embarrassment of History," in Bieringer, Pollefeyt, and Vandecasteele-Vanneuville, *Anti-Judaism and the Fourth Gospel,* 41–60; David Rensberger, "Anti-Judaism and the Gospel of John," in *Anti-Judaism and the Gospels,* ed. William R. Farmer (Harrisburg, PA: Trinity Press International, 1999), 120–57; Craig S. Keener, *The Gospel of John,* vol. 1 (Peabody, MA: Hendrickson, 2003), 214–32.

73. Typical of this perspective is the following from Raymond Brown: "It is this situation in which the Gospel was written that explains the use of the term 'the Jews.' . . . For the most part, the Jews who had accepted Jesus were now simply Christians and part of the Church, so that when Christians spoke of the Jews without qualification they were referring to those who had rejected Jesus and remained loyal to the Synagogue." Raymond E. Brown, *The Gospel According to John I–XII* (New York: Doubleday, 1966), lxxii.

74. Adele Reinhartz combines the historical and literary approaches in *Befriending the Beloved Disciple* (New York: Continuum, 2001).

(i.e., Gentile Yeshua-believers) in a translation that renders *Ioudaioi* always as "Jews" (rather than "Judeans" or "Jewish leaders"), the Gospel of John obviously contributes to anti-Jewish sentiment. When read by non-Yeshua-believing Jews in such a translation, the book produces a sense of alienation from its subject.

In contrast to this literary method of analysis, our canonical-theological approach will focus, not on ways in which the book might affect its readers, but instead on its explicit teaching. As stated above, we do not know what John's original intention was in using the term *Ioudaioi* as he does. We do know its effect on second- or third-century Gentile readers with no historical bond to the Jewish people, and on post-Constantinian Christian readers with political power over Jewish minorities in their midst. Whatever John's original intention was, it is hard to imagine his being pleased with what later history made of his text. In light of that history, John himself would likely find this use of *Ioudaioi* disturbing. Whatever the overall literary effect of his writing when read in a later context, as Yeshua-believers our commitment to the authority of the text binds us only to its explicit teaching. A canonical-theological approach may require that we resist the literary potential of the text in the interest of following its fundamental message.

John's Teaching Concerning Israel

What does John teach about the people of Israel, i.e., the Jewish people? In an important verse cited earlier, Yeshua states: "You [Samaritans] worship what you do not know; we [Jews] worship what we know, for salvation is from the Jews" (John 4:22). Alan Culpepper sees this verse as the beginning of a proper reading of John:

> In the context of conversation with the Samaritan woman, Jesus affirms the historical primacy of Israel. The heritage and experience of Judaism are foundational to salvation.[75]

For our purposes, it is crucial to recognize that here Yeshua unambiguously speaks about the Jewish people as a whole and its spiritual heritage. In another text he may charge a particular set of Jewish leaders in Jerusalem with being the devil's children because they seek to kill him (John 8:44). But here Yeshua *teaches* about the Jewish people as a people. This positive theological use of *Ioudaioi* resembles John's references to *Israel*. The Baptist announces that he

---

75. R. Alan Culpepper, "Anti-Judaism in the Fourth Gospel as a Theological Problem for Christian Interpreters," in Bieringer, Pollefeyt, and Vandecasteele-Vanneuville, *Anti-Judaism and the Fourth Gospel,* 74.

has come so that Yeshua "might be revealed to Israel" (John 1:31). A few verses later Yeshua hails Nathaniel as "an Israelite in whom there is no deceit" (John 1:47), and Nathaniel responds by acclaiming Yeshua as "the King of Israel" (John 1:49). John thus employs the term *Israel* with no trace of ambivalence.

At the beginning of John a disciple sincerely calls Yeshua the King of Israel. Near the end of John a Gentile ruler ironically asks if he is "the King of the Jews."

> Then Pilate entered the headquarters again, summoned Jesus, and asked him, "Are you the King of the Jews?" Jesus answered, "Do you ask this on your own, or did others tell you about me?" Pilate replied, "I am not a Jew, am I? Your own nation and the chief priests have handed you over to me." (John 18:33–35)

Pilate addresses Yeshua as a Jew and calls the Jewish people "your own nation." This recalls the dialogue between Yeshua and another non-Jew (i.e., the Samaritan woman), in which Yeshua is also identified as a Jew and his relationship to his people is highlighted. The title cited by Pilate, "King of the Jews," plays a central role in John's version of the decision to crucify Yeshua:

> He [Pilate] said to the Jews, "Here is your King!" They cried out, "Away with him! Away with him! Crucify him!" Pilate asked them, "Shall I crucify your King?" The chief priests answered, "We have no king but the emperor." Then he handed him over to them to be crucified. (John 9:14–16)

Pilate mocks the Jewish leaders by presenting Yeshua as their King. He finally evokes a response that pleases him: their only king is the Roman emperor. In order to accomplish their purpose, the chief priests are willing to deny not only Yeshua but also the fundamental article of Jewish faith, which states that God is Israel's only ultimate Sovereign.[76]

The title King of the Jews continues to play an important role in John's narrative of the crucifixion:

> Pilate also had an inscription written and put on the cross. It read, "Jesus of Nazareth, the King of the Jews." Many of the Jews read this inscription, because the place where Jesus was crucified was near the city; and it was written in Hebrew, in Latin, and in Greek. Then the chief priests of the Jews said to Pilate, "Do not

---

76. Rabbinic tradition understands the Shema (Deuteronomy 6:4) to be an acknowledgement of God's unique kingship (*M. Berachot* 2:2), even though the Shema does not refer explicitly to God as King. This understanding of the Shema was probably common to first-century Judaism.

write, 'The King of the Jews,' but, 'This man said, I am King of the Jews.'" Pilate answered, "What I have written I have written." (John 19:19–22)

The inscription itself is an element of early tradition found also in the other Gospels. However, the dispute between Pilate and the Jewish leaders over the inscription is unique to John. John makes explicit what the synoptics only imply: Pilate has this inscription placed on the cross in order to mock the Jewish leaders and people, and the leaders bristle at what they rightly take to be an insult. John tells of the incident in an ironic tone. Just as he was willing to describe Yeshua as the King of Israel at the beginning of the book, so now he proudly acclaims the crucified Messiah as the King of the Jews. In order to underline the positive meaning of "the Jews" in this unit, John describes the hostile Jewish leaders as "the chief priests of the Jews" rather than as "the Jews."

John's description of the dialogue with Pilate and the inscription on the cross radiates outward and connects with other parts of his gospel. We have already noted the link to Nathaniel's acclamation and Yeshua's conversation with the Samaritan woman. There is also a link to the words of Caiaphas concerning Yeshua's death. As we have already seen, Pilate states in his dialogue with Yeshua, "Your own nation and the chief priests have handed you over to me" (John 18:35). This reference reminds the reader of the words of Caiaphas described in John 11:49–52 (italics added):

> But one of them, Caiaphas, who was high priest that year, said to them, "You know nothing at all! You do not understand that it is better for you to have one man die for the *people* [*laos*] than to have the whole *nation* [*ethnos*] destroyed." He did not say this on his own, but being high priest that year he prophesied that Jesus was about to die for the *nation* [*ethnos*], and not for the *nation* [*ethnos*] only, but to gather into one the dispersed children of God.

That John wanted us to see these texts together is evident from his allusion to Caiphas's prophecy in 18:14 (italics added), just before the dialogue with Pilate:

> Caiaphas was the one who had advised the Jews that it was better to have one person die for the *people*.

The "nation" hands him over to be executed, yet he dies for their benefit. John endorses the words of Caiaphas, seen as an unintended and misunderstood prophecy that points to Yeshua's death as a sacrifice for both Israel (the nation, the people) and the Gentiles (the other children of God). Yeshua is the King of the Jews and displays his love for those he rules by willingly giving his life for them. In contrast, John portrays the chief priests as apostate leaders who deny God before Pilate and demand the death of God's anointed.

This is John's teaching about the Jewish people. It is not very extensive, but it certainly fits well with what is found elsewhere in the New Testament. But does it fit well with John's teaching on other matters? John is often seen as soteriologically dualist, holding that only those who believe in Yeshua in this life will share in the life of the world to come. Such a teaching would exclude all non-Yeshua-believing Jews from that life. While space constraints prevent me from treating this topic adequately in the present volume, I would concur with Alan Culpepper that John need not be read in such an exclusivist and dualist manner:

> John 1:9, "The true light, which enlightens everyone, was coming into the world," is the most radically inclusive statement in the New Testament. Working since the creation as light enlightening every person, the Logos was active in the history of Israel and was confessed by her heroes: Abraham, Moses, and Isaiah. One who worships the God of Abraham, Isaac, and Jacob, therefore, worships the God revealed by the Logos, the same Logos that became flesh in Jesus. The Johannine Jesus who said, "No one comes to the Father except through me" (14:6), also said, "Before Abraham was, I am" (8:58). . . . There is no doubt that John does not condemn the Jewish people as a people. Indeed, the Gospel holds forth the hope of universal salvation, at least in a general sense. Jesus is "the Lamb of God who takes away the sin of the world" (1:29), and when he is lifted up, he will draw all people to himself (12:32).[77]

John does not provide a comprehensive teaching on soteriology. The book fails to tell us about the fate of the vast multitudes who have not rejected Yeshua but who have also not explicitly embraced him. We should therefore be reluctant to assume that John's soteriology implies a divine rejection of the Jewish people.

The above interpretation of John requires us to read somewhat across the grain. However, the basic thesis of a canonical and theological interpretation of scripture is that our reading of each text and each book should be guided by the vision of the canon as a whole, as viewed within the life of the believing community in the context of its journey through history. If our presentation of Mark, Matthew, Luke-Acts, and Paul has been convincing, and if the hermeneutical considerations discussed in chapter 1 are taken into consideration, then such a reading of John seems eminently reasonable.

77. Culpepper, "Anti-Judaism," 74–75.

Conclusion

We began this chapter with the premise—based on the previous chapter—that the New Testament as a canonical whole assumes that a distinctive Jewish communal presence is important for the outworking of the divine purpose in the world. We then suggested that the body of observant Jewish Yeshua-believers was insufficient in itself to constitute such a communal presence, on the historical and theological grounds that there has been no continuous communal presence of such a body. This means that the wider Jewish community, consisting mainly of non-Yeshua-believing Jews, must play an essential positive role in God's purpose for the world. We proposed in this chapter to test this hypothesis against the data supplied by the New Testament. Can New Testament teaching be plausibly construed in such a way that it affirms the continuing covenantal significance of the Jewish people, even as it orders its life without explicit Yeshua-faith?

Our examination of the major New Testament books has yielded a positive answer to this question. Mark presumes the ongoing role of the Jewish people. Matthew, Luke-Acts, and Paul emphatically affirm it. John can reasonably be construed in such a way that it at least permits such a thesis.

Luke-Acts and Paul should serve as our main guides on this topic. Both authors treat it explicitly and give it a special place in their overall theological schemes. For both of them the Jewish people are still Israel, a holy people, upon whom the redemption of the world ultimately hinges.

4

Bilateral Ecclesiology in Solidarity with Israel

Our conclusions from chapters 2 and 3, taken together, have profound implications for our understanding of the transnational ekklesia established to embody and proclaim the faith of Yeshua.

We have concluded that, according to New Testament teaching, the ekklesia does not replace Israel. The Jewish people as a whole retains its position as a community chosen and loved by God. While, in Pauline language, Israel has experienced a "partial hardening" that temporarily prevents her from corporately embracing Yeshua-faith, she nevertheless remains a holy people, set apart for God and God's purposes.

We have also concluded that, according to New Testament teaching, the ekklesia contains at its core a portion of Israel. Paul calls this portion "the remnant" and describes it as a representative and priestly component of Israel that sanctifies Israel as a whole. In order to fulfill its vocation, this portion of Israel must truly *live as Israel*—that is, it must be exemplary in observing those traditional Jewish practices that identify the Jewish people as a distinct community chosen and loved by God.

Three implications follow naturally from these conclusions. The first concerns the basic structure of the ekklesia. Jewish practice is inherently corporate in nature. Circumcision is a social rite, performed by a trained official within the community. Sabbath observance requires social support and communal expression. The dietary laws require kosher meat processing and a network of related families following similar food customs. The practical need for communal support reinforces the underlying meaning of all Jewish practice, which is to be an effective sign marking Israel as a people set apart for God.

At the same time, the New Testament also emphasizes the importance of Gentiles becoming part of the ekklesia without becoming Jews. The text presents the ekklesia as itself an ordered community, a network of household units bound together in committed relationships. However, the leadership of the Yeshua movement determined at an early stage that the ekklesia as an eschatological extension of Israel was to be an essentially transnational reality in which the cultural particularities of different regions and ethnicities would be expressed within the broad framework of Israel's messianic faith. The Jewish members of the ekklesia—who in the beginning held all positions of authority and influence—were to avoid exerting overt or subtle pressure on Gentile adherents to become Jews.

Only one structural arrangement would allow for distinctive Jewish communal life within the context of a transnational community of Jews and Gentiles: the one ekklesia must consist of two corporate subcommunities, each with its own formal or informal governmental and communal structures. Thus the first implication of chapters 2 and 3 is that the ekklesia is bilateral—one reality subsisting in two forms.

Given that the Jewish people as a whole remains a community set apart for God, and that the Jewish segment of the ekklesia represents and sanctifies Israel, and that faithful Jewish practice requires extensive communal support, a second implication arises out of the first: the Jewish branch of the twofold ekklesia must identify with the Jewish people as a whole and participate actively in its communal life.

These two implications then suggest a third. If the Jewish branch of the ekklesia maintains solidarity with the Jewish people as a whole, then the Gentile ekklesia is thereby brought into meaningful relationship with "all Israel." Without becoming Jewish, it is joined to an extended multinational commonwealth of Israel and can legitimately identify with Israel's history and destiny. This provides the Gentile branch of the ekklesia with a way of sharing in Israel's life and blessings without succumbing to supersessionism. On this point it is noteworthy that the rise of Christian supersessionism is correlated with schism between the Jewish and Gentile branches of the ekklesia, schism between the Jewish branch and the wider Jewish people, and the demise of Jewish Yeshua-faith as a viable corporate reality.

At first, Gentile Yeshua-believers apparently expressed their solidarity with the Jewish people by participating along with Jewish Yeshua-believers in the wider

Jewish world. They attended synagogue gatherings and experienced Jewish life directly. Only Yeshua-believing Jews would have accepted them as equals and as sharers in Israel's eschatological blessings, but this need not have prevented them from active involvement with the rest of the Jewish community.

If one accepts our reading of the New Testament in chapters 2 and 3 and ponders the conclusions reached there, the ecclesiology embodied in these three implications should make sense in theological terms. A bilateral ecclesiology in solidarity with Israel as a whole takes up all the elements affirmed so far and assembles them into a coherent structure that effectively addresses the problem of Christian supersessionism. But how does it square with the actual ecclesiological teaching of the New Testament? These three assertions may seem to be logically implied by the New Testament teaching we have examined so far, but does the New Testament provide any evidence that such an ecclesiology was ever actually upheld and practiced? In this chapter we will argue that the answer to this question is yes.

James and the Jerusalem Congregation

In chapter 3 we discussed the role of Jerusalem within the geographic structure of Acts. The story begins in Jerusalem and then continually returns to Jerusalem. We proposed that by ending his narrative in Rome, Luke implied that the story was unfinished. It would end when Jerusalem was redeemed and the kingdom was restored to Israel (Luke 2:38; Acts 1:6).

For Luke, as for all first-century Jews, Jerusalem was the center of the world.[1] As Robert Brawley suggests, Luke's concern for the temple shows that he shared the widespread Jewish conviction that the Jerusalem sanctuary constituted the *axis mundi*, the meeting place of heaven and earth.[2] This is why Yeshua's death, resurrection, and return must take place in Jerusalem. This is why the twelve apostles establish their base of operations in Jerusalem. This is why the city remains central to the narrative of Acts, even when the twelve no longer reside there.

The centrality and the holiness of Jerusalem also explain the special role played by its ekklesia. The Yeshua-believers in Antioch send aid to the Jerusalem congregation in a time of famine (Acts 11:27–30). After each of his journeys, Paul returns to Jerusalem, visiting both the temple and the Jerusalem congregation

---

1. Richard Bauckham, "James and the Jerusalem Church," in *The Book of Acts in Its Palestinian Setting*, ed. Richard Bauckham, vol. 4 of *The Book of Acts in Its First Century Setting*, ed. Bruce W. Winter (Grand Rapids: Eerdmans, 1995), 417–27.

2. Robert L. Brawley, *Luke-Acts and the Jews* (Atlanta: Scholars, 1987), 127–32.

(Acts 9:26–29; 15:2; 18:22; 21:17–23:11). The head of the Jerusalem congregation, James the brother of Yeshua, also holds a unique position of authority within the Yeshua movement. According to Luke, the crucial leadership meeting that determines the requirements for Gentiles entering the movement takes place under the presidency of James, even though Peter is present (Acts 15:7, 13, 19). James and the Jerusalem elders give Paul direction on how to improve his image within the Jerusalem congregation, and Paul willingly complies (Acts 21:18–26).

The letters of Paul confirm Luke's picture of the importance of the Jerusalem congregation and its main leader, James. Paul invests much effort in collecting funds from the Gentile members of the Yeshua movement to aid the Jerusalem congregation, which he refers to as "the holy ones" (Galatians 2:10; 1 Corinthians 16:1–4; 2 Corinthians 9:1–15; Romans 15:25–27). This collection has been compared to the temple tax that Jews throughout the world paid annually to support the functioning of the Jerusalem sanctuary.[3] It is clear from Romans 15:27 that Paul treats it as an acknowledgement by the Gentile Yeshua-believers of their debt to the people of Israel.[4] Thus the Jerusalem congregation represents the Jewish portion of the Yeshua movement to the Gentile portion and thereby also represents the Jewish people as a whole.

Paul's letters likewise bear witness to the stature of James among mid-first-century Yeshua-believers. When recounting the resurrection appearances of Yeshua, Paul says that he "appeared to James, then to all the apostles" (1 Corinthians 15:7). One could infer from this text that Paul considered James an apostle. This plausible inference is confirmed by Galatians 1:19, where Paul mentions a visit to Jerusalem in which he had seen none of the apostles except James. It is especially significant that Paul lists James (along with Peter and John) as one of the three "pillars," and in that list James appears first (Galatians 2:9). Paul also implies that Peter deferred to James and gave him precedence, in practice if not in principle (Galatians 2:12). Though Paul asserts that his own appointment as an apostle derived directly from Yeshua rather than from the Jerusalem leadership (Galatians 1:1, 12), he nevertheless acknowledges that he needed their approval for his work to succeed (Galatians 2:2).

3. Donald Harman Akenson, *Saint Saul* (Oxford: Oxford University Press, 2000), 163–65.

4. "This contribution was especially important in Paul's ministry since it was a gift from Gentiles to Jews and was regarded as a sacrificial offering and an expression of appreciation for the initial role the Jews had played in providing the gospel for them (Romans 15:16, 25–27). The Gentiles were in debt to the Jews and needed to acknowledge it." John McRay, *Paul* (Grand Rapids: Baker Academic, 2003), 187. I would add that the appreciation would have been not only for the gospel but for the full riches of Israel's heritage that these Gentiles had tasted.

The unique authority of James came in part from his physical relationship to Yeshua. His reputed piety, character, and competence also added prestige. However, we should not underestimate the influence associated with his role as the head of the Jerusalem congregation. Richard Bauckham sees this clearly:

> As the permanent head of the mother church, he continued to symbolize the center while other apostles now represented the movement of the gospel out from the center. James in the period of his supremacy in Jerusalem was no merely local leader, but the personal embodiment of the Jerusalem church's constitutional and eschatological centrality in relation to the whole developing Christian movement, Jewish and Gentile.[5]

This congregation truly was "the mother church" for the whole movement, and its leader was inevitably put in a position of central importance.

Given the special role of the Jerusalem congregation and its leader within the worldwide Yeshua movement, it is noteworthy that Luke stresses its strict adherence to Jewish practice and its active participation in the religious life of the wider Jewish community. As faithful Jews, members of the Jerusalem congregation observe the Sabbath (Acts 1:12), gather for worship on the holiday of Pentecost (Acts 2:1), and pray at the times ordained by Jewish custom (Acts 3:1). They include among their ranks many priests and Pharisees (Acts 6:7; 15:5). They are a community "zealous for the Torah" (Acts 21:20). They attend the temple (Acts 2:46; 3:1) and meet in its courts (Acts 5:12; 5:42), and the people of the city hold them in high regard (Acts 2:47; 5:13).

Like Bauckham, Jacob Jervell perceives the centrality of the Jerusalem community for the worldwide Yeshua movement. However, he also sees this centrality in relation to its role as the representative of Israel and of Judaism within the transnational ekklesia:

> At the end of the book [of Acts] this congregation [in Jerusalem] is decisive for the church as a whole. According to Luke, Jerusalem has authority over all the Christian churches. There is no church disconnected from Jerusalem and so from Israel.[6]

For Jervell, the centrality of the Jerusalem congregation in Acts represents for Luke the ongoing role of the Jewish segment of the Yeshua-movement as the point of connection between the Gentile Yeshua-believers and the heritage of Israel:

---

5. Bauckham, "James and the Jerusalem Church," 450.
6. Jacob Jervell, *The Unknown Paul* (Minneapolis: Augsburg, 1984), 18–19.

"Israel" does not refer to a church that is made up of Jews and Gentiles, but to the repentant portion of "empirical" Israel; they are Jews who have accepted the gospel, to whom and for whom the promises have been fulfilled. For Luke this relationship is the presupposition for the Gentiles sharing in the promises.[7]

The Gentiles, however, are not Israel, but have been associated with Israel.[8]

Luke conceives of the Jewish Christian element in the church as the center and kernel of the church.[9]

Jervell's reading of Acts does justice to the place of Israel and of the Jerusalem congregation in that book. Thus the role of the Jerusalem congregation in Acts supports our thesis that the New Testament teaches a bilateral ecclesiology in solidarity with Israel.

The unique position of James in the early Yeshua movement is also reflected in the New Testament letter bearing his name. Scholars dispute whether the letter was actually written by James the brother of Yeshua. However, there is no doubt that it is attributed to him. Thus the letter presents itself as instruction from the head of the Jerusalem congregation, the preeminent leader of the Jewish portion of the ekklesia. The most interesting part of the letter for our purposes is the superscription: it is addressed to "the twelve tribes in the Dispersion" (James 1:1). Several recent commentators agree that this designation can refer only to Jewish people.[10] Most likely, it refers to groups of Jewish Yeshua-believers who are located outside the land of Israel. This is significant, for elsewhere in the New Testament such groups are found only in the land. Here the leader of the Jewish ekklesia addresses an encyclical to the congregations under his authority located outside the land of Israel. This implies a consciousness of a distinct corporate identity among the Jewish congregations within the one Messianic ekklesia.

Early in the canonical process the letter of James was combined with letters attributed to Peter and John. These are traditionally called the "catholic" or "general" epistles. Richard Bauckham thinks that the canonical arrangement of these books reveals awareness in the early Yeshua movement of the priority of Israel and the special role of the Jewish portion of the ekklesia:

7. Jacob Jervell, *Luke and the People of God* (Minneapolis: Augsburg, 1972), 43.

8. Jervell, *Luke*, 67.

9. Jervell, *The Unknown Paul*, 42–43.

10. Richard Bauckham, *James* (London: Routledge, 1999), 21, 105, 112; John Painter, *Just James* (Minneapolis: Fortress, 1999), 243–45; Ralph P. Martin, *James* (Waco, TX: Word, 1988), 8–10; Luke Timothy Johnson, *Brother of Jesus, Friend of God* (Grand Rapids: Eerdmans, 2004), 7; Patrick J. Hartin, *James of Jerusalem* (Collegeville, MN: Liturgical Press, 2004), 94–95.

If we read the catholic epistles in the order which at an early date came to be the accepted canonical order, with James in first place and 1 Peter immediately following, then we read first a letter addressed only to Jewish Christians as the twelve tribes in the Diaspora and then a letter apparently addressed only to Gentile Christians as "exiles of the diaspora," to whom defining descriptions of Israel as God's people are applied. One effect is to portray the inclusion of Gentiles in the eschatological people of God, which retains through its Jewish Christian members its continuity with Israel and yet is also open to the inclusion of those who had not hitherto been God's people (1 Peter 2:10). . . . The sequence and relationship of James and 1 Peter portrays the priority of Israel . . . , Gentile Christians' indebtedness to Jewish believers . . . , and also the full inclusion of Gentiles in the people of God.[11]

Bauckham also finds this message expressed in the ancient order of the canon, found in most of the earliest biblical codices and still used in the Eastern churches, which places the catholic epistles before the Pauline epistles.

The order which places the catholic letters (with James at their head) before the Pauline corpus maintains the priority of the centre over the movement out from the centre.[12]

John Miller goes further, viewing the arrangement of the entire New Testament canon (in its Eastern form) as a response to Marcionism that recontextualizes Paul by giving precedence to the three pillars who represent the Jewish ekklesia.[13]

Though emerging as a canon within the Gentile ekklesia, the New Testament nevertheless gives special honor to the Jerusalem congregation and preserves the memory of the unique role of James among the leaders of the early Yeshua movement. In doing so, it bears witness to the bilateral ecclesiology of the movement's founders and to their consciousness of standing in solidarity with the people of Israel.

11. Bauckham, *James*, 156–57. David Trobisch observes that "unlike the Pauline Letters, the Catholic Epistles are not arranged according to their length." *The First Edition of the New Testament* (Oxford: Oxford University Press, 2000), 135–36, n. 37. According to Trobisch's computer assisted calculation, 1 John is the longest, followed by 1 Peter, and then James. Trobisch follows Dieter Luhrmann ("Gal 2,9 und die katholischen Briefe," *Zeitschrift für die neutestamentliche Wissenschaft* 72 [1981], 71) in asserting that the general letters are arranged in accordance with the sequence in which the three pillar apostles are named in Galatians 2:9. Trobisch, 57, 60, 135, n. 37.

12. Bauckham, *James*, 116.

13. John W. Miller, *How the Bible Came to Be* (New York: Paulist Press, 2004), 60–65.

James and the Jerusalem Council

Luke articulates explicitly his bilateral ecclesiology in an account that occupies a central place in his narrative: his report on the Jerusalem council. In the previous chapters Luke had described the conversion of Cornelius (Acts 10–11), the beginning of the Gentile mission in Antioch (Acts 11:19–21), and the first Gentile mission journey of Paul and Barnabas (Acts 13–14). As a result of these momentous events, some Judean members of the Yeshua movement travel to Antioch and insist that Gentile Yeshua-believers should be circumcised (i.e., convert to Judaism) and should live as Torah-observant Jews (Acts 15:1, 5). Paul and Barnabas object fiercely to this initiative, and the controversy leads to a meeting in Jerusalem that includes Paul, Barnabas, Peter, James, and the other main leaders of the young movement.

The discussion begins with heated debate (Acts 15:7). Peter then rises and recounts his experience with Cornelius as an argument against compelling the Gentiles to become Jews. Next Barnabas and Paul tell about the extraordinary results of their work among the Gentiles. Finally James pronounces an authoritative decree based on exegesis of a text from Amos 9:

> After they finished speaking, James replied, "My brothers, listen to me. Simeon has related how God first looked favorably on the Gentiles, to take from among them a people for his name. This agrees with the words of the prophets, as it is written, 'After this I will return, and I will rebuild the dwelling of David, which has fallen; from its ruins I will rebuild it, and I will set it up, so that all other peoples may seek the Lord—even all the Gentiles over whom my name has been called. Thus says the Lord, who has been making these things known from long ago.' Therefore I have reached the decision that we should not trouble those Gentiles who are turning to God, but we should write to them to abstain only from things polluted by idols and from fornication and from whatever has been strangled and from blood. For in every city, for generations past, Moses has had those who proclaim him, for he has been read aloud every sabbath in the synagogues." (Acts 15:13–21)

Two preliminary points from this text should be noted. First, Peter and James offer different types of argument in support of the final ruling. Peter bases his argument on experience and supernatural intervention. While this carries weight, only the subsequent argument offered by James—based on scripture—is definitive. As Richard Bauckham comments, these leaders deliberate in the manner of a rabbinic council issuing halakhic rulings: "The issue is a matter of halakhah, which can only be decided from Scripture."[14] Second, it is James who issues the

---

14. Bauckham, "James and the Jerusalem Church," 452.

authoritative decree. James does not merely persuade, he judges.[15] Thus Luke underlines the unique authority of James as the leader and embodiment of the Jerusalem congregation.

Jacob Jervell comments on the substance of James's decision, reasoning, and exegesis as follows:

> For James the event shows "how God first visited the Gentiles, to take out of them a people for his name" (v. 14). This episode is justified and confirmed on the basis of scriptural interpretation, namely, by prophetic utterances (vv. 16–18). It is, however, not only this episode or even the Gentile mission that is established by the scriptural reference. With the admission of Gentiles to the people of God, there are now two groups within this people. No doubt 14b is meant to correspond with 17: "to take out of them (=Gentiles) a people for his name" and "all the Gentiles who are called by my name." "A people of the Gentiles" is related to "the rebuilding of the dwelling of David which has fallen," the restoration of Israel (v. 16). James asserts that two groups exist within the church. The conversion of the Gentiles is the result of the conversion of Israel, as is demonstrated by the numerous references to Jewish mass conversions.
>
> This division of the church into two groups is the presupposition for the apostolic decree, or better yet, James' decree. The entire argument is carried by the difference between the two groups. It is presupposed that Jewish Christians keep the law; this point of view harmonizes with the account in Acts as a whole. On the other hand, Gentile Christians need not keep the law in its entirety. James supports this by appealing to Moses as a witness for his decision (v. 21). The apostolic decree is nothing but Mosaic law, which is applied to Gentiles living together with Israel. Actually, Luke at this point has two authorities for the decree: Moses and James.[16]

Jervell notices what most commentators miss. James's exegesis of Amos 9 leads to the immediate conclusion that "two groups exist within the church." The first group consists of the Jewish Yeshua-believers, who constitute Israel's eschatological firstfruits. As we showed in chapter 2, the controversy in Acts 15 makes sense only if all parties assumed that this Jewish group is obligated to live according to the Torah. The second group consists of the Gentile Yeshua-believers, the "people" whom God took for himself from among the nations. Amos 9 treats

---

15. "James is portrayed as more than just another rhetor; he is portrayed as a judge or authority figure who can give a ruling that settles a matter. Unlike a rhetorician who merely proposes a certain course of action, James is portrayed as one who can take action." Ben Witherington III, *The Acts of the Apostles* (Grand Rapids: Eerdmans, 1998), 457.

16. Jervell, *Luke*, 190. On James's speech in Acts and its use of scripture, see also Bauckham, "James and the Jerusalem Church," 452–62.

this as a distinct group, related to Israel but also distinct from it.[17] Therefore it cannot be presumed that the commandments incumbent on Israel are also incumbent on this group. According to the implicit Torah exegesis of James, based on Leviticus 17–18, this group associated with Israel is obligated to keep only a limited number of commandments from the Torah.[18] Thus James roots his halakhic decision in the bilateral ecclesiology he derives from Amos 9.

Many commentators perceive that, according to Acts, Jews and Gentiles within the early Yeshua-movement lived according to different customs (*ethne*). However, few have seen that these distinct customs presume and require distinct communal expressions (they are *national* customs), and that this connection between communal expression and way of life is central to the logic of James's speech. There is one ekklesia, but it contains within it two distinct communal entities: a Jewish ekklesia (representing and serving as a bridge to Israel as a whole) and a Gentile ekklesia.[19]

Paul and Bilateral Ecclesiology

One could respond to our argument by asserting that even if James and Luke both espoused bilateral ecclesiology, Paul clearly opposed it. According to the common view, Paul considered a mixed community of Jews and Gentiles to be the ideal expression of the ekklesia in any given location, and sought to found such communities.[20] In these groups, Jewish members would be permitted to maintain Jewish practice but only insofar as such practice did not conflict with unrestricted community relationships with their Gentile brothers and

17. Bruce Chilton interprets Acts 15:14 similarly: "James' perspective here is not that all who believe are Israel . . . but that *in addition* to Israel God has established a people in his name." Bruce Chilton and Jacob Neusner, *Judaism in the New Testament* (New York: Routledge, 1995), 105.

18. Exegetes commonly recognize that the requirements for Gentiles found in the apostolic decree are based on the commandments incumbent upon Gentiles living among the people of Israel as found in Leviticus 17–18; see Bauckham, "James and the Jerusalem Church," 458–62. It is noteworthy that the reading from the prophets (the *haftorah*) for Leviticus 17–18 in the traditional Ashkenazic Jewish lectionary is Amos 9.

19. "The verdict of the first Jerusalem Council then is that the Church is to consist of two segments, united by their faith in Jesus. However, with respect to the Mosaic Law, Jewish Christians would remain under it while gentile Christians would come under the Noachide commandments." Michael Wyschogrod, "Letter to a Friend," *Modern Theology* 11:2 (April 1995), 171, in *Abraham's Promise* (Grand Rapids: Eerdmans, 2004), 209.

20. "If Paul's call for unity is taken seriously, he did not merely want to be the apostle to the gentiles. He wanted to be an apostle of all the church, for his vision was for a new community formed of all gentiles and Jews. . . . Paul's attempt to organize that community, parallel to his attempt to gain acceptance as an apostle, also ironically publicized his ritual position as apostasy and worse." Alan F. Segal, *Paul the Convert* (New Haven, CT: Yale University Press, 1990), 265.

sisters.[21] Exponents of this view see the Antioch incident narrated in Galatians 2 as demonstrating that, in Paul's mind, any conflict in a mixed community that pitted Jewish particularity against Gentile inclusion must be resolved in favor of the latter.[22]

This reading of Paul presumes that his teaching permitted Jewish practice among Jewish Yeshua-believers but did not mandate such practice. We argued against such an interpretation of Paul in chapter 2. One can make a solid case for the view that Paul saw Jewish practice as an obligation rather than an option for Jews. If this is true, what are the implications for our understanding of Pauline ecclesiology?

Terence Donaldson accepts the premise that Paul saw Jewish practice as normative for Jewish Yeshua-believers. However, he also accepts the premise that Paul saw a mixed community of Jews and Gentiles to be the ideal expression of the ekklesia. Donaldson himself wonders how these two convictions can be combined:

> I have identified [Paul's] basic convictions concerning *membership requirements* [membership is granted through faith in Christ, and therefore not through Torah observance], *status* [Jew and Gentile are on equal terms in Christ; there is no distinction], and *identity* [all those in Christ are members of Abraham's family]. How can we add to these the additional conviction [also held by Paul] that an ethnically identified Israel, differentiated from the Gentiles in traditional Torah-determined ways, continues to have significance within the new sphere of reality determined by Christ?[23]

Donaldson answers this question in a way that highlights the inevitable conflict that would arise between these two premises:

> With the benefit of hindsight, we can easily discern a certain instability in such a set of convictions. They could not be held together in any consistent way for very long. . . . [I]nevitably as time goes on and one generation succeeds another,

21. See, for example, E. P. Sanders, *Paul, the Law, and the Jewish People* (Philadelphia: Fortress, 1983), 177–78.

22. Jacob Jervell agrees that Paul sought to found communities of Jews and Gentiles, and saw these communities as ideal expressions of the *ekklesia*. However, he departs from the usual reading of Paul in arguing that Jews and Gentiles in the Pauline congregations lived as two distinct bodies: "A look at the Pauline churches shows that Jews and Gentiles live together as distinct groups. They have not mingled in such a way as to become some kind of a *tertium genus*. This is so even in a late letter like Romans (see e.g. 11:13ff.; 15:7ff.). The concept of the Jewish Christians constituting the center of the church, that is the idea of Romans 11, demands that it is actually possible to distinguish between Jewish and Gentile Christians." *The Unknown Paul*, 38.

23. Terence L. Donaldson, *Paul and the Gentiles* (Minneapolis: Fortress, 1997), 185 (brackets added).

any distinction between Jew and Gentile would inevitably fall away, identifiably Jewish portions of the community would inevitably become assimilated, and "Israel" would inevitably become (as it did by the time of Justin Martyr) a purely allegorical or nonliteral designation for a decidedly non-Jewish entity.[24]

Thus, according to Donaldson, Paul tried to combine two principles of community formation that were ultimately incompatible. How could he have made such a mistake? Donaldson offers the following answer:

> How is it that he can remain so committed to an Israel defined in traditional, Torah-based terms, while at the same time insisting on a redefinition of Abraham's family (Israel) based instead on Christ—a redefinition which, if followed through consistently, would sooner or later surely mean the disappearance of an ethnically identifiable Israel?
>
> As argued earlier, an answer suggests itself in the phrase "sooner or later." For Paul, there *was* no "later"![25]

Donaldson contends that the Pauline model makes sense in light of Paul's expectation that this age was drawing to a close. He was not planning for a multigenerational community. He did not consider the possibility that nineteen hundred and fifty years might pass and the present order of the world remain intact.

Donaldson deserves credit for seeing what many other commentators miss: Paul's continued commitment to "an ethnically identified Israel, differentiated from the Gentiles in traditional Torah-determined ways." Donaldson also perceives a sociological reality of great importance for us in this book: that mixed communities of Jews and Gentiles, formed according to Paul's supposed ecclesiology, would inevitably fail to preserve Jewish life for future generations. However, he mistakenly accepts the common interpretation of this Pauline pattern. More convincing is an alternative understanding of Paul's ecclesiological vision, offered by many recent scholars, that stresses his specific vocation: he was called to be an apostle to the Gentiles.[26] While he never ceased to pray for his fellow Jews

24. Ibid., 185.
25. Ibid., 246.
26. See Galatians 1:16; 2:2, 7–9; Romans 1:5, 13–15; 15:15–21; Ephesians 3:1–9. The importance of recognizing Paul's specific vocation as directed to Gentiles has been noted and emphasized by Johannes Munck, *Paul and the Salvation of Mankind* (Richmond: John Knox, 1959); Krister Stendahl, *Paul Among Jews and Gentiles* (Philadelphia: Fortress, 1976), and *Final Account: Paul's Letter to the Romans* (Minneapolis: Fortress, 1995); Paul van Buren, *A Theology of the Jewish-Christian Reality,* vol. 2, *A Christian Theology of the People Israel* (San Francisco: Harper & Row, 1983), 277–82; Lloyd Gaston, *Paul and the Torah* (Vancouver: University of British Columbia Press, 1987); Peter J. Tomson, *Paul and the Jewish Law* (Minneapolis: Fortress, 1990); Stanley Stowers, *A Rereading of Romans* (New Haven, CT: Yale University Press, 1994); Mark Nanos, *The Mystery*

and to attempt to win them to Messiah whenever possible, his basic task in life lay elsewhere.[27] That the communities he formed were overwhelmingly Gentile was not a mark of his failure but of his success. That the few Jews associated with those communities may have de-emphasized in some respects their daily Jewish practice for the sake of their Gentile brothers and sisters was not a universal law of the ekklesia but a consequence of the particular character of these congregations: they were Gentile communities founded by the apostle to the Gentiles.

This perspective on Paul's practical ecclesiology finds support in his description of the agreement reached in Jerusalem concerning his mission to the Gentiles:

> Seeing that I had been entrusted with the good news of the uncircumcision, just as Peter had been entrusted with the good news of the circumcision (for he who worked through Peter making him an apostle of the circumcision also worked through me in regard to the Gentiles), and recognizing the divine gift that had been given to me, James and Cephas and John, who were acknowledged pillars, extended to Barnabas and me the right hand of partnership, agreeing that we should go to the Gentiles and they to the circumcision. They asked only one thing, that we remember the poor, which very thing I was eager to do. (Galatians 2:7–10, translation mine)

The full implications of the wording of this agreement often go unnoticed. The agreement demarcates two distinct corporate spheres of responsibility: the circumcision (the Jewish people) and the uncircumcision (the non-Jewish nations). It implies, not only two distinct missions, but also two distinct networks of communities resulting from those missions and two distinct leadership structures overseeing those missions and communities. If our reading of James 1:1 is correct, and James (or the one writing in his name) addressed his letter to the Jewish Yeshua-believing congregations of the Diaspora, then this implication is confirmed.

Such a reading of Galatians 2 was known in the first centuries of the church.[28] Archeologist Fr. Bellarmino Bagatti begins his volume *The Church from the Circumcision* with the following words:

> In the mosaic of the Church of St. Sabina in Rome, made under Pope Celestine (422–432), at the sides of the great historical inscription there are two female

---

of Romans (Minneapolis: Fortress, 1996); and John G. Gager, "Paul's Contradictions: Can They Be Resolved?" *Bible Review* 14:6, December 1998, 32–39, and *Reinventing Paul* (Oxford: Oxford University Press, 2000).

27. However, as seen in Romans 9–11, Paul may have been motivated in his mission to the Gentiles by the belief that it was an essential precondition for the restoration of Israel. Thus he was serving Israel even as he labored among the Gentiles.

28. See Jervell, *Paul*, 41–42 and 163, n. 35.

figures, the "Ecclesia ex circumcisione" on the left and the "Ecclesia ex gentibus" on the right. Each has a book in her hand. Over the former is St. Peter, in the act of receiving the law from God's hand; over the latter is St. Paul. Evidently as a basis of the composition is the saying of St. Paul to the Galatians (2, 7): "to me was committed the gospel for the uncircumcised, as to Peter that for the circumcised.". . . From these and other like compositions we can conclude that, in the mind of the mosaicists, the two churches, represented under the female forms, were equal both in teaching and in future recompense.[29]

These mosaics make clear that Galatians 2 was understood as implying more than just the establishment of two missions. The agreement speaks of "the good news of the circumcision" and "the good news of the uncircumcision," but it implies the existence of "the ekklesia of the circumcision" and "the ekklesia of the uncircumcision." The one ekklesia of Messiah Yeshua is not made up of individual Jews and Gentiles, mixed together in an undifferentiated collective, but of two distinct corporate entities joined in what should have been an indissoluble bond of love and mutual commitment.

This bilateral picture of Pauline ecclesiology draws further support from the work of Mark Nanos, who argues that the Gentile ekklesia*i* that Paul addresses in Romans and Galatians are attached to Jewish communities in their cities.[30] According to Nanos, Paul preferred to form such a connection between his fledgling congregations and the established Jewish world. Favoring such a thesis is 2 Corinthians 11:24, in which Paul states that he received the severe synagogue discipline of forty lashes minus one on five occasions. As E. P. Sanders rightly concludes, this proves that Paul himself continued to be committed to Judaism and the Jewish community, since "had he wished he could have withdrawn from Jewish society altogether and thus not have been punished."[31] If Paul himself continued to participate in diaspora Jewish life as

29. Fr. Bellarmino Bagatti, *The Church from the Circumcision* (Jerusalem: Franciscan, 1971), 1.

30. See Mark D. Nanos, *The Mystery of Romans*, and *The Irony of Galatians* (Minneapolis: Fortress, 2002). See also Douglas Harink, *Paul among the Postliberals* (Grand Rapids: Brazos, 2003), 218–225. Harink accepts Nanos's thesis and probes its theological implications.

31. E. P. Sanders, *Paul, the Law, and the Jewish People*, 192. Sanders continues: "The most important point to be derived from 2 Corinthians 11:24 is that both Paul and the Jews who punished him regarded the Christian movement as falling within Judaism. Paul's converts were taken seriously enough by synagogue authorities to lead them to discipline the one who brought them into the people of God without requiring circumcision. . . . Thus we see again that Paul was not consciously aiding in the foundation of a new religion. None of the parties who emerge in Paul's letters—Paul himself, his Gentile converts, the 'false brethren,' Peter and the other Jerusalem apostles, and the non-Christian Jews—looked on the Christian movement as outside the bounds of Judaism. *Punishment implies inclusion.* If Paul had considered that he had withdrawn from Judaism, he would not have attended synagogue. If the members of the synagogue had considered him an outsider, they would not have punished him."

he traveled, and if the Gentile congregations he founded likewise sought as much connection as possible to the Jewish communities in their areas, then ideally the local synagogue itself would have provided a framework in which an incipient bilateral ecclesiology could have been expressed. The Jewish Yeshua-believers would participate as full members of the synagogue, which gave them a support system for their life as Jews. The Gentile Yeshua-believers would likewise share in the life of the wider Jewish community, though without full membership. In addition, there would be supplementary gatherings of the Jewish and Gentile Yeshua-believers, either separately or together. Wherever this type of arrangement obtained, the Yeshua movement's solidarity with the people of Israel would have been assured. Unfortunately, in many places it was not practically feasible.[32]

Peter Tomson draws similar conclusions to ours based on his study of Pauline halakhah. While we have called the underlying New Testament paradigm *bilateral* ecclesiology, Tomson prefers to speak of Paul's *pluriform* ecclesiology (italics added):

> What is constant is Paul's attachment to the practical situation in each case and his resolute commitment to *a pluriform church of Jews and gentiles*. . . . The "rule for all the churches" [1 Corinthians 7:17–24] . . . states Paul's *pluriform ecclesiology*.[33]

Since Paul expected Jews to live as Jews but required that Gentiles not become Jews, he respected the sort of ecclesiological "pluriformity" that allowed such distinct paths to be walked corporately and not just individually. Far from opposing bilateral ecclesiology, Paul's teaching actually presumes it.[34]

"One New Humanity" and Bilateral Ecclesiology

Though scholars debate whether Paul wrote Ephesians, the book appears under his name and seeks to convey a vision of the ecclesiology championed

32. Harink, *Paul among the Postliberals*, 225–26.

33. Tomson, *Paul*, 269–70.

34. Michael Wyschogrod presents Paul's bilateral ecclesiology in this way: "As I read it, Paul thought of the church as made up of two complementary portions. One portion of the church was to consist of former gentiles who were bound by the Noachide Laws and believed in Jesus as the Christ. The other portion was to consist of Jews bound by the Torah and believing that Jesus was the Christ. These two segments of the church had their faith in Jesus in common and, for Paul, this was the decisive factor. But there was also a difference in that Jews in the church remained loyal to the Torah. They were the original household to which the gentiles had, through Christ, been admitted." *Abraham's Promise*, 197–98.

by the apostle to the Gentiles. How does that ecclesiology fit with the bilateral perspective presented above?

According to traditional interpretation, Ephesians decisively rejects any hint of bilateral ecclesiology. The key verse cited to support this reading is Ephesians 2:15: "He has abolished the law with its commandments and ordinances, that he might create in himself one new humanity in place of the two."[35] The "two" refers to Jews and Gentiles. Thus God acted in Yeshua to end Israel's distinctive identity and way of life ("abolished the law") and to create one new humanity consisting of Jews and Gentiles together. This one new humanity brings to an end the distinction between Jew and Gentile. There is no longer room for "the two" in the newly created "one."

This traditional reading likewise minimizes the significance of the Jewish people in Ephesians. Andrew Lincoln's commentary is an excellent case in point:

> Unlike the Gentile Christians in Rom 11, they [i.e., the Gentile audience of Ephesians] are not told that they have been added to a given Jewish base. The Gentiles' former disadvantages have been reversed, not by their being incorporated into Israel nor even by their joining a renewed Israel of Jewish Christians, but by their being made members of a new community which transcends the categories of Jew and Gentile, an entity which is a new creation. The two former groupings have not simply merged, but one new person has been created in place of the two (2:15). In Ephesians, then, the emphasis is on discontinuity with Israel, and the concept of the Church is in fact, if not in name, that of the "third race."[36]

Such an interpretation of Ephesians makes of the book a direct refutation of all that we have argued to this point. As Lincoln frankly notes, it also asserts a stark difference between Paul's teaching in Romans and that found in Ephesians.

35. In chapter 2 we deliberately avoided the complicated exegetical and theological issues surrounding the continuing validity of the Torah and focused instead on the continuing obligation of Jewish covenantal practice. Therefore we did not there undertake the task of explaining verses such as this one, which appears to state that Yeshua "abolished the Torah." At this point I would only note that the Greek of this verse is not so unambiguous in its view of the Jewish law as the NRSV might lead one to conclude. In fact, one could easily interpret the Greek as stating that it is the *enmity* between Jew and Gentile that is abolished rather than the Torah. That enmity is in some way related to the Torah, but the nature of that relationship is not explicated in the text. For alternative translations, see the Jerusalem Bible, J. B. Phillips, and the Jewish New Testament. John Howard Yoder translates the verse as follows: "He destroyed in his person the hostility caused by the rules of the Law." See John Howard Yoder, *The Jewish-Christian Schism Revisited*, ed. Michael G. Cartwright and Peter Ochs (Grand Rapids: Eerdmans, 2003), 26.

36. Andrew T. Lincoln, *Ephesians* (Dallas: Word Books, 1990), xciii.

The traditional reading of Ephesians has not gone unchallenged by New Testament scholars. The most thorough and effective attack has come from Markus Barth.[37] In his two-volume commentary on Ephesians, Barth advances the thesis that the *categories* of Jew and Gentile are not transcended but only the hostility between the two. He affirms what Lincoln denies: "It is the distinctive message of Ephesians that no Gentile can have communion with Christ or with God unless he also has communion with Israel."[38]

Barth sees the honor bestowed on Israel as already expressed in Ephesians 1. When the author switches between first- and second-person plural pronouns, Barth interprets the shift as a contrast between Jews and Gentiles. Thus he translates Ephesians 1:11–13 as follows:

> As resolved by him who carries out all things after his will and decision, we [Jews] were first designated and appropriated in the Messiah. We, the first to set our hope upon the Messiah, were to become a praise of God's glory. You [Gentiles] too are [included] in him. For you have heard the true word, the message that saves you.[39]

He interprets these verses as meaning that "even before their baptism the Jews were (unlike the Gentiles . . .) not apart from the Messiah but held together by him to whom they were looking forward."[40] He also sees significance in the fact that "Paul sets the *recent* conversion of Gentiles through the gospel in contrast to the hope and destiny that were *previously* given to the Jews!"[41]

Ephesians expresses Israel's honor in more explicit fashion in 2:11–12:

> Remember, then, that in the past [and] in the realm of flesh you, the Gentiles— called The Uncircumcision by those who call themselves The Circumcision, that handmade operation in the realm of flesh . . . [Remember] that at that time you were apart from the Messiah, excluded from the citizenship of Israel, strangers to the covenants based upon promise. In this world you were bare of hope and without God.

37. For a recent volume that adopts a position similar to that of Barth, see McRay, *Paul*, 334–51.

38. Markus Barth, *Ephesians 1–3* (Garden City, NY: Doubleday, 1974), 337. Elsewhere Barth writes: "According to Ephesians 2:15 and 3:6, the Gentiles became members of the one body of Christ only by their insertion into Israel." *Israel and the Church* (Richmond: John Knox, 1969), 90.

39. All quotes from Barth's translation of Ephesians are taken from *Ephesians 1–3*, xxvii–xxxiv. Brackets are in the original. In defense of this way of interpreting the pronouns, see 130–33.

40. Barth, *Ephesians 1–3*, 132.

41. Ibid.

Barth notes the progression in the types of concepts used here to differentiate
Jews and Gentiles:

> At first the difference between Jews and Gentiles was described in ceremonial and
> external terms of "Circumcision" and "Uncircumcision"; then it was designated
> by the political, legal, sociological, and psychological concepts, "apart from the
> Messiah," "excluded from the citizenship of Israel," "strangers," "bare of hope."
> Now, at the conclusion, the difference is depicted as soteriological and theo-
> logical. God himself had not shown he cared for the Gentiles! They have been
> God-forsaken people.[42]

Barth sees this progression as a caution against interpreting the reference to
circumcision in a negative light:

> The combination of seemingly external features with basic theological grounds
> for division reveals that the weight of ceremonial elements should not be belittled.
> Circumcision manifests much more than an incidental historical difference; the
> difference between Jews and Gentiles is grounded in God's own history with
> mankind, i.e., in the first election of Israel alone and the corresponding temporary
> exclusion of the Gentiles from his blessing.[43]

According to Barth, these verses assert the privileges of Israel in terms reminis-
cent of Romans 9:4–5.[44] It appears that Romans and Ephesians may resemble
one another more than Lincoln would allow.

Furthermore, Barth argues that Ephesians 3:4–6, like Romans 11, shows
that the Gentiles attain life with God only through being joined to Israel. He
translates these verses as follows:

> Correspondingly, by reading [this] you are able to perceive how I understand the
> secret of the Messiah. In other generations it was not made known to the Sons of
> Men as it is now revealed through the Spirit to his holy apostles and prophets: In
> the Messiah Jesus [and] through the gospel, the Gentiles are joint heirs, members
> in the same body, fellow beneficiaries in all that is promised.

---

42. Ibid., 260.

43. Ibid., 275. Franz Mussner sees these verses in a similar light: "If one formulates these five
sentences on the unsaved condition of the Gentiles in a positive way with a view to Israel, then they
would sound as follows: Israel possesses the hope of the Messiah. Israel forms a 'commonwealth'
(*politeia*): the *qehal* YHWH. To Israel belong the covenants of the promise. Israel possesses thereby
hope. Israel lives in community with God and in the knowledge of God in the world." *Tractate on
the Jews* (Philadelphia: Fortress, 1984), 25.

44. Mussner sees the similarity of these two passages (23–26).

In his commentary Barth paraphrases the final verse in this way: "together with Israel the Gentiles are now 'heirs, members, beneficiaries.'"[45] He then notes the similarity between this message and Paul's teaching in Romans:

> It is the distinctive message of Ephesians that no Gentile can have communion with Christ or with God unless he also has communion with Israel. With this doctrine Ephesians does not contradict Romans or Galatians, for according to Romans 11:17 the Gentiles are grafted onto Israel.[46]

Ephesians 3:4-6 also brings us back to the earlier verses in the book that spoke of the privileges of Israel and the former alienation of the Gentiles:

> The last term, lit. "co-partakers of the promise," harks back to 1:12–13 and 2:12, i.e. to the passages that speak of the hope first held by the Jews alone, of the "covenant of promise" from which the Gentiles were excluded, and of the "earnest" or "seal" of "the promised Holy Spirit."[47]

Once again, Ephesians appears as reflection in the spirit of Romans on the relationship between Jews and Gentiles rather than as a radical departure from the message of that letter.

But what does Barth make of Ephesians 2:15? According to the NRSV, this verse tells us that Yeshua creates in himself "one new humanity in place of the two." Barth renders this verse quite differently: "[This was] to make peace by creating in his person a single new man out of the two."

In the NRSV the new humanity replaces and ends the Jew-Gentile distinction. In Barth God creates the new humanity "out of the two" rather than "in place of the two."[48] This implies that "the two" may remain in the midst of the "one." Barth's commentary makes clear that this is his understanding of the text:

> The new man is "one . . . out of the two." . . . The new creation is not an annihilation or replacement of the first creation but the glorification of God's work. . . . Ephesians alone calls God's covenant partner "one new man" and emphasizes that this man consists of two, that is, of Jews and Gentiles. . . . The incorporation of the Gentiles into Israel and the formation of one people consisting of Jews and Gentiles certainly does not mean that the Gentiles must become Jews, or the Jews Gentiles! . . . Their historic distinction remains true and recognized even within

---

45. Barth, *Ephesians 1–3*, 337.
46. Ibid.
47. Ibid., 337–38.
48. The Greek is ambiguous and permits either translation. It could be rendered literally as "in order to create the two in him into one new humanity."

their communion. . . . Ephesians 2:15 proclaims that the people of God is different from a syncretistic mixture of Jewish and Gentile elements. The members of the church are not so equalized, leveled down, or straitjacketed in a uniform as to form a *genus tertium* that would be different from both Jews and Gentiles. Rather the church consists of Jews and Gentiles reconciled to one another by the Messiah who has come and has died for both.[49]

The one humanity *consists of* two. In other words, Ephesians 2:15 advocates rather than refutes bilateral ecclesiology!

Support for this reading of Ephesians comes from Luke Timothy Johnson. He comments on the lengthy section of the book devoted to husbands and wives (Ephesians 5:22–33). These verses focus on the love of the husband for his wife, the unity they are supposed to share as "one flesh," and the way this love and unity reflect both the teaching of Genesis 2:24 and its typological embodiment in the relationship between the Messiah and his ekklesia. Johnson notes that the passage ends with Paul's referring to the Genesis text and asserting, "This mystery is a profound one, and I am saying that it refers to Christ and the church." Johnson then suggests that this mystery is related to the mystery of Ephesians 3:4–6:

> We remember that Paul's "mystery" is that Jews and Greeks are reconciled and made one in the church. The relationship between husband and wife, therefore, symbolizes the mystery of unity in plurality and makes it present within the community. This completes the Pauline perception of "neither Jew nor Greek, neither male nor female." . . . Man and woman submit to each other in respect and love and service, finding unity and peace not in a false identification but in a pluralistic unity. So should Jew and Greek celebrate their unity in service to each other, so that God's purpose might be fulfilled, "to unite all things in him, things in heaven and things on earth" (1:10).[50]

In other words, the unity of Jew and Gentile does not imply the elimination of all distinction between the two, any more than the unity of husband and wife eliminates all gender differentiation. Instead, the unity envisioned is one of mutual "respect and love and service."

Barth's interpretation appears especially compelling when its theological substance is seriously considered. The message of Ephesians is that the unity and mutual love of Jews and Gentiles in Messiah express the reconciling power

49. Barth, *Ephesians 1–3*, 310.
50. Luke T. Johnson, *The Writings of the New Testament* (Phildelphia: Fortress, 1986), 378–79.

of Yeshua's death and resurrection. This act of reconciliation serves as a model and pledge of Yeshua's power to overcome the deepest of human divisions and hostilities. However, if Jew and Gentile blend together in such a way that the distinction between them is utterly effaced, how can their unity be a sign of anything? The extraordinary action of God in bridging the chasm and ending the hostility becomes a mere historical remembrance rather than a miracle that is continually renewed. As the leaders of the early Yeshua movement recognized at the council of Jerusalem, to make Gentiles into Jews would negate this sign of reconciliation. It remains the task of a later generation to finally recognize that to make Jews into Gentiles produces the same result.

Once again, upon closer inspection we find that what was purported to provide a refutation of bilateral ecclesiology can be interpreted persuasively as espousing that very teaching.[51]

Mark and Revelation

Two additional New Testament texts deserve consideration here. These texts offer no clear window into the ecclesiological realities of the early Yeshua movement. However, they do present ecclesiological imagery that points in a similar bilateral direction. The first text is Mark 8:1–10, which describes the feeding of the four thousand. In an earlier chapter (6:30–44) Mark tells of the feeding of the five thousand. As pointed out by Larry Hurtado, the first feeding miracle contains a number of allusions to Moses and Israel as depicted in the Torah: three references to the location as a "deserted area" (Mark 6:31, 32, 35; see Exodus 16), the description of the crowd as "like sheep without a shepherd" (Mark 6:34; see Numbers 27:17), the organization of the crowd into groups of a

51. It could be objected that this reading of Ephesians fails to take account of Ephesians 4's concern for practical unity on a local level, and its possible implication that the practical unity between Jew and Gentile requires a single local ecclesial context. I would answer this objection by pointing to Ephesians 4:17 ("you must no longer live as the Gentiles live"), which presumes—like the rest of the letter (see 3:1)—that the addressees are all non-Jews. Thus those who are exhorted to live in unity with one another on a local level are all part of the Gentile ekklesia. Moreover, the diverse "gifts" that serve that unity in Ephesians 4 do not reside in each local congregation but are invested in translocal officials (apostles, prophets, etc; Ephesians 4:11), who in the early Yeshua-movement were (like Paul) usually Jewish! Thus the local Gentile ekklesia would be able to express its unity with the Jewish ekklesia by honoring the Jewish apostles and prophets who linked them to Israel. Finally, the content of this letter—interpreted as I have done in this chapter—would fit perfectly a Gentile audience that maintained active involvement with the wider Jewish community of their region. Such involvement, providing a natural meeting point for Jewish and Gentile Yeshua-believers, would provide an excellent setting for expressing unity within the one body of Messiah.

hundred and of fifty (Mark 6:40; see Exodus 18:21 and Deuteronomy 1:15), and the symbolic numbers of the five loaves (for the five books of the Torah) and the twelve baskets left over (for the twelve tribes).[52] The Greek word used in Mark 6:41 for Yeshua's blessing of the food is *eulogesan*, which customarily translates the Hebrew verb *barakh* employed in traditional Jewish table blessings.[53]

In contrast, Mark 8:1–10 is part of a set of stories that take place outside predominantly Jewish areas (Tyre and Sidon in 7:24–30, the Decapolis in 7:31–37).[54] It lacks the Mosaic and Torah allusions of the earlier account. In Mark 8:3 Yeshua remarks that some of the crowd have come "a long way" (*apo makrothen*), better translated as "from afar," which, as Hurtado notes, "renders a term frequently used in the Greek OT to describe foreign (Gentile) areas."[55] The Greek word used in Mark 8:6 for Yeshua's blessing of the food is *eucharistesas*, from which the Christian term Eucharist derives. The numbers found in Mark 8 may also, like those in Mark 6, have symbolic significance: there are seven loaves and seven baskets left over, and many commentators have seen a connection here to the seventy nations of the earth in Genesis 10 and possibly the seven leaders of the Hellenists in Acts 6:1–7.[56]

John Painter sees in Mark 6 and 8 a similar pattern to what we found in Galatians 2:

> Just as Jesus had fed a Jewish crowd of five thousand, he now fed a Gentile crowd of four thousand. Mark implies a twofold mission and this is one reason for the two parallel feeding stories.[57]

However, Painter does not go far enough. As we saw in our comments on Galatians 2, a twofold mission implies a twofold ekklesia. Mark 6 and 8 do not speak merely of mission. The narrative presents Yeshua's feeding of the multitudes as an anticipation of the Messianic banquet in the world to come, which will likewise be anticipated after his resurrection in the eucharistic meals celebrated by the ekklesia. As Paul recognizes in 1 Corinthians 10:17, this meal both expresses and establishes the community of the Messiah in its oneness. However, this united community is twofold, and therefore Mark relates two incidents in Yeshua's life that prefigure this twofold community.

---

52. Larry W. Hurtado, *Mark* (A Good News Commentary: San Francisco: Harper & Row, 1983), 88–90.
53. Ibid., 93.
54. John Painter, *Mark's Gospel* (New York: Routledge, 1997), 114.
55. Hurtado, *Mark,* 110, 115–16.
56. Painter, *Mark's Gospel,* 118; Hurtado, *Mark,* 111, 116.
57. Painter, *Mark's Gospel,* 118.

The other New Testament text that fits the bilateral pattern described above is Revelation 7. The first eight verses of this chapter tell of the sealing of the 144,000 from the twelve tribes of Israel. Then verses 9–17 picture "a great multitude that no person could number, from every nation, from all tribes and peoples and tongues." Many commentators see these two images as referring to the same group of people—the one community of the Messiah, which follows him on the way of martyrdom.[58] However, many others find here images pointing to the twofold nature of the people of God.[59] This reading is supported by the description of New Jerusalem in Revelation 21, where the names of the twelve tribes of Israel are inscribed on the city gates (21:12) and the nations and their kings bring their glory through those gates (21:24, 26). Further, the city also contains the tree of life bearing twelve kinds of fruit (corresponding to the twelve tribes, 22:2), with leaves that bring healing to the nations (22:2). Additional support comes from the allusions to the feast of Booths found in Revelation 7:9–17 and the connection this forges with Zechariah 14, which, like Revelation 21–22, speaks of the nations making pilgrimage to Jerusalem in the world to come.[60] The formation of the twofold Messianic ekklesia is thus an anticipation of the eschaton, when the nations will join with Israel in the worship of the God of Israel.

Michael Goulder has grasped these implications of Revelation 7 and has articulated them in language similar to that used here in formulating a bilateral eccesiology:

> Revelation is a book written by a seer with sympathies for both missions. In Revelation 7 there are two great wings of the church. There are 144,000 sealed "out of every tribe of the sons of Israel"; the twelve tribes are named, and there are 12,000 sealed from each tribe. But then, "After this I looked, and behold, a great multitude which no man could number, from every nation, from all tribes and peoples and tongues, standing before the Lamb" (7.9). In other words there

---

58. G. B. Caird, *The Revelation of Saint John* (Peabody, MA: Hendrickson, 1966), 94–95; G. E. Ladd, *A Commentary on the Revelation of John* (Grand Rapids: Eerdmans, 1972), 116–17; B. M. Metzger, *Breaking the Code* (Nashville: Abingdon, 1993), 61.

59. G. Quispel, *The Secret Book of Revelation* (New York: McGraw Hill, 1979), 60–61; M. R. Mulholland, Jr., *Revelation* (Grand Rapids: Francis Asbury, 1990), 182; C. Rowland, *Revelation*, Epworth Commentaries (London: Epworth, 1993), 91; J. Moltmann, *The Coming of God* (Minneapolis: Fortress, 1996), 198; Robert W. Jenson, "Toward a Christian Theology of Israel," *Pro Ecclesia* 9, no. 1 (Winter 2000): 52, 54, 56.

60. On the allusions to the feast of Booths in Revelation 7:9–17, see A. Edersheim, *The Temple* (Peabody, MA: Hendrickson, 1994), 227–28; Jean Daniélou, *The Theology of Jewish Christianity* (Chicago: Henry Regnery/London: Darton, Longman & Todd, 1964) 328; Rowland, *Revelation*, 91.

is a Jewish Christian church and a Gentile church—and the latter is beginning
to outnumber the former.[61]

The one ekklesia consists of "two great wings"—one Jewish, one Gentile. What
Goulder finds in Revelation 7 is what we have already found in Acts, James, the
Pauline corpus, and Mark.

Karl Barth and Bilateral Ecclesiology

While some historians and biblical scholars have noticed the bilateral ecclesiology of the New Testament, few theologians have taken it seriously. Probably
the main reason for this is the fact that such an ecclesiology has little practical
significance in a church almost exclusively Gentile in composition. If one takes
the New Testament model as in any sense normative, the theological consequences are profoundly disturbing.

It is therefore striking that the exception to this rule is the most influential
theologian of the twentieth century, Karl Barth. As we will soon see, Barth offers
no practical proposals for ecclesiological reform, nor does he find fault with the
way the church has dealt with its Jewish constituents. However, he approaches
the theoretical issues in a way that could—in new circumstances—encourage
such discussion to proceed in a fruitful direction.[62]

Barth treats the topic of Israel and the church under the heading of "The
Election of God." Characteristically, he begins with Christology. In Barth's teaching, divine election is preeminently God's choice of Yeshua. In an ingenious
transformation of the Reformed concept of double predestination, Barth sees
the election of Yeshua as having a twofold meaning.

---

61. M. Goulder, *St. Paul versus St. Peter* (Louisville: Westminster John Knox, 1995), 66. Goulder
has championed anew the nineteenth-century thesis of F. C. Baur that Paul's message to the Gentiles
and Peter's message to the Jews were in conflict. It should be evident that we are not advocating
such a position. However, Goulder sees in Revelation 7 an attempt to view the two messages and
ecclesial spheres as complementary. What Goulder affirms for Revelation 7, we affirm for the
New Testament as a whole.

62. In this section we will not discuss Barth's teaching as a whole on the relationship between
Israel and the church, but only examine those elements that have a direct bearing on the thesis of
this chapter. For a critical assessment of that teaching along with a summary of how subsequent
theologians have responded to it, see Stephen R. Haynes, *Prospects For Post-Holocaust Theology*
(Atlanta: Scholars, 1991), 47–102. For a more appreciative perspective, see Eberhard Busch, "The
Covenant of Grace Fulfilled in Christ as the Foundation of the Indissoluble Solidarity of the Church
with Israel: Barth's Position on the Jews During the Hitler Era," *Scottish Journal of Theology* 52
(1999): 476–503.

> If the teachers of predestination were right when they spoke always of a duality, of election and reprobation, of predestination to salvation or perdition, to life or death, then we may say already that in the election of Jesus Christ which is the eternal will of God, God has ascribed to man the former, election, salvation and life; and to Himself He has ascribed the latter, reprobation, perdition and death.[63]

In Yeshua God elects to humble and empty himself unto death for the sake of human beings, so that they might be raised with Yeshua to life with God. Yeshua's twofold election is thus associated with the two aspects of his reconciling work, his crucifixion and resurrection.

Barth then proceeds to speak about the election of "the community of God." The election of this community derives from the election of Yeshua. It is "the human fellowship which in a particular way provisionally forms the natural and historical environment of the man Jesus Christ."[64] The election of this community also has the same twofold reality as Yeshua's election:

> To this unity and twofold form of Jesus Christ Himself there corresponds that of the community of God and its election. It exists according to God's eternal decree as the people of Israel (in the whole range of its history in past and future, *ante* and *post Christum natum*), and at the same time as the Church of Jews and Gentiles (from its revelation at Pentecost to its fulfillment by the second coming of Christ). In this its twofold (Old Testament and New Testament) form of existence there is reflected and repeated the twofold determination of Jesus Christ Himself. The community, too, is as Israel and as the Church indissolubly one. It, too, as the one is ineffaceably these two, Israel and the Church.[65]

We therefore have a bilateral community: it is both "indissolubly one" and "ineffaceably two." It is both "united" and "differentiated."[66] The two components are the people of Israel and the assembly of the church. As Eberhard Busch explains, the "*one* difference between the two forms is that Israel is a 'people', of which one usually becomes a member through birth, whereas one becomes a member of the church by being called."[67] While Barth links Israel to the Old Testament and the church to the New, he also states explicitly that Israel continues to exist as

---

63. Karl Barth, *Church Dogmatics* II.2 (Edinburgh: T&T Clark, 1957), 162–63.

64. Ibid., 196.

65. Ibid., 198. The connections Barth makes between Yeshua's crucifixion and Israel, and between Yeshua's resurrection and the church, are highly problematic in the way he develops them. Nevertheless, as noted above, the deficiencies in his overall treatment of Israel and the church need not occupy us here.

66. Barth, *CD* II.2, 207, 233.

67. Busch, "Covenant of Grace," 490.

the elect people within the one community of God after the coming of Yeshua (*post Christum natum*).

Barth sees the Jewish people as a whole, whether Yeshua-believing or non-Yeshua-believing, as bound inseparably to its Messiah. As part of the community of God, it is also part of Messiah's body.[68] When Israel does not believe in Yeshua, it resists its own election. However, it cannot cancel that election nor cut itself free from its Messiah.[69] Barth even asserts that Israel is now sanctified through its physical connection to Yeshua as his "kinsmen."[70]

Since the true identity and destiny of the Jewish people derive from its relationship to its Messiah, Yeshua-believing Jews have a special place in Barth's ecclesiology. He can speak of them as both "the Church in Israel" and "Israel in the Church."[71] As "the Church in Israel," they (like Paul) maintain solidarity with their "kinsmen" and confirm Israel's election. As "Israel in the Church," they enable the whole church to share in that solidarity with Israel, and they serve as the church's "secret origin, as the hidden substance which makes the Church the community of God."[72]

The terminology used by Barth here is noteworthy. He does not focus on Jewish Yeshua-believers as individuals, but instead focuses on their corporate identity. They fulfill their appointed role when they are the ekklesia in Israel, and Israel in the ekklesia. Barth can define the church as "the gathering of Jews and Gentiles called on the ground of its election."[73] By its very nature, therefore, it includes both Jews and Gentiles. However, he can also speak of "the Gentile Church," that corporate entity that is established by "the Gentile mission."[74] This implies that Barth saw "the gathering of Jews and Gentiles" in the ekklesia as consisting of two corporate entities, the Jewish ekklesia and the Gentile ekklesia.

---

68. Barth, *CD* II.2, 199.

69. In keeping with the exegesis of Romans 11 offered by Richard Hays (see chapter 3), Barth sees Israel's "hardening" as itself a mysterious participation in Yeshua's suffering: "There falls, therefore, on their hardening . . . a reflection of the glory of the divine act of love which did not spare the only-begotten Son but delivered Him up for us all." *CD* II.2, 279.

70. Barth bases this claim on his interpretation of Romans 11:16. He sees the "root" and "first fruits" of that verse as both referring to the Messiah. See *CD* II.2, 285–87.

71. "It is by God's mercy that again and again there is . . . a remnant which by its work . . . attests and confirms in and with its own election the election of all Israel. The remnant does this . . . because of the fact that it is already the Church in Israel." *CD* II.2, 273. "If it were to believe and therefore to be obedient to its election . . . it could then really be Israel *in* the Church. . . . It would then be precisely Israel (the 'Jewish' element) in the Church which by its special contribution would see to it that the Church remains the Church." *CD* II.2, 235.

72. Ibid., 201.

73. Ibid., 199.

74. Ibid., 281.

Of course, no such Jewish ekklesia existed in Barth's experience, nor did he advocate the reestablishment of such an entity. He probably had not thought through the matter in terms of practical ecclesiology. As Stephen Haynes observes, "Barth does not explain how Israel is to enter the church and remain Israel. . . ."[75] He intuited from the New Testament that it was not enough for individual Jewish Yeshua-believers to join the ekklesia; they need to "remain Israel," which implies that they need to have a distinct communal existence and to participate actively in the life of the Jewish people as a whole. However, Barth did not take the next step—the step we are taking—and propose that the ekklesia reconsider its fundamental constitution in light of this intuition.

Conclusion

At the beginning of this chapter we presented three apparent implications from the conclusions reached in the previous chapters: (1) the one ekklesia of Messiah consists of two distinct but united communal networks, one Jewish and one Gentile; (2) the Jewish segment of the ekklesia shares fully in the life of the wider Jewish world, living according to its national customs and taking concern for its welfare; (3) the Gentile segment enters into a portion of Israel's heritage through its unity with the Jewish segment, and thereby also assumes concern for the welfare of Israel as a whole. We called this ecclesiological vision *bilateral ecclesiology in solidarity with Israel.*

In the course of this chapter we examined the New Testament to see if it showed explicit signs of such an ecclesiology. We have seen that it does indeed. The Acts of the Apostles presents the Jerusalem community under the leadership of James as the mother congregation for the worldwide ekklesia. It thereby sets the Gentile Yeshua-movement in relationship to the Jewish Yeshua-movement and brings both into solidarity with Israel as a whole. Paul's collection for the Jerusalem congregation confirms this witness of Acts. At the Jerusalem council James speaks of the Gentile portion of the Yeshua movement as a distinct "people for his name." Galatians 2 reports a Jerusalem agreement (with James again taking precedence) which demarcates two distinct fields of outreach (and thus two networks of congregations). The book of Ephesians proclaims the one new humanity in Messiah consisting of two differentiated but united parts, and celebrates the fact that the Gentile Yeshua believers have been given a share in Israel's riches.

75. Haynes, *Post-Holocaust Theology,* 65.

We then looked at the bilateral ecclesiology of Karl Barth, arrived at in a completely different manner from our own but having much in common with the conclusions reached in this chapter.

Before ending this chapter, we should cite perhaps the clearest statement of bilateral ecclesiology articulated by a biblical scholar. It comes from the distinguished Jewish Christian scholar David Noel Freedman. Freedman wrote the following in 1969:

> Paul's ingenious and effective exegesis created a single citizenship in the Christian commonwealth; it was divided into two classes, equal but separate: Jews and Gentiles. Jews who became Christians would continue to be Jews, while Gentiles would become Christians without also becoming Jews. All would share the same promises and perquisites, receive the same status and rights, but each community would order its own polity and practice.
>
> Thus, a two-house theory of Christianity emerged from the first generation experience, a provisional solution to an immediate problem. In principle and ultimately in fact there was no distinction between Jew and Gentile in the Church, but there was in practice, for it was at least as important to maintain the integrity and continuity of the Jewish group as to establish the freedom and autonomy of the Gentile community. As a result, the Jewish Christians were able to have active and effective relations with Gentile Christians and at the same time retain operating status in the non-Christian Jewish community. Thus a link was forged, however tenuous, between Christianity and Judaism, and it persisted as long as the Jewish Christian community continued to exist. This halfway house with conduits to both sides could serve as meeting place and mediator, communication center and symbol of the continuity to which both enterprises belonged.[76]

Freedman recognizes that the New Testament presumes two subcommunities, each with its own "polity and practice," "equal but separate."[77] As a Jew, he also makes a monumental claim that few Christian commentators would even consider: "It was at least as important to maintain the integrity and continuity of the Jewish group as to establish the freedom and autonomy of the Gentile community."[78] As seen above, Terence Donaldson pointed out the problem with a "homogeneous" ecclesiology: "Identifiably Jewish portions of the community

---

76. David N. Freedman, "An Essay on Jewish Christianity" (1969), reprinted in *Divine Commitment and Human Obligation: Selected Writings of David Noel Freedman*, vol. 1, *Ancient Israelite History and Religion* (Grand Rapids: Eerdmans, 1997), 246–47.

77. "Distinct" would be more accurate.

78. This insightful half sentence undercuts the statement made in the first part of the same sentence: "In principle and ultimately in fact there was no distinction between Jew and Gentile in the Church, but there was in practice." How could it be so important to "maintain the integrity and continuity of the Jewish group" if "there was no distinction between Jew and Gentile in the

would inevitably become assimilated."[79] Unfortunately, few Christians have viewed this eventuality as problematic.

Freedman concludes by referring to the Jewish portion of the Yeshua movement as a "link between Christianity and Judaism." Peter von der Osten-Sacken has employed a similar image, calling the Jewish branch of the ekklesia "the ecclesiological bridge joining Israel and the Gentiles."[80] In this way the Gentile ekklesia was brought into solidarity with Israel.

Freedman sees this "two-house theory" as "a provisional solution to an immediate problem." In historical terms it certainly was provisional in the sense that it did not last. But should we see it as provisional in the sense that it should not have lasted? If it is the only way to safeguard and uphold an ongoing Jewish existence within the ekklesia, and if—as we have argued—such an ongoing Jewish existence is crucial to the identity of the ekklesia, then bilateral ecclesiology may be the only way to keep the ekklesia from schism. In that case, it should be regarded as normative rather than provisional.

Church"? Donaldson has it right on this point: Paul's "no distinction" principle applied only to entrance requirements and fundamental status. It did not nullify the actual distinction between Jews and Gentiles nor detract from its importance.

79. Donaldson, *Paul and the Gentiles,* 185.

80. Peter von der Osten-Sacken, *Christian-Jewish Dialogue* (Philadelphia: Fortress, 1986), 105.

5

The Christian No to Israel

Christian Supersessionism and Jewish Practice

We have argued so far that the New Testament affirms the validity and importance of Jewish practice for all Jews and the validity and importance of the covenant between God and the Jewish people. We have also argued that the New Testament bears witness to a bilateral ecclesiology in solidarity with Israel that follows naturally from these first two affirmations. We are thus placing the New Testament's yes to Israel within the context of its yes to Jewish practice, and also within the context of a particular understanding of the ekklesia and its relationship to both the Jewish people and Jewish practice.

Our reading of the New Testament is not shared by the traditional teaching of the Christian church. That tradition is almost uniformly supersessionist. It sees the church as replacing genealogical Israel as the people of God and views the Jewish people as now just like another ethnic or non-Christian religious group, or as distinctive only in being the object of a uniquely horrific curse.[1]

Many post-Holocaust Christian theologians have faced this tradition honestly and have sought to revise Christian teaching about the Jewish people. The Roman Catholic Church has officially renounced supersessionism, acknowledging the

---

1. Some forms of traditional supersessionism also teach that the Jewish people will be "converted" before Yeshua returns. While this hope provides a positive dimension to Israel's future existence, it does nothing to attenuate its "cursed" condition in the present age.

teaching of the apostle Paul that "the Jews remain very dear to God, for the sake of the patriarchs, since God does not take back the gifts he bestowed or the choice he made" (*Nostra Aetate* 4).[2] Other churches have followed suit.[3] We should celebrate this reappropriation of New Testament teaching and the new relationship it makes possible between Christians and Jews.

At the same time, I would argue that this reappropriation has not gone far enough. While most Christian churches and theologians now recognize the irrevocable nature of the covenant between God and Israel, few have considered the implications of this recognition for the validity and importance of Jewish practice for all Jews (including those who believe in Yeshua), and even fewer have considered the implications for ecclesiology and the church's own self-definition.

R. Kendall Soulen is among those who have begun to see these implications. It is striking that he has done so under the influence of a Jewish theologian, Michael Wyschogrod:

> For Wyschogrod, the acid test of the church's theological posture toward Israel's election is the church's conduct toward Jews in its own midst, that is, toward Jews who have been baptized. For it is here that the church demonstrates in an ultimate way whether it understands itself in light of God's eternal covenant with the seed of Abraham. If the church acknowledges the abiding reality of Israel's corporeal election, it will naturally expect baptized Jews to maintain faithfully their Jewish identity. But if the church truly believes that it has superseded God's covenant with Israel, it will prohibit or discourage Jews from preserving their identity as Jews and members of the Jewish people. In short, the problem of supersessionism turns on the church's capacity to acknowledge the abiding religious significance of Israel's corporeal election and hence the abiding religious significance of the distinction between Gentile and Jew.[4]

Soulen and Wyschogrod both understand that if Yeshua-believing Jews are "to maintain faithfully their Jewish identity," they must observe the Jewish practices rooted in the Torah and defined by Jewish tradition, and they must participate actively as "members of the Jewish people."[5] In fact, Wyschogrod has devoted

2. See *Documents of Vatican II*, Austin P. Flannery, ed. (Grand Rapids: Eerdmans, 1975), 741. At the same time, Roman Catholic ecclesiology maintains the use of traditional language (e.g., "the new people of God," *Nostra Aetate* 4) that could (but need not) be understood in a supersessionist manner.

3. See *The Theology of the Churches and the Jewish People* (Geneva: WCC Publications, 1988).

4. R. Kendall Soulen, *The God of Israel and Christian Theology* (Minneapolis: Fortress, 1996), 11.

5. Soulen, 11–12; Michael Wyschogrod, "Letter to a Friend," *Modern Theology* 11:2 (April 1995), 165–71.

much of his ecumenical writing to the goal of alerting Christians to the crucial connection between supersessionism and Christian disrespect for the Torah and Jewish practice.[6] As both Wyschogrod and Soulen recognize, the Gentile ekklesia's no to Israel was expressed and embodied in its no to Jewish practice, and both these denials were made concrete in its no to the Jewish ekklesia. In this way it severed its living connection to the Jewish people and opened a tragic schism in the heart of the people of God.

In this chapter we will examine the early signs of this schism in the second century CE and its mature theological and canonical expression in the post-Constantinian era. Our purpose is not to condemn the church or its revered teachers but to understand what occurred, and—to the limited extent possible—why it happened. In the process of this study, we will also see how these teachers preserved a theological inheritance that contained within it the vital seeds of its own non-supersessionist reformation.

The Second Century: Anti-Judaism and the Marcionite Crisis

The end of the first and beginning of the second century CE brought formidable new challenges to the ekklesia. The Jewish war against Rome and its brutal conclusion (66–74 CE) undermined the unique and central role of the Jerusalem community within the ekklesia. Though a Jewish Yeshua-believing community was apparently reestablished in Jerusalem after the war and continued to function until the devastating defeat of Bar Kochba in 135 CE, it never regained its former place in the structure or the imagination of the wider ekklesia.

A distinct Jewish communal expression of Yeshua-faith continued to exist for several centuries.[7] However, by the second century it was already small and geographically limited. It was also becoming increasingly marginalized in both the wider Jewish world and the wider ekklesia.

In addition to the wars of 66–74 and 132–135, there was an extensive Jewish revolt against Rome outside the land of Israel in 115–117 CE. In the wake of these conflicts between Jews and Roman authority, anti-Jewish sentiment

6. Michael Wyschogrod, "A Jewish Reading of St. Thomas Aquinas on the Old Law," in *Understanding Scripture,* ed. Clemens Thoma and Michael Wyschogrod (New York: Paulist, 1987), 125–38; "A Jewish View of Christianity," in *Toward a Theological Encounter,* ed. Rabbi Leon Klenicki (New York: Paulist, 1991), 116–19 (this article is now included in *Abraham's Promise,* [Grand Rapids: Eerdmans, 2004], 149–64); "Christianity and the Jewish Law," *Pro Ecclesia* 2 (1993): 451–59; "Paul, Jews, and Gentiles" in *Abraham's Promise,* 188–201.

7. Richard Bauckham, *Jude and the Relatives of Jesus in the Early Church* (Edinburgh: T&T Clark, 1990); Ray A. Pritz, *Nazarene Jewish Christianity* (Leiden: Brill, 1988); Fr. Bellarmino Bagatti, *The Church from the Circumcision* (Jerusalem: Franciscan Press, 1971).

increased throughout the empire.[8] This was not an easy time to be a Jew or a friend of Jews.[9]

In the first century, outsiders had seen Gentile Yeshua-believers as participants in a Jewish movement. These Gentile members of the ekklesia evidently had understood themselves in similar fashion. Association with the Jewish community had brought legal protection (since Judaism was a recognized licit religion in the Roman Empire) and a measure of respect (since Judaism had an ancient and venerable pedigree). In the second century this situation changed dramatically. Association with the Jewish world was now a liability rather than an asset.

Christian writers of the second and third centuries also report anti-Christian sentiment among Jews of the period.[10] The reliability of accounts that connect Jews to particular anti-Christian incidents has been called into question.[11] Nevertheless it is reasonable to assume that many Jews held a very low opinion of the Yeshua-movement, and of that movement's granting of full covenant status to Gentile members without requiring compliance with all the covenant stipulations of the Torah. In Justin's narrative of his conversation with a Jewish interlocutor in the mid-second century, the Jew's first words to Justin (a Gentile Yeshua-believer) consist of an exhortation to be circumcised and observe the entire Torah.[12] Justin's dialogue may be fictional, but the initial comments of Trypho probably capture the normal Jewish response of the period to Gentiles claiming to be heirs of Israel's covenant. This response intensified the growing alienation of many Gentile Yeshua-believers from the Jewish world.

8. This does not mean that Judaism lost all attraction for Gentiles in this period. Peter Schafer (*Judeophobia* [Cambridge, MA: Harvard University Press, 1997], 115, 183–85, 192–94) and Shaye J. D. Cohen (*From the Maccabees to the Mishnah* [Philadelphia: Westminster, 1987], 49, 57–58) both argue that Judaism continued to win the sympathies of some Romans and that this attraction intensified the anti-Jewish rhetoric of Roman writers such as Tacitus and Juvenal.

9. Seth Schwartz sees the period following the Bar Kochba revolt as a time in which "Judaism shattered." *Imperialism and Jewish Society, 200 BCE to 640 CE* (Princeton, NJ: Princeton University Press, 2001), 175. "Probably everywhere . . . the failure of the revolts had led to disaffection with and attrition from Judaism." Ibid., 108. "In the second and third centuries the Jewish communities in the Diaspora experienced a decline comparable, and related, to the disintegration of Palestinian Jewish society in the same period." Ibid., 114. "Whether or not large numbers of Jews regularly worshiped the Greek gods, their ubiquity as symbols is profoundly important as an indication of the postrevolt collapse of any normatively Jewish ideological system." Ibid., 159.

10. Edward H. Flannery, *The Anguish of the Jews* (New York: Paulist, 1999), 35–38.

11. James Parkes, *The Conflict of the Church and the Synagogue* (Jewish Publication Society, 1934; repr. New York: Atheneum, 1969), 125–50; Judith M. Lieu, *Neither Jew Nor Greek?* (Edinburgh: T&T Clark, 2002), 135–50.

12. *Dialogue with Trypho*, chapter 8.

These conditions made it possible for a new and virulently anti-Jewish form of faith to emerge within the Gentile ekklesia of the mid-second century.[13] Its champion was Marcion, a Gentile from Asia Minor. As early as 140 (only five years after the suppression of the Bar Kochba revolt), he was propounding the view that the God of Yeshua was different from and superior to the God of Israel. Marcion rejected the authority of the Jewish Bible and established a scriptural canon that included only an expurgated version of the gospel of Luke and ten Pauline letters (Galatians, 1–2 Corinthians, Romans, 1–2 Thessalonians, Ephesians, Colossians, Philemon, Philippians, in that order). Paul was the only true apostle, and Pauline thought was captured preeminently in the letter to the Galatians.[14]

The Bishop of Rome excommunicated Marcion in 144. Unrepentant, he proceeded to found a new church. His efforts were successful, and his church grew in numbers and influence. This success reveals the depth of anti-Jewish feeling that existed at the time, both within the Gentile ekklesia and in Roman society as a whole. The times were propitious for a message of redemption that repudiated any positive connection to the Jewish people and its ancestral God.

The Christian response to Marcion proved to be a crucial event in the history of the church. It produced an unequivocal affirmation of the Jewish Bible as Christian scripture. Thus the church proclaimed that the Father of Jesus Christ was the God of Israel, and the God of Israel was the Father of Jesus Christ. In this way the church preserved its essential connection to the Jewish tradition. While it did not immediately grasp the full significance of this connection, its affirmation at this formative stage of its history established the conditions that would make the eventual renunciation of supersessionism an inner process of theological recovery rather than merely a reaction to external events and priorities.

The Christian response to Marcion also contributed substantially to the formation of the New Testament canon. John Miller has argued convincingly that the contents and shape of the New Testament canon should be understood as the church's recontextualizing of the Marcionite canon so as to repudiate its

13. "When looked at in the context of Greco-Roman prejudices against Jews, . . . Christian supersessionism seems almost philosemitic. There were multitudes of gentile Christians who rejected it, not because of its anti-Judaism, but because it was not anti-Jewish enough." George Lindbeck, "The Church as Israel," in *Jews and Christians*, ed. Carl E. Braaten and Robert W. Jenson (Grand Rapids: Eerdmans, 2003), 84.

14. On Marcion and Marcionism, see Jaroslav Pelikan, *The Christian Tradition,* vol. 1, *The Emergence of the Catholic Tradition* (Chicago: University of Chicago Press, 1971), 71–81. On the relationship between Marcionism and Gnosticism, see Kurt Rudolph, *Gnosis* (San Francisco: HarperCollins, 1987), 313–16.

On the Marcionite canon of scripture, see John Miller, *How the Bible Came to Be* (New York: Paulist, 2004), 48–75.

anti-Jewish principle. Thus Romans—a more balanced treatment of the Jewish people and Torah—begins the Pauline corpus rather than Galatians, which is now set at the middle of the letter collection where it is paired with Ephesians. This rearranged set of letters is preceded, not by an expurgated Gospel of Luke, but by four Gospels and the book of Acts. As Miller states, "The reader of this canon-codex is introduced to Paul . . . as one apostle among others and part of a larger movement stemming from the historic mission of Jesus himself to his own people."[15] As noted in the last chapter, the oldest biblical codices also place the general letters before (rather than after) the Pauline corpus. These letters are attributed to the pillar apostles of the Jerusalem community (James, Peter, John, Jude), three of whom are referred to in Paul's letter to the Galatians (1:16–2:9). Thus those apostles representing the ekklesia of the circumcision are given precedence to Paul and set the context for reading his writings. Moreover, at the end of one of the general letters—2 Peter—readers are urged to interpret Paul's writings carefully, since "there are things in them hard to understand, which the ignorant and unstable twist to their destruction, as they do the other scriptures" (2 Peter 3:16). Miller comments on this verse as follows:

> These words imply an existent, influential collection of Paul's letters that is circulating in the churches and is being seriously misconstrued along with "the rest of the scriptures." This is precisely what those who created the Christian Bible believed was happening in the wake of the Marcionite movement. Thus, these words bear explicit and compelling witness to the felt concerns of those who fashioned this Bible in the fight against heresies.[16]

Finally, this entire "New Testament" is joined to the Jewish Bible in a single codex. In this way the church affirmed that Yeshua could be understood only within the context of Israel's history and destiny.

The Marcionite crisis thus stimulated a partial yes to Israel's heritage in the Gentile church.[17] Unfortunately the conditions that provided fertile soil for the Marcionite movement also made it difficult for the church authorities and teachers to realize the full implications of that affirmation. Like the Marcionites,

---

15. Ibid., 64.

16. Ibid., 64.

17. "The communities oriented to the Old Testament were perhaps a minority among gentile Christians [in the second century], but they led the way. It is to them that we owe the anti-Marcionite selection from older writings to form the New Testament. Moreover, they read the ancient scriptures through the lens of Jesus Christ as witnessed to by this new addition to the canon, and they came to view the church, Christ's body, in increasingly Israel-like terms. . . . Jaroslav Pelikan reflects a historians' consensus when he speaks of 're-judaization.'" Lindbeck, "The Church as Israel," 85.

they had imbibed the anti-Jewish sentiment of the times, and the interpretation they gave to Israel's heritage was one that denied Israel any legitimate rights as heirs. They said yes to Israel's heritage, but only in a radically revised form. They then said no to Israel itself and to its ancestral way of life.

The Second Century: Anti-Judaism and Christian Teaching

The most influential Christian writers of the second century agree in teaching that the Jewish people no longer enjoy the privileges of the covenant and that Jewish practice (e.g., circumcision, Sabbath observance, dietary laws) is an invalid expression of the life of the covenant. In this section we will examine the teaching of five of these writers: Ignatius of Antioch, the author of the *Epistle of Barnabas*, Justin Martyr, the author of the *Epistle to Diognetus*, and Irenaeus.

Ignatius of Antioch

Ignatius, bishop of Antioch, wrote a set of letters to congregations in Asia Minor as he was being transported to Rome for execution around 114 CE. His major concern in these letters is to urge his hearers to maintain their unity and to order themselves under their bishops. He also combats a docetic Christology, according to which Yeshua suffered only in appearance and not in reality. A third theme emerges in two of his letters, *Philadelphians* and *Magnesians*. In these letters Ignatius warns against the dangers of "Judaism."

In his letter to the *Philadelphians* Ignatius addresses a situation resembling that which Paul confronted in Galatia. Apparently he had heard that there were Gentiles in this congregation who had adopted "Judaism" and were promoting it among other Gentile congregants. This greatly disturbed Ignatius:

> But if anyone interpret Judaism (*Ioudaismos*) to you do not listen to him; for it is better to hear Christianity (*Christianismos*) from the circumcised than Judaism from the uncircumcised.[18] (*Philadelphians* 6:1)

Like Paul, Ignatius discourages Gentiles from assuming a full-orbed Jewish life and from teaching such a life to other Gentiles. Unlike Paul, however, Ignatius contrasts "Judaism" as a systemic way of life and thought with an entity he calls "Christianity." As far as we know, this term originates with Ignatius. It shows for the first time a self-conscious awareness of Judaism and Christianity as two

---

18. All citations from the letters of Ignatius are from Kirsopp Lake, *Apostolic Fathers*, vol. 1 (Cambridge, MA: Harvard University Press, 1912).

separate religious systems. According to Ignatius, it is good to hear a Jew promoting Christianity. This certainly implies that such a Jew no longer follows or promotes Judaism, since Ignatius sees the two as mutually exclusive. However, in *Philadelphians* Ignatius focuses not on Jews but on Gentiles. He is agitated at the idea that Gentiles are following and promoting Judaism.

In *Magnesians* Ignatius has a broader concern about Judaism. As *Philadelphians* implies but does not state, Ignatius finds it just as offensive when Jewish Yeshua-believers practice Judaism as when Gentiles do.

> If then they who walked in ancient customs came to a new hope, no longer living for the Sabbath, but for the Lord's Day, on which also our life sprang up through him and his death, . . . how then shall we be able to live without him of whom even the prophets were disciples in the Spirit and to whom they looked forward as their teacher? (*Magnesians* 9:1–2)

Ignatius here claims that the early Jewish Yeshua-believers gave up the "ancient customs" such as Sabbath observance and assumed a different way of life. In accordance with the above translation, the majority of interpreters see a reference here to honoring Sunday in some manner—at least through gathering with the ekklesia for worship. Thus, according to Ignatius, the apostles and their Jewish disciples forsook the Sabbath, which is a sign of God's covenant with Israel, and oriented their lives instead around Yeshua's resurrection and the new reality he initiated.

Ignatius continues:

> Put aside then the evil leaven, which has grown old and sour, and turn to the new leaven, which is Jesus Christ. . . . It is monstrous to talk of Jesus Christ and to practice Judaism [*ioudaizein*]. For Christianity did not base its faith on Judaism, but Judaism on Christianity, and every tongue believing on God was brought together in it. (*Magnesians* 10:2–3)

The term *ioudaizein* ("to judaize") may refer to Gentiles adopting Jewish identity and practice. This is certainly its meaning in Paul (Galatians 2:14). However, the sentence that follows implies that Ignatius would have found it just as "monstrous" for Jewish Yeshua-believers to practice Judaism as for Gentiles. After all, Christian faith does not believe in Judaism, but instead Jewish faith believes in Christianity. Therefore Judith Lieu should be taken seriously when she suggests that Ignatius may have used the term "judaize" to refer to anyone who lived as a Jew: "Ignatius may not have made the distinction, finding both equally unacceptable and meriting the negative resonances of the description."[19]

19. Judith Lieu, *Image and Reality* (Edinburgh: T&T Clark, 1996), 31.

Fifty years after the deaths of Peter and Paul, a prominent Christian bishop speaks disparagingly of Judaism and Jewish practice as "the evil leaven, which has grown old and sour." He exhorts all, Jews and Gentiles, to reject any attempt to combine Yeshua and Judaism: "It is monstrous to talk of Jesus Christ and practice Judaism." Sadly, we have come a long way in a short time.

The Epistle of Barnabas

The *Epistle of Barnabas* is likely written by a Gentile Yeshua-believer to other Gentile Yeshua-believers.[20] It may have been composed as early as the end of the first century, but it is more likely from the years just before the Bar Kochba revolt (i.e., 130–32).[21] The main purpose of the letter is to prevent its Gentile audience from taking on a Jewish identity and way of life, "that we should not be shipwrecked by conversion to their law" (*Barnabas* 3:6).[22]

The pronouns in this clause speak volumes. *Barnabas* does not employ the terms Judaism and Christianity, but it does present Jews as "them" and Yeshua-believers as "us."[23] As in the letters of Ignatius, we find here a vision of two mutually exclusive communities. *Barnabas* combats fiercely the notion that Yeshua-believers and the Jewish people share a common covenant: "Be not like unto some, heaping up your sins and saying that the covenant is both theirs and ours" (4:6; see 13:1–2). The author asserts that the covenant was offered to Israel at Sinai, but Israel rejected it by sinning with the golden calf, and the offer was never renewed (4:7-8; 14:1–5). God showed his great love by sending Yeshua to Israel (5:8), but Israel completed its full measure of sins by putting him to death (5:11–12; 14:5) and was definitively abandoned (4:14).

Ignatius pays scant attention to Jewish scripture. *Barnabas*, on the other hand, consists mainly of exhortation based on biblical commentary. In keeping with what will soon be the anti-Marcionite stance of the church, *Barnabas* affirms

---

20. Reidar Hvalvik, *The Struggle for Scripture and Covenant* (Tübingen: J. C. B. Mohr/Paul Siebeck, 1996), 43–45; Stephen G. Wilson, *Related Strangers* (Minneapolis: Fortress, 1995), 128; Oskar Skarsaune, *In the Shadow of the Temple* (Downers Grove, IL: InterVarsity, 2002), 218–21. Some scholars have argued that both the author and the original audience were Jewish Yeshua-believers; see Hvalvik, 43, n. 5, for a list. They base their conclusion mainly on midrashic traditions employed in the letter; see Daniélou, *The Theology of Jewish Christianity,* 33–36. However, the presence of such traditions can be explained by the author's use of source material.

21. In support of the earlier dating, see Wilson, *Related Strangers,* 135, 139. Hvalvik makes the case for 130–32 CE.

22. All citations from the *Epistle of Barnabas* are from Kirsopp Lake, *Apostolic Fathers,* vol 1.

23. "The author does not use the term 'Jews.' . . . The distinctive way he chooses to refer to Jews, past and present, is by pairing pronouns. For there is never any doubt who the contrasted entities are—Christians and Jews—nor that the latter are presented in negative and hostile terms." Wilson, *Related Strangers,* 129.

the authority of Jewish scripture and sees the Father of Yeshua as the God who appeared to Abraham, Isaac, Jacob, and Moses. However, the author also wants to deny Israel's share in the covenant. As we have already seen, he does this by portraying the golden calf incident and the breaking of the first set of tablets as the revocation of that covenant. However, after this incident the Pentateuch describes God's commandments to Israel, and *Barnabas* knows that the Jewish way of life is rooted in those biblical commandments. If the Jewish Bible is accepted as authoritative, how can *Barnabas* dismiss that way of life and the Jewish people who live it?

This was the great problem posed for the second century Gentile ekklesia as it sought both to affirm the Jewish Bible and to reject Judaism and the Jewish people. *Barnabas* adopts a twofold strategy for solving this problem. First, he draws upon the Hellenistic Jewish tradition of spiritualizing, allegorical exegesis. Thus he sees the commandment of circumcision as a directive to hear the divine word and believe (9:1–3), the dietary laws as instructions on the kind of people one should avoid (10:1–11), and the Sabbath commandment as requiring the total sanctification of life that will only be attainable in the world to come (15:1–9). This initial move becomes standard in later Christian exegesis.

The second move is more daring. *Barnabas* insists that commandments related to Jewish practice, such as circumcision, dietary laws, and the Sabbath, were never intended to be observed in a literal manner. When Israel began circumcising their sons, restricting their diets, and setting apart the seventh day of the week, they showed that they had failed to understand the commandments they had received.

> For he declared that circumcision was not of the flesh, but they erred because an evil angel was misleading them. (9:4)

> Moses received three doctrines concerning food and thus spoke of them in the Spirit; but they received them as really referring to food, owing to the lust of their flesh. (10:9)

Thus *Barnabas* does not see the Jewish way of life as a valid preparatory stage leading to the coming of the Messiah. Instead, the letter portrays Jewish practice as invalid from the beginning. Such practice constitutes proof of the Jewish people's blindness, hardness of heart, and demonic deception.[24]

---

24. This teaching of *Barnabas* bears some resemblance to that of Jews in Alexandria who clung to the spiritual meaning of the commandments while disregarding their literal observance (Philo, *On the Migration of Abraham*, 89–92). They differ, however, in purpose. We have no evidence that the Alexandrian spiritualizers ridiculed those who observed the commandments literally or

Barnabas addresses Gentiles and seeks to dissuade them from identifying or living as Jews. In this purpose it resembles the Pauline letters. However, the implications of its arguments and rhetoric display a vision that is inconsistent with that of the apostle to the Gentiles. According to *Barnabas*, Jews and Yeshua-believers are two mutually exclusive groups. Jews are part of a sinful people who rejected the covenant, misunderstood the commandments, and killed the Messiah. As a result, God has abandoned them. If a Jew becomes a Yeshua-believer, he or she thereby makes a decisive break with the Jewish people. In the language of *Barnabas*, such a person leaves "them" and becomes part of "us." Moreover, that break entails a dramatically altered way of life. If literal observance of circumcision, the dietary laws, and the Sabbath demonstrates hardness of heart and demonic deception, those who are enlightened by becoming part of "us" will necessarily break with such practice.

Justin Martyr

Justin wrote his *Dialogue with Trypho* between 155 and 160 CE. However, it purports to be an account of an extended conversation that took place soon after the Roman suppression of the Bar Kochba revolt two decades before. In fact, we learn in the first chapter that Trypho is a refugee from that conflict. The suffering and humiliation of the Jewish people thus provide the dramatic backdrop for Justin's argument against Jewish interpretation of scripture and Jewish observance.

Ignatius rarely refers to the Jewish Bible. *Barnabas* gives its full attention to explaining that book but does not see the church as Israel. Israel is the Jewish nation, whom God has rejected. God has chosen a new people, the church, to replace Israel. In contrast, Justin asserts what will become a staple of Christian theology and exegesis: "We are the true spiritual Israel, and the descendants of Judah, Jacob, Isaac, and Abraham."[25] Justin thus sees a greater measure of continuity between the Israel of the Jewish Bible and the church of the New Covenant. Nevertheless the final result is the same as in the *Epistle of Barnabas*: the Jewish people are no longer the beloved heirs of the divine promises. The church, the "true spiritual Israel," supersedes the Jewish people, unfaithful carnal Israel.

---

portrayed such observance as evidence of demonic deception. They only saw it as unnecessary. *Barnabas*, on the other hand, employs this motif in order to emphasize Jewish stupidity and hardness of heart. To circumcise your sons, keep the dietary laws, and observe the Sabbath is to demonstrate your membership in the stiff-necked people God has rejected.

25. *Dialogue*, 11. All citations from the *Dialogue with Trypho* are from *The Fathers of the Church*, vol. 6, *Writings of Saint Justin Martyr*, trans. Thomas B. Falls (Washington, DC: Catholic University of America Press, 1948).

Like *Barnabas*, Justin builds his case on the authority of the Jewish Bible. He claims that the church interprets it truly, whereas the Jews misunderstand their own sacred text. Justin also follows the first part of the twofold interpretive strategy of *Barnabas*, reading the "ceremonial" commandments of the Torah in a spiritual, allegorical manner. His discussion of the prohibition of eating leaven at Passover illustrates this mode of exegesis:

> This is the symbolic meaning of unleavened bread, that you do not commit the old deeds of the bad leaven. You, however, understand everything in a carnal way, and you deem yourselves pious if you perform such deeds, even when your souls are filled with deceit and every other kind of sin. (Chap. 14)

The "symbolic meaning" of ceremonial observances such as circumcision and the Sabbath provides perpetual instruction for the people of the New Covenant. Justin argues that the church embodies this symbolic meaning in its conduct.

However, Justin refuses to follow the second part of the interpretive strategy of *Barnabas*. He does not suggest that Israel was mistaken in taking the ceremonial commandments literally. Justin realizes that such a forced reading of the text would undermine the credibility of Christian exegesis. Therefore he needs to find a way of affirming the literal intent of the commandments while at the same time explaining why they are no longer applicable. His solution captures the polemical spirit of *Barnabas* in a more persuasive exegetical argument: God gave these commandments to Israel because of its uniquely sinful orientation. Thus the Sabbath commandment was necessary because Israel was incapable of remembering God daily (Chap. 19). Observance of the Sabbath ensured that they would at least remember God weekly! The dietary laws had a similar purpose:

> You were likewise forbidden to eat certain kinds of meat, so that when you ate and drank you would keep God before your eyes, for you have always been disposed to forget Him, as Moses himself testifies. (Chap. 20)

This is why those who have received the New Covenant no longer observe these practices:

> We, too, would observe your circumcision of the flesh, your Sabbath days, and, in a word, all your festivals, if we were not aware of the reason why they were imposed upon you, namely, because of your sins and your hardness of heart. (Chap. 18)

Justin proclaims Yeshua to be the New Law (Chap. 11) and asserts that those who receive him live a more exemplary and pious life than the Jews. Spiritual

Israel no longer needs those commandments whose purpose was to compensate for carnal Israel's stubborn hardness of heart.

Justin is a perceptive enough reader to recognize that some of the ceremonial commandments have an additional purpose: they serve as distinguishing ethnic markers, separating and preserving Israel as a nation. In a daring move, Justin turns this positive purpose on its head, contending that Israel was singled out in this way so that it might receive more punishment than other nations!

> Indeed the custom of circumcising the flesh, handed down from Abraham, was given to you as a distinguishing mark, to set you off from other nations and from us Christians. The purpose of this was that you and only you might suffer the afflictions that are now justly yours. (Chap. 16)

> As I stated before, it was by reason of your sins and the sins of your fathers that, among other precepts, God imposed upon you the observance of the Sabbath as a mark. (Chap. 21)

Justin thus accepts the continuing applicability of these commandments to the Jewish people, but only insofar as they continue to rebel against God and merit divine wrath. He implies here that all Jews who become Yeshua-believers should give up these practices and no longer be distinct from other nations, since they no longer merit divine judgment.

The ongoing existence of carnal Israel serves no positive purpose other than to witness to what happens to those who disobey God. Justin says nothing about Israel's future salvation. In fact, his system excludes it. He does embrace a millennial eschatology with a thousand-year reign in the city of Jerusalem. However, those who reign in the city are Christians, not Jews (Chap. 80)! Spiritual Israel inherits the blessings, while carnal Israel receives the curses.

In the *Dialogue with Trypho* Justin lays the foundation for all future Christian treatments of the Jewish people and Jewish observance. He also comments explicitly on the topic of Jewish Yeshua-believers and Jewish practice. His views deserve to be quoted at length:

> "But," Trypho again objected, "if a man knows that what you say is true, and, professing Jesus to be the Christ, believes in and obeys Him, yet desires also to observe the commandments of the Mosaic Law, shall he be saved?"
>
> "In my opinion," I replied, "I say such a man will be saved, unless he exerts every effort to influence other men (I have in mind the Gentiles whom Christ circumcised from all error) to practice the same rites as himself, informing them that they cannot be saved unless they do so. . . .

"But why," pressed Trypho, "did you say, 'in my opinion such a man will be saved?' There must, therefore, be other Christians who hold a different opinion."

"Yes, Trypho, " I conceded, "there are some Christians who boldly refuse to have conversation or meals with such persons. I don't agree with such Christians. But if some [Jewish converts], due to their instability of will, desire to observe as many of the Mosaic precepts as possible—precepts which we think were instituted because of your hardness of heart—while at the same time they place their hope in Christ, and if they desire to perform the eternal and natural acts of justice and piety, yet wish to live with us Christians and believers, as I already stated, not persuading them to be circumcised like themselves, or to keep the Sabbath, or to perform any other similar acts, then it is my opinion that we Christians should receive them and associate with them in every way as kinsmen and brethren. (Chap. 47; bracketed material original)

This chapter contains several noteworthy features. First, Trypho's question—can a Jewish Yeshua-believer who lives as a practicing Jew be saved?—employs the language of Acts 15, but with inverted meaning. In Acts 15 the question was, can a Gentile Yeshua-believer who is not converted to Judaism be saved? Circumstances have so changed in one century that Trypho now must ask Justin if (in Christian opinion) a Jewish Yeshua-believer who does not forsake Judaism can be saved! Second, Justin's answer indicates that some Christians actually hold that such Yeshua-believing Jews are not saved! (This may have been the view of Ignatius and Barnabas.) As we will see, this strict position, while not endorsed by Justin, will later become normative Christian teaching. Thus, while the early Jewish Yeshua-movement decided that a Gentile did not need to become a Jew in order to be saved, the growing consensus among Christians was that in effect a Jew did need to become a Gentile to be saved! Third, while Justin adopts a more tolerant view and accepts such Jews as legitimate Yeshua-believers—on the condition that they do not seek to persuade Gentile Yeshua-believers to live as Jews—he clearly sees their attachment to Jewish identity and practice as a character defect. Such conduct expresses "instability of will."

Rather than seeing a Jewish Yeshua-believing branch of the ekklesia as an essential component in the ekklesia's constitution, binding it to the people of Israel, Justin shows only that he is broadminded enough to tolerate its existence. Even such toleration will soon be a thing of the past.

The Epistle to Diognetus

The *Epistle to Diognetus* is a defense of "the religion of the Christians" written within a decade or two of Justin's *Dialogue with Trypho*. As in the other Christian texts we have examined, the author treats this "religion" as completely distinct from that of the Jews.

In fact, *Diognetus* begins by distinguishing Christian religion from that of the Greeks and from that of the Jews. First, the author ridicules idolatry. Then he proceeds to ridicule Judaism. The terms in which he does the latter have more in common with *Barnabas* than with Justin. He aims his barbs initially at the temple sacrifices, which he sees as little better than the pagan variety:

> The Jews indeed, by abstaining from the religion already discussed, may rightly claim that they worship the one God of the Universe, and regard him as master, but in offering service to him in like manner to those already dealt with they are quite wrong. For just as the Greeks give a proof of foolishness by making offerings to senseless and deaf images, so the Jews ought rather to consider that they are showing foolishness, not reverence, by regarding God as in need of these things. . . . For after all, those who think that they are consecrating sacrifices to him by blood and burnt fat, and whole burnt offerings, and that they are reverencing him by these honours, seem to me to be in no way better than those who show the same respect to deaf images. For it seems that the one offer to those who cannot partake of the honour, the others to him who is in need of nothing.[26] (3:1–3, 5)

The author then attacks circumcision, dietary laws, holiday fasting, and Sabbath and festival observance as involving "arbitrary distinctions" and imposing useless restrictions:

> Moreover I do not suppose that you need to learn from me that, after all, their scruples about food and superstition about the Sabbath, and their pride in circumcision and the sham of their fasting and feast of the new moon, are ridiculous and unworthy of any argument. For how can it be anything but unlawful to receive some of the things created by God for the use of man as if well created, and to reject others as if useless and superfluous? And what can it be but impious falsely to accuse God of forbidding that a good deed should be done on the Sabbath day? And what does it deserve but ridicule to be proud of the mutilation of the flesh as a proof of election, as if they were, for this reason, especially beloved by God? And their attention to the stars and moon, for the observance of months and days, and for their arbitrary distinctions between the changing seasons ordained by God, making some into feasts, and others into occasions of mourning;—who would regard this as a proof of piety, and not much more of foolishness? So then I think that you have learnt sufficiently that the Christians do rightly in abstaining from the general silliness and deceit and fussiness and pride of the Jews. (4:1–6)

---

26. All citations from the *Epistle to Diognetus* are from Kirsopp Lake, *Apostolic Fathers*, vol. 2 (Cambridge, MA: Harvard University Press, 1913).

Barnabas and Justin both realized the need to explain why Christians disregard commandments contained in texts they consider sacred. This author recognizes no such need. The reader would have no idea from this presentation that the "general silliness" of Jewish observance was rooted in scripture common to Jews and Christians.

The approach taken in the *Epistle to Diognetus* derives from the rhetorical setting of the document. The author addresses educated pagans, seeking to persuade them of the legitimacy and credibility of the Christian religion. He probably assumes anti-Jewish sentiment among his intended audience and is therefore eager to distinguish Christian from Jewish religion. Rather than acknowledging a common Jewish and Christian scripture, and then explaining how Jews and Christians interpret differently the "ceremonial" commandments found there, the author evades the issue and pretends it does not exist.

The *Epistle to Diognetus* illustrates again how far Yeshua-faith has come from its first-century Jewish beginnings. For an author such as this, an ecclesiological bridge is unthinkable. The Jews and the Christians are two different races, and the latter want nothing to do with the former.

Irenaeus

Irenaeus, Bishop of Lyons, wrote his classic work, *Against Heresies*, at the very end of the second century CE. Most consider this book the summit of second-century Christian theology, and it is worthy of such praise. Irenaeus here undertook the daunting task of describing and refuting the complex Gnostic systems that proliferated in his era. He thereby contributed enormously to the rejection of Marcionism and the enduring affirmation of the Jewish Bible as foundational to Christian faith.

In dealing with Jewish practice and the Jewish people, Irenaeus follows the substantive pattern established by his predecessors. Like the *Epistle of Barnabas*, he views the statutes of the Torah as given only because of the sin of the golden calf (4.15.1). God originally gave Israel only the Decalogue, representing the "natural precepts." In addition, they received circumcision and the Sabbath as signs, that they might be preserved as a distinct nation (4.16.1; see also 3.12.11). Then, after the sin of the golden calf, God gave Israel the corporeal regulations of the Torah, which were temporary measures intended for a period of "slavery" (4.13.2). When the Divine Word came as a human being, he fulfilled the law and rendered obsolete the national signs and regulations linked to servitude (4.13.2; 4.16.5).

At the same time, the tone of Irenaeus differs radically from that of his predecessors. As defender of the Jewish Bible and adamant opponent of Gnosticism and Marcionism, he argues insistently for the dignity of the "Old Covenant." He never denigrates Jewish practice. In keeping with his overall theological perspective, he sees the Sinai regulations as part of the educational process of humanity by which human beings gradually grow to maturity in the Messiah. Therefore the Jewish people are viewed, not as uniquely degenerate, but instead as representatives of a world moving from childish servitude to freedom and consummation.

In fact, Irenaeus even acknowledges that Yeshua and his immediate followers continued to observe the Jewish law (4.12.4; 3.12.15). He implies that this was appropriate until the destruction of Jerusalem, at which time Jewish practice became obsolete (4.12.4; 4.4.1–2). From that point forward, the Jewish people no longer had any special significance in the divine economy.

Irenaeus therefore presents a more positive perspective on the Jewish people and Jewish practice. Nevertheless, in the final analysis his conclusions are not substantively different from those of his second-century Christian predecessors. The covenant with Israel has been revoked, Jewish practice and Jewish national life are obsolete, and the church has been liberated from its Jewish ecclesiological bonds.

Ecclesiology "on the Ground"

Before leaving these second-century authors, it is important to note that the situation "on the ground" appears to have been considerably different from what they portray as normative. For the past fifteen years many historians have begun reading these texts against the grain, asking what they reveal not only of their authors' vision but also of the actual ecclesiological conditions they faced. Their conclusions are both surprising and important. While these second-century authors are anti-Jewish supersessionists, who see Judaism and Christianity as airtight and mutually exclusive religious systems, many second-century Yeshua-believers held a different view.[27] For them, Yeshua-faith was a variety of Judaism, and adherence to that faith required a living relationship to the wider Jewish community.

James Dunn has argued this point concerning Ignatius, Barnabas, and Justin, and concluded that these writings actually implied the opposite of what they explicitly stated: "Talk of a clear-cut or final parting of the ways at 70 CE is distinctly premature."[28] Stephen Wilson has interpreted Barnabas as indicating

---

27. See Adam H. Becker and Annette Yoshiko Reed, eds., *The Ways That Never Parted* (Tübingen: Mohr-Siebeck, 2003), for recent essays that point in this direction.

28. James D. G. Dunn, *The Partings of the Ways* (Philadelphia: Trinity Press International, 1991), 237–38.

the existence of second-century "Christians who had begun to rethink their relationship with Judaism, who wished to create room for coexistence within a single covenant, and who were attracted to Jewish ways."[29] Wilson speaks of this as the document's "secondary voice" and sees it as important because "it demonstrates that the views that Christians took of Judaism were far more diverse than the monochrome, negative portrait that was later to dominate the Christian tradition."[30] Judith Lieu makes a similar point about Ignatius:

> For Ignatius, Judaism and Christianity share no common ground and it is inconceivable that anyone should partake in both. Yet the very force of his argument demonstrates that this was precisely what was happening, or perhaps what was happening was that his clear definition of Judaism and Christianity did not match the life of the churches.[31]

Daniel Boyarin reads Ignatius in the same way:

> I am not suggesting, for instance, that there was no distinction at all between "Judaism" and "Christianity" by the second century, only that the border between the two was so fuzzy that one can hardly say precisely at what point one stopped and the other began. "It is monstrous to talk of Jesus Christ and to practice Judaism," thunders Ignatius, thus making both points at once, the drive of the nascent orthodoxy to separation and the lack thereof "on the ground."[32]

These second-century authors exert their energies to draw a thick, black line between Christians and Jews, Christianity and Judaism, and thereby unwittingly show that such a line did not yet exist.

Earlier in this chapter we spoke of the Jewish wars with Rome and the anti-Jewish sentiment they generated as factors explaining how such a dramatic ecclesiological change could occur in the Yeshua-movement in such a relatively short time. Attentiveness to the "secondary voice" in the writings we have examined helps us to see that this dramatic ecclesiological change did not take place smoothly and without opposition. Not only did many Jewish Yeshua-believers continue to live as observant Jews, as Justin reluctantly admits, but many Gentile Yeshua-believers continued to maintain contacts with the Jewish community

29. Wilson, *Related Strangers,* 139.

30. Ibid., 141. Oskar Skarsaune has recently read *Barnabas* in the same way, indicating that the letter points "to a situation in which the lines of demarcation between Jews and Christians are not that clear-cut; the author wants to make them so." *In the Shadow of the Temple,* 220–21.

31. Judith Lieu, *Image and Reality,* 40. The name of Lieu's book itself points to this contrast between a "primary" and a "secondary" voice.

32. Daniel Boyarin, *Dying For God* (Palo Alto, CA: Stanford University Press, 1999), 10–11.

and to adopt elements of Jewish practice. Supersessionism triumphed, but the victory was not won easily.

The Quartodeciman Controversy

At the end of the second century a controversy arose that manifested the desire of the Gentile ekklesia to break free from all Jewish connection and influence. At the same time, this controversy also showed how strong the connection and influence remained.

The point of disagreement was this: should the Gentile ekklesia commemorate the death and resurrection of Yeshua on the fourteenth of Nisan, when the Jews celebrate the Passover? Those who said yes were called the Quartodecimans (from the Latin word for "fourteenth"). Their practice likely derived from the early Jewish ekklesia.[33] The small communities of Jewish Yeshua-believers in the second century almost certainly maintained this custom. However, their practice would not have caused this controversy, since they were already treated with hostility or suspicion by the Gentile ekklesia. The problem came from the fact that the Gentile ekklesia of the province of Asia (in Asia Minor) was Quartodeciman and claimed that their practice was of apostolic origin.[34]

The Quartodeciman observance was disturbing, since (if followed) it would obligate the entire ekklesia to order its liturgical calendar in accordance with the decisions of the Jewish community. In a matter of great practical import it expressed dependence upon and even solidarity with the wider Jewish world. That this was the point of controversy is quite evident from the documents of the period. Thus the fourth-century bishop Epiphanius asserts that the Quartodecimans attributed the following instruction to the apostles:

> As for you, do not make calculations [to determine the New Moon or the proper month]. But when your brothers of the circumcision celebrate the Passover, celebrate yours also. . . . And even if they are wrong in their calculation, do not worry about it.[35]

As Boyarin recognizes, this text is "astonishing." It expresses exactly the type of identification and solidarity with Israel that we saw in the bilateral ecclesiology of the New Testament. But such an ecclesiology was no longer tolerable in the late second century.

---

33. Wilson, *Related Strangers,* 236.
34. See the *Ecclesiastical History* of Eusebius, 5.24.1–3.
35. Cited in Boyarin, *Dying For God,* 13; see also 144, n. 57.

In the first half of the second century it appears that most of the Gentile ekklesia outside Asia Minor did not celebrate an annual commemoration of Yeshua's death and resurrection.[36] The Quartodeciman practice of Asia Minor was thus a curiosity, but it did not provoke attack from the rest of the Gentile ekklesia. Eusebius describes a visit of Polycarp to Rome in the 150s, where the Asian bishop and the Bishop of Rome discussed the matter and agreed to disagree (5.24.15–17). However, at some point in the following decades an annual celebration of Yeshua's resurrection did develop in the Gentile ekklesia outside Asia Minor, and this celebration took place on a Sunday. According to Stephen Wilson, "the Gentile bishops devised Easter Sunday as an alternative to the Quartodeciman festival in the aftermath of the Bar Cochba rebellion."[37] Thus, in the midst of widespread anti-Jewish sentiment, the Quartodeciman practice suddenly became a matter of controversy.

The tensions reached a fever pitch in the 190s, when Bishop Victor of Rome attempted to excommunicate the congregations of the province of Asia for their observance of the fourteenth of Nisan. This action stirred much protest, even from authorities that shared Roman practice. Thus Irenaeus wrote a letter rebuking Victor for his action.[38] It is not clear how Victor responded to the protests. It is clear that Victor's initiative did not put an end to Quartodeciman practice.

This is evident from the decision of the Nicene Council in 325. This council of bishops officially embraced the position that Victor had advocated 130 years before, outlawing Quartodeciman observance. Of course, they would not have even taken up the question if such observance had ceased. An official synodal letter from the Council announces their decision:

> We further proclaim to you the good news of the agreement concerning the holy Easter, that this particular also has through your prayers been rightly settled; so that all our brethren in the East who formerly followed the custom of the Jews are henceforth to celebrate the said most sacred feast of Easter at the same time with the Romans and yourselves and all those who have observed Easter from the beginning.[39]

36. Wilson argues persuasively for this position (*Related Strangers*, 235–41). J. N. D. Kelly agrees, at least in the case of Rome. *The Oxford Dictionary of Popes* (Oxford: Oxford University Press, 1986), 10–11.

37. Wilson, *Related Strangers*, 238. For other explanations, see Kenneth A. Strand, "John as Quartodeciman: A Reappraisal," *Journal of Biblical Literature* 84 (1965): 251–58; Roger T. Beckwith, "The Origin of the Festivals Easter and Whitsun," *Studia Liturgica* 13 (1979): 1–20.

38. Eusebius, *Ecclesiastical History* 5.24.10–18.

39. *Nicene and Post-Nicene Fathers of the Christian Church,* second series, vol. 14, *The Seven Ecumenical Councils,* ed. Philip Schaff and Henry Wace (Grand Rapids: Eerdmans, 1983), 54.

The concern of the council is not just with obtaining uniformity of practice in the celebration of Yeshua's death and resurrection. Above all, they seek to end a situation where Christians follow "the custom of the Jews." That this was the primary intent becomes even clearer in the letter written by the Emperor Constantine announcing the results of the Council:

> It was declared to be particularly unworthy for this, the holiest of all festivals, to follow the custom [the calculation] of the Jews, who had soiled their hands with the most fearful of crimes, and whose minds were blinded. In rejecting their custom, we may transmit to our descendants the legitimate mode of celebrating Easter, which we have observed from the time of the Saviour's Passion to the present day [according to the day of the week]. We ought not, therefore, to have anything in common with the Jews, for the Saviour has shown us another way; our worship follows a more legitimate and more convenient course (the order of the days of the week); and consequently, in unanimously adopting this mode, we desire, dearest brethren, to separate ourselves from the detestable company of the Jews, for it is truly shameful for us to hear them boast that without their direction we could not keep the feast . . . it would still be your duty not to tarnish your soul by communications with such wicked people [the Jews].[40]

Constantine's language is almost embarrassingly direct. The Council acted to effect separation between Christians and Jews, and in particular to end a situation where a segment of the Christian community relied upon decisions of the Jewish community for liturgical direction.

Even the authoritative action of the Nicene Council was unable to effect such a separation in a final and definitive manner. This is demonstrated by the virulent sermons of John Chrysostom in Antioch near the end of the fourth century and by the canons of later councils.[41] The bonds tying the ekklesia to the Jewish people were so strong that they continued to resist utter dissolution, even in the face of the decrees of popes, councils, and emperors.

After Constantine: The Prohibition of Jewish Practice for Jewish Yeshua-Believers

The Quartodeciman controversy reveals the struggle of the Gentile ekklesia to break free from Jewish practice and influence. It has, however, taken us be-

---

40. Ibid.

41. See The Fathers of the Church, vol. 68, Saint John Chrysostom—Discourses Against Judaizing Christians, trans. Paul W. Harkins (Washington, DC: Catholic University of America Press, 1977). On later conciliar canons, see Canons 37–38 from the Council of Laodicea in 360 and Canon 40 from the Council of Agde (France) in 506.

yond our primary object of concern, which is the validity or invalidity of Jewish practice for Jewish Yeshua-believers. On this matter, second-century writings reveal a broad consensus within the Gentile ekklesia. All authorities agree that such practice is unnecessary. All authorities agree that it is also unwise and to be discouraged. However, beyond this broad consensus, disagreement emerges. Some Gentile Christian leaders (such as Justin) think that Jewish Yeshua-believers who remain observant Jews should be accepted as legitimate members of the ekklesia, provided they do not proselytize for Judaism among Gentile Yeshua-believers. Others think that Jewish practice excludes these Jews from the ekklesia. For them, Jewish practice—even for Jews—is utterly incompatible with Yeshua-faith.

By the end of the fourth century it is clear that the less tolerant view has prevailed, at least among church authorities. We can see this new consensus, and also how it copes with the New Testament material that appears to point in a different direction, by studying a remarkable exchange of letters between Augustine and Jerome.[42] Augustine wrote to Jerome to express concern about Jerome's views on the book of Galatians. Jerome held that Paul's rebuke of Peter in Galatians 2 was feigned, whereas Augustine insisted that it was genuine. As the debate developed, the main topic soon became whether the early Jewish Yeshua-believers truly maintained Jewish practice and, if so, why.[43]

Augustine's second letter insists that even Paul continued to live as an observant Jew.

> He [Paul] was, after all, a Jew, but having become a Christian, he had not abandoned the sacraments of the Jews, which that people had suitably and legitimately received at the time when they were necessary.[44]

It was appropriate for Jewish Yeshua-believers in that generation to observe Jewish customs, but only if they "no longer place the hope of salvation in them," and only if they accept "that they should in no way be imposed upon the Gentiles."[45] These are the same qualifications found in Justin's acceptance of second-century

---

42. In 394 or 395 Augustine wrote a letter to Jerome criticizing some of Jerome's writings on the book of Galatians. Receiving no reply, he wrote a second letter on this topic in 397. A full response does not come from Jerome until 404. In this letter, Jerome finally defends his views and attacks those of Augustine. In 405 Augustine replies to Jerome, answering the latter's attacks and clarifying his own position.

43. A new English translation of these letters is available in *The Works of Saint Augustine: Letters 1–99*, trans. Roland Teske, S.J. (Hyde Park, NY: New City, 2001). All quotations included here are from this translation. For recent discussion of this letter exchange, see the references in Shaye J. D. Cohen, *The Beginnings of Jewishness* (Berkeley: University of California Press, 1999), 368, n. 13.

44. Letter 40 in *Works of St. Augustine*, 149.

45. Ibid., 149–50.

Jewish Yeshua-believers. Like Justin, Augustine recognizes that these Jewish practices were "now superfluous," but he sees them as causing no damage to those in that generation who were observant "because of the habit of celebrating them."

Jerome responds to Augustine's exegesis by misrepresenting it. His summary of Augustine's view is actually what we presented in chapter 2 as the New Testament teaching on the topic: the Gentile Yeshua-believers were "free from the burden of the law," but the Jewish Yeshua-believers were obligated to obey it.[46]

> The sense of your whole discourse . . . is that Peter did not make a mistake insofar as he thought that those who came to believe from the Jews should observe the law, but that he deviated from the right path because he forced the Gentiles to live like Jews.[47]

As we have seen, this was not Augustine's view. He had only stated that it was permissible and even appropriate for the first generation of Jewish Yeshua-believers to observe Jewish practice. He had not said that they were obligated to do so. Furthermore, Jerome accuses Augustine of implying that what was true in that first generation remained the case in the generations that followed.

> This is the essence of the question, in fact of your view, namely, that after the coming of the gospel of Christ Jewish believers act correctly if they observe the commandments of the law, that is, if they offer the sacrifices that Paul offered, if they circumcise their sons, if they keep the Sabbath, as Paul with Timothy and all the Jews have observed them. If this is true, we slip into the heresy of Cerinthus and of Ebion; though they believed in Christ, they were condemned by our fathers for the sole reason that they mixed the ceremonies of the law with the gospel of Christ and professed the new teaching without giving up the old. . . . Up to the present there exists among the Jews in all the synagogues of the East a heresy that is called the heresy of the Minaei, and it is condemned by the Pharisees up to the present. They are commonly called Nazareans; they believe that Christ, the son of God, was born of the Virgin Mary, and they say that he is the one who suffered under Pontius Pilate and rose, in whom we also believe. But insofar as they want to be both Jews and Christians, they are neither Jews nor Christians. . . . But if the necessity is imposed upon us to accept the Jews with their legal observances and if it will be permissible for them to observe in the churches of Christ what they practiced in the synagogues of Satan—I am going to say what I think—they will not become Christians, but will make us Jews.[48]

46. Letter 75 in *Works of St. Augustine*, 284.
47. Ibid., 288.
48. Ibid., 288–89.

Jerome assumes that the position of Augustine inevitably leads to an endorsement or at least toleration of the party of the Nazarenes, the small Jewish Yeshua-believing community of his own day. Justin had been willing to offer such toleration in the second century, but for Jerome this was impossible. In his oft-quoted words, the Nazarenes "want to be both Jews and Christians," but in reality they "are neither Jews nor Christians." Jerome challenges Augustine to realize the implications of his exegesis, for in fact he knows that Augustine could never condone or tolerate the Nazarene approach:

> Again I say, "You are a bishop, a teacher of the churches of Christ; prove that what you say is true. Take one of the Jews who, after having become Christian, has his newly born circumcised, who observes the Sabbath, who abstains from *foods that God created to be used with thanksgiving* (1 Tm. 4:3), who sacrifices a lamb in the evening on the fourteenth day of the first month. When you do this, or rather when you do not do this—for I know that you are a Christian and will not do something sacrilegious—whether you want to or not, you will condemn your view.[49]

Jerome's argument is instructive. He assumes that if he can show that Augustine's exegesis leads to condoning or tolerating the Nazarene approach to Jewish identity and practice, he has succeeded in undermining that exegesis.

How does Jerome interpret the Jewish practice of the apostles and their followers? He contends that Peter and Paul only "pretended to observe the commandments of the law."[50] They did so in order to make it easier for Jews to believe in Yeshua. They were thus adopting an evangelistic and pastoral tactic, in giving the appearance of living according to Jewish practice. In reality, they believed "that the law was not to be observed after the coming of the gospel," and that "the ceremonies of the Jews are dangerous and deadly for Christians . . . whether from the Jews or from the Gentiles."[51]

Augustine replies by clarifying his own interpretation, and distinguishing his views from the caricature that Jerome has sketched. The reason it was appropriate for even Paul to live according to Jewish practice was "so that he would not be thought to condemn, like the idolatry of the Gentiles, those rites that God had commanded in the earlier times, as was fitting, to foreshadow things to come."[52] While the first generation of Jewish Yeshua-believers was permitted to observe Jewish customs, Augustine now makes clear that "Christian teaching

49. Ibid., 291.
50. Ibid., 288.
51. Ibid., 285, 289.
52. Letter 82 in *Works of St. Augustine*, 318.

would not now force them to do so."[53] Furthermore, this permission extended only to that first generation.

> Later, bit by bit and little by little, the preaching of the grace of Christ, of course, grew more widespread. . . . Thus, with the calling of those Jews at the time of the presence of the Lord in the flesh and during the apostolic times, all that observance of the symbols would be brought to an end. . . . Thus I believe, however, that the apostle Paul truthfully observed all those practices, and I do not, nonetheless, force or allow a Jew who has become a Christian to practice those rites in a sincere manner, just as you, who thought that Paul practiced them as a pretense, do not force or allow such a person to pretend to practice them.[54]

Jerome's assumption was correct. Augustine agrees with him (and not with Justin) in thinking that the Nazarene approach is *now* totally unacceptable. In order to explain how he can think it proper for Peter and Paul to have lived as Jews and yet condemn the contemporary Nazarenes for doing the same, Augustine employs a vivid metaphor.

> For, when the faith had come that was foretold earlier by those observances . . . they lost the life, as it were, of their function. And yet, like dead bodies of parents, they had to be carried as if to their burial, not as a pretense, but with respect, but were not to be immediately abandoned or thrown to the abuse of their enemies, as if to the teeth of dogs. Hence, any Christian of the present time, even though formerly a Jew, who wants to observe them in a like manner, as if disturbing ashes already at rest, will not be devoutly accompanying or carrying the body, but wickedly violating its burial.[55]

Judaism is like an honored parent who has died. The Jewish practice of the first generation of Yeshua-believers was a way of expressing genuine respect and appreciation for that deceased parent. However, for a later generation to live in this way would be tantamount to desecrating the parent's bones.

Augustine teaches in the tradition of Irenaeus. Like that pioneering theologian, he shows great respect for the Jewish "sacraments" of the law, and displays none of the contempt for literal Jewish observance seen in the earlier writers of the second century. Like Irenaeus, Augustine also acknowledges the Jewish observance of Yeshua and his Jewish followers, but sees that observance as valid only for the first generation. Irenaeus appears to see the destruction of the

53. Ibid., 320.
54. Ibid., 322–23.
55. Ibid., 323.

temple as the decisive turning point, after which Jewish observance is no longer appropriate. Augustine is vague about the precise timing of the transition, but it seems to correspond roughly with 70 CE. Augustine's theological position thus benefits from the achievement of Irenaeus. However, his exegesis is far more thorough and penetrating than that of Irenaeus, and therefore his views as expressed in these letters become the classic statement of Christian theology on the topic of Jewish practice in the New Covenant.[56]

That this is the case is seen by the use made of these letters by Thomas Aquinas in his treatment of the topic in the *Summa* (Ia Iiae Q 103 Article 4). As usual, Aquinas articulates the issue at hand clearly and succinctly: "Whether since Christ's Passion the legal ceremonies [of the Mosaic law] can be observed without committing mortal sin?"[57] Employing the technical language of the medieval church, Aquinas raises the same question that Trypho posed to Justin. The answer he gives reflects the consensus of the Gentile ekklesia from the fourth century to his own:

> Just as it would be a mortal sin now for anyone, in making a profession of faith, to say that Christ is yet to be born, which the fathers of old said devoutly and truthfully; so too it would be a mortal sin now to observe those ceremonies which the fathers of old fulfilled with devotion and fidelity.[58]

Like Irenaeus and Augustine (whom Aquinas here quotes as a supporting authority), Aquinas seeks to combine reverence for the ceremonies of the Mosaic law with the firm conviction that their observance is no longer valid.[59] He does this by comparing Jewish observance to biblical prophecy. Like prophecy, Jewish observance points forward to the coming of the Messiah. Once the Messiah has come, Messianic prophecy can be remembered, but it cannot be restated in the future tense. Similarly, Jewish observance can be remembered, but it cannot be relived.

56. For an excellent overview of the development of Augustine's thinking regarding the Jewish people and Judaism, see Jeremy Cohen, *Living Letters of the Law* (Berkeley: University of California Press, 1999), 19–71.

57. All citations from Thomas are from *Summa Theologica*, vol. 2 (Westminster, MD: Christian Classics, 1981), 1086–87.

58. To support this statement, Aquinas cites Augustine: "Such is the teaching of Augustine (Contra Faust. xix. 16), who says, It is no longer promised that He shall be born, shall suffer and rise again, truths of which their sacraments were a kind of image: but it is declared that He is already born, has suffered and risen again; of which our sacraments, in which Christians share, are the actual representation."

59. Cohen argues that Augustine's later writings acknowledge the ongoing importance of literal Jewish Torah observance (outside, of course, the ekklesia). In contrast, Cohen contends that Aquinas sees all such observance as improper. *Living Letters,* 39, 364–89.

Before proceeding further, we should listen to the questions that Wyschogrod puts to Thomas in response to this comparison between prophecy and observance:

> For even if there is, from the point of view of Christian faith, a large element of prefigurement of Christ in the Old Testament, does it have to follow that someone who refrains from eating pork or who fasts on the Day of Atonement is committing a mortal sin? Must his actions be interpreted as saying that "Christ was to be born" (103, 4 Reply) rather than that he had been born, thereby denying Christ? Could adherence to the Mosaic Law not be interpreted much more benevolently, as love of God and his commandments, as fidelity to a holy way of life out of which—for Christian faith—the Redeemer was born? If the commandments before Christ predicted him, could they not after Christ celebrate the prediction that came true and point to the final fulfillment that both Jews and Christians await? In short, the argument that the Mosaic commandments predict Christ and that to adhere to them after Christ is a mortal sin because one is denying that he has come by so doing is a rather thin reed on which to hang the case for the ceremonial commandments turning into mortal sin after Christ. It is almost as if Thomas starts with that conviction and then looks around for some justification of it which he achieves by the ingenious argument of the prediction that turns into a denial.[60]

Wyschogrod's final statement is to the point. Both Thomas and Augustine (the patristic source of the "ingenious argument") begin with their conclusion, which is for them an incontrovertible article of ecclesiastical tradition, and then work backward. They struggle to find theological justification for an established teaching that is difficult to defend.

The most formidable argument against this established teaching is the one raised in the letter exchange between Augustine and Jerome. Aquinas gives it pride of place as "Objection 1":

> It would seem that since Christ's Passion the legal ceremonies can be observed without committing mortal sin. For we must not believe that the apostles committed mortal sin after receiving the Holy Ghost. . . . But the apostles observed the legal ceremonies after the coming of the Holy Ghost.

In response, Aquinas summarizes skillfully the positions taken by Jerome and Augustine in their letters.

---

60. Michael Wyschogrod, "A Jewish Reading of St. Thomas Aquinas on the Old Law," in *Understanding Scripture,* ed. Clemens Thoma and Michael Wyschogrod (New York: Paulist, 1987), 136.

Jerome distinguished two periods of time. One was the time previous to Christ's Passion, during which the legal ceremonies were neither dead, since they were obligatory, and did expiate in their own fashion; nor deadly, because it was not sinful to observe them. But immediately after Christ's Passion they began to be not only dead, so as no longer to be either effectual or binding; but also deadly, so that whoever observed them was guilty of mortal sin. Hence he maintained that after the Passion the apostles never observed the legal ceremonies in real earnest; but only by a kind of pious pretense, lest, to wit, they should scandalize the Jews and hinder their conversion. . . .

Augustine more fittingly distinguished three periods of time. One was the time that preceded the Passion of Christ, during which the legal ceremonies were neither deadly nor dead: another period was after the publication of the Gospel, during which the legal ceremonies are both dead and deadly. The third is a middle period, viz., from the Passion of Christ until the publication of the Gospel, during which the legal ceremonies were dead indeed, because they had neither effect nor binding force; but were not deadly, because it was lawful for the Jewish converts to Christianity to observe them, provided they did not put their trust in them so as to hold them to be necessary to salvation, as though faith in Christ could not justify without the legal observances. On the other hand, there was no reason why those who were converted from heathendom to Christianity should observe them.

Aquinas accepts Augustine's threefold chronological scheme rather than the twofold pattern of Jerome. This allows the interpreter to take seriously the evidence from the Acts of the Apostles and the Pauline letters, and yet also to affirm the unequivocal supersessionist theological and canonical legacy of the Gentile ekklesia.

Augustine's explanation, summarized well by Aquinas, became classic because it was the best that could be offered. Nevertheless, like the comparison between Jewish practice and Messianic prophecy, it will only persuade those who are already committed to the conclusion on other grounds. As we have seen in chapter 2, there is no basis in the New Testament for viewing the apostolic period of Jewish observance as a transitional phase in the life of the ekklesia. In the book of Acts there is no gradual diminution in dedication to a Jewish way of life within the ekklesia of the circumcision. Such dedication is visible from beginning to end. The New Testament presents bilateral ecclesiology in solidarity with Israel as normative, and no temporal limit is stated or implied. Only a preexisting theological commitment to supersessionism could lead one to be satisfied with the explanation of the relevant biblical texts offered by Augustine and accepted by Aquinas.

As we have already seen, Jerome and Augustine agree on the basic point at issue: in the language of Aquinas, it is a "mortal sin" for Jewish Yeshua-believers to live as Jews. They only disagree on how to explain the New Testament data that seem to teach otherwise. We cannot hold Jerome, Augustine, or Aquinas responsible for creating the Christian consensus on this topic. It existed before any of them picked up a pen. They are all interpreting an authoritative ecclesiastical tradition whose roots go back to the early second century. This tradition became an official part of the canonical heritage of the Gentile ekklesia at the second council of Nicea in 787. Canon 8 of the decisions of this council (which is considered the last of the seven ecumenical councils) states the following:

> Since certain, erring in the superstitions of the Hebrews, have thought to mock at Christ our God, and feigning to be converted to the religion of Christ do deny him, and in private and secretly keep the Sabbath and observe other Jewish customs, we decree that such persons be not received to communion, nor to prayers, nor into the Church; but let them be openly Hebrews according to their religion, and let them not bring their children to baptism, nor purchase or possess a slave. But if any of them, out of a sincere heart and in faith, is converted and makes profession with his whole heart, setting at naught their customs and observances, and so that others may be convinced and converted, such an one is to be received and baptized, and his children likewise; and let them be taught to take care to hold aloof from the ordinances of the Hebrews. But if they will not do this, let them in no wise be received.[61]

For a Jew to "keep the Sabbath and observe other Jewish customs" is to "mock at" and "deny" the Jewish Messiah. Such people are to be excommunicated. Only those Jews willing to "set at naught" Jewish "customs and observances" are to be accepted as fitting candidates for baptism.

The eventual consensus position of the Gentile ekklesia makes Justin look like a paragon of toleration. This is a church that has no place for Judaism and no place for Jews. It has retained the Jewish Bible and believed in the Jewish Messiah, but it has said no to the Jewish people and its ancestral way of life.

---

61. *Nicene and Post-Nicene Fathers,* vol. 14, 561. This canon was institutionalized through a vow taken by Jewish candidates for baptism, by which they solemnly renounced Jewish practice. For a sampling of such baptismal vows, see James Parkes, *The Conflict of the Church and the Synagogue* (Jewish Publication Society, 1934: repr. New York: Atheneum, 1981), 394–400.

Supersessionism, Jewish Practice, and the Primal Schism

The traditional Christian consensus regarding Jewish practice fits well with the theological and pastoral perspective of a supersessionist church. In a church which does not value the continuing existence of the Jewish people (other than as a historical sign of God's curse on disobedience or as a character in the future eschatological drama), Jewish practice and Jewish identity have no positive significance. Once again, Wyschogrod sees the picture clearly:

> In fact, throughout the centuries, Jews who entered the Church very quickly lost their Jewish identity. Within several generations they intermarried and the Jewish traces disappeared. . . . In short, if all Jews in past ages had followed the advice of the Church to become Christians, there would be no more Jews in the world today.[62]

The question is: What are the theological and pastoral implications of renouncing supersessionism? Does it not require a reconsideration of the traditional consensus regarding Jewish practice? Wyschogrod states the question baldly:

> Does the Church really want a world without Jews? Does the Church believe that such a world is in accordance with the will of God? Or does the Church believe that it is God's will, even after the coming of Jesus, that there be a Jewish people in the world? . . . If, from the Christian point of view, Israel's election remains a contemporary reality, then the disappearance of the Jewish people from the world cannot be an acceptable development. Closely related to the survival of the Jewish people is the question of the Mosaic Law.[63]

Christians who now affirm the irrevocable nature of the covenant between God and Israel must rethink their approach to Jewish practice as rooted in the Torah—for all Jews, including Jewish Yeshua-believers. Once they have done so, they will then have to ask whether traditional ecclesiology, in which a Gentile church stands over against the Jewish people, must give way to a bilateral ecclesiology in solidarity with Israel.

Looking at the sad history surveyed in the present chapter, George Lindbeck argues that the ekklesia can claim to be (part of) Israel only if it contains within it "Torah-observant" Jews:

> As they became the great majority, gentile Christians increasingly looked askance at the continued Torah observance of their Jewish fellow believers. Ultimately the

---

62. Wyschogrod, "Letter to a Friend," 169.
63. Ibid.

few Jews within the church were canonically compelled to be non-practicing, that is, assimilated and in effect deprived of their Jewish identity. Completely forgotten was the need for Torah-observant Jewish participation in the church if it is to be truly Israel in the new age. Instead it was affirmed by universal practice . . . that the church can be Israel without Jews, and from there it is but a short step to the supersessionist absurdity condemning Christian Jews for Torah-observance, that is, for worshiping God as did Jesus and the apostles.[64]

In forbidding rather than requiring Torah observance from its Jewish members, the ekklesia annulled its right to claim continuity with biblical Israel. Its leaders may have thought they were striking a blow only against Judaism and the Jewish people, but in fact they were also wounding themselves by undermining their own ecclesiological identity.

Supersessionism and the crumbling of the ecclesiological bridge, i.e., the Jewish ekklesia, damaged the church in a profound way. But we must avoid the temptation to see church history in purely negative terms. The Gentile ekklesia preserved the essential message entrusted to it. It continued to proclaim Israel's risen Messiah. It rejected Marcionism and accepted the Jewish Bible as inspired, authoritative, and canonical. It collected the books of the New Testament and arranged them in a manner that further countered Marcionite anti-Judaism. The most virulent forms of anti-Jewish teaching in the second century did not carry the day but were moderated by Irenaeus and later by Augustine. The church faithfully preserved and carried within it the truths that would allow it eventually to reexamine its history and recognize supersessionism as an error demanding correction.

At the same time, the triumph of supersessionism and the crumbling of the ecclesiological bridge produced a schism in the heart of the people of God. Ultimately the schism was between the multinational ekklesia and the Jewish people. However, this basic schism was precipitated by an internal schism *within* the Messianic ekklesia—between the Gentile ekklesia and its Jewish counterpart, whose role was to bridge the gap between Israel and the Yeshua-believing Gentile community. As Dunn notes, "The parting of the ways was more between mainstream Christianity and Jewish Christianity than simply between Christianity as a single whole and rabbinic Judaism."[65]

Those committed to ecumenical healing and reconciliation often overlook this primal schism. Thomas Torrance rightly claims that the separation and enmity between Jews and Christians "still constitutes the deepest ecumenical problem for the whole Christian Church."[66] He believes that all other ecclesial divisions are secondary, and their healing depends on the healing of this original rift:

64. Lindbeck, "The Church as Israel," 83–84.
65. Dunn, *The Partings of the Ways*, 239.
66. Thomas F. Torrance, *Theology in Reconciliation* (London: Geoffrey Chapman, 1975), 27.

> The deepest schism in the one People of God is the schism between the Christian and the Jewish Church, not that between East and West or Roman and Protestant Christianity. The bitter separation between the Catholic Church and the Synagogue that set in after the Bar Cochba revolt in the second century after Christ was one of the greatest tragedies in the whole of our history, not only for the people of God but for all western civilization. . . . Only with the healing of that split in a deep-going reconciliation will all the other divisions with which we struggle in the ecumenical movement finally be overcome.[67]

The preacher of the papal household of Pope John Paul II, Raniero Cantalamessa, employs the same language as Torrance, seeing the Messianic Jewish movement as a reminder of the primal schism and a sign that it can be overcome:

> Quite a few in the Jewish religion have started to acknowledge Jesus as "the glory of Israel." They openly acknowledge Jesus as the Messiah and call themselves "Messianic Jews." . . . These help us to overcome certain gloomy prospects of ours, making us realize that the great original schism afflicting the Church and impoverishing it is not so much the schism between East and West or between Catholics and Protestants, as the more radical one between the Church and Israel.[68]

Cantalamessa is not envisioning here a mere conversion of Israel. He realizes that the schism originates in both parties and requires change in both parties.

> We are not saying this in a spirit of proselytism but in a spirit of conversion and obedience to the Word of God because it is certain that the rejoining of Israel with the Church will involve a rearrangement in the Church; it will mean a conversion on both sides. It will also be a rejoining of the Church with Israel.[69]

It is striking to hear these words from an eminent Roman Catholic. The healing of the church requires its reunion with Israel. The reunion with Israel requires the Jewish ekklesia. And the Jewish ekklesia will emerge again as a constructive ecumenical force only when the Gentile ekklesia addresses and reverses its past teaching regarding Jewish identity and practice within the twofold community of the Messiah.

---

67. Thomas F. Torrance, "The divine vocation and destiny of Israel in world history" in *The Witness of the Jews to God,* ed. David W. Torrance (Edinburgh: Handsel, 1982), 92. Torrance contends that "schism between Christians and Jews is the deepest schism and the root cause of all other schism in the one People of God" (87).

68. Fr. Raniero Cantalamessa, *The Mystery of Christmas* (Sydney: St. Paul's Publications, 1988), 101.

69. Ibid.

6

JEWISH TRADITION
AND THE CHRISTOLOGICAL TEST

I n our last chapter we examined the church's no to the Jewish people and the Jewish way of life, expressed in its rejection of both the Jewish ekklesia and solidarity with the Jewish people as a whole. We argued that this no helped precipitate a schism within the people of God, and we assessed the damage inflicted on the church's own life through this schism. Of course, every schism involves two parties, and both sides inevitably contribute to the rift. Therefore in this chapter we will look at the other side of the split—the apparent Jewish no to Yeshua, expressed in its rejection of both the Jewish ekklesia and the Yeshua movement as a whole. Our aim will be to answer one crucial question: how should Yeshua-believers assess the Jewish religious tradition of the past nineteen centuries?

It is important to add the word "apparent" to the phrase "the Jewish no to Yeshua." John Howard Yoder has argued that neither the Jewish people as a whole nor Judaism as a religion ever "rejected Jesus."[1] If Yoder is right, why do

---

1. John Howard Yoder, *The Jewish-Christian Schism Revisited,* ed. Michael G. Cartwright and Peter Ochs (Grand Rapids: Eerdmans, 2003), 51–61, 76–77. He bases his argument on the judgment, accepted by an increasing number of historians, that the definitive division between "Judaism" and "Christianity" did not occur before the Bar Kochba revolt (135 CE), and perhaps not till Constantine. By the time the Jewish people and Judaism offered an unequivocal communal rejection of "Christianity," the "Christ" to whom it said no was thoroughly dejudaized. This last point was articulated already in the 1930s by James Parkes: "And they [the early Jewish ekklesia]

Paul (in Romans 9–11) and the book of Acts, while acknowledging a sizable and influential body of Jewish Yeshua-believers, seem to imply a general rejection of Yeshua by the wider Jewish community? The answer may be related to their conviction that a generalized communal acceptance of Yeshua by the Jewish people was necessary for Israel's redemption and the world's consummation. In light of the stakes, they may have interpreted the lack of such acceptance as de facto rejection. In this chapter we will speak of an apparent Jewish no to Yeshua. Such careful language allows us to take seriously what most Jews in the world for the past fifteen centuries have thought about their own response to "Jesus," without uncritically absorbing the traditional Christian interpretation of that response.

We concluded in the last chapter that the church's no to the Jewish people and to Judaism wounded the church, but it did not nullify its identity or vocation, nor did it utterly corrupt its message. Thus we can and should appreciate the theological riches in the writings of Irenaeus, Athanasius, and Augustine; the heroism of the church's martyrs; and the charity and humility of her saints. We can and should gratefully recognize the church's preservation of the good news in the reception and transmission of the New Testament canon and in the formulation of the early creeds. We can and should esteem highly the tradition of worship embodied in the liturgies of the church and her dedication to the task of proclaiming the reign of the God of Israel to the nations of the world.

If the church's *actual* no to the Jewish people and to Judaism does not vitiate the richness of Christian tradition, then the Jewish people's *apparent* no to Yeshua need not vitiate the richness of Jewish tradition. This tentative conclusion runs counter to a view still prevalent in some circles of the Christian world. According to this view, the Jewish people may retain covenantal status, but the religious tradition of rabbinic Judaism is invalidated by its rejection of Yeshua.[2] However, once we acknowledge the continuing obligation of Yeshua-believing Jews to live according to Jewish practice, and the Gentile ekklesia's devaluation of this obligation through much of its history, the corresponding Christian devaluation of rabbinic Judaism as a religion that promotes Jewish

---

on their side might well say—paradoxical as it may appear to us now—that the Gentile Church by its attitude made the acceptance of the Messianic claims of Jesus impossible to the Jew; and that the perpetual statement of the Gentile leaders that the Jews continued to reject Christ was fundamentally untrue, because they were being offered Him only upon conditions which were false and impossible for a loyal Jew to accept—in other words, an attitude to the whole of Jewish history and the Law which was based upon Gentile ignorance and misunderstanding, and was quite unsupported by the conduct of Jesus Himself." James Parkes, *The Conflict of the Church and the Synagogue* (New York: Atheneum, 1969; originally published in 1934), 93.

2. As we will see in chapter 8, such a view has sometimes been expressed in both the Hebrew Christian and Messianic Jewish movements.

practice is called into question. If we are facing a schism within the people of God rather than an unfaithful, apostate Judaism that has fallen away from a faithful, orthodox Christianity, we must be open to the possibility that we gain access to the fullness of the divine purpose only when we appreciate the riches of both traditions. Each tradition might complement the other.

The conclusions we have already reached in this book suggest that this is likely the case. The New Testament affirms the irrevocable covenant with Israel and likewise affirms Jewish practice—rooted in the Torah—as a sign of that enduring covenant and as a means of preserving Israel's distinct covenantal existence in the world. In other words, the New Testament affirms the validity of what we would today call Judaism. A particular type of Judaism emerged in the early centuries of the common era—rabbinic Judaism—and won the adherence of the Jewish people as a whole. This particular expression of Judaism—and only this particular expression of Judaism—succeeded in preserving both the Jewish people and its covenantal way of life. Its crucial role in what is evidently a divinely appointed task points to its inherent value.

Moreover, while numerous rival Jewish religious movements vie with one another in the twenty-first century, all claim some measure of continuity with rabbinic Judaism. One cannot build a contemporary Judaism exclusively on either the Bible or modern (or postmodern) sensibility. Without some connection to the historical experience of the Jewish people, Judaism evaporates into thin air. As Peter Ochs states,

> there is, in one sense, no other Judaism for Jews than that which comes by way of Rabbinic Judaism, or the Judaism of *Mishnah*, Talmud, synagogue, prayer book, and Torah study that emerged after, in spite of, and in response to the loss of the Second Temple. All of the new Judaisms that have appeared since have appeared from out of and in terms of this Rabbinic Judaism.[3]

Judaism is not a religious artifact from biblical times but a dynamic way of life embodied in and transmitted by a living community. The abstract affirmation of Judaism has no meaning unless it is expressed as a practical affirmation of the actual religious tradition of the Jewish people. If one denies the legitimacy of historical Judaism, one in effect asserts that the divine purpose for the Jewish people found in the New Testament has been definitively thwarted. The theological problems raised by this conclusion should make us wary of the premise from which it is inferred.

---

3. Peter Ochs in Yoder, *Jewish-Christian Schism Revisited*, 3.

Bruce Marshall argues a similar case. He begins from the conviction—shared widely today among the churches—that Israel's covenantal election is permanent. He infers from this that the distinction between Jew and Gentile is likewise permanent.

> The permanent election of Israel seems to require that the identifiable existence of the Jewish people also be permanent. . . . The permanence of Israel's election thus entails the permanence of the distinction between Jew and Gentile.[4]

He proceeds to ask a crucial question: "How then is the distinct identity of the Jews, and so Israel's election, to be maintained?" His answer confirms what we have already concluded regarding Jewish practice, and extends that conclusion further:

> The obvious answer is by Jewish observance of the full range of traditional Jewish law (halachah, which embraces both the written and oral Torah, that is, both biblical and rabbinic law . . .). This observance, in which the Gentiles will surely have no interest and to which God's electing will does not obligate them, will be the chief means by which Abraham's descendants can be identified, and indeed will keep the Gentiles at a certain distance, thus ensuring that Abraham's children do not, through intermarriage, vanish into the sea of nations. The ancient and distinctive responsibilities of the Jewish people towards God are, as it were, the mark of Israel's primordial and permanent election which remains post Christum.[5]

Marshall summarizes his argument succinctly:

> The Jewish people cannot be permanently elect unless they can be distinguished at all times from the nations, and the observance of traditional Jewish law seems to be the one mark by which this distinction can be sustained post Christum.[6]

Marshall's reasoning is simple, clear, and compelling. If we recognize its force, we will be disposed to affirm the legitimacy of Jewish religious tradition, even before examining its substance or its stand in relation to Yeshua.

---

4. Bruce D. Marshall, "Christ and the Cultures: The Jewish People and Christian Theology," in *The Cambridge Companion to Christian Doctrine,* ed. Colin E. Gunton (Cambridge: Cambridge University Press, 1997), 91.

5. Ibid., 91–92.

6. Ibid., 92. For a similar viewpoint, see Robert W. Jenson, "Toward a Christian Theology of Judaism," in *Jews and Christians,* ed. Carl E. Braaten and Robert W. Jenson (Grand Rapids: Eerdmans, 2003), 9–11.

However, contemporary Yeshua-believers—whether Gentile or Jewish—will never wholeheartedly acknowledge the legitimacy, value, and importance of Jewish religious tradition without such an examination. Those who embrace the faith taught by the apostles will be justifiably reluctant to acknowledge the legitimacy of a religion from which Yeshua, the incarnate Word, is absent. According to that faith, Yeshua functions as the universal mediator of creation, revelation, reconciliation, and redemption. He constitutes the permanent embodiment of the Divine Presence. Therefore, if Yeshua is present, God is present; if Yeshua is absent, God is absent.

This means that our argument for the legitimacy, value, and importance of Jewish religious tradition cannot persuasively assert that the Jewish people have a way to God that bypasses Yeshua.[7] Instead, we must be able to affirm that Yeshua abides in the midst of the Jewish people and its religious tradition, despite that tradition's apparent refusal to accept his claims. We must be able to conclude, with Bruce Marshall, that "there is at this point a divinely willed disharmony between the order of knowing and the order of being."[8]

In our view there are good biblical, historical, and theological reasons for reaching just this conclusion. Let us examine those reasons and assess their weight.

Yeshua as One-Man Israel

The New Testament employs many biblical images in its attempt to explore the meaning and significance of Yeshua. One of those images has special relevance to our topic of study: Yeshua as representative and individual embodiment of the entire people of Israel.[9]

This perspective on Yeshua is particularly prominent in the opening chapters of the Gospel of Matthew. The initial verses of the book present Yeshua not only

7. After proposing that the church should recognize the divine mandate underlying historical Judaism, Robert Jenson proceeds to assert that this recognition must have an ultimate christological basis: "Christian theology cannot . . . regard such proposals as true, unless they can be Christologically founded—unless, that is, their truth is upheld by the truth about who and what the risen Christ is." Jenson, "Christian Theology of Judaism," 11.

8. Marshall, "Christ and the Cultures," 90.

9. Will Herberg, a Jewish theologian, sees this concept as crucial for explaining how the Gentile members of the church are related to the Jewish people. He speaks of Yeshua as a "one-man Israel": "Christ appears in early Christian thinking as, quite literally, an incarnate or one-man Israel, the Remnant-Man." Fritz A. Rothschild, "General Introduction," in *Jewish Perspectives on Christianity*, ed. Fritz A. Rothschild (New York: Continuum, 1996), 244. In contrast to our treatment here, Herberg fails to see the implications of this concept for Yeshua's ongoing relationship to the Jewish people.

as the messianic "son of David" but also as the "son of Abraham," i.e., the one who like Isaac and Jacob embodies the whole people through all generations, and who transmits blessing to the nations of the earth.[10] This sets the stage for the next chapter, which informs us of King Herod's efforts to locate and destroy the newborn Messiah. To escape from Herod, Joseph and Mary take Yeshua to Egypt:

> Then Joseph got up, took the child and his mother by night, and went to Egypt, and remained there until the death of Herod. This was to fulfill what had been spoken by the Lord through the prophet, "Out of Egypt I have called my son." (2:14–15)

The text cited by Matthew (Hosea 11:1) is not a straightforward Messianic prophecy. Instead, the prophet speaks of Israel's filial relationship with God and about God's redemption of Israel from Egypt.[11] Matthew evidently sees Yeshua's filial relationship with God, and God's protection of Yeshua from an oppressive king, as expressing his identity as Israel's representative and individual embodiment.

In the next chapter Matthew describes the mission and message of John the Baptist. John summons Israel to repentance and baptism and announces the imminent arrival of one who "will baptize you with the Holy Spirit and fire" (Matthew 3:11). John baptizes in the Jordan River, perhaps as a way of associating his work with that of Moses and Joshua and with Israel's entry into the Promised Land. When Yeshua appears on the scene, John recognizes him as the one of whom he had been speaking. Therefore, John seeks to be baptized by him. Yeshua refuses and instead insists on being baptized by John, "to fulfill all righteousness" (Matthew 3:15). In this way Matthew portrays Yeshua's identification with the people of Israel and implies that he must first represent Israel in its repentance and obedience, and probably also in its suffering, before he can act as the effective agent of Israel's renewal.[12]

When Yeshua emerges from the Jordan, a voice from heaven is heard, saying, "This is my Son, the beloved, with whom I am well pleased" (Matthew 3:17). The reference to Yeshua as "my Son" recalls Matthew 2:15 and its use of Hosea 11:1. As Yeshua identifies with Israel and assumes his role as Israel's representative,

---

10. Thanks to Daniel Keating for pointing out to me the significance of Matthew's genealogy in this context.

11. "When Israel was a child, I loved him, and out of Egypt I called my son." Hosea 11:1.

12. The synoptic Gospels speak of Yeshua's suffering death as a "baptism" that he must undergo (Mark 10:38–39; Luke 12:49–50). In this light, his being baptized by John indicates his identification not only with Israel's sinful condition but also with the judgment that such a condition elicits.

God addresses him just as God addressed Israel. The additional phrase, "the beloved," probably alludes to Genesis 22:2, where Isaac is spoken of as Abraham's beloved. In this way the baptism of Yeshua is linked to the binding of Isaac and anticipates Yeshua's sacrificial death.[13] The allusion likewise associates Yeshua with Isaac as the individual embodiment of the seed promised to Abraham. Finally, the phrase "with whom I am well pleased" is drawn from Isaiah 42:1:

> Here is my servant, whom I uphold, my chosen, in whom my soul delights; I have put my spirit upon him; he will bring forth justice to the nations.

The baptismal theophany thus presents Yeshua as the servant of Isaiah. The previous chapter of Isaiah employs similar language but makes clear that the servant in question is Israel:

> But you, Israel, my servant, Jacob, whom I have chosen, the offspring of Abraham, my friend; you whom I took from the ends of the earth, and called from its farthest corners, saying to you, "You are my servant, I have chosen you and not cast you off." (41:8–9)

In summary, this one brief sentence, addressed to Yeshua from heaven, includes a condensed cluster of biblical allusions, all of which point to Yeshua as the representative and individual embodiment of the people of Israel.

Following his baptism, Yeshua goes into the wilderness for a period of forty days. He fasts and endures a set of tests by the devil. The forty days of testing in the wilderness recapitulate Israel's forty years of testing before entering the Promised Land. The devil's first two tests begin with the words, "If you are the Son of God" (Matthew 4:3, 6). Thus the tempter challenges Yeshua to prove the truth of the words of the baptismal theophany, which had confirmed Yeshua's role as Israel's representative. Yeshua responds to all three of the devil's challenges by citing verses from Deuteronomy (6:13; 6:16; 8:3) that summon Israel to obedience and faith. The context of Deuteronomy 8:3 deserves particular attention:

> Remember the long way that the LORD your God has led you these forty years in the wilderness, in order to humble you, testing you to know what was in your heart, whether or not you would keep his commandments. He humbled you by letting you hunger, then by feeding you with manna, with which neither you

---

13. In Jewish tradition the binding of Isaac is seen as both exemplary of and including within itself the future martyrs of Israel. See Shalom Spiegel, *The Last Trial* (Woodstock, VT: Jewish Lights, 1993).

nor your ancestors were acquainted, in order to make you understand that one does not live by bread alone, but by every word that comes from the mouth of the LORD. The clothes on your back did not wear out and your feet did not swell these forty years. Know then in your heart that as a parent disciplines a child so the LORD your God disciplines you. (8:2–5)

Here the connection to Israel's forty years of testing in the wilderness is made explicit. The mention of God's parental concern for Israel in Deuteronomy 8:5 reinforces the view that Yeshua's identity as God's Son in Matthew 4 has the God-Israel relationship as its primary background. In striking fashion the temptation narrative brings to a climax the Gospel's introductory presentation of Yeshua as the representative and individual embodiment of Israel.

We have seen that Yeshua's identity as Son of God and servant of the Lord imply his role as one-man Israel.[14] This is also true of his identity as the Son of Man of Daniel 7. While New Testament scholars disagree about the intent of the historical Yeshua in calling himself the "Son of Man," it is clear that the Gospels see the term as an allusion to the heavenly figure of Daniel 7.[15] That figure represents Israel, "the holy ones of the Most High," particularly those who suffer as martyrs (Daniel 7:14, 18, 22, 27). It is likely that the Gospel writers remain fully conscious of the corporate significance of the term "Son of Man" in Daniel 7, and expect their readers to understand Yeshua in light of that usage. Thus Yeshua's suffering sums up and includes within itself all the suffering of Israel's martyrs, who are themselves but the priestly representatives of the entire community; and his resurrection anticipates the vindication and glorification of God's covenant people.[16]

N. T. Wright has argued that this view of Yeshua as the representative and individual embodiment of Israel is central to the New Testament's theological vision. He sees this as fundamental to the Gospel genre itself:

What must therefore be said about the literary genre of the gospels, which is after all a principal key to how they are to be read? As we have seen, they tell the story of Jesus in such a way as to convey the belief that this story is the climax of Israel's story. They therefore have the *form* of the story of Israel, now reworked in terms of a single human life. Since, then, Israel's story has been embodied in one man, the gospels have also the form of what we must call quasi-biography.

14. For the view that the earliest use of the term "Son of God" as applied to Yeshua included an allusion to Israel's corporate filial relationship to God, see Richard N. Longenecker, *The Christology of Early Jewish Christianity* (Grand Rapids: Baker, 1981), 93–99.

15. In many cases the allusions to Daniel 7 are unmistakable (e.g., Mark 8:38; 13:26; Matthew 19:28; 25:31).

16. See Morna D. Hooker, *The Son of Man in Mark* (London: SPCK, 1967).

Modern study of ancient secular biography has shown, as we saw, that the gospels are *at least* biographies. But they are more than that. They are, in fact, Jewish-style biographies, designed to show the quintessence of Israel's story played out in a single life. . . . The gospels are therefore the story of Jesus *told as the history of Israel in miniature*: the 'typology' which is observed here and there by critics is simply a function of this larger purpose of the evangelists.[17]

As his final remark in the above paragraph implies, Wright also sees this perspective as fundamental to the claim of the early Yeshua movement that Yeshua's death and resurrection occurred "according to the scriptures":

That is why Paul and others keep insisting that Jesus' death and resurrection happened "according to the scriptures," or in fulfillment of them. People often write of such phrases . . . as if they meant that the early church could find proof-texts to show that Israel's god had predicted the resurrection long before. . . . As we saw, . . . however, the point of such ideas is that Israel's scriptures *as a whole* tell of the covenant; of the exile as the result of Israel's god punishing his people for their sins; and of the great "return" that will happen when that dark period is finally over and done. What the early church is saying, when telling the story of Jesus' resurrection and announcing it to the world as the summons to obedient faith, is that the history of, and promises to, Israel had come true in Jesus, that in his death he had taken the exile as far as it could go, and that in his resurrection he had inaugurated the real return from that real exile. Once again, therefore, we are driven to the conclusion: to announce the resurrection, and to do so (in shorthand) "according to the scriptures," is *to tell Israel's story in the form of Jesus' story.*[18]

Wright argues elsewhere that Paul's emphasis on Yeshua as the new Adam should be understood in light of Second Temple Jewish thinking, which presented Israel itself in that role. In reversing Adam's disobedience and its penalty of death, Yeshua demonstrates that he is the true representative and individual embodiment of the people of Israel.[19]

What does Yeshua's role as one-man Israel imply about his ongoing relationship to the Jewish people? The answer to this question will be determined in large part by a theologian's preexisting view of Israel's present covenantal status. On the one side, Wright combines a vivid appreciation for Yeshua as one-man Israel with the denial that the Jewish people remain in covenant with

17. N. T. Wright, *The New Testament and the People of God* (Minneapolis: Fortress, 1992), 401–2.

18. Wright, *New Testament*, 400–401.

19. N. T. Wright, *The Climax of the Covenant* (Minneapolis: Fortress, 1991), 18–40.

God after Yeshua's death and resurrection. Wright interprets Romans 11 in a supersessionist manner.[20] He thinks that Paul has surrendered all faith in a national restoration of Israel at the end of the age. Therefore he understands Yeshua's role as one-man Israel in terms of a displacement of national Israel. This role does not imply that the risen Yeshua has any special relationship with the Jewish people and its religious tradition. On the other side, R. Kendall Soulen, who affirms Israel's present covenantal status and reads Romans 11 in a non-supersessionist manner, sees Yeshua's resurrection as an anticipatory pledge of God's eschatological fidelity to Israel:

> If Jesus is the proleptic enactment of God's eschatological fidelity to the work of consummation, then Jesus is by this very fact the carnal embodiment of God's end-time fidelity toward Israel and toward Israel's future as the place of unsurpassable blessing for Israel, for the nations, and for all creation. By its nature, then, Jesus' resurrection from the dead anticipates a future event whose character as victorious fidelity can no longer be in doubt. That event is God's intervention on behalf of all Israel in keeping with God's promises, such that God's final act of covenant faithfulness toward Israel redounds not only to the blessing of Israel but also to the blessing of the nations and all of creation. Jesus, the firstborn from the dead, is also the first fruits of God's eschatological vindication of Israel's body. In light of Jesus' bodily resurrection, it is certain not only that God will intervene on behalf of the whole body of Israel at the close of covenant history but also that by this very act God will consummate the world.[21]

Both Wright and Soulen recognize the connection between the national resurrection of Israel, foretold in scripture and expected by many first-century Jews, and the resurrection of the one Jew Yeshua of Nazareth. However, the theological implications they draw from this connection are radically divergent, because they begin with different views of the enduring covenantal status of the Jewish people.[22]

Soulen speaks of Yeshua's relationship to Israel in eschatological terms. Yeshua is the "first fruits of God's eschatological vindication of Israel's body." This implies a mysterious connection between Yeshua and Israel in the present time before the eschaton, but does not speak about this connection outright. Messianic Jewish

---

20. Wright, *Climax*, 246–57. For a critique of Wright's supersessionism, see Douglas Harink, *Paul among the Postliberals* (Grand Rapids: Brazos, 2003), 153–84.

21. R. Kendall Soulen, *The God of Israel and Christian Theology* (Minneapolis: Fortress, 1996), 166.

22. For another non-supersessionist interpretation of Yeshua's identity as a one-man Israel, see Mussner, *Tractate on the Jews*, 130–31.

Bible translator David Stern has commented provocatively and unequivocally on the contemporary significance of Yeshua's role as one-man Israel:

> This concept, that the Messiah embodies the Jewish people, should not seem strange to believers, who learn precisely that about Yeshua and the Church. . . . But the Church has not clearly grasped that the Holy One of Israel, Yeshua, is in union not only with the Church, but also with the Jewish people.[23]

Stern's view resembles that of Karl Barth, who sees the church and the Jewish people as bound indissolubly to the person of the Messiah. Such extraordinary theological claims make sense when we view the New Testament picture of Yeshua as one-man Israel in light of the New Testament teaching on Israel's irrevocable covenant. However, before making these claims ourselves, we will consider additional evidence which points in the same direction.

Israel's No and Yeshua's Yes

In order to accept Stern's assertion that "Yeshua is in union not only with the church, but also with the Jewish people," we must be able to show how it is compatible with the fact that the Jewish people as a community have apparently said no to Yeshua and his Messiahship. What basis do we have for concluding that Yeshua has said yes to those who have said no to him?

We should begin with Paul's treatment of this subject in Romans 11. In chapter 3 we saw how Paul depicted Israel's "partial hardening" as a form of suffering imposed by God so that God's redemptive purpose for the world might be realized. We examined the numerous parallels between Romans 8 and Romans 9–11, and the likelihood that Paul sought to assert indirectly a relationship between Israel's "partial hardening," the eschatological suffering of Yeshua-believers, and the redemptive death of the Messiah. We suggested that this relationship is part of the "mystery" that Paul speaks of in Romans 11:25. For the most striking and consequential of the parallels between Romans 8 and Romans 9–11, we cited the work of Richard Hays, who looks at Romans 11:21 in light of Romans 8:32 and concludes that, for Paul, Israel's no *to* Yeshua can properly be viewed as a form of participation *in* Yeshua!

> By describing the fate of unbelieving Israel in the same language that he had used to describe Jesus' death, Paul hints at a daring trope whose full implications subsequent Christian theology has usually declined to pursue. What Paul has done,

---

23. David Stern, *Messianic Jewish Manifesto*, 108.

in a word, is to interpret the fate of Israel christologically. . . . Israel undergoes rejection for the sake of the world, bearing suffering vicariously.[24]

This is not the only way that Paul looks at Israel's no. Like other New Testament authors, Paul also believes that the leaders of the Jewish people in his day are culpable for failing to accept Yeshua. However, the more positive appraisal of Israel's no has special significance when seen in the context of later history.

We surveyed that history in the previous chapter. As seen in chapters 2, 3, and 4, the message of Yeshua came to the first generation of Jewish hearers as a proclamation of how the God of Israel had acted and was acting in Yeshua for the redemption of Israel and the world. It told of how Israel's covenant had been renewed and confirmed in the Messiah, and how the way was now also open for Gentiles to share in Israel's eschatological riches without becoming Jews. As seen in chapter 5, the message about Yeshua that came to Jews in the second century was radically different. It spoke of how Israel's covenant and way of life had been annulled in the Messiah, and it claimed that Jewish identity and practice were of no value or even prohibited. Any Jew who was loyal to the covenant would conclude that such a message could not possibly come from the God of Israel. To reject such a purported Messiah would be an act of fidelity to God rather than infidelity! Paul van Buren states this point clearly:

> The Gospel met Gentiles as a demand to abandon their pagan ways and the service of gods that are not God. The Gospel met the Jews, as the church after Paul's time preached it, as the demand to abandon the express commands and covenant of the very God whom the church proclaimed! Here is a profound incoherence that has arisen because of the lack of a proper Christian theology of Israel. The theological reality which such a theology must address, then, is that Israel said No to Jesus Christ out of faithfulness to his Father, the God of Israel.
>
> What the Jewish people were taught by their Rabbis to deny was a church which taught that Israel's covenant with God had been superseded. The church was asking Israel to agree that its faithfulness to Torah had no longer any meaning, because God's faithfulness to his people had come to an end. For Israel to have accepted such a church would have been a betrayal of the covenant and a denial of the faithfulness of God![25]

24. Richard B. Hays, *Echoes of Scripture in the Letters of Paul* (New Haven, CT: Yale University Press, 1989), 61. See also his *The Moral Vision of the New Testament* (San Francisco: Harper, 1996), 433.

25. Paul M. van Buren, *A Theology of the Jewish-Christian Reality*, vol. 2, *A Christian Theology of the People Israel* (San Francisco: Harper & Row, 1983), 34, 276.

Van Buren rightly sees the Jewish response to this distorted message as an expression of covenant faithfulness to God. However, a perspective shaped by Yeshua-faith can and should go further than this. If the obedience of Yeshua that led him to death on the cross is rightly interpreted as the perfect embodiment and realization of Israel's covenant fidelity, then Jewish rejection of the church's message in the second century and afterward can rightly be seen as a hidden participation in the obedience of Israel's Messiah.

This remarkable conclusion receives tragic confirmation in the post-Constantinian era. Once the Roman Empire became officially Christian, it proceeded to limit the rights and privileges of Jews. Eventually it took advantage of its power to compel Jews to listen to Christian sermons. In some places and times Christian authorities went further, and Jews were given the choice between conversion to Christianity and expulsion. At other times the choice was even starker—between conversion to Christianity and death. Many devout Jews chose the latter, and their martyrdom would live on in the consciousness of future generations of Jews as the exemplar of perfect covenant fidelity. In this way the Jewish no to Yeshua became inextricably and tragically associated in the Jewish collective memory with the supreme, heroic yes to "his Father, the God of Israel."

All contemporary Christians cringe upon hearing of these crimes. Such deeds are indefensible, and Christian leaders have recognized the need to acknowledge them as such. However, Christians seldom look at these appalling acts of violence in light of the enduring covenant with Israel, the continuing validity of Jewish practice, and the traditional Christian denial of both these truths. When Christians sought to compel Jews to become Christians, they were also seeking to compel them to deny Judaism and the Jewish people—and thus God himself! Viewed in this light, the death of Jews murdered for refusing to convert to Christianity takes on the full significance of martyrdom—even from a Christian perspective. For one who believes in Yeshua, all true martyrdom—faithful witness to the God of Israel at the cost of one's life—involves participation in the suffering and death of the ultimate "faithful witness" (*ho martys ho pistos*).[26] In this case, saying no to the Yeshua proclaimed by the church became a way of sharing in his perfect yes to God.

Beginning with the New Testament teaching concerning Israel's irrevocable covenant, proceeding to its teaching on Yeshua as one-man Israel, then considering Paul's hints on the mysterious Christological significance of Israel's no to Yeshua in light of the church's history of supersessionism, anti-Judaism, and violent persecution, Stern's claims about Yeshua's ongoing union with the Jew-

26. Revelation 1:5.

ish people grow in credibility. Paradoxically, the Jewish no to Yeshua becomes a sign of his presence in Israel rather than of his absence.

The Holocaust and Christian Reassessment of Judaism

The destruction of six million Jews at the hands of Nazi executioners elicited a profound reaction among Christians in the Western world. Though this monumental act of genocide was not perpetrated in the name of Christ or Christianity, and though it was directed against a race and not a religion, it was evident to all that it never could have occurred apart from nearly two millennia of entrenched Christian anti-Judaism. Of course awareness of the Holocaust stirred Christian sympathy for Jews and Judaism; more importantly, however, it moved Christians to reexamine their own history and tradition and to ask old questions in a new way. What is the significance of the Jewish people in the divine plan? How should their apparent no to Yeshua be assessed? Is it possible that the risen Messiah lives among them? When persecuting Jews in the name of Yeshua, were Christians actually persecuting Yeshua himself?

The fact that Nazi anti-Semitism was racial rather than religious, and that Christians were also victimized by the brutal regime, made it easier for Yeshua-believers to see this violent outburst of hatred for Jews in a new light. We find such a new perspective exemplified in the life of Edith Stein, a Jewish convert to Catholicism. While she apparently inherited some of the anti-Judaic prejudices of her Catholic environment, these did not prevent her from seeing the Jewish suffering around her in a christological perspective.[27] Stein entered the Carmelite convent in 1933, at the beginning of the Nazi regime in Germany. The opportunity for her to do so arose because Nazi legislation forced her out of her teaching position. She saw what was on the horizon. The new name she took upon becoming a Carmelite—Teresa Benedicta a Cruce (of the Cross)—expressed her convictions about the suffering of the Jewish people and its relation to the suffering of Yeshua. Reflecting five years later upon her 1933 experience, she wrote:

> I must tell you that I already brought my religious name with me into the house as a postulant. I received it exactly as I requested it. By the cross I understood the destiny of God's people which, even at that time, began to announce itself. I

27. Regarding these prejudices, see Daniel Krochmalnik, "Edith Stein: A Jew's Path to Catholicism," in *Never Forget,* ed. Waltraud Herbstrith, O.C.D. (Washington, DC: I.C.S. Publications, 1998), 74–75.

thought that those who recognized it as the cross of Christ had to take it upon themselves in the name of all.[28]

As Daniel Krochmalnik rightly observes, "The cross is, for Edith Stein, originally a symbol of her community of fate with Judaism, but with a Christian interpretation."[29] The Jewish people were now participating in the sufferings of their unrecognized Messiah. Edith Stein saw her own sharing in the suffering of her people as a way of likewise participating in the Messiah she knew and loved.

As a Jew and a Catholic, Edith Stein saw the suffering of her people at the hands of the Nazis as a sign of their indissoluble bond with their Messiah. Many Gentile Yeshua-believers reached the same conclusion. Richard John Neuhaus writes, "It is said that when John XXIII, then papal nuncio in Paris, first saw the pictures of the Jewish corpses at Auschwitz, he exclaimed, 'There is the Body of Christ!'"[30] Clemens Thoma expresses a similar view:

> Auschwitz is the most monumental modern sign for the most intimate bonding and unity of Jewish martyrs—representing all Judaism—with the crucified Christ, although this could not have been conscious for the Jews concerned. The Holocaust is for believing Christians, therefore, an important sign of the unbreakable unity, grounded in the crucified Christ, of Judaism and Christianity despite all divisions, individual paths, and misunderstandings.[31]

Thomas Torrance has made this assertion on more than one occasion.

> Certainly the fearful holocaust of six million Jews in the concentration camps of Europe, in which Israel seems to have been made a burnt-offering laden with the guilt of humanity, has begun to open Christian eyes to a new appreciation of the vicarious role of Israel in the mediation of God's reconciling purpose in the dark underground of conflicting forces within the human race. Now we see Israel, however, not just as the scapegoat, thrust out of sight into the despised ghettos of the nations, bearing in diaspora the reproach of the Messiah, but Israel drawn into the very heart and center of Calvary as never before since the crucifixion of Jesus.[32]

In faithfulness to the God and Father of our Lord Jesus Christ the Christian Church can never be the same after the Holocaust, for all its understanding of

---

28. Ibid., 73.
29. Ibid., 73.
30. Richard John Neuhaus, "Salvation is from the Jews," in *Jews and Christians,* 70.
31. Clemens Thoma, *Christian Theology of Judaism* (New York, 1980), 159.
32. Thomas F. Torrance, *The Mediation of Christ* (Colorado Springs: Helmers & Howard, 1992), 38–39.

divine revelation and salvation, mediated through Israel, must be, and cannot but be, affected by the *Eli, Eli, lama sabachthani?* in which Israel and Jesus Christ are for ever forged together in a new and quite irreversible way.[33]

For these Christians, Auschwitz signals a turning point in the way Yeshua-believers perceive the Jewish people. The terrible reality of the Holocaust has opened their eyes to the truth of Stern's proposition: "The Holy One of Israel, Yeshua, is in union not only with the church, but also with the Jewish people."

Auschwitz has also raised questions about the theological interpretation of Isaiah 53. Since the Middle Ages, Jewish reading of this text has largely followed the classic commentary of Rashi, who views the suffering servant described in the chapter as the people of Israel. Traditional Christian commentators, on the other hand, see this figure as the Messiah and consider the suffering, death, and resurrection of Yeshua to be the fulfillment of the prophecy. In light of the Holocaust, some Yeshua-believing interpreters are suggesting that the two readings should be combined. Joel Marcus, a Yeshua-believing Jewish exegete, devotes an entire volume to this theme.[34] Like other Christian thinkers, Marcus sees the crucifixion paintings of Chagall as indications even within the Jewish world of a sense of analogy between Yeshua's suffering and Israel's suffering.[35]

> Might there not be a way to combine these two interpretations? Might one not suggest that there is an analogy, a likeness, a mysterious identification between the redemptive sufferings of Jesus and . . . Holocaust victims? . . . Even some Jewish writers and artists have expressed a similar sort of intuition of an identification between Christ's sufferings and that of the martyrs of the Holocaust. One thinks, for example, of the crucifixion scenes painted by Marc Chagall in the late thirties and early forties—scenes in which the crucified one is always an identifiably Jewish figure, and the background is usually a burning Jewish settlement or shtetl of Eastern Europe.[36]

> This, then, is the theme that we will explore together: the likeness between the suffering and death of Jesus on the cross and the suffering and death of his relatives according to the flesh during the Nazi era.[37]

33. Thomas F. Torrance, "The Divine Vocation and Destiny of Israel in World History," in *The Witness of the Jews to God,* ed. David W. Torrance (Edinburgh: Handsel, 1982), 96.

34. Joel Marcus, *Jesus and the Holocaust* (New York: Doubleday, 1997).

35. Franz Mussner is another case in point. "The crucified Christ is not separated by Chagall from the people from whom he comes; rather the suffering of Israel flows together with the suffering of Christ and the suffering of Christ together with the suffering of Israel. Chagall has thereby penetrated deeply into the mystery of the 'collective figure' of the 'servant of God.'" *Tractate on the Jews,* 44.

36. Marcus, *Jesus and the Holocaust,* 28–29.

37. Ibid., 32.

Marcus concludes the book by narrating his experience of walking through an ancient Jewish cemetery in Prague:

> As I wandered past the tottering gravestones, this sense of contact with the past became palpable. . . . I sensed a continuity, an unbroken chain of Jewish existence that reached all the way back to Sinai. And I saw myself as part of that chain.
>
> But I also experienced another sort of communion as I wandered through the graveyard on the morning of my departure from Prague . . . , communion in another . . . central facet of the brokenness of the world—the body of Jesus that was broken on the cross. . . .
>
> It is the central intuition of this book that these two forms of communion—with the tragedies of Jewish history, culminating in the Holocaust, and with Jesus' death on the cross—are inextricably bound up with each other. A corollary is that the tikkun of the world, its repair, restoration, and redemption—including the redemption of Israel—has already been decisively inaugurated in Jesus' resurrection from the dead.[38]

At the end, Marcus recognizes that he is dealing with more than just an analogy. He is dealing with two realities that are "inextricably bound up with each other." He also recognizes that he is dealing with more than just the Holocaust. He is dealing with all "the tragedies of Jewish history," which reach their culmination in the Holocaust.[39] The inexpressible horror of the Holocaust has opened Yeshua-believing eyes to see what they were previously blind to: the presence of Yeshua among his flesh-and-blood brothers and sisters.

As a Jew, Marcus also perceives the irony in his thesis:

> There is, of course, a terrible irony in such a suggestion, since Jews have been persecuted down through the ages as the supposed killers of Christ. Indeed, Holy Week has always been a particularly dangerous time for Jews for this reason, for it is then especially that Christian mobs have gone on the rampage against their Jewish neighbors out of revenge for their alleged crime of murdering God. In this light we can understand why, for many Jews, the cross stands not so much for the death of Jesus nearly two thousand years ago as for the deaths, down through the ages, of the Jewish men, women, and children who have been murdered in Jesus' name.[40]

38. Ibid., 135–36.

39. Traditional Jewish theology would not consider all "the tragedies of Jewish history" to be sacrificial and redemptive. In keeping with the corporate rewards and punishments promised in the Torah, Jewish thinking has always acknowledged a disciplinary component in the sufferings of Jewish history. However, such a perspective has never been adequate to cover the full scope of Jewish suffering, nor to account for the fact that it was often the most pious and faithful who endured the worst hardships.

40. Marcus, *Jesus and the Holocaust*, 30–31.

When Christians stormed through Jewish neighborhoods during Holy Week and murdered innocent Jews in the name of Yeshua, they were reenacting the passion narrative with themselves in the place of those who crucified Yeshua—and demonstrating that the martyred Yeshua still lived among his martyred brothers and sisters. This is the burden of the powerful prayer attributed by some to Pope John XXIII:

> We understand that a mark of Cain is inscribed on our foreheads. In the course of centuries our brother Abel lay in the blood that we have shed or he wept tears that we have caused because we forgot Your love. Forgive us the curse that we wrongfully attached to the name "Jew." Forgive us that we crucified you, in their flesh, for the second time.[41]

The Holocaust opened eyes to the living and enduring relationship between Yeshua and the Jewish people. However, it is only when we see the Holocaust against the backdrop of the long history of Christian anti-Judaism—as Marcus and John XXIII do—that the full implications of this revelation become evident. It implies that Israel's apparent no to Yeshua resulted in Israel's intimate participation in Yeshua's yes to God.[42]

The Jewish People as "the Body of Messiah"

The Holocaust has opened Christian eyes to the significance of Christian anti-Judaism and to the reality of Yeshua's presence among his flesh-and-blood brothers and sisters, even when they appear to reject him. In this way it has also intensified exegetical sensitivity to New Testament teaching about Yeshua as one-man Israel. With eyes now open to previously unseen horizons, some theologians have recently proposed that Yeshua's ongoing presence in Israel is implicit in the truth at the very heart of Yeshua-faith: the Incarnation.

Bruce Marshall argues that the doctrine of the Incarnation implies that God assumes *Jewish* flesh, and that Yeshua's identity as a Jew continues after his resurrection. However, as with all Jews, Yeshua's Jewishness depends on his active participation in a Jewish community! He is a Jew by virtue of his relationship to other Jews. Marshall presents his case as follows:

41. Krochmalnik, "Edith Stein," 74–75.
42. My point in this section is certainly not to suggest that the Holocaust was a divinely orchestrated opportunity for Israel to participate in Yeshua's sacrifice. Nor am I suggesting that the Jewish people have lived and suffered blamelessly through the centuries. The point of this section is to merely show how reflection on the Holocaust has enabled some Christian theologians to recognize the ongoing intimate relationship between Yeshua and the Jewish people.

According to the traditional Christian doctrine of incarnation . . . , in the person of the Logos God makes his own the flesh of the particular Jew, Jesus of Nazareth. God's ownership of this Jewish flesh is permanent. In the end, when all flesh shall see the glory of the Lord, the vision of God will, so the traditional Christian teaching goes, be bound up ineluctably with the vision of this Jew seated at God's right hand. So in willing his own incarnation, it seems that God wills the permanence, indeed the eschatological permanence, of the distinction between Jews and Gentiles. But Jesus cannot be a Jew, or be identified as such (as he will be in the eschaton), all by himself, in isolation from his people. He is a Jew, like any other, only in virtue of his descent from Abraham, and thus in virtue of his relationship to the Jewish people as a whole.[43]

Taking up a proposal from Michael Wyschogrod, Marshall argues further that God's incarnate presence in Yeshua resembles God's presence among Yeshua's flesh-and-blood brothers and sisters.[44]

And this suggests that in owning with unsurpassable intimacy the particular Jewish flesh of Jesus, God also owns the Jewish people as a whole, precisely in their distinction from us Gentiles; he cannot own the one without also owning the other. The two forms of ownership are not identical—the one involves nothing short of union, the other something like indwelling—but neither are they totally disparate. As both Jewish and Christian theologians have sometimes observed, the Christian doctrine of incarnation is an intensification, not a repudiation, of traditional Jewish teaching about the dwelling of the divine presence in the midst of Israel.[45]

The doctrine of the Trinity implies that if God is present in Israel, Yeshua is also present there. Therefore Marshall reaches the same conclusion as Stern, though he begins from the doctrine of the Incarnation rather than from the New Testament teaching on Yeshua as one-man Israel.

Robert Jenson follows a similar course of reasoning. Jenson first argues that Yeshua's Jewish identity is integral to his risen eschatological humanity, and that this identity consists of a relationship to the Jewish people:

The risen Jesus is also flesh, in that he is risen bodily, for to be an embodied creature is to be flesh. Now, flesh is never an individual possession; that we are

43. Bruce D. Marshall, *Trinity and Truth* (Cambridge: Cambridge University Press, 2000), 178.
44. Michael Wyschogrod, "Incarnation," *Pro Ecclesia* 2 (1993): 210–17. See also "Incarnation and God's Indwelling in Israel," in *Abraham's Promise* (Grand Rapids: Eerdmans, 2004), 165–78.
45. Marshall, *Trinity*, 178.

flesh means among other things that we have parents and ancestors, who—at least until we get to Adam—are not everyone's parents and ancestors. The Word who has come in the flesh belongs to the lineage of Abraham and Sarah, and this fact belongs to his identity, to what traditional Christology calls the "one hypostasis" of the Word who is Jesus.[46]

Jenson moves from this premise to an ecclesiological conclusion: the church is the body of Christ only in association with the Jewish people:

> Paul teaches, and the church follows his teaching, that the church is the body of the risen Christ, and Paul does not initially mean that as a trope. As my body is myself as I am present and available to you, so the church is Christ's presence to the world. . . . But what sort of flesh is this body?
>
> Can there be a present body of the risen Jew, Jesus of Nazareth, in which the lineage of Abraham and Sarah so vanishes into a congregation of gentiles as it does in the church? My final—and perhaps most radical—suggestion to Christian theology . . . is that . . . the embodiment of the risen Christ is whole only in the form of the church *and* an identifiable community of Abraham and Sarah's descendants. The church and the synagogue are together and only together the present availability to the world of the risen Jesus Christ.[47]

Like Marshall, Jenson reaches his radical conclusion through theological reflection on the implications of the Incarnation. He does not base his conclusion on exegesis concerning Yeshua as one-man Israel, nor does he base it on consideration of the tragic history of Christian anti-Judaism and of the Holocaust. Nevertheless he reaches the same point in the end: "the Holy One of Israel, Yeshua, is in union not only with the Church, but also with the Jewish people."

Conclusion

In chapter four we presented a bilateral ecclesiology in solidarity with Israel. According to such an ecclesiology, the ekklesia requires a living connection to the Jewish people. In the first generation of the Yeshua movement, the ekklesia of the circumcision provided such a link. It was a visible, sociological reality. In the generations that followed, this ecclesiological bridge collapsed, and the two corporate entities—the church and the Jewish people—apparently went their own separate ways. In the last chapter, we described this separation as a schism

46. Robert W. Jenson, "Toward a Christian Theology of Judaism," in *Jews and Christians*, 12.
47. Ibid., 12–13.

within God's people. In the present chapter we have argued that this tragic schism has not utterly destroyed the inner bond that holds together the two parts of the one people of God. Yeshua maintains his relationship with the Jewish people and continues to live among them—though in a hidden, obscure fashion. At the same time, the Jewish people live on in the risen Yeshua, and through his ongoing Jewish identity as one-man Israel he mediates Israel's presence to the church—albeit in a hidden, obscure fashion. The (apparent) Jewish no to Yeshua has not expelled his Messianic presence from Israel, and the (actual) Christian no to the Jewish people and Judaism has not expelled Israel's presence from the church's inner sanctum.

The Second Vatican Council appears to have had some inkling of these truths. The fourth paragraph of *Nostra Aetate*, which deals with the Jewish people, begins in this way: "Sounding the depths of the mystery which is the church, this sacred Council remembers the spiritual ties which link the people of the New Covenant to the stock of Abraham." Pope John Paul II finds this introduction to be particularly significant:

> The Church of Christ discovers her "bond" with Judaism by "searching into her own mystery." The Jewish religion is not "extrinsic" to us, but in a certain way is "intrinsic" to our own religion.[48]

Richard John Neuhaus offers a similar comment on the beginning of *Nostra Aetate* 4: "The church does not go outside herself but more deeply within herself to engage Jews and Judaism."[49] This could be read as an arrogant, triumphalist interpretation of Judaism and the Jewish people. However, that is clearly not its intent. Instead, it is intended as recognition that the church has life only because it retains a connection to Israel through Yeshua. As the church ponders its own inner constitution and deepens its understanding of itself, it realizes its essential bond to Judaism and the Jewish people. As Yeshua lives on in Israel, so the Jewish people live on in the church, as the root without which the branches would wither and die (Romans 11:18).

In conclusion, the apparent Jewish no to Yeshua is no obstacle to our accepting the legitimacy and value of Jewish religious tradition, just as the actual Christian no to Judaism and the Jewish people has not negated the riches of Christian tradition. Thankfully, the Jewish and Christian no's are weaker than God's—and Yeshua's—gracious yes.

48. Pope John Paul II, *Spiritual Pilgrimage* (New York: Crossroad, 1995), 63.
49. Richard John Neuhaus, "Salvation is from the Jews," 73.

7

JEWISH TRADITION
AND THE BIBLICAL TEST

Our thesis—that Jewish religious tradition has legitimacy, value, and importance for both the Jewish people and for the Christian church—has in our view passed the christological test. We must now subject it to the biblical test. Are the claims of Jewish religious tradition compatible with the teaching of scripture? Is there any room in the teaching of Yeshua and his apostles for the type of religious way of life that eventually becomes rabbinic Judaism?

We are not arguing here for a seamless continuity between rabbinic Judaism and the Judaism of the Bible. We are not contending that the written Torah directly authorizes rabbinic tradition, nor that Yeshua and his apostles anticipated and prophetically approved of that tradition. The question we are asking is far more limited in scope. We are merely inquiring into the compatibility of Jewish religious tradition and scripture, including the New Testament.[1]

We will begin by looking at the central idea at the heart of developed rabbinic thought, the doctrine of the oral Torah, and argue that a certain form of that teaching has a reasonable basis in the written Torah. We will then examine the New Testament to see what it has to say about first-century religious currents that played a key role in the eventual emergence of rabbinic Judaism. Finally,

---

1. On the notion of compatibility in the theological sphere, see George Lindbeck, "A Question of Compatibility: A Lutheran Reflects on Trent," in *Justification by Faith*, ed. H. George Anderson, T. Austin Murphy, and Joseph A. Burgess (Minneapolis: Augsburg, 1985), 230–40.

we will look at some of the criticisms of rabbinic Judaism offered historically by Christians on the basis of the New Testament, and assess their weight.

The Oral Torah: A Biblical Basis for Its Legitimacy?

In previous chapters we have made the case that the Jewish people as a whole have a religious obligation to observe the Jewish way of life rooted in the Torah. While the New Testament offers dramatic new perspective on the Torah, it does not deny the premise, central to all forms of Judaism, that the Torah contains authoritative practical instruction for the people of Israel as it seeks to fulfill its covenantal vocation as a holy nation. But once we affirm this proposition, we face a challenge: how are Jews to understand the Torah and live according to it in the postbiblical world? According to Eliezer Berkovits, to respond to this question is to enter the realm of oral Torah: "How to face the confrontation between the text and the actual life situation, how to resolve the problems arising of this confrontation, is the task of . . . the Oral Law."[2]

The Insufficiency of the Written Torah

Is the written Torah sufficient for instructing the Jewish people in how to live as individuals, families, and local communities? While it is certainly foundational and indispensable, it is not sufficient. The Torah requires a living tradition of interpretation and application if it is to be practiced in daily life. This is due in part to the lack of detail in its legislation. As Michael Fishbane notes, "Frequent lacunae or ambiguities in their legal formulation tend to render [biblical] . . . laws exceedingly problematic—if not functionally inoperative—*without interpretation.*"[3] But lack of practical legislative detail is not the only problem. There are also numerous inconsistencies and even apparent contradictions.[4] If

2. Eliezer Berkovits, *Not in Heaven: The Nature and Function of Halakha* (Hoboken, NJ: Ktav, 1983), 1.

3. Michael Fishbane, *Biblical Interpretation in Ancient Israel* (Oxford: Oxford University Press, 1985), 92 (emphasis original). Examples are plentiful. The Torah forbids all "work" on the Sabbath (Exodus 20:10; Deuteronomy 5:14), but it nowhere defines the meaning of work. Similarly, it commands that Jews "afflict themselves" on the Day of Atonement (Leviticus 16:31), but it does not stipulate what this means in practice. When the Torah teaches about unclean birds (Leviticus 11:13–19; Deuteronomy 14:11–18), it does not provide any criteria for distinguishing the clean from unclean (as it does for mammals and for fish), but only lists examples. Is this a complete list? What about unlisted birds of prey?

4. Numbers 18:21–32 commands that Israelites give their tithe to the Levites, who then offer a tithe of the tithe to the priests. However, Deuteronomy 12:22–29 instructs Israelites to eat their own tithe at the central sanctuary and to give it to the poor every three years. Exodus 21:7 indicates that a female slave is not freed in her seventh year as is a male slave, whereas Deuteronomy 15:17

Jews of the Second Temple period were to keep these laws, they would need to have an interpretive tradition that would allow them to address the apparent discrepancies.[5]

David Weiss Halivni concludes from such tensions in the Pentateuch that an oral interpretive tradition must have existed, at least by the time the people as a whole accepted the text in its current form as authoritative:

> Both modern and traditional scholarship have noted in their respective ways that the text of the Pentateuch contains apparent inconsistencies, gaps, and even contradictions, sometimes in the most essential matters of observance. . . . The problem is not only that the laws of the festivals and Sabbaths are nowhere detailed enough that they might immediately be put into practice . . . without extensive guidance beyond the written word. Even more challenging than the frequent lack of detail is the fact that those details that are spelled out are not always congruous from one part of the Pentateuch to the other. . . . Coherent observance at the time of canonization cannot have been based on the scriptures alone. Some oral guidance must have accompanied the text as soon as observance was instituted.[6]

Fishbane goes further, arguing that an oral legal tradition must have originated much earlier:

> There need be no reasonable doubt that the preserved written law of the Hebrew Bible is but an expression of a much more comprehensive oral law. Such an oral legal tradition would have both augmented the cases of our collections and clarified their formulations to the scope and precision necessary for viable juridical decisions. Accordingly, the biblical law collections may best be considered as prototypical compendia of legal and ethical norms rather than as comprehensive codes. . . . The received legal codes are thus a literary expression of ancient Israelite legal wisdom: exemplifications of the "righteous" laws upon which the covenant was based.[7]

---

appears to treat the female and male slave alike. Exodus 12:1–13 seems to presume that Passover will be observed in the home, whereas Deuteronomy 16:2 requires that it be observed in the central sanctuary. Exodus 12:5 says that the Passover offering can be a sheep or a goat, whereas Deuteronomy 16:2 permits it also to be a bull. See David Weiss Halivni, *Revelation Restored* (Boulder, CO: Westview, 1997), 24–26; Fishbane, *Biblical Interpretation,* 136–37.

5. We find evidence of such a tradition in Chronicles. Exodus 12:9 indicates that the Passover offering is to be roasted in fire, whereas Deuteronomy 16:7 says "*u-vi-shal-ta*" (which usually means "you shall boil"). The two passages are brought together in 2 Chronicles 35:13, which states that the Passover sacrifice is to be "cooked [*b-sh-l*] in fire." Thus, the word *b-sh-l* is understood to mean "cooked" rather than "boiled." See Halivni, *Revelation Restored,* 25; Fishbane, *Biblical Interpretation,* 135–36.

6. Halivni, *Restoration Restored,* 23–24.

7. Fishbane, *Biblical Interpretation,* 95.

Neither Halivni nor Fishbane contend that this oral legal tradition was identical to what is later found in the rabbinic corpus. However, they both rightly recognize that the written Torah not only permits supplemental instruction—it requires it.

The Central Judiciary: A Mosaic Office for Torah Interpretation

Does the Torah establish or envision an institutional framework for providing such necessary supplemental instruction? There are good reasons for thinking that it does. In a text set at a key juncture in the narrative of Exodus—at "the mountain of God" just before the Sinai theophany—Jethro visits Moses and offers him important advice (Exodus 18:5, 13–27). The people of Israel have been coming to Moses with their disputes, and he has been inquiring of God, deciding (*shafat*) the disputes, and making known the relevant statutes and laws (*torot*). However, this activity is exhausting both Moses and the people. Therefore Jethro recommends that Moses establish tribal judges to handle the day-to-day disputes of the people. Only the major cases, too difficult for them to decide, should be brought to Moses. Moses accepts the advice of his father-in-law, and a new institution of subordinate and higher courts is born.

The significance of this incident is underlined by the position it occupies in the Deuteronomic retelling of the Exodus-Sinai-Wilderness narrative. It is the first event reported by Moses (Deuteronomy 1:9–18). There the subordinate leaders are called "magistrates" (*shoftim*) and "officials [*shotrim*] for your tribes" (Deuteronomy 1:15–16). Conceptual and verbal parallels suggest that the wilderness judicial system depicted at the beginning of the book serves as key background for the book's later section that establishes the fundamental institutions of Israel's future government (Deuteronomy 16:18–18:22). This section begins with the command to appoint "magistrates [*shoftim*] and officials [*shotrim*]" in every town, who shall "judge [*shaftu*] the people with righteous judgment" (Deuteronomy 16:18–20). Thus the local judges of the future are identified with the tribal magistrates of the desert past. Deuteronomy then proceeds to institute a central judiciary in "the place that the LORD your God will have chosen" that hears cases too difficult for the local courts (Deuteronomy 17:8–13). The prominent placement of Deuteronomy 1:9–18 and its verbal resemblance to Deuteronomy 16:18-20 imply that the central judiciary carries on Moses's function just as the local courts carry on the function of the tribal courts of the wilderness period.

The importance of this central judiciary and its role as the latter-day expression of the Mosaic office becomes clearer with a careful study of the pericope. The passage begins by directing that certain types of cases should be brought from the local courts to the central court. These are cases that are "too difficult for you," and that involve homicide (*beyn dam le-dam*), personal injury, or disputes over the appropriate law to apply (Deuteronomy 17:8). The central court shall hear the case and render a decision. The persons involved are not free to disregard this decision but "must carefully observe all that they instruct you to do" (Deuteronomy 17:10). The words "carefully observe" (*shamarta la'asot*) appear frequently in various forms in Deuteronomy, always enjoining obedience to the words of the Torah itself (e.g., Deuteronomy 6:3; 16:12). Here they enjoin obedience to the high court. The verb used to characterize the decision of the judges is also significant: y*oru* ("they will instruct") shares the same consonantal root as *Torah*. This is no accident, as becomes evident in the subsequent verse commanding the concerned parties to "act according to the word of *Torah* that they teach you (*yoru-cha*)" (Deuteronomy 17:11). As if these exhortations to obedience were not enough, the passage proceeds to urge that the parties "not turn aside from the decision that they declare to you, neither to the right nor to the left," and warns that those who arrogantly disobey the central court shall be put to death so that evil might be purged from Israel and so that all the people might hear and fear and not act in a similar manner (Deuteronomy 17:11–13). Though such warnings appear frequently in Deuteronomy (Deuteronomy 13:6; 17:7; 19:19; 21:21; 22:21; 24:7), they are usually a way of urging compliance with the Torah itself rather than with those who administer it.

Thus the judgment of the central court is described in a manner that implies a scope beyond that of merely rendering verdicts in particular cases. In addressing difficult cases they are teaching Torah. They are functioning in the role that Moses occupied during the wilderness wandering, and their words have an authority analogous to that of the Mosaic Torah itself.

As Frank Crusemann astutely observes,

> *The conclusion we must draw from this is absolutely clear: The decisions of the court have the same significance and the same rank as the things that Moses himself said—which means Deuteronomy itself.* The Jerusalem high court rendered decisions with the authority of Moses and it had his jurisdiction. It spoke in the name of Moses and extrapolated forward the will of YHWH.

> The development and structure of deuteronomic law cannot be separated from the institution of the Jerusalem central court. . . . According to Deut 17:8f. this court speaks with the same authority as Deuteronomy itself—the authority of Moses.[8]

8. Frank Crusemann, *The Torah* (Edinburgh: T&T Clark, 1996), 97, 269.

Crusemann may overstate his conclusion. Nevertheless, his essential thesis remains valid. Deuteronomy establishes an institution that carries on the Mosaic role of interpreting and applying the Torah in new and unforeseen circumstances.

According to 2 Chronicles 19, such an institution actually existed in ancient Israel. This chapter describes how King Jehoshaphat appointed magistrates (*shoftim*) in all the fortified cities of Judah and then established a high court in Jerusalem (2 Chronicles 19:5, 8). The high court would hear cases sent to them "from your brothers living in their cities" (2 Chronicles 19:10). As in Deuteronomy 17:8, prominent among these would be cases of homicide (*beyn dam le-dam*). The identical wording demonstrates that the author of 2 Chronicles 19 sees the action of King Jehoshaphat as the realization of the intent of Deuteronomy 17. In addition to difficult cases of homicide, the high court should render judgment in disputes "between Torah and commandment, statutes and ordinances." This phrase corresponds to "between one kind of legal right and another" in Deuteronomy 17:8 and helps explain that enigmatic formulation. Crusemann interprets the expanded version of 2 Chronicles 19:10 as referring to "cases that involve a 'collision of norms' and thus automatically involve something like precedents."[9] Sometimes compliance with one law may lead one to disobey another. In such cases one encounters a "collision of norms"—and an authorized interpretive agency is required in order to clarify what is permissible and what is required. Such clarification involves more than just rendering a verdict in a particular dispute. Such precedent-setting cases also provide new instruction on how the Torah is to be lived out. Thus the high court teaches, interprets, and establishes Torah.[10]

The relationship between the future high court and Moses may also be implicit in Numbers 11. In this chapter, as in Exodus 18 and Deuteronomy 1, Moses

9. Crusemann, *The Torah*, 94.

10. The role of the central judiciary, patterned on the role of Moses during the wilderness wandering, may be illustrated by the five instances in the Torah where new laws are given in response to unforeseen legal questions posed by the people (Leviticus 24:10–23; Numbers 9:6–14; Numbers 15:32–36; Numbers 27 and 36). These laws are unusual in the Torah. Normally, the Torah's narrative presents legal material as rooted solely in the divine initiative. God summons Moses and gives him laws. No human circumstances on the ground provide a context to which God responds. However, in these five instances the initiative comes from the people, and the result is not merely the resolution of particular cases but the promulgation of new legislation. These five narratives thus provide the Mosaic paradigm for the interpretive work of the central court in Jerusalem. The central court will not derive its rulings in oracular fashion (as does Moses), and this distinction preserves the primary and unique status of the Mosaic legislation. However, apart from this fact the central court will function as did Moses, and its authority to clarify and interpret the Torah derives from Moses himself. On these five legal narratives and their importance, see Fishbane, *Biblical Interpretation*, 99–106; Crusemann, *The Torah*, 100–101.

is burdened by his task of leading the people of Israel and, as in those other chapters, his burden is relieved by the appointment of other leaders to assist him (Numbers 11:11–15, 16–17, 24–25). However, there are also differences between the Exodus/Deuteronomy helpers and those described in Numbers 11. First, the leaders of Numbers 11 are not explicitly assigned responsibility for subordinate groupings (thousands, hundreds, fifties, tens), nor is their role restricted to local judgment. Second, their number is given, and that number is "seventy." They are thus identified with the seventy elders who ascended Sinai with Moses and "saw the God of Israel" (Exodus 24:9–11). In this way they are more closely associated with Moses than are the subordinate judges of Exodus 18 and Deuteronomy 1. Third, just as they ascended Sinai with Moses, so their appointment occurs at the Tent of Meeting, corresponding to the future temple in Jerusalem (Numbers 11:16, 24). Fourth and finally, they receive a measure of the prophetic spirit that Moses possesses (Numbers 11:17, 25–30). This also associates the seventy elders closely with Moses himself. Just as Elisha will receive the spirit that is upon Elijah, so the seventy receive the spirit of Moses (2 Kings 2:9–10, 15).

All of these factors indicate that the seventy elders of Numbers 11 prefigure the central court of Deuteronomy 17 and 2 Chronicles 19 rather than the subordinate courts of the cities of Judah. The connection with Elijah and Elisha offers especially strong support for this thesis. Just as Elisha received Elijah's spirit and succeeded him in his role of prophet, so the seventy elders receive Moses's spirit and prefigure the institution that will succeed Moses in his role as teacher of the Torah. If a Sanhedrin of seventy elders ever existed during the Second Temple period as claimed by rabbinic literature, its numerical composition would have implied that it was the divinely sanctioned successor to Moses, extending the Mosaic office of interpreting and applying the Torah just as the seventy elders did in Numbers 11 and just as Jehoshaphat's high court did in 2 Chronicles 19.[11]

The Basis of Authority

Numbers 11 also points to the basis of authority for the Jerusalem high court. The seventy are empowered by God to act in the role of Moses, but before their official appointment and empowerment they were already "elders and officials

11. E. P. Sanders (*Judaism: Practice and Belief, 63 BCE—66 CE* [Philadelphia: Trinity Press International, 1992], 472–88) argues that such a Sanhedrin did *not* exist during the Second Temple period, though various "councils," with diverse functions, did play a role in government. For a more traditional perspective, see S. Safrai, "Jewish Self-Government," in *The Jewish People in the First Century*, vol. 1, ed. S. Safrai and M. Stern (Philadelphia: Fortress, 1974), 379–404.

[*shotrim*] of the people" (Numbers 11:16, 24). As we have seen, a group of seventy elders represented the people earlier at Sinai (Exodus 24:9–11). Thus in a sense authority is vested in the people of Israel as a whole. This view draws further support from the Deuteronomic instructions regarding Israel's governmental institutions (Deuteronomy 16:18–18:22). Deuteronomy 16:18 begins this section with the foundational law of government: "You shall appoint magistrates and officials." Who is the singular "you" of this verse? It evidently stands for the hearers of Deuteronomy—the people as a whole. Similarly, the hearers of Deuteronomy are also told that they are permitted to have a king, if they so decide (17:14–15). That king must fit certain criteria (including a conviction among the people that God himself has chosen the man), but the people themselves decide whether to have a king and who that king should be.[12]

The authority vested in the people of Israel as a whole to act as Moses's successor can also be seen in the book of Esther. After the Jewish people escape the destruction plotted by Haman, Mordecai and Esther urge them to celebrate an annual feast (Purim) to commemorate the event. The book—which never mentions the name of God—then describes the people's response:

> The Jews established and accepted as a custom for themselves and their descendants and all who joined them, that without fail they would continue to observe these two days every year, as it was written and at the time appointed. (Esther 9:27)

One Talmudic interpretation of "established and accepted" understands it to mean, "they [i.e., the heavenly court] upheld above what they [i.e., the Jewish people] had accepted below."[13] Or, in David Novak's paraphrase, "God confirmed what the Jewish authorities on earth had themselves decreed for the people."[14] This is probably not so far removed from the intent of the author. Just as the book of Esther depicts the providential power of God at work in the world through human action, without ever mentioning the divine Name, so it presents a divinely ordained institution established apparently by human authority. And that authority is not merely invested in the leaders, as Novak's paraphrase might suggest. Instead, it is the people as a whole who "established and accepted as a custom for themselves and their descendants and all who joined them" the celebration of Purim. And, by incorporating the book of Esther into the biblical canon, the Jewish people made clear their determination

---

12. Crusemann, *The Torah*, 238, 247.
13. *b. Megillah* 7a.
14. David Novak, *The Election of Israel* (Cambridge: Cambridge University Press, 1995), 169–70.

that in fact God had confirmed in heaven what the Jewish people had decreed and accepted on earth.

We thus may conclude that (1) because of its lack of legal detail and its abundance of apparent legal inconsistency, the Torah requires supplemental legal instruction; (2) the Torah itself recognizes this fact and envisions a Mosaic teaching office whose role is to interpret and apply the Torah's regulations to new circumstances; and (3) this Mosaic teaching office, while having its ultimate authority from God, receives its immediate sanction from the affirmation of the Jewish people as a whole. While the Torah itself nowhere uses the term, there is no reason why the tradition of supplemental instruction in the Mosaic succession should not be called "oral Torah." It is thereby both distinguished from the written Torah and identified with it—just as the high court of Deuteronomy 17 and the seventy elders of Numbers 11 are both distinguished from Moses and identified with him.

Oral Torah in Rabbinic Tradition

We have seen that it is possible to find in the written Torah a justification for a certain kind of oral Torah. How does this biblically rooted doctrine compare with the traditional rabbinic understanding? What, in fact, is the rabbinic doctrine of the oral Torah?

The Talmudic sages distinguish two types of law—which they call "scriptural law" (*d'oraita*) and "rabbinic law" (*d'rabbanan*). The latter is also divinely authorized, so that commandments ordained by "rabbinic law" can be treated as commandments of God. Why is this the case? Not because the rabbis are simply repeating laws received through a chain of teachers going back to Moses, but because "scriptural law" in Deuteronomy 17 gives them the authority to act on behalf of God. This is clearly stated in the midst of a discussion concerning the lighting of Hanukkah candles—a custom commemorating a victory that occurred more than a thousand years after the giving of the Torah at Sinai:

> What blessing is recited? "Who sanctified us by His commandments and com-
> manded us to kindle the light of Chanukkah." And where [in the written Torah]
> did He so command us? Rav Avi'a said: [It derives] from, "You shall not turn
> aside [from the ruling that they declare to you, to the right or to the left]" (Deu-
> teronomy 17:11).[15]

Thus, the fundamental Talmudic claim to authority is not based on a myth of origins but on a text in the Pentateuch that, as we have already seen, had as

---

15. *b. Shabbat* 23a (translation mine).

its purpose the sanctioning of an ongoing Mosaic office of interpretation and application of the Torah.

The Talmud consistently distinguishes between obligations that are scriptural law and those that are rabbinic law, treating the former as taking precedence over the latter. As Halivni notes, "There are differences with respect to severity of observance between a law which is biblically commanded and a law which is rabbinically ordained."[16] Thus, to the extent that we may equate oral Torah with rabbinic law, we may also assert that rabbinic tradition decisively subordinates the oral Torah to the written Torah.

In what sense are the rabbinic decisions, authorized by the written Torah in Deuteronomy 17, themselves related to oral instruction given to Moses at Sinai? According to the fifteenth-century scholar Joseph Albo, only a very general connection exists between the two: "Therefore Moses was given orally certain general principles, only briefly alluded to in the Torah, by means of which the Sages may work out the newly emerging particulars in every generation."[17] Many modern Jewish theologians pass over even such a minimal link and stress instead the practical, concrete, and contingent quality of the oral Torah. The written Torah stands as an unchanging norm, but the oral Torah is dynamic, flexible, reflecting the infinite diversity of circumstances that face the Jewish people in the course of its journey through history. According to Eliezer Berkovits, this is the heart of the oral Torah's job description.[18]

Both Berkovits and Michael Wyschogrod stress the essential *oral* dimension of the oral Torah. Berkovits mourns over the fact that the oral Torah was ever consigned to written form, calling this "the exile of the oral Torah into literature."[19] The appearance of the oral Torah in written form could easily lead to a

---

16. David Weiss Halivni, *Peshat and Derash* (Oxford: Oxford University Press, 1991), 14. Thus a *kal va-chomer* argument (i.e., from the greater to the lesser) is employed to demonstrate that one may interrupt one's recitation of the *Hallel* (Psalms 113–118) in order to greet someone in authority—for if one may interrupt one's recital of the *Shema*, which is obligatory according to "Scriptural Law," one may surely interrupt the *Hallel*, which is obligatory only according to "Rabbinic Law" (*b. Berachot* 14a). It is likewise decreed that in order to show respect for those in authority it is generally permitted to set aside rules ordained by "Rabbinic Law"—but not commandments that are ordained by "Scriptural Law" (*b. Berachot* 19b). These are not exceptions to the Talmudic approach, but typical. See *b. Berachot* 15a, 16b, 20b, 21a; *b. Nidah* 4b; *b. Sukkah* 44a; *b. Bava Kama* 114b, and Rashi's commentary on *b. Berachot* 17b and 20b. See also Novak, *The Election of Israel*, 172–73; and Michael Wyschogrod, *The Body of Faith* (Northvale, NJ: Jason Aronson, 1996), xxxii.

17. Cited in Rabbi Dr. Moshe Zemer, *Evolving Halakhah* (Woodstock, VT: Jewish Lights, 1999), 43.

18. "How to face the confrontation between the text and the actual life situation, how to resolve the problems arising of this confrontation, is the task of the *Torah she'baal'Peh*, the Oral Law." Berkovits, *Not in Heaven,* 1.

19. Ibid., 88.

misunderstanding of its essential nature as the flexible, contingent application of the written Torah to new situations. Wyschogrod goes so far as to describe the oral Torah as the Torah's power to enter into Jewish life and shape it from the inside—so that Israel becomes "the incarnation of the Torah":

> In spite of the writing down of the oral law, it would be a grave mistake to erase the distinction between the written and oral law. Theologically speaking, the oral law can never be written down. The oral law is that part of the law carried in the Jewish people. The law does not only remain a normative domain that hovers over the people of Israel and judges this people. It does that, too, of course. But the Torah enters the being of the people of Israel. It is absorbed into their existence and they therefore become the carriers or the incarnation of the Torah. The oral law reflects this fact.[20]

Such a description of the oral Torah resembles Pauline teaching on the role of the Holy Spirit, an internal principle that fashions the community of faith into a living and incarnate Torah.[21]

Thinkers who adopt such a perspective on the oral Torah often emphasize the role played by the Jewish people as a whole in the halakhic process. Thus David Novak argues that the Jewish people have a more active part to play in the development of rabbinic law than in the development of scriptural law:

> Finally, there is the factor of popular consent. In the area of Scriptural law, this factor does not seem to be at work. Although it is assumed that the law of God is for the good of man, nevertheless, its authority is assumed whether one sees the good the law is intending or not. . . . With rabbinic law, on the other hand, popular consent is indeed a major factor *ab initio*. Thus the Talmud assumes that "a decree . . . cannot be decreed unless it is obvious that the majority of the community will abide by it" (*b. Avodah Zarah* 36a). In other words, not only the Rabbis but the ordinary people too have more power in the area of man-made law than they do in the area of God-made law. Nevertheless, the fact that this power is not construed to be for the sake of autonomy *from* the covenant but to be more like autonomy *for* the covenant enables one to look to the Jewish people themselves as a source of revelation. . . . In cases of doubt about what the actual law is, where there are good theoretical arguments by Rabbis on both sides of the issue, one is to "go out and look at what the people are doing" (*b. Berachot* 45a).[22]

20. Wyschogrod, *The Body of Faith*, 210.

21. Romans 8:3–8; 2 Corinthians 3:1–18. For an insightful exegesis of 2 Corinthians 3, see Richard B. Hays, *Echoes of Scripture in the Letters of Paul* (New Haven, CT: Yale University Press, 1989), 122–53.

22. Novak, *The Election of Israel*, 174–75.

This brings us back to what we saw earlier in the book of Deuteronomy. Biblical law is rooted in divine revelation, but it must be administered, interpreted, and applied by human authorities, and those authorities gain their legitimacy through being chosen by the covenant people. Thus we find that the view of the oral Torah seen in at least one important strand of rabbinic tradition has much in common with the basic premises inherent in the written Torah.

The Pharisees in the New Testament

Historians of rabbinic Judaism writing at the end of the twentieth and beginning of the twenty-first century usually emphasize the novelty and creativity of rabbinic Judaism.[23] As a religious system, rabbinic Judaism originates in the era following the first Jewish revolt (66–74 CE), matures with the codification of the Mishnah (200 CE), but does not gain full recognition in the Jewish world until after the completion of the two Talmuds (600 CE). Nevertheless, all acknowledge that the rabbinic movement draws substantially from currents that existed during the Second Temple period. Jacob Neusner isolates three groups who together formed the rabbinic coalition:

> Rabbinic Judaism . . . did not begin in 70. It drew in part upon teachings and traditions of the Pharisees, who had formed a sect within the larger Judaic world of the land of Israel. After 70, the Pharisees formed the single most influential group. . . . But the rabbinic Judaism that was aborning took within itself a second group, the heirs and continuators of the scribes from the period before 70. . . . The sect of the Pharisees and the profession of the scribes—together with the surviving priests who joined them—framed a Judaism to take the place of the Judaism of temple and cult.[24]

The scribes contributed their expertise with the written Torah and their orientation to study as worship. The priests brought with them their practical knowledge of the workings of the Jerusalem temple. But the key to the success of the coalition was the Pharisees, with their concern for the holiness of all Israel, and with their distinctive practices (such as ritual handwashing) and teachings (such as the resurrection of the dead).[25]

---

23. See, for example, Alan F. Segal, *Rebecca's Children* (Cambridge, MA: Harvard University Press, 1986), and Jacob Neusner, *A Short History of Judaism* (Minneapolis: Fortress, 1992); Seth Schwartz, *Imperialism and Jewish Society, 200 BCE to 640 CE* (Princeton, NJ: Princeton University Press, 2001).

24. Neusner, *Short History*, 51–52.

25. Shaye Cohen notes that the authors of the Mishnah do not explicitly identify themselves as the descendants of the Pharisees. He explains this by arguing that the rabbinic movement sought

The late emergence of rabbinic Judaism means that we cannot ask about the attitude of Yeshua or his apostles toward it. However, we can ask about the New Testament's view of the Pharisees. While the answer to this question is not sufficient for the purpose of assessing rabbinic Judaism as a developed system, it is surely relevant to that purpose. If we are to draw any conclusions from the New Testament in regard to what will become rabbinic tradition, we must pay close attention to the way those writings treat the Pharisees and their teaching.

In studying the New Testament view of the Pharisees, we must pay attention not only to what the authors say but also to what they presume. We must go beyond noting the existence of polemics and ask if the various writings of the New Testament—read in historical context—tell us anything about the reason for those polemics. We must also distinguish among the New Testament writings and recognize the heterogeneous viewpoints of the authors. As canonical readers, we begin with the assumption that the New Testament writings present a coherent message. However, the canonical perspective does not oblige us to expect a uniform, undifferentiated text.

Matthew as Polemicist

The New Testament view of the Pharisees displays far more complexity than is normally imagined. The Pharisees do not play a major role in Mark.[26] This situation changes in the other Gospels. Matthew and John portray the Pharisees in an intensely negative light, whereas Luke-Acts treats them in a more benevolent manner. Upon closer examination, we find that the anti-Pharisaic polemics in Matthew and John differ substantially. Matthew attacks Pharisaism as an insider who shares many of the same ideological positions when seen within the broader spectrum of Jewish life, whereas John simply equates Pharisees and Jewish authorities, with slight attention given to the distinctive Pharisaic perspective.

Let us begin by looking at Matthew's harsh treatment of the Pharisees. When we compare Matthew with Mark and Luke in their handling of common material, Matthew's preoccupation with the Pharisees becomes evident. Whereas Luke and Mark distinguish between scribes/lawyers/Torah teachers, on the one hand, and Pharisees, on the other, Matthew lumps them together. For Matthew,

---

to be all-embracing and nonsectarian, and was thus reluctant to acknowledge its sectarian roots. See Shaye J. D. Cohen, *From the Maccabees to the Mishnah* (Philadelphia: Westminster, 1987), 154–59; 226–27. On the relationship between the Pharisaic movement and rabbinic Judaism, see Peter Tomson, *"If this be from Heaven"* (Sheffield: Sheffield Academic Press), 50–55.

26. As Gunter Stemberger notes, "the Pharisees assume a dominant role only in the later Gospels." *Jewish Contemporaries of Jesus* (Minneapolis: Fortress, 1995), 22. In Mark, the Pharisees oppose Yeshua (Mark 3:6), and Yeshua finds fault with their tradition (7:1–13). However, they play no role in Yeshua's arrest or trial.

scribe means Pharisaic scribe.[27] This equating of scribes and Pharisees explains a distinctive feature in Matthew's narrative. Mark speaks of the Sanhedrin as "the chief priests and scribes [and elders]" (Mark 8:31; 10:33; 11:18; 11:27; 14:1; 14:43; 14:53; 15:1). Matthew normally follows this Markan terminology, but in two cases he coins a new phrase: "the chief priests and the Pharisees" (Matthew 21:45; 27:62). This Matthean phrase makes sense if the author sees virtually all scribes as Pharisees and all Pharisees as scribes. The scribes in the Sanhedrin then must all be Pharisees, and the Sanhedrin can be called either "the chief priests and scribes" or "the chief priests and Pharisees." The scribe-Pharisee equation likewise would explain Matthew's unusual linking of the Pharisees with the Sadducees (Matthew 3:7; 16:1; 16:6; 16:11–12). If the author considered the chief priests to be Sadducees, then the phrase "Pharisees and Sadducees" would be equivalent to "Pharisees and chief priests." By explicitly connecting the Pharisees to the Sanhedrin, Matthew does what Mark and Luke avoid doing: he implicates the Pharisees in the arrest, trial, and execution of Yeshua.

Matthew and Proto-Rabbinic Halakhah

Yet Matthew's harsh polemic against the Pharisees is only half of the story. The whole story is far more complex—and far more interesting. While Matthew is undoubtedly the New Testament's most polemically anti-Pharisaic book, it is also the most substantively Pharisaic—or proto-rabbinic—text in the early history of the Yeshua-movement.[28] The proto-rabbinic character of Matthew

27. Mark reports that "scribes from Jerusalem" attack Yeshua as a magician (Mark 3:22), whereas Matthew presents the accusers as Pharisees (Matthew 9:34; 12:24). (In Luke 11:15 the charge is made by "some of them," with the identity of "them" left uncertain.) In Mark 12:28 "one of the scribes" approaches Yeshua with the question, "Which commandment is the first of all?" and Yeshua commends him as one "not far from the kingdom of God" (v. 34). In the parallel passage in Matthew, a Pharisaic lawyer asks the question in order to test Yeshua (Matthew 22:34–35) and receives no commendation. Both Mark and Matthew then narrate a pericope in which Yeshua inquires how the Messiah can be David's son if David calls him "Lord" (Psalm 110:1). In Mark's account (12:35) Yeshua says, "How can *the scribes* say that the Messiah is the son of David?" whereas in Matthew (22:41) Yeshua addresses the question to *the Pharisees*. In Luke 11, Yeshua pronounces a set of "woes"—first upon the Pharisees (vv. 37–44), and then upon "lawyers" (vv. 45–48). In Matthew's version of the woes (23:1–36), placed immediately after Yeshua's teaching on the great commandment and the Davidic descent of the Messiah, the woes are pronounced upon one group: the "scribes and Pharisees."

28. We are here commenting on similarities between Matthew and later rabbinic writings. We are unable to assert conclusively that these common elements derive from Pharisaism. Some of them may derive from non-Pharisaic scribal tradition. However, it is likely that these Pharisaic and scribal traditions had already fused by the final decades of the first century, when Matthew was written. Regardless, we are on safe ground if we refer to these characteristics as proto-rabbinic and if we recognize that Matthew learned them from contemporaries whom he sees as the latter-day heirs of the "scribes and Pharisees."

is reflected especially in the book's concern for halakhah, that is, the practical outworking of the Jewish way of life rooted in the commandments of the Torah. Matthew shows not only a proto-rabbinic concern for halakhah but also knowledge of terminology, ways of thinking, and particular disputes that would later appear in rabbinic literature. He even shows surprising agreement with certain halakhic positions formulated in the early rabbinic movement.

As in rabbinic literature, communal leaders in Matthew have the authority to "bind and loose," i.e., forbid or permit certain behavior in accordance with halakhic standards (Matthew 16:19; 18:18).[29] As in rabbinic literature, the whole Torah is summed up in terms of a limited number of commandments (Matthew 7:12; 22:40).[30] As in rabbinic literature, some commandments are seen as "light" and others as "weighty," yet they are all valid and binding (Matthew 5:19; 23:23).[31] As in rabbinic literature, principles derived from biblical texts are employed to resolve practical conflicts between competing Torah obligations (Matthew 9:13; 12:7).[32]

Matthew appears to be aware of halakhic disagreements that exist internal to the proto-rabbinic world. In Mark 10:2, Pharisees ask Yeshua, "Is it lawful for a man to divorce his wife?" In Matthew 19:3, they ask, "Is it lawful for a man to divorce his wife for any cause?" In Mark, Yeshua answers, "No." In Matthew, he answers, "Whoever divorces his wife, except for unchastity, and marries another commits adultery" (Matthew 19:9). Peter Tomson views this difference between Matthew and Mark against the background of proto-rabbinic disagreements between the school of Shammai and the school of Hillel. The school of Hillel permitted divorce for any cause whatsoever ("even if she spoiled a dish for him"), whereas the school of Shammai ruled that divorce was allowed only in cases where the wife was guilty of sexual immorality.[33]

> The question of the Pharisees is no longer "whether a person is allowed to send his wife away," but, "Is a person allowed for every reason to send his wife away?" (Mark 10.2; Matthew 19.3). . . . The question amounts to asking whether Jesus is in agreement with the standpoint of the Hillelites that divorce could be based "on every ground." Equally surprising is the fact that the answer is in conformity with the Shammaite standpoint: marriage can only be disbanded for unchastity

29. W. D. Davies and Dale C. Allison, Jr., *A Critical and Exegetical Commentary on the Gospel According to Saint Matthew,* vol. 2 (Edinburgh: T&T Clark, 1991), 787; David C. Sim, *The Gospel of Matthew and Christian Judaism* (Edinburgh: T&T Clark, 1998), 197; Anthony J. Saldarini, *Matthew's Christian-Jewish Community* (Chicago: University of Chicago Press, 1994), 119.

30. *b. Makkoth* 23b–24a.

31. *Avot* 2:1.

32. See Berkovits, *Not in Heaven,* 24–32, 76–84.

33. *m. Gittin* 9:10.

or sexual license. In other words, in Matthew Jesus chooses sides in an intra-Pharisaic discussion.[34]

We cannot be certain whether Matthew interpreted earlier Yeshua-tradition in light of proto-rabbinic teaching or uniquely preserved Yeshua-tradition that itself had special affinity with proto-rabbinic currents. In any case, it is clear that Matthew inhabits a world that has much in common with that of the scribes and Pharisees he attacks.

Matthew's affinity for proto-rabbinic halakhah is also seen in Matthew 23:23–24:

> Woe to you, scribes and Pharisees, hypocrites! For you tithe mint and dill and cummin, and have neglected the weightier matters of the law, justice and mercy and faith. It is these you ought to have done, without neglecting the others.

Matthew presents here a theme that is common to all the synoptic Gospels: Yeshua's emphasis on proper conduct in human relationships. As noted in chapter 2, this text also affirms the ritual component of the Torah ("without neglecting the others"). However, Yeshua's teaching here goes beyond such an affirmation. The ritual norms that Yeshua upholds in this text are not found in the written Torah, but instead derive from Pharisaic tradition![35] The tithing of small herbs such as mint, dill, and cummin was a Pharisaic extension of the written Torah. Yet, according to Matthew, Yeshua not only urges compliance with this practice—he treats it as a matter of the Torah (though of lesser weight than the injunctions to love, justice, and faithfulness).[36]

Matthew's proto-rabbinic orientation must be taken fully into account as we read Matthew 23:2–3, a central text about the Pharisees that traditional Christian commentators have found difficult to interpret: "The scribes and the Pharisees sit on Moses' seat; therefore, do whatever they teach you and follow it" (literally: "carefully observe [poiesate kai tereite] all that they say to you").

Seeing only the anti-Pharisaic polemics of Matthew and not his own proto-rabbinic orientation, most commentators have been unable to make sense of this text. This perspective has also prevented them from recognizing a biblical

---

34. Tomson, *Heaven,* 287.

35. See W. D. Davies and Dale C. Allison, Jr., *A Critical and Exegetical Commentary on the Gospel According to Saint Matthew,* vol. 3 (Edinburgh: T&T Clark, 1997), 295.

36. Luke's version of this saying is as follows: "But woe to you Pharisees! For you tithe mint and rue and herbs of all kinds, and neglect justice and the love of God; it is these you ought to have practiced, without neglecting the others" (11:42). Like Matthew, Luke both affirms Pharisaic tithing practices and subordinates them to weightier concerns. However, only Matthew's version explicitly makes the Pharisaic tithing practices and the moral imperatives "matters of Torah."

allusion in the text and its radical implications. A Jewish exegete, Samuel Lachs, sensitive to the halakhic significance of the allusion, has recognized the biblical text undergirding Matthew 23:2–3: "This is based on Deuteronomy 17:10, which is the biblical basis for rabbinic authority replacing that of the priests."[37] Whatever synagogue architecture was like in Yeshua's day, the "seat of Moses" in this verse refers primarily to the correspondence between the high court of Deuteronomy 17 and the role of Moses during Israel's time in the wilderness.[38] Thus, Matthew's Yeshua states that the Pharisaic teachers occupy the position of the judges in Deuteronomy 17—they are the legitimate heirs of Moses and have authority to interpret and apply the Torah in their generation as Moses did in his. This way of reading Matthew 23:1–3 is confirmed by what Yeshua says about how their words are to be received: "carefully observe all that they say to you." This is a paraphrase of Deuteronomy 17:10: "carefully observe all that they instruct you to do."

The importance of this text for our purpose cannot be overestimated. Yeshua here employs the same verse to justify the halakhic legitimacy of the Pharisaic teachers as is later used in rabbinic tradition to justify the halakhic legitimacy of the rabbis. As in the examples cited above, it is highly likely that this commonality reflects Matthew's intimate knowledge of the inner workings of the early rabbinic movement and his own affirmation of much of its traditional teaching. The rabbinic and Matthean reading suits well Deuteronomy 17's original function within the Pentateuch as presented above. Though Matthew 23 proceeds to castigate those very same Pharisees for unworthy conduct, this fact only throws the initial verses into bolder relief. Matthew apparently approves of the central Pharisaic tradition but cannot stomach the Pharisees themselves—whose spiritual descendants are presumably now opposing his post-70 community of Jewish Yeshua-believers.

Matthew and "The Tradition of the Elders"

Is it possible to reconcile such an interpretation of Matthew 23:2–3 with the apparent rejection of the "tradition of the elders" in Matthew 15:1–20? In chapter 2 we argued that Matthew edited Mark's version of the controversy over hand-

37. Samuel Tobias Lachs, *A Rabbinic Commentary on the New Testament* (Hoboken, NJ: Ktav, 1987), 366.

38. "We must remember here to see the people's representatives and especially the elders as we find them in the exilic/postexilic variants of the story from Ex 18 in Deut 1 and Num 11 as functioning in the line of Moses, as established and imbued with his spirit. The pronouncement and interpretation (or application) of law made by them is thus a part of a comprehensively interpreted Mosaic office. When, in Matt 23:2, the Pharisees and the Scribes sit on the seat of Moses, this goes far beyond the question of the existence of a seat of Moses in the synagogue—an actual piece of furniture—and it refers to the same phenomenon." Crusemann, *The Torah*, 103.

washing in order to make clear that the dispute concerned Pharisaic custom rather than basic biblical commandments (i.e., the dietary laws). At this point we should take another look at these two versions of the story in order to see how they deal with the Pharisaic "tradition of the elders."[39]

In Mark 7:5 the Pharisees begin by asking Yeshua, "Why do your disciples not live [literally: walk] according to the tradition of the elders?" The word "walk" in its Hebrew root is related etymologically—at least in the popular mind of Jewish antiquity—to the rabbinic term halakhah. Thus the question could be understood to imply that Yeshua's disciples in general ignore distinctive Pharisaic traditions. Yeshua responds to the question (Mark 7:6–7) by citing Isaiah 29:13 in a way that appears to treat the Pharisaic tradition as a mere "human precept." He then draws a general conclusion from the biblical text, in reference to the Pharisees: "You abandon the commandment of God and hold to human tradition" (Mark 7:8).[40] After citing the biblical text and applying it to the Pharisees, Yeshua offers a specific example of this habitual pattern of conduct (Mark 7:9–12).[41] He concludes the example by stating that in so teaching and acting, the Pharisees are "making void the word of God" through their tradition (Mark 7:13a).[42] He also adds a final flourish: "And you do many things like this" (Mark 7:13b). These final words capture the heart of Yeshua's charges in Mark 7. By leading with the biblical text, paraphrasing its words as a criticism of Pharisaic tradition, providing a particular case as an example of abuse, and then concluding with a general statement that explicitly indicates the case was but an example of a pattern of conduct, Mark 7 raises fundamental questions about the Pharisaic tradition as a whole.[43]

39. See Appendix A at the end of this chapter for the parallel texts of Matthew 15:1–14 and Mark 7:1–2, 5–15 in synoptic form.

40. The word translated "abandon" (*aphentes*) is a present participle, implying here continuous, habitual action.

41. "You have a fine way of rejecting [*atheteite*] the commandment of God in order to keep your tradition!" (Mark 7:9). The word translated "rejecting" is in the present tense, again implying habitual action.

42. "Making void" (*akurountes*)—again, a present participle.

43. At the same time, even Mark 7 falls short of a definitive rejection of Pharisaic tradition. Two points are of special significance. First, the Pharisees would not attack Yeshua for permitting his disciples to act contrary to the tradition of the elders if he had not given them grounds to think of him as one sympathetic to Pharisaic norms. Would Pharisees criticize a Sadducean teacher for permitting his disciples to neglect Pharisaic customs? Thus, the complaint itself reveals an underlying affinity. Second, the Pharisees single out "some of Yeshua's disciples"—they do not criticize the conduct of *all* the disciples, nor Yeshua himself. Does this suggest that Yeshua practiced ritual handwashing (as did some of his disciples) but did not insist that *all* his disciples follow the custom? If so, Yeshua does not reject Pharisaic custom in itself, but only its level of importance and authority. These subtle reminders of Yeshua's affinity for the Pharisees (and vice versa) were probably built into the narrative received by Mark. While the evangelist himself does nothing to highlight them, he also does not eliminate them from the text.

The differences in Matthew's version of the confrontation are subtle but striking. In Matthew the Pharisees ask, "Why do your disciples break the tradition of the elders?" (Matthew 15:1). The disciples are charged with violating the tradition of the elders in a particular instance.[44] Matthew avoids the word "walk," which could imply a general disregard for the tradition. He also uses the same word ("break") in Yeshua's reply: "And why do you break the commandment of God for the sake of your tradition?" (Matthew 15:3). The verbal repetition underscores Matthew's central point in dealing with the tradition of the elders—it becomes problematic when it takes precedence over fundamental biblical commandments. In the next two verses (Matthew 15:4–5), Yeshua immediately presents the particular case of honoring parents and dedicating property to the sanctuary (unlike Mark, who first cites Isaiah 29:13). He concludes from this case: "So, for the sake of your tradition, you have made void (*ekurosate*) the word of God" (Matthew 15:6 RSV). In Mark 7:13 the same verb is found, but in the present tense. Here the verb is an aorist, implying a particular judgment regarding a particular case. Only after all this does Yeshua cite Isaiah 29:13 (Matthew 15:7–9). In Matthew the biblical reference provides support for a prophetic critique of a specific halakhic abuse. It does not constitute an attack on the Pharisaic tradition as a whole. This assessment is further buttressed by the elimination of the final Markan flourish: "And you do many things like this." Matthew does add verses that denounce the Pharisees themselves as "blind guides" (Matthew 15:12–14), but this is consistent with his pattern of affirming Pharisaic tradition while finding fault with the character and leadership of the Pharisees themselves.

Matthew's approach to Pharisaic tradition resembles his approach to the ritual commandments of the written Torah. Just as he places ritual commandments at a lower level than the commandments of "justice, mercy, and faith," so that the latter must take precedence when norms collide, so he subordinates Pharisaic tradition to the written Torah. At the same time, he affirms the authority of the ritual commandments, announcing that "whoever breaks one of the least of these commandments, and teaches others to do the same, will be called least in the kingdom of heaven" (Matthew 5:19). The parallels between Matthew's halakhic language and judgments and later rabbinic material, along with the puzzling affirmation of Pharisaic authority in Matthew 23:2–3, make it likely that Matthew treated Pharisaic tradition with similar respect.

---

44. The term "break" also presumes recognition of the authority of the rules that are violated.

Matthew's "Polemic Affinity"

The commonalities between Matthew and proto-rabbinic tradition extend beyond specifically halakhic concerns. Like rabbinic texts, Matthew favors the use of circumlocutions (such as "heaven") in place of the word "God." Like the Mishnah, Matthew follows a topical method of organization rather than the more dramatic narrative form found in Mark and Luke. Like rabbinic texts, Matthew shows a fondness for numerical patterning (five discourses, ten mighty deeds, seven petitions, seven parables, seven woes), *gematriya* (fourteen generations and the numerical value of the name "David" in Yeshua's genealogy), and mnemonic devices (such as parallelism). Matthew's version of the Lord's Prayer includes material—absent in Luke—that resembles later synagogue liturgy.[45]

How can Matthew combine such discordant Pharisaic and anti-Pharisaic tendencies? We can best understand this feature of Matthew according to what Peter Tomson calls "polemic affinity." In commenting on Matthew 5:17–20, Tomson writes:

> The typically Matthaean polemics against the superficial piety of the "scribes and Pharisees" is recognizable. Polemics is a negative sign of affinity, and the latter betrays itself in the characteristically Pharisaic notions that this passage also contains. Jesus admits here to a more radical version of the Pharisaic observance of the law ["unless your righteousness exceeds that of the scribes and Pharisees . . ."]. . . .
>
> The polemic affinity with the Pharisees is expressed in the technical terminology. In rabbinic literature as well the "jot and the crotchet"—the smallest letter yod and the small curls that decorate the letters—are proverbial for the great significance of small details. . . . Jesus is on Pharisaic turf and uses the appropriate terminology.[46]

Thus the polemic intensity derives not from distance but from proximity. David Sim has also noted this aspect of Matthew:

> It is now well recognized that polemical and stereotypical language such as we find in Matthew does not reflect the distance between the two parties. On the contrary, it indicates both physical and ideological proximity between the disputing groups. . . . A general sociological rule of thumb is that the closer the relationship between dissenting groups, the more intense the conflict and the sharper the resultant polemic.[47]

---

45. "[May your Name be sanctified] on earth as in heaven" is identical to the reader's repetition of the *kedushah* in the daily morning *Amidah.* See Birnbaum, *Daily Prayer Book,* 83–84.

46. Tomson, *Heaven,* 284–85.

47. Sim, *Matthew and Christian Judaism,* 121.

Matthew's anti-Pharisaic polemic is not only consistent with his own Pharisaic orientation, and with the common ground he shares with Pharisaic tradition; the one actually derives from the other. The heated polemic exists because of the intimate proximity.

In light of this, we should not hesitate to interpret Matthew 13:52 in a bold manner. This verse consists of a saying of Yeshua found only in Matthew:

> Therefore every scribe who has been trained for the kingdom of heaven is like the master of a household who brings out of his treasure what is new and what is old.

It is often suggested that this saying captures the evangelist's own sense of identity as a scribe "trained for the kingdom of heaven."[48] We should recall that elsewhere in Matthew "scribe" equals "Pharisee." Is this not also what Matthew means here? All that we have seen points to the fact that the author of this Gospel is steeped in proto-rabbinic modes of speech and thought. Thus he may well be a "Pharisaic scribe" who has become a student of Yeshua ("trained for the kingdom of heaven") and is now able to present both what is new (i.e., the eschatological reality of Yeshua's teaching and work) and what is old (i.e., the Pharisaic scribal traditions that he had formerly mastered). His adherence to Yeshua has now put him and his community at odds with his former teachers and friends, and tempers are flaring hot. He can no longer use the term *Pharisee* in a neutral or positive manner. Nevertheless, he sees himself as a "[Pharisaic] scribe" whose distinctive Pharisaic knowledge and perspective enrich his understanding of the Messiah and his capacity to convey the Messiah's message.

Luke-Acts and John

The author of Luke-Acts appears to have less intimate knowledge of Pharisaic thought and practice than does the author of Matthew. However, these books also approach the Pharisees with more sympathy and appreciation. Many Pharisees invite Yeshua to their homes for meals—even though he regularly uses such occasions to admonish them (Luke 7:36–50; 11:37–52; 14:1–24).[49] These invitations

---

48. See, for example, Davies and Allison, *Matthew,* vol. 2, 445. Matthew's distinctive reference to Yeshua-believing scribes is also found in Matthew 23:34 (see Luke 11:49).

49. "Jesus will criticise the Pharisees at every opportunity, but they nonetheless continue to treat him as a respected colleague." Steve Mason, "Chief Priests, Sadducees, Pharisees and Sanhedrin in Acts," in *The Book of Acts in Its Palestinian Setting,* ed. Richard Bauckham, vol. 4 of *The Book of Acts in Its First Century Setting,* ed. Bruce W. Winter (Grand Rapids: Eerdmans, 1995), 135. Peter Tomson sees more reciprocity in the relationship: "The Pharisees in the story of 'Luke' are portrayed as having mixed feelings about Jesus. They do not fundamentally reject him, but neither do they trust him completely. Jesus' reserved attitude towards them corresponds to this: he agrees with them on the essentials, but has serious criticism on details." Tomson, *Heaven,* 224.

are significant, since the Pharisees emphasized table fellowship among those sharing a common code of ritual purity. Meal invitations from Pharisees thus signify respect for Yeshua's piety and Torah observance. Some Pharisees warn Yeshua that Herod Antipas wants to arrest and execute him; they evidently seek to protect him from harm (Luke 13:31–33).[50] Yeshua tells some Pharisees that "the reign of God is among you"—and this may imply that God is especially among them *because* they are Pharisees (Luke 17:20–22).[51]

Luke's account of the early Yeshua movement in Acts depicts the Pharisees in an even more favorable light. Gamaliel speaks in the Sanhedrin on their behalf and succeeds in winning the release of the imprisoned apostles (Acts 5:34–40). Many Pharisees become members of the Jerusalem ekklesia (Acts 15:5). In Acts, Paul proudly identifies himself as a Pharisee, and does so in the present rather than the past tense: "I am a Pharisee, a son of Pharisees" (Acts 23:6; see also Acts 26:4–8). When he appears before the Sanhedrin, the Pharisaic members of the council come to his defense, even as Gamaliel earlier defended the apostles (Acts 23:9). In summary, the Lukan writings do not present the Pharisees as the enemies of Yeshua, of his followers, or of the good news. Instead, Luke sees them as those Jews most open, sympathetic, and helpful to the new movement.[52]

As in its approach to the Jewish people as a whole, the Gospel of John is a special case. Like Matthew, John treats the Pharisees as a leadership group linked to the chief priests (John 7:32, 45; 11:47, 57; 18:3). Unlike Matthew, they are not explicitly identified as scribes. In fact, John tells us nothing about the Pharisees that would enable us to distinguish them from the chief priests other than the fact that they apparently have some connection to the synagogue (John 12:42). At times, John sees the Pharisees as identical to the ill-defined leadership group he calls "the Jews."[53]

In reality, we learn nothing from John about the Pharisees as a distinct group whose particular tradition we are seeking to assess. Like Matthew, John portrays

50. "While in this Gospel [i.e., the Gospel of Luke] . . . the Pharisees are not at all involved in Jesus' trial and execution, here they even want to save his life!" (Tomson, *Heaven,* 223)

51. "Jesus' most compassionate statement to the Pharisees comes when they inquire of him, still the respected teacher, 'when the kingdom of God comes' (17:20). In responding that 'the kingdom of God is *within you*' (17:22), Jesus is declaring that the Pharisees have the kingdom in themselves, as the 'older brother' [Luke 15: 25–32] with heaven's resources at their disposal, as the righteous and healthy of society; but as we have seen time and again, they squander their potential." Mason, 142.

52. Though he uses anachronistic and misleading terminology, Robert Brawley nonetheless accurately perceives Luke's attitude toward the Pharisees: "Luke ushers the Pharisees right up to the portals of the Christian faith. . . . Paul himself then becomes the example of a Pharisee most faithful to the hopes of Israel." Robert L. Brawley, *Luke-Acts and the Jews* (Atlanta: Scholars, 1987), 158.

53. John 1:24 (see 1:19); 8:13 (see 8:22); 9:13, 15, 16, 40 (see 9:18, 22); 12:42 (see 9:22).

the Pharisees (with the exception of Nicodemus) as the opponents of Yeshua. However, these Pharisees are colorless and featureless, and John's only criticism of them is that they do not welcome Yeshua. We cannot base an evaluation of the Pharisees on John's depiction of them any more than we can base an evaluation of the Jewish people as a whole on John's portrayal of "the Jews."[54]

We hope we have made our point: the New Testament treatment of the Pharisees and of Pharisaic tradition is far more complex than it might first appear. They play a relatively minor role in the Markan narrative. They become enormously important in Matthew as villains, yet a deeper analysis demonstrates that Matthew's polemic derives from proximity: Matthew contains the most anti-Pharisaic rhetoric in the New Testament because it also contains the New Testament's most Pharisaic vision of Yeshua and his teaching. Luke and Acts minimize the negative features of the Pharisees and maximize the positive, seeing them as Yeshua-believers *in potentia*. Finally, John presents them as dark, shadowy figures who oppose Yeshua, but have no clear features by which they can be identified.

In 1985 the Vatican Commission for Religious Relations with the Jews issued a document that included discussion of Yeshua's relationship to the Pharisees.[55] The document makes many of the same observations found here and draws similar conclusions. It notes the many commonalities between Yeshua's teaching and that of the Pharisees, and it underlines the absence of the Pharisees "in accounts of the Passion."[56] The document also stresses that the New Testament sometimes presents Pharisees in a positive light. Addressing the adversarial quality of some of the biblical narratives, the Vatican Commission explains them in terms of polemic affinity: "It may also be stressed that, if Jesus shows himself severe toward the Pharisees, it is because he is closer to them than to other contemporary groups."[57]

54. See our discussion of John in chapter 3.

55. "Notes on the Correct Way to Present the Jews and Judaism in Preaching and Catechesis in the Roman Catholic Church," in *The Bible, the Jews, and the Death of Jesus* (Washington, DC: United States Conference of Catholic Bishops, 2004), 48–53.

56. Ibid., 50–51.

57. Ibid., 51. In 1988 the U.S. National Conference of Catholic Bishops issued its own document on the same topic, in which it restated the position of the Vatican document: "Jesus was perhaps closer to the Pharisees in his religious vision than to any other group of his time. The 1985 *Notes* suggest that this affinity with Pharisaism may be a reason for many of his apparent controversies with them. . . . In some cases, Jesus appears to have been participating in internal Pharisaic debates on various points of interpretation of God's law." "God's Mercy Endures Forever: Guidelines on the Presentation of Jews and Judaism in Catholic Preaching" (Bishops' Committee on the Liturgy, National Conference of Catholic Bishops, September 1988), in *The Bible, the Jews, and the Death of Jesus*, 68.

The New Testament view of the Pharisees has more positive elements than one might at first expect. Luke offers a model for a balanced assessment of the Pharisaic movement as a whole. Matthew 23:2–3 provides support for the legitimacy of the proto-rabbinic halakhic tradition. Though one could not base an endorsement of later rabbinic Judaism on the New Testament alone, the place of the Pharisees in that document presents no obstacle to such an endorsement.

Rabbinic Judaism from a New Testament Perspective

It would be helpful at this point in our study to offer a detailed examination of rabbinic Judaism as a religious tradition, and then to compare and contrast that tradition with a canonical reading of New Testament teaching. Unfortunately we cannot possibly undertake such an examination in the space here available. Instead, as we conclude these two chapters, we will ask a more modest question: is there any insuperable obstacle, from a New Testament perspective, in affirming rabbinic Judaism as a divinely sanctioned religious tradition appointed for the purpose of preserving the Jewish people, God's covenant with the Jewish people, and the way of life stipulated by that covenant?

As it turns out, we have already dismissed the most common objections to rabbinic Judaism lodged by Christians through the centuries. These objections were usually based on a reading of the New Testament that we have found severely wanting. Thus Christian critics have accused rabbinic Judaism of being fixated on external ritual because it holds tightly to circumcision, the Sabbath, and the dietary laws. However, we have seen that the New Testament itself affirms the validity and importance of these practices for the Jewish people. Christian critics have accused rabbinic Judaism of maintaining a religious-ethnic distinction that had been abrogated by the coming of the Messiah. However, we have seen that the New Testament itself upholds the ongoing ethnic distinctiveness of the Jewish people and witnesses to a bilateral ecclesiology in solidarity with Israel that expands the boundaries of the covenant without obliterating Israel's unique position within it. Christian critics have charged rabbinic Judaism with the crime of rejecting the Messiah sent to the Jewish people and with developing a religious system that prevents Jewish people from entertaining his claims. However, we have seen that the resistance to accepting Yeshua in mature rabbinic Judaism (i.e., the Judaism of the Mishnah and Talmud) involved an act of loyalty to the covenant that paradoxically brought the Jewish people into deeper union with the one they were ostensibly denying. Christian critics have attacked the rabbinic doctrine of the oral Torah, arguing that it necessarily implies a supplanting of biblical authority with mere human teaching. However, we have seen that the written Torah itself provides the basis for the doctrine of the oral Torah, and that the rabbinic justification for this doctrine (built upon Deuteronomy 17) has a sound exegetical foundation that is even recognized in the New Testament (e.g., Matthew 23:2–3). Christian critics have adopted Matthew's polemic against the Pharisees and turned it against rabbinic Judaism as the later embodiment of Pharisaic tradition. However, we have seen that Matthew's rhetoric derives from polemic affinity and demonstrates his proximity to Pharisaism rather than his distance from it, and that Luke-Acts takes a far friendlier view of the Pharisees and their tradition.

Until recently Protestant Christian critics viewed rabbinic Judaism through the lens of Reformation disputes and attacked it as a later manifestation of the Jewish "works righteousness" religion that the apostle Paul allegedly denounced. E. P. Sanders decisively undermined this caricature of rabbinic Judaism in his landmark volume, *Paul and Palestinian Judaism*, and today most Protestant scholars refrain from this attack.[58] As Sanders demonstrated, rabbinic Judaism sees God's relationship with the Jewish people as rooted in God's gracious initiative and guaranteed by God's gracious promise.

The traditional Christian attacks on rabbinic Judaism, supposedly based on New Testament teaching, turn out to be questionable at best. Going beyond this assessment, John Howard Yoder has argued provocatively that rabbinic Judaism in the age of Christendom displayed a way of life that was closer to the teaching and example of Yeshua than what was generally found in the church of the same period: "For over a millennium the Jews of the diaspora were the closest thing to the ethic of Jesus existing on any significant scale anywhere in Christendom."[59] As an Anabaptist, Yoder focuses especially on rabbinic Judaism's communal ethos, its approach to the external governments that ruled the territories in which Jews lived, its resistance to the Zealot temptation of forcing God's hand, and its regard for the sanctity of human life.[60]

As an additional argument for the legitimacy of rabbinic Judaism, we may recall that the entire people of Israel, according to the Torah and other biblical books such as Esther, serves as the earthly agent in conferring halakhic authority. It is striking that Pharisaic tradition receives as positive and prominent treat-

---

58. E. P. Sanders, *Paul and Palestinian Judaism* (Philadelphia: Fortress, 1977), 33–238. Krister Stendahl also captured the attention of New Testament exegetes when he argued that the Reformation construal of Paul's teaching on this topic distorted the apostle's meaning and intent. Krister Stendahl, *Paul Among Jews and Gentiles* (Philadelphia: Fortress, 1976). Stendahl's reading of Paul has not established the same kind of consensus as Sanders's characterization of rabbinic Judaism, but it has succeeded in putting the issue on the table.

59. John Howard Yoder, *The Jewish-Christian Schism Revisited*, ed. Michael G. Cartwright and Peter Ochs (Grand Rapids: Eerdmans, 2003), 81–82.

60. Ibid., 75–89.

ment as it does in the New Testament, since it had not achieved full acceptance among the Jewish people as a whole during the first century. Postbiblical Jewish institutions that had achieved such acceptance—such as the synagogue with its attendant pattern of public scripture reading, or the recitation of blessings before eating bread or drinking wine—are received without question by Yeshua, the apostles, and the New Testament authors. By the early Middle Ages, the entire Jewish world recognized rabbinic tradition—the Judaism of the written and oral Torah—to be the authorized, legitimate expression of Jewish religious life. From the perspective of both the written Torah and the New Testament, this gives rabbinic Judaism a greater stature than Pharisaic tradition enjoyed during the Second Temple period and immediately thereafter.

We are not arguing here that New Testament teaching and the teaching of rabbinic Judaism are the same. We are also not arguing that the New Testament directly legitimates rabbinic Judaism.[61] Because we have strong theological grounds, articulated at the beginning of the previous chapter, for accepting the legitimacy of rabbinic Judaism, we do not require such a direct endorsement. All we need is the assurance that the New Testament presents no insuperable obstacles in this path. In our view, this low bar has been leapt with ample room to spare. Our thesis—the legitimacy, value, and importance of rabbinic Judaism—remains intact.

That thesis is crucial. If rabbinic Judaism is not valid, then no Judaism is valid. It is the only Judaism available—at least for the overwhelming majority of Jews in the world.[62] It is the Judaism that preserved the Hebrew language, the Hebrew scripture, the synagogue and home liturgy, the Jewish way of life grounded in the Torah, and the Jewish people themselves. Like every tradition transmitted and nurtured by human communities, including the Christian tradition, rabbinic Judaism is imperfect and requires continual renewal, development, and contextual reapplication. Nevertheless, it is *rabbinic Judaism* that is being renewed, developed, and contextually reapplied. We cannot affirm the election and way of life of the Jewish people without likewise affirming the tradition that has sustained them both.

61. Nor, of course, are we arguing that rabbinic Judaism is a "pure" tradition, entirely without defect. Loyal Jews would not assert this about Judaism any more than loyal Christians would assert it of Christianity, considered as a historical tradition.

62. There are small pockets of Jews who have preserved nonrabbinic forms of Judaism, such as the Karaites and the Ethiopian Jews (some might also place the Samaritans in this category). However, these forms of Judaism are not viable options for most twenty-first-century Jews, who have no living contact with them. Nor is it reasonable to think that extinct nonrabbinic forms of Judaism (such as Qumran Judaism, or even first-century Yeshua-believing Judaism), available to us only through fragmentary documents, can be reconstructed out of thin air.

Appendix A

Matthew 15	Mark 7
¹Then Pharisees and scribes came to Jesus from Jerusalem and said,	¹Now when the Pharisees and some of the scribes who had come from Jerusalem gathered around him,
	²they noticed that some of his disciples were eating with defiled hands, that is, without washing them.
²"Why do your disciples break the tradition of the elders? For they do not wash their hands before they eat."	⁵So the Pharisees and the scribes asked him, "Why do your disciples not live according to the tradition of the elders, but eat with defiled hands?"
³He answered them, "And why do you break the commandment of God for the sake of your tradition?	⁶He said to them, "Isaiah prophesied rightly about you hypocrites, as it is written, 'This people honors me with their lips, but their hearts are far from me;
⁴For God said, 'Honor your father and your mother,' and, 'Whoever speaks evil of father or mother must surely die.'	⁷in vain do they worship me, teaching human precepts as doctrines.'
⁵But you say that whoever tells father or mother, 'Whatever support you might have had from me is given to God,' then that person need not honor the father.	⁸You abandon the commandment of God and hold to human tradition." ⁹Then he said to them, "You have a fine way of rejecting the commandment of God in order to keep your tradition!
⁶So, for the sake of your tradition, you make void the word of God.	¹⁰For Moses said, 'Honor your father and your mother'; and, 'Whoever speaks evil of father or mother must surely die.'
⁷You hypocrites! Isaiah prophesied rightly about you when he said: ⁸'This people honors me with their lips, but their hearts are far from me; ⁹in vain do they worship me, teaching human precepts as doctrines.'"	¹¹But you say that if anyone tells father or mother, 'Whatever support you might have had from me is Corban' (that is, an offering to God)— ¹²then you no longer permit doing anything for a father or mother,
	¹³thus making void the word of God through your tradition that you have handed on. And you do many things like this."
¹⁰Then he called the crowd to him and said to them, "Listen and understand:	¹⁴Then he called the crowd again and said to them, "Listen to me, all of you, and understand:
¹¹it is not what goes into the mouth that defiles a person, but it is what comes out of the mouth that defiles."	¹⁵there is nothing outside a person that by going in can defile, but the things that come out are what defile."
¹²Then the disciples approached and said to him, "Do you know that the Pharisees took offense when they heard what you said?"	

Matthew 15	Mark 7

[13]He answered, "Every plant that my heavenly Father has not planted will be uprooted.

[14]Let them alone; they are blind guides of the blind. And if one blind person guides another, both will fall into a pit."

8

FROM MISSIONARY TO POSTMISSIONARY
MESSIANIC JUDAISM

Many contemporary Christians and Jews view the division of Judaism and Christianity into two separate religious communities and traditions as a healthy historical development. Such a view enables them to validate both communities and traditions, while giving personal loyalty to only one of them. We have argued here for a different thesis: the division of Judaism and Christianity was a tragic schism within the one people of God that badly damaged both sides.

Most Christians and Jews of the last two thousand years have viewed the emergence of their two separate communities neither as a natural and beneficial evolution nor as a schism crippling them both. Instead, they have considered their own community and tradition to be the only authentic heir of the promise to Abraham, Isaac, and Jacob, and have seen the other as an apostate people, alienated from the covenant. In the Christian church—with its missionary origins and its position of political and cultural dominance—this view produced a missionary posture toward the Jewish people.[1] That posture included the wish that Jews would renounce the error of "Judaism," embrace the truth of "Christianity," and enter the Christian church. In the process, they would forsake their religious identity as Jews and become part of a universal faith community.

---

1. The *missionary posture* existed even when no *missionary program* was initiated.

This Christian missionary posture to Jews has no precedent in the New Testament. Undoubtedly the early Yeshua movement expanded because of the dynamic missionary impulse at its heart. That impulse led the apostles to go to the Gentiles, urging them to forsake idolatry and to turn to the God of Israel, the only living and true God. Upon doing so, these Gentiles would enter the twofold ekklesia and thereby share in Israel's identity and destiny. However, the apostolic approach to the Jewish people was another matter. The apostles were Jews addressing other Jews, announcing that Israel's Messiah had come and that Israel's destiny was soon to be realized—if the community of Israel would only welcome its Messiah. Accepting this message entailed a new Jewish affiliation, but not one that required a rupture with the wider Jewish community or its generally accepted norms.

The ecclesiological vision presented in this book calls into question the traditional Christian missionary posture toward the Jewish people. Our ecclesiology can be summarized in five basic principles: (1) the perpetual validity of God's covenant with the Jewish people; (2) the perpetual validity of the Jewish way of life rooted in the Torah, as the enduring sign and instrument of that covenant; (3) the validity of Jewish religious tradition as the historical embodiment of the Jewish way of life rooted in the Torah; (4) the bilateral constitution of the ekklesia, consisting of distinct but united Jewish and Gentile expressions of Yeshua-faith; (5) the ecumenical imperative of the ekklesia, which entails bringing the redeemed nations of the world into solidarity with the people of Israel in anticipation of Israel's—and the world's—final redemption. In short, we have argued for a *bilateral ecclesiology in solidarity with Israel that affirms Israel's covenant, Torah, and religious tradition.* According to this pattern, the Jewish ekklesia serves the wider Jewish community by constituting its eschatological firstfruits, sanctifying the whole and revealing the eschatological meaning of Jewish identity and destiny. It also serves the wider Jewish community by linking the redeemed of the nations to Israel's corporate life and spiritual heritage, thereby enabling Israel to fulfill its mission as a light to the nations. This ecclesiology stands in stark contrast to the Christian church's missionary posture toward the Jewish people, especially in the post-Constantinian era. In that setting, the Christian church approached the Jewish people from outside, as an external community opposed to Jewish national existence and the Jewish way of life. In effect, it treated the Jewish people the way the early Yeshua movement treated the idolatrous Gentiles—only with greater contempt.

Two centuries ago the Christian church's missionary posture toward the Jewish people became for the first time an aggressive, concerted, and organized missionary program. Paradoxically, this new programmatic initiative coincided with and derived from a dramatic change in the nature of the missionary posture itself. The Protestant church's Jewish missions both grew out of and further stimulated a new perspective on the Jewish people that would eventually affirm the basic principles of the bilateral ecclesiology articulated above. Thus the new missionary movement carried within it the seeds of its own demise—or, rather, its own transformation.

In this chapter we will look at the Christian missionary program of the past two centuries and the resultant emergence of Hebrew Christianity and Messianic Judaism. As a parallel development that has received too little attention, we will also examine the surprising appearance of Hebrew Catholicism. We will assess these movements in order to discern the development of a *bilateral ecclesiology in solidarity with Israel that affirms Israel's covenant, Torah, and religious tradition.* Looking at recent currents in Messianic Judaism, we will argue that the movement's trajectory points to an unexpected destination: a fully postmissionary form of Messianic Judaism that reveals the mystery of Israel in the heart of the ekklesia, and the mystery of Yeshua in the heart of Israel.

The Missionary Movement and Hebrew Christianity

The Birth of a New Movement

Before the nineteenth century, a Jew's entry into the Christian church led invariably to the dissolution of his or her Jewish identity. As seen in chapter 5, the church demanded that the new Christian renounce all Jewish practice and sever all ties with the Jewish community. The sincere convert came to see Jewish religious tradition as profane, blind, and even wicked. Thus, after becoming Bishop of Burgos in 1414, the former Rabbi Solomon Halevi could describe his religious journey in these words:

> I was . . . brought up in Jewish blindness and incredulity; while learning Holy Scripture from unsanctified teachers, I received erroneous opinions from erring men, who cloud the pure letter of Scripture by impure inventions. . . . But when it pleased Him whose mercies are infinite to call me from darkness to light, and from the depth of the pit to the open air of heaven, the scales seemed as it were to fall from the eyes of my understanding.[2]

The ex-Rabbi's extreme language reveals the mentality of the times: Judaism was blind, unbelieving, unholy, erroneous, and impure, and Jews lived in "darkness" and "the depth of the pit."

2. Dan Cohn-Sherbok, *Messianic Judaism* (New York: Cassell, 2000), 9.

Knowledgeable Jewish converts to Christianity such as Rabbi Halevi did not actually sever all ties with the Jewish community and assimilate quietly into their new Gentile environment. The Jewish community would have been happier if they had done so. Instead, they employed their understanding of Jewish texts and life in attempting to bring their former coreligionists along the same path they had trodden. In other words, they became missionaries. Given their low opinion of Judaism, their missionary zeal sometimes led them to denounce rabbinic writings as blasphemous and even to seek papal or imperial sanction to censor or burn these sacred Jewish texts. In this way Jewish converts such as Nicholas Donin (thirteenth century), Pablo Christiani (thirteenth century), Geronimo de Santa Fe (fifteenth century), and Johannes Pfefferkorn (sixteenth century) earned a place of infamy in the annals of Jewish history. As the Hebrew Christian scholar Jacob Jocz notes, "some of the converts, especially in the Middle Ages, showed a fanatic hatred to Jewry and were the cause of great tribulation."[3] As a result, the image of the Jewish convert to Christianity and missionary to "the Jews" was tainted in the Jewish popular imagination not only with apostasy but also with treachery.

Christian attitudes toward Judaism began to change with the Renaissance (fifteenth and sixteenth centuries). The brilliant humanist Giovanni Pico della Mirandola (1463–1494) became a devoted student of Jewish mysticism, which he saw as ancient wisdom preserved through the centuries by the Jewish people. In 1490 he met with Johann Reuchlin in Florence and urged the German scholar to pursue the study of rabbinic literature. Reuchlin heeded the advice, and more than two decades later became the champion of Jewish writings against the slanders of Johannes Pfefferkorn. Like Pico della Mirandola, Reuchlin saw rabbinic literature as confirming rather than denying the truths of Christianity. His response to Pfefferkorn elicited the support of Christian humanists throughout Europe and signaled that a new orientation toward Judaism was possible in the Christian world, at least among the scholarly elite. This new orientation, reflected in Christian study of kabbalah in the sixteenth century, continued to gain ground in the seventeenth century with the emergence of appreciative Christian scholarship on the Talmud.[4]

---

3. Jakob Jocz, *The Jewish People and Jesus Christ* (London: SPCK, 1954), 201. Jocz adds the following: "That some converts in the past have behaved treacherously, there is no denying.... No less an authority than Dr. H. C. Lea, the historian of the Inquisition, observes: 'From early times the hardest blows endured by Judaism had always been dealt by its apostate children, whose training had taught them the weakest points to assail and whose necessity of self-justification led them to attack these mercilessly'" (225).

4. Lev Gillet, *Communion in the Messiah* (London: Lutterworth, 1942; repr. Eugene, OR: Wipf and Stock, 1999), 23–27.

Some of the greatest Christian scholars of Judaism of the nineteenth century, such as Hermann Strack, Gustaf Dalman, Franz Delitzsch, and G. H. Box, were also champions of missionary efforts among the Jewish people. Their new attitude toward Judaism changed the way Christian missionaries to the Jews presented their message. Jocz notes this change:

> The effort at an honest appreciation of Judaism has had a salutary effect upon the whole missionary enterprise. The repeated admonitions by eminent scholars . . . who have pressed for a closer study of Judaism, have not been in vain. The result was not only a more adequate presentation of Christianity to Judaism and Judaism to Christianity, but, what is more important, a deeper understanding of the significance of the Gospel.[5]

> A definite reaction against such one-sided and partisan presentation of Christianity [as was offered by Christian missionaries to Jews in previous eras] marks the modern missionary approach. Here Judaism is presented not as an erroneous religion, devoid of all truth, separated in letter and spirit from the Old Testament, but as of the same essence as Christianity, yet at a less developed stage.[6]

The perception of Judaism as a positive religious reality did not dull missionary fervor, but it did alter the missionary message and methodology.

On the popular level more favorable Christian attitudes toward Jews and Judaism arose mainly in connection with Protestant religious movements of the seventeenth, eighteenth, and nineteenth centuries. The English Puritans of the seventeenth century focused on the Pentateuch and its legislation as few Christians had done before, creating an environment in which Christians could see Jewish devotion to the Torah in a different light.[7] In the same period German pietists took special interest in the Jewish people and their religion. Philip Jacob Spener (1635–1705), a key figure in this movement, even argued for what would later be called "Jewish emancipation."[8] However, the most potent force for changing Christian attitudes toward Jews and Judaism was the passion for eschatology that grew steadily in the seventeenth and eighteenth centuries and reached a crescendo in the nineteenth. The eschatological scenarios common in that period often included belief in the Jewish people's return to the land of their ancestors and national acceptance of Yeshua as the Messiah. Jocz notes the effect of this belief on attitudes toward the Jewish people:

5. Jocz, *Jesus Christ*, 223.
6. Ibid., 216.
7. "What the revival of Hebrew learning had done in a small intellectual minority was accomplished among the English masses by Puritanism." Gillet, *Communion*, 28.
8. See Jocz, *Jesus Christ*, 222.

Instead of maintaining, as the old Church did, that the Jewish people is utterly rejected by God, it was now recognized that Israel had still a great future. This change was to a large extent effected by the revival of eschatological interest and the intensive . . . study of prophecy which accompanied the pietist movement in Germany and the Evangelical revival in England. . . . A theology in which the Jews played a vital part came into existence.[9]

With the emergence of dispensationalism in the nineteenth century, the Jewish people became not only a part of the eschatological scenario but its structural center. Pioneered in England by John Nelson Darby (1800–1882), dispensationalism held as its fundamental tenet the distinction between the Jewish people and the church. It saw this distinction as becoming especially critical at the eschaton, since the church would be removed ("raptured") from the earth at the beginning of the "great tribulation," and the Jews who remained (the 144,000) would become Messiah's representatives in the world. This theology fostered a Christian view of the Jewish people unlike anything seen in the previous history of the church. In fact, Yaakov Ariel considers it a unique development in the history of religion:

> In no other case has one religious community assigned a predominant role to another religious community in its vision of redemption or claimed that the other group held a special relationship with God. Similarly, in no other situation has one religious group invested so much hope in another group as the key brokers on the road to universal salvation.[10]

On a popular level, the spread of dispensationalism, especially among twentieth-century American evangelicals, did more than any other movement to foster a positive attitude toward Jews among conservative Christians.[11]

Just as scholarly appreciation of Judaism supported rather than undermined missionary activity, so the popular movements mentioned above paradoxically both improved Christian attitudes toward Jews and stimulated mis-

---

9. Ibid., 221.

10. Yaakov Ariel, *Evangelizing the Chosen People* (Chapel Hill: University of North Carolina Press, 2000), 287.

11. "The new dispensationalist understanding of the role of the Jewish people in God's plans for humanity demonstrated itself in the way the missions presented the Christian belief to the Jews. They promoted the idea that the acceptance of the Christian faith was compatible with the Jewish faith and heritage. Throughout the centuries, Christians expected Jews who had embraced Christianity to turn their back on their Jewish heritage and identity. Their Jewishness had been looked upon as a deficiency, an obstacle to be overcome. . . . The new evangelical missions, on the other hand, presented the acceptance of Christianity as a fulfillment of one's Jewish destiny." Ibid., 15.

sionary efforts to convert them. Thus Spener was one of the first to advocate complete religious freedom for the Jews, and also one of the first to propose a detailed missionary agenda for winning the Jews to Christianity.[12] At the University of Halle, a center of German pietism in the eighteenth century, Johannes Heinrich Callenberg established the *Institutum Judaicum* in 1728 for the purpose of training missionaries to the Jewish people.[13] But it was the eighteenth-century evangelical revival in England and its increasing preoccupation with eschatology that made that country the center of Christian missions to the Jews in the nineteenth century.[14] In 1809 the first missionary society devoted to Christian missions to the Jews was established there—the London Society for Promoting Christianity Amongst the Jews. The torch was passed to America as the twentieth century dawned, and American initiative in this sphere derived mainly from the rapid spread of dispensationalism among American evangelicals.[15]

The combination of Christian missionary zeal and heightened esteem for the Jewish people made it possible for a self-conscious "Hebrew Christian" movement to arise in the nineteenth century. Historical developments internal to the Jewish world also contributed to the creation of an environment in which such a movement could flourish. In traditional European society Jews lived for the most part in their own communities, segregated from their Christian neighbors, governing their own political and judicial affairs under the overall jurisdiction of Christian authorities. As Stephen Wylen notes, in this setting "religion was only one aspect of the Jewish way of life, inseparable from law, custom, and culture. There is not even a word for *religion* in the Hebrew language."[16] The blending of nationality and religion that had been a hallmark of Judaism from its beginnings reinforced this arrangement. With the dawning of the European Enlightenment, this situation changed dramatically. In the world at large a new sphere of public life opened up in which Jews could participate

12. Jocz, *Jesus Christ*, 222.

13. Gillet, *Communion*, 173.

14. "The early nineteenth century saw a dramatic rise in attempts to convert Jews in Britain, which was witnessing a strong evangelical and premillennialist resurgence, including hope for the national rejuvenation of the Jews." Ariel, *Evangelizing the Chosen People*, 9.

15. The central thesis of Yaakov Ariel's work is that Christian missionary efforts among the Jewish people in twentieth-century America were impelled primarily by the pervasive influence of dispensationalist theology. As he states in his introduction, "The driving force for a strong movement of American Christians laboring at missionizing the Jews has been a new school of premillennialist hope: dispensationalism. . . . From the widespread acceptance of this belief in America during the 1870's, its adherents took great interest in the Jewish people, the prospect of their national restoration, and religious conversion." Ariel, *Evangelizing the Chosen People*, 2–3.

16. Stephen M. Wylen, *Settings of Silver* (New York: Paulist, 2000), 331.

without forsaking Jewish identity. Then the Jewish Enlightenment, called the *Haskalah*, broke down the walls of the ghetto from within and encouraged Jews to enter the wider flow of European culture.

The *Haskalah* introduced something new into Jewish life: the distinction between Jewish nationality and religion. Exponents of the *Haskalah*, known as *Maskilim*, saw this distinction as essential to their program of reform. In Western Europe, *Maskilim* such as Moses Mendelssohn (1729–86) promoted a view of Judaism as a philosophy and religion rather than a nationality. This principle became an integral part of Reform Judaism in the nineteenth century, permitting Jews to live as loyal Germans or Americans in public life while practicing Judaism in the domestic sphere. In Eastern Europe the *Maskilim* drew the same distinction between nationality and religion but identified Jewish life with the former rather than the latter. In multiethnic, multilingual states such as Russia and Austria-Hungry, it was easy to conceive of the Jews as a people, with their own national identity. Whereas the *Maskilim* in Western Europe affirmed Judaism as a religion and denied its national character, the *Maskilim* in Eastern Europe rejected traditional Jewish religious life and asserted instead the primacy of Jewish nationality.[17] Zionism arose among the Eastern European *Maskilim* as the ultimate expression of a movement emphasizing Jewish nationality over Jewish religion.[18]

Given the new distinction between Jewish nationality and religion, it was now conceivable in Jewish terms that a Jew could enter the church (i.e., accept the Christian religion) and still retain some measure of Jewish national identity. Given the new esteem for the Jewish people existing among the missionaries who were bringing the message of Yeshua to them, this was now also conceivable in Christian terms. As a result, in 1813, four years after the founding of the London Society for Promoting Christianity Amongst the Jews, forty-one Jewish Yeshua-believers formed an association in London called *Beney Abraham* (the Children of Abraham). In 1866 the Hebrew Christian Alliance was established, again in Britain. This was followed by the Hebrew Christian Prayer Union in 1882. The appearance of such institutions represented a radical innovation in the history of Jewish-Christian

17. Ibid., 328–31.

18. "The Zionists rejected the notion that modern Judaism should be a religion. Many Zionists believed that religion is not relevant in the modern world. The Zionists believed that the Jews are above all a nation. Rather than seek acceptance in modern nation-states as citizens of the Jewish faith, Jews ought to seek to restore their own status as a nation among the nations of the world. Religious Judaism became the dominant mode of modern Judaism in Germany, the United States, and other Western countries. In Eastern Europe, with its multinational empires, Zionism was the most appealing movement to Jewish modernists." Wylen, *Settings of Silver*, 382.

relations. For the first time since the early centuries of the common era, Jewish Yeshua-believers were seeking to remain a part of the Jewish people. Jocz sees this as the great divide separating Medieval "baptized Jews" from "modern Hebrew Christianity":

> It is here that the vast difference appears between the modern Hebrew Christian and the baptized Jew of the Middle Ages. Modern Hebrew Christianity is impelled by a desire to remain loyal to the Jewish people so long as such loyalty does not clash with its religious convictions. It is essentially a movement *towards* the Jewish people and is marked by the effort to find a place in its life.[19]

The "baptized Jews" of the pre-modern period consciously turned away from the Jewish people; modern "Hebrew Christians" reversed course and sought to integrate their new faith with loyalty to their nation.[20]

Hebrew Christians received their faith from the missionaries. In turn, they earnestly supported missions to the Jews. The American Hebrew Christian Alliance, founded in 1915, stressed the importance of the missionary enterprise in its constitution. Of its three stated objectives, two dealt with the missions:

- To propagate more widely the gospel . . . by strengthening existing Jewish missions, and fostering all other agencies to that end
- To provide for evangelical Christian churches of America an authoritative and reliable channel [of] how best to serve the cause of Jewish evangelization[21]

Hebrew Christianity was inseparable from the missionary movement. Hebrew Christians tried to remain part of their people, but one of their main motives in doing so was the desire to win other Jews to Christianity. In this way they represented the interests and concerns of the church to the Jewish people.

However, that was not the end of the story. As Ariel underlines, these avid missionaries also represented Jewish interests and concerns to the church. They did so first by energetically supporting the establishment of a Jewish homeland

---

19. Jocz, *Jesus Christ,* 233.

20. At the first meeting of the Hebrew Christian Alliance, A. M. Meyer made this point clear: "Let us not sacrifice our identity. When we profess Christ, we do not cease to be Jews. . . . We cannot and will not forget the land of our fathers, and it is our desire to cherish feelings of patriotism." Cohn-Sherbok, *Messianic Judaism,* 17.

21. Ibid., 27–28. "Two years after the [founding] Conference, Arthur Kuldell described the achievements of this meeting in an article, 'The Spiritual Aims of the HCAA': . . . Its chief aim and ultimate goal is to reach American Jewry with the Gospel." Cohn-Sherbok, *Messianic Judaism,* 29.

in what was then Palestine. These efforts were in keeping with their dispensationalist theology, but also served to express their Jewish national identity. In the 1920s and 1930s the Hebrew Christian Alliance even sought admission to the Zionist Organization of America. In doing so, Alliance spokesmen presented their movement as another branch of Judaism and contended that they were ambassadors for Zionism to the Christian community.[22] Second, Hebrew Christians battled against anti-Semitism in the evangelical church, even when it put their own reputations and organizations at risk.[23] They saw such prejudice as undermining the message they were carrying to their fellow Jews—that genuine Yeshua-faith and love of Israel go hand in hand. Third, they showed deep concern for the plight of European Jews with the rise of Hitler. Ariel pays tribute to their response:

> It is a noteworthy fact that missions to the Jews in America were among the bodies most concerned with the fate of Jews in Nazi Germany and, later on, in Nazi-occupied Europe. They tried to alert the evangelical community and were among the first to grasp the full scope of the horrors.[24]

While one can detect a missionary motive even in their support of Jewish causes, the Hebrew Christians were not merely Christians masquerading as Jews. Their loyalty to their people was sincere, even if others thought it misguided.

Where did Hebrew Christianity stand in relation to the five ecclesiological principles proposed in this book? The novelty of the movement consisted in its adherence to the first principle, the validity of Israel's covenant and election. This was the cardinal doctrine upon which Hebrew Christianity took its stand. For the most part Hebrew Christians rejected our second principle, the validity

22. "'We are contending for a vital principle, the official recognition of the Hebrew Christians as an integral part of the Jewish nation,' wrote the editor of the *Hebrew Christian Alliance Quarterly* in explaining the request to be accepted into the Zionist organization. In his appeals to the Zionist leadership, the alliance representative, John Zacker, declared that 'the Hebrew Christian Alliance . . . has placed itself on record as favoring earnest efforts for the realization of Palestine as a Jewish homeland' [October 1921]. He demanded full rights for converted Jews in the Zionist organization and presented them as a division within Judaism. 'Any Jew, be he Orthodox, Conservative, Reform, Messianic, Rationalist, . . . should without shadow of doubt, be cordially received into your organization' [January 1922]. Zacker further claimed that the Hebrew Christian Alliance served as a representative of the Zionist cause in the Christian community." Ariel, *Evangelizing the Chosen People,* 173–74.

23. "Well aware of anti-Jewish prejudices, missionaries emphasized the importance of the Jews in God's plans for humanity. They condemned anti-Semitism and discrimination against Jews worldwide. Some of them made a particular effort to combat such anti-Semitic accusations as the blood libel of ritual murder, which was still alive at the turn of the century." Ibid., 14; see also 111–12; Cohn-Sherbok, *Messianic Judaism,* 35, 50.

24. Ariel, *Evangelizing the Chosen People,* 129–30.

and obligation of Jewish practice rooted in the Torah. There were exceptions, and we will speak about them below. But in general Hebrew Christians forsook Sabbath observance and the dietary laws and took pride in their "freedom from the Mosaic Law."[25] If this was the case with the rules of the written Torah, then how much more so with the oral Torah of the Rabbis (our third principle)! Their ecclesiology was emphatically homogeneous rather than bilateral—though, as we will see below, significant figures within the movement argued for the establishment of a distinct Jewish ekklesia. These figures loom large because of the later movement they prefigure—but in their own time they were always minority voices.[26] Finally, Hebrew Christians showed some measure of solidarity with the Jewish people, but their loyalty was national rather than religious. Their primary religious identity was unambiguously Christian, and they saw themselves as bringing the Jewish people into the church, not as bringing the church to Israel.

In their own time, the Hebrew Christians of the nineteenth and early twentieth centuries were pioneers opening up virgin territory. It is unfair to fault them according to the standards of a later time. As usual, Ariel judges their achievement with fairness and sympathy:

> The remarkable thing about the attitudes of the Jewish Christian activists of the early twentieth century was not their unwillingness to build new modes of Jewish Christian life but rather that they did get together and find the courage to build an organization of their own in which they gave expression to their mutual concerns. Such a development would have been unheard of for converted Jews throughout most of Christian history. . . . The foundations of Messianic Judaism of later years were laid in this early period.[27]

A new religious movement had been born, straddling the borders of two related but feuding communities. Even today its full promise has not been fully recognized or realized.

A Hebrew Christian Church?

In the 1880s Joseph Rabinowitz appeared on the Hebrew Christian scene, introducing a vision previously inconceivable: the establishment of an autonomous, indigenous Jewish ekklesia. While the ecclesiology and missiology of

---

25. They also forsook circumcision, at least as a covenantal obligation.

26. The majority position was voiced by Sabbati Rohold, first president of the Hebrew Christian Alliance of America: "The HCAA has made it clear as daylight that it is absolutely against anything which savours a distinction between Jew and Gentile." Cohn-Sherbok, *Messianic Judaism,* 32.

27. Ariel, *Evangelizing the Chosen People,* 51.

Rabinowitz failed at first to win over the majority of Hebrew Christians, his work received worldwide attention and made the question of a Hebrew Christian church a matter of serious debate at missionary conferences and Hebrew Christian gatherings. The genie would never again be put back in the bottle.

Joseph Rabinowitz was born in Bessarabia in 1837. He was raised in a Hasidic environment but was exposed to the *Haskalah* as a young man and, setting aside his traditional religious upbringing, became a fervent *Maskil* and Jewish nationalist. He contributed articles to Hebrew language periodicals and gained a reputation as a learned writer, dedicated to the welfare of the Jewish people. In 1882 he journeyed to Jerusalem with the intent of investigating settlement possibilities. While there, he came to the conclusion that Israel's hope for national restoration could be realized only in "Yeshua, our brother." He returned to Bessarabia and began to proclaim this message, gathering a small community called "Israelites of the New Covenant" (*Beney Israel, Beney Brit Chadashah*).

In 1885 Rabinowitz traveled to Germany to explain and defend his program to a small meeting of leading figures from the Christian missions to the Jews, including the world-renowned biblical scholar Franz Delitzsch. He succeeded in winning their support, and they agreed to his being baptized in such a manner that he would afterward "be regarded as a member of the church of Christ and not as a member of the denomination to which his baptizer might belong."[28] Membership in a Christian denomination was inconsistent with his vision for Israelites of the New Covenant, a body of loyal Jews who were to live within the confines of the Jewish people. The missionaries also agreed to give Rabinowitz total freedom to lead the movement, without interference from the denominations or missionary societies. Clearly these eminent men were impressed by Rabinowitz and saw the work he was doing as profoundly significant.

What was Rabinowitz's vision for the way of life of the Israelites of the New Covenant? His views on this question were even more controversial than his commitment to a distinct Jewish ekklesia. Rabinowitz insisted that the Israelites of the New Covenant should practice circumcision, honor the Sabbath, and keep the Passover and other Jewish holidays. Delitzsch and his colleagues were reluctant to agree to this. Kai Kjaer-Hansen notes the tension produced by this topic at the 1885 meeting:

> The question of the Sabbath was discussed once more, probably raised by Delitzsch. Other sources make it clear that even though Delitzsch did not wish to make this into a test question, he found it difficult to accede to it. . . . Circumcision and the

28. Kai Kjaer-Hansen, *Joseph Rabinowitz and the Messianic Movement* (Grand Rapids: Eerdmans, 1995), 82.

Sabbath were to be national distinctives, which however must not obscure that Christ is the end of the law and that justification is solely through faith in him.[29]

The legacy of seventeen centuries of Christian theology weighed heavily on these men. In a letter written by Delitzsch, the scholar acknowledged the importance of preserving Israel's national identity but asserted that this could be done apart from traditional practices instituted by the Torah: "Israel's national distinctiveness must be maintained and will be maintained without circumcision and with Sunday instead of the Sabbath."[30] This remarkable statement shows both how far the Christian world had come in recognizing the role of the Jewish people, and how far it had yet to go in recognizing the legitimacy of Judaism as the way of life of the Jewish people. Even with these misgivings, Delitzsch and company endorsed Rabinowitz and the work he was undertaking.

Did Rabinowitz view circumcision, the Sabbath, and the holidays as integral aspects of Jewish national identity or as optional practices to be encouraged for pragmatic reasons? As noted earlier in this book, the Jerusalem Council presumed that Jewish observance was *obligatory* for Jewish Yeshua-believers. One century later Justin explained to Trypho that the issue in the church debates of his time was whether Jewish Yeshua-believers were *free* to observe such practices. In arguing his case before Gentile Christian authorities, Rabinowitz first puts the question in terms of liberty.[31] Kjaer-Hansen reports on an 1884 meeting in Bessarabia between Rabinowitz and some visiting missionaries:

> Rabinowitz was also called upon to give his views on the observing of Jewish customs. The cause of this was that at the meeting he had stressed that he and those like-minded with him desired liberty to observe Jewish customs handed down from their fathers in so far as these were not at variance with the spirit of Christianity.[32]

Rabinowitz proceeds to distinguish between two types of obligation: religious and national.

---

29. Ibid., 84.

30. Ibid., 113.

31. In speaking of Rabinowitz's view of Jewish practice, Kjaer-Hansen underlines the theme of liberty: "Hereby Gentile Christians were obligated to weigh up why they would not give Jews a liberty corresponding to that Paul had won for Gentiles, as regards the relationship to the law. For his own part, Rabinowitz desired this liberty, but without denouncing other Hebrew Christians who chose to be assimilated in a Christian church." Hansen, *Joseph Rabinowitz*, 233. While this summary of Rabinowitz's perspective is accurate, it is also incomplete because it fails to deal with the complementary theme (also prominent in Rabinowitz's writings) of Jewish obligation.

32. Ibid., 56.

From a "religious" point of view, he and his adherents believed that the law had been perfectly fulfilled by the Messiah. But from a "patriotic" point of view, they felt obligated to keep the law as far as nationality and circumstances made it possible.[33]

The reintroduction of the notion of obligation concerned the missionaries. What sort of obligation was this?

To reach clarity about Rabinowitz's attitude, the question was put whether a Christian Jew who did not circumcise his child would be committing a sin. Rabinowitz's reply was: "He does not commit a sin, but he thereby estranges himself from his people." He gave a similar reply to the question whether Christian Jews who do not keep the Sabbath were committing a sin.[34]

From confessional materials composed by Rabinowitz, it is evident that he considered circumcision and the Sabbath to be divine commandments that Jews were still obligated to obey.[35] The distinction between *religious* and *national* does not, therefore, imply that the national obligations are of merely human origin or sanction. In response to the question of the missionaries, Rabinowitz indicates that violation of these divinely imposed national obligations is not a sin. Thus, in making a distinction between religious and national obligations, Rabinowitz retains the belief that Jewish practice is divinely commanded and obligatory for Jews while portraying the nature of that commandment/obligation as qualitatively different from and lesser than the essential "moral" commandments/obligations.

While Rabinowitz broke new ground in the respect he showed to the commandments of the written Torah, his attitude toward the oral Torah resembled that of the medieval Jewish converts to Christianity. In one of the confessional documents for the Israelites of the New Covenant, he wrote as follows:

The Mishna and Talmud are not to be used for establishing any doctrines, but regarded only as an everlasting memento of the spirit of deep slumber which God

33. Ibid.
34. Ibid.
35. "[As] we are the seed of Abraham according to the flesh, who was the father of all those who were circumcised and believed, we are bound to circumcise every male-child on the eighth day, as God commanded him. And as we are the descendants of those whom the Lord brought out of the land of Egypt, with a stretched out arm, we are bound to keep the Sabbath, the feast of unleavened bread, and the feast of weeks, according as it is written in the law of Moses, whilst the (Gentile) Christians celebrate them only in commemoration of the resurrection of the Messiah from the dead, and the outpouring of the Holy Spirit from heaven." Kjaer-Hansen, *Joseph Rabinowitz*, 104.

has permitted to fall upon us; so that the "Shulchan Aruch" [i.e., the authoritative code of traditional Jewish Law] . . . became a net, a snare, and a stumbling-block to us, and have darkened our eyes so that we failed to see the ways of the true and life-giving Faith.[36]

Here Rabinowitz and Delitzsch reversed roles, with Delitzsch taking the part of the defender of Judaism:

Delitzsch criticizes Rabinowitz for this, considering that in the Talmud and other Jewish traditional literature there are ideas which are akin to the Christian faith. Delitzsch would wish that on this point Rabinowitz expressed himself with greater balance![37]

Delitzsch was the enlightened Western European Christian scholar and missionary who had learned to appreciate rabbinic literature, whereas Rabinowitz was the enlightened Eastern European *Maskil* who had distinguished traditional Jewish religion from Jewish nationality, being loyal to the latter while contemptuous of the former.[38]

Joseph Rabinowitz gained international attention for his endeavor to reestablish an autonomous, indigenous Jewish expression of the ekklesia. Nevertheless his efforts ended in failure. While he succeeded in gathering a small group of Jewish Yeshua-believers, he never received permission from the Russian government to baptize and form a congregation. When he died in 1899, he did not leave behind a Jewish Yeshua-believing community. However, he did leave behind an example that would continue to stir passionate debate among missionaries and participants in the Hebrew Christian movement for many decades to come.[39]

How does the Rabinowitz program match up with our five ecclesiological principles? First, Rabinowitz emphatically affirms Israel's enduring covenant and election. Second, he likewise affirms the enduring importance of Jewish

36. Ibid.

37. Ibid., 109.

38. Kjaer-Hansen notes that Rabinowitiz's contempt for rabbinic tradition preceded his faith in Yeshua and derived not from Christian prejudice but from the principles of the Jewish *Haskalah*: "Rabinowitz had questioned the significance of Talmudic study and the binding character of the Talmud, already before he came to faith in Jesus. In an article in Haboker Or in 1879 he gives expression to this critical attitude to Talmud. Other Haskala Jews had done the same." Ibid., 109.

39. The influence of Rabinowitz even during his lifetime can be seen in the efforts of two Methodist missionaries, Arno Gaebelein and Ernest Stroeter, who attempted to found a Jewish Christian church following Jewish practice in the Lower East Side of Manhattan in the 1890s. Gaebelein visited Rabinowitz in Bessarabia in 1895 and translated, published, and distributed one of his books. See Ariel, *Evangelizing the Chosen People*, 19–20.

practice, though his attitude toward the obligatory quality of that practice remains ambiguous. Third, he denies the value and validity of rabbinic tradition. Fourth, he takes the initial steps toward the formation of a bilateral ecclesiology. Fifth, though he demonstrates a radical solidarity with the Jewish people, his ecclesiology still reflects a missionary orientation in its disregard for historical Jewish religious experience and its focus on Israel entering the (universal) church (without a corresponding emphasis on the church joining Israel).

While Rabinowitz was the first to take this path, he did not walk it alone. In his own time his name was often associated with that of Isak Lichtenstein (1824–1909), a Hungarian rabbi who became a Yeshua-believer in 1883—one year after Rabinowitz—but did not publicly announce his faith for several years. He resigned from his position as an officiating rabbi in 1892. Like Rabinowitz, he was a controversial figure among missionaries and Hebrew Christians.[40] This was the case for three reasons. First, he refused to be baptized (though he reputedly baptized himself in the name of Yeshua in a Jewish ritual bath). He made this decision in order to retain his religious status as a Jew, with the rights and privileges it entailed within the Jewish world (e.g., burial in a Jewish cemetery). Second, Lichtenstein continued to live in a pious Orthodox manner. If the basic Torah observance of Rabinowitz provoked heated discussion, one can imagine the response to the traditional practice of Lichtenstein! Third, as a contemporary writer reported, Lichtenstein refused "to attach himself to any agency that brings converts into membership in denominational churches."[41] Lichtenstein himself lived as a Jew among Jews, and he would not ally himself with missionaries whose efforts resulted in fellow Jews taking a different course.

Lichtenstein and other likeminded figures (such as Theodore Lucky in Galicia) extended the Rabinowitz model in the direction of our five ecclesiological principles.[42] In the generation that followed, one sees a similar extension in the thinking of Paul Levertoff. A descendant of Shneur Zalman, the founder of Chabad Hasidism, Levertoff was born in Russia in 1879. He became a Yeshua-believer in 1897, two years before the death of Rabinowitz. Levertoff devoted himself to a life of scholarship, holding the chair of Hebrew and Rabbinics at the *Institutum Judaicum* (founded by Franz Delitzsch) in Leipzig before emigrating to Britain,

40. Rabinowitz met Lichtenstein in 1891 in Budapest. Based on their meeting and on Lichtenstein's writings, Rabinowitz faulted the Hungarian rabbi for his unwillingness to break with traditional Judaism. As Kjaer-Hansen notes, "Rabinowitz . . . here uses similar expressions in his criticism of Lichtenstein to those others might use against himself." Kjaer-Hansen, *Joseph Rabinowitz*, 174–75.

41. A. E. Thompson, *A Century of Jewish Missions* (Chicago: Fleming H. Revell, 1902), 162.

42. Like Lichtenstein, Lucky lived as an orthodox Jew and called into question the practices of the Christian missionary societies. See Jocz, *Jesus Christ,* 255–56; Gillet, *Communion,* 202; Cohn-Sherbok, *Messianic Judaism,* 24–25, 45–46.

where he was ordained a minister of the Church of England. In so tying himself to a particular church, Levertoff departed in practice from the ecclesiological principles espoused by Rabinowitz, Lichtenstein, and Lucky. Nevertheless, it appears that his long-term vision was greatly influenced by their teaching and example. Lev Gillet says this about Levertoff's ecclesiological goal:

> He holds the ideal of a Jewish Christian community, which he conceives as ". . . a Jewish branch of the Catholic Church in a congenial Jewish traditional environment, where the essentials of Christian Faith and worship are expressed, as much as possible, in Jewish terms."[43]

From Levertoff's point of view, the most "congenial Jewish traditional environment" for a "Jewish Christian community" was the mystical Hasidic world of his ancestors. Levertoff believed that Yeshua-faith could easily be integrated with the best in Hasidic spirituality.[44]

Levertoff gathered a small group of Jewish Christians in Stepney for Sabbath worship, employing traditional Jewish music and a Hebrew-language liturgy.[45] Nevertheless, Levertoff was not a missionary, and he appears to have had misgivings about the entire Christian missionary posture toward the Jews. Gillet states that he "devoted himself to the task, not of mission to the Jews, but of intellectual contact and practical co-operation with them."[46] Illustrative of this approach was his participation as translator in the Soncino English edition of the Zohar (the central text in the Jewish mystical tradition).[47]

In Gillet's *Communion in the Messiah*, written in England during the Second World War by a Russian Orthodox priest who was a refugee from Nazi-controlled France, we probably have a faithful presentation of the thought of Paul Levertoff. In this volume Gillet explicitly confesses his respect for Levertoff: "We think that the most important contemporary approach to the formation of Jewish Christianity has been the work of Paul Levertoff."[48] Writing only a few years after

43. Gillet, *Communion*, 203.

44. "Dr. P. P. Levertoff, a great exponent of *hasidic* thought, has devoted his energies to working out the essential unity between Jewish (viz. *hasidic*) and Christian points of view in matters of worship and doctrine." Jocz, *Jesus Christ*, 209.

45. Cohn-Sherbok, *Messianic Judaism*, 55.

46. Gillet, *Communion*, 203.

47. *The Zohar*, vol. 3, 2nd ed., trans. Harry Sperling, Maurice Simon, and Dr. Paul P. Levertoff (London: Soncino, 1984); and *The Zohar*, vol. 4, 2nd ed., trans. Maurice Simon and Dr. Paul P. Levertoff (London: Soncino, 1984). The original publication of these volumes was in the 1930s. Vol. 3 includes a publisher's note acknowledging Levertoff's role: "The Soncino Press desire to acknowledge the services of Dr. Paul P. Levertoff, whose work in collaboration with the translators of the first two volumes has materially helped to expedite publication of Volume III."

48. Gillet, *Communion*, 203.

the publication of *Communion in the Messiah*, Jocz discerns Levertoff's influence on Gillet.[49] The book is of great intrinsic interest, whether or not it reflects the thinking of Levertoff. However, the probability that it offers a window into the thinking of one of the most visionary and erudite Jewish Christians of the twentieth century adds immensely to its importance for our purposes.

Gillet begins with a brief sketch of the New Testament approach to Judaism. He views Yeshua as a Pharisaic-leaning, Torah-observant Jew.[50] Likewise, he presents Paul as combating only the necessity of Gentile, not Jewish, Torah observance.[51] Gillet then turns to his true theme: the total compatibility between authentic Yeshua-faith and post-first-century Jewish religious tradition.

> The Gospel is the fruit and completion and crown of Judaism. . . . To bring to the Jews the crown of their faith means to show them the continuity between Christianity and the whole line of Jewish religious thought, rabbinical as well as Scriptural. . . .
>
> The whole message of Israel is an authentic part of God's Revelation and can be, without the abolition of a single jot, brought together with the message of Jesus. Nothing of the true Jewish tradition—from Hillel to modern Hasidism—needs to be altered in order to adjust itself to the Gospel: it needs only to be complemented.[52]

Following the teaching of Jacques Maritain, Gillet sees the Jewish people as a *corpus mysticum*—a mystical body, like the church. However, he goes beyond Maritain in arguing that Israel's "mystical" role transcends "the limits of secular history":

> Maritain is careful to restrict the Jewish task of "activation" of the world to "the plane" and "the limits of secular history." We shall go further and say that these true Israelites [i.e., those faithful to the divine Law and a prophetic vision] belong to sacred history and achieve a redeeming work in the *diaspora*.[53]

Such a perspective explains Gillet's readiness to recognize the legitimacy of Jewish religious tradition. It also explains his readiness to discern in Jewish

49. Jocz, *Jesus Christ*, 209.
50. "Jesus himself was nearer to genuine Pharisaism than to any other religious school in Israel." Gillet, *Communion*, 6.
51. "Paul fought for the right of the Gentile Christians not to be bound by the Jewish law. But he never questioned the legitimacy of Judaeo-Christianity or the obligation of the circumcised Christian to keep the Law." Gillet, *Communion*, 7.
52. Ibid, 180, 186.
53. Ibid., 157.

suffering—so visible at the time he was writing—the prophetic and redemptive presence of Isaiah's suffering servant:

> If we do ascribe a religious significance and purpose to the existence of the Jews, we must consider their sufferings as part of this purpose. . . . We must interpret Israel's woes in the light of the teaching about the Suffering Servant. . . . By its many sufferings, Israel may help the consummation of the divine purpose in history.[54]

Gillet—and, we presume, Levertoff—thus approach Jewish history and tradition with enormous sympathy and appreciation.

For Gillet, Christian thinking about the Jewish people and Judaism must be primarily ecclesiological rather than missiological. He does not view the Jewish people as an external field for church mission, but as intimately bound to the church's inner reality:

> The *corpus mysticum Christi* [i.e., the mystical Body of Christ] is not a metaphor; it is an organic and invisible reality. But the theology of the Body of Christ should be linked with a theology of the mystical Body of Israel.[55]

In effect, Gillet portrays the divide between Judaism and Christianity as a schism and argues that healing this schism is crucial to any healing of the divisions afflicting the Christian churches:

> Are the promoters of this movement [i.e., the ecumenical movement] aware that no scheme of reunion can succeed if it is not vertical as well as horizontal? Can the daughter Churches, i.e., the Christian Churches, become reconciled if they make no step towards their mother, the Church of Israel? We firmly believe that, in the plan of God, the mother will be—some day still far off—the center and the instrument of unity.[56]

Gillet—and, we presume, Levertoff—thus make the leap from a missionary to a postmissionary posture toward the Jewish people.

Yet Gillet makes this leap without losing his christological bearings. He does not present Yeshua as the Messiah only for the Gentiles. Yeshua is the *Jewish* Messiah, even though his name is honored mainly among the Gentiles. Gillet argues that the Jewish tradition preserves a vivid sense of the Messianic Kingdom,

54. Ibid., 160.
55. Ibid., 215.
56. Ibid., 188–89.

a renewed world of peace and justice, under the reign of the God of Abraham, Isaac, and Jacob. When Jews orient their actions toward the establishment of this Kingdom, they are in reality acting "for and in the Messiah":

> Speaking again from the strict Christian standpoint . . . there is no action whatever, sincerely made for the sake of the Messianic Kingdom, which is not made for and in the Messiah. . . . The Jews who work for the Kingdom may perhaps not know with Whom they have to do. When the Messianic Kingdom appears, they will learn the truth and the Messiah will manifest Himself.[57]

Yet would it not be better if these Jews knew the truth of their Messiah's identity now, rather than having to wait till "the Messianic Kingdom appears"? This is where Gillet reintroduces the missionary imperative—but in a radically revised form. He acknowledges that the church has a mission to the Jewish people and that that mission consists of making known the identity of the Messiah "for and in" whom faithful Jews have always lived and died. Yet he proceeds to add a complementary assertion that essentially dissolves the traditional missionary paradigm: the Jewish people also have a mission to the church!

> We think (and in this we differ from most Christian missionaries) that the word "mission," used in connection with Israel, has a twofold meaning: there is, and there ought to be, a mission of the Christian Church to Israel; but there is also a Mission of Israel to the Christian Church, and this (as we think) divinely appointed mission must not be overlooked.[58]

The Jewish people's mission to the church is also Messianic. Insofar as the church is ignorant of Judaism and the Jewish people, it is also ignorant of the Jewish Messiah. Thus both the church and the Jewish people have at present an imperfect "communion in the Messiah" that can only be completed by the witness of the other:

> What about the pious Jew who (without any guilt) has not accepted Jesus? What about the pious Christian entirely unconscious of his Jewish inheritance? Is there no communion between them? . . . The Messiah Jesus is Himself the substance of all Messianic faith, all Messianic hope, all Messianic love, all Messianic grace. A true Christian and a true Israelite communicate in the same Messiah. This communion is partial and implicit. God will make it some day total and explicit. . . .

57. Ibid., 107.
58. Ibid..172.

A Jew who accepts (not only intellectually) Jesus as Messiah enters into communion with the Messiah *as Jesus*, and with the community of the followers of Jesus. Reciprocally, a Christian who becomes aware of the Jewish contents of his own faith and inwardly responds to this new awareness enters into communion with Jesus *as Jewish Messiah* and invisibly with the Messianic community of Israel, insofar as the Messiah displays an immanent activity inside it. Thus the Mission—the two-fold Mission—ends in communion.[59]

Fr. Raniero Cantalamesa speaks of a dual "conversion" involving both the "rejoining of Israel with the Church" and "a rejoining of the Church with Israel."[60] Gillet rejects the term "conversion," since it implies to him (on the Jewish side) that Jews must reject Judaism in order to embrace Yeshua-faith.[61] Despite the difference over terminology, the message of Cantalamesa and Gillet is the same: each body has something that the other needs, and each can be whole only by being properly related to the other.

Gillet adds two further qualifications to the church's mission to the Jewish people that similarly undermine the traditional missionary paradigm. First, he argues that the church cannot bear witness to Yeshua among the Jewish people as though it had no history of brutalizing Jews and attacking Judaism:

We have no right to approach the Jew now as if our hands were clean. We must first of all atone for our gross violation of the law of our Master and deserve the forgiveness and confidence of Israel. We shall speak of our faith only when we have proved our love. . . . At the same time we should make it clear that we love the Jew not in order to win him over, but because we, as Christians, must unconditionally love him.[62]

Awareness of the history of Christian treatment of Jews and Judaism will reinforce the humility required by recognition of the church's need to receive the message and mission directed to it by Israel. Second, in accordance with his positive assessment of Jewish religious tradition, Gillet insists that Yeshua-faith must be presented to Jews as the "the fruit and completion and crown of Judaism" rather than as its nullification. For Gillet this is not a matter of effective marketing but of theological truth. Jews who believe in Yeshua should be urged to practice Judaism rather than become part of a denominational church, not

---

59. Ibid, 196.
60. See the end of chapter 5.
61. Ibid., 195. By "conversion," Cantalamesa means a sincere change of mind and heart, rather than the exchange of one religion for another.
62. Ibid., 189–90.

in order to maximize evangelistic opportunities, but as a matter of religious loyalty and theological integrity.

This brings us to Gillet's endorsement of the program of Rabinowitz, Lichtenstein, and Lucky—the establishment of a "Jewish Christian Church."

> Generally speaking, we are very far from considering the adhesion of a Jew to one of the Gentile Christian Churches as an ideal solution. It may sometimes be the only possible one, but we do not think it either normal or desirable. The appearance and diffusion of a Jewish Christianity, inside the Church universal, is, as we believe, the only true solution.[63]

Gillet offers two models for how such a Jewish Christianity could operate. He calls the first model "unsynagogued" Jewish Christianity.

> "Unsynagogued" Jewish Christianity means a Jewish Christianity which has broken its ties with the Synagogue. Such a Jewish Christian group might exist under two forms. It could be a special and autonomous branch of one of the present Christian Churches. . . . Or the Jewish Christian group could become an independent Christian Church.[64]

He calls the second model "synagogued" Jewish Christianity:

> "Synagogued" Jewish Christianity means a Jewish Christianity which keeps, as far as possible, its ties with the synagogue.[65]

As an example of synagogued Jewish Christianity, Gillet cites Rabbi Isak Lichtenstein. He recognizes the many problems a Jew or group of Jews would encounter in seeking to participate in traditional synagogue life as Yeshua-believers, but he argues that such an arrangement is theoretically possible and poses no problems from a Christian theological perspective (of the sort he presents in his book).

In keeping with the overall vision enunciated in *Communion in the Messiah*, Gillet sees the importance of Jewish Christianity as primarily ecclesiological rather than missiological. It is not a tactical or strategic move adopted for the sake of "spreading the good news." Instead, it is an essential part of the church's ecclesiological self-discovery and an essential step toward the unity of the *corpus mysticum*:

63. Ibid., 191.
64. Ibid., 206.
65. Ibid.

We believe that the development of a Jewish Christianity is inseparably linked with the development, among Christians, of a new ecumenical consciousness.[66]

Gillet—and, we presume, Levertoff—envision a Jewish expression of Yeshua-faith that binds the church to Israel and Israel to the church, and that brings reconciliation in place of conflict. In other words, they envision a postmissionary Messianic Judaism. In fact, they come remarkably close to envisioning a full-orbed bilateral ecclesiology in solidarity with Israel that affirms Israel's covenant, Torah, and religious tradition.

While Rabinowitz, Lichtenstein, Lucky, and Levertoff influenced many and caused the issues of Jewish practice and a Hebrew Christian church to be matters of ongoing debate, the Hebrew Christian movement as a whole did not follow their lead. Thus, Mark Levy, a Jewish Episcopal priest (like Levertoff), proposed to the third national conference of the Hebrew Christian Alliance of America in 1917 that the following resolution regarding Jewish practice be adopted:

Resolved, that the Hebrew Christian Alliance of America endorse the resolution that our Jewish brethren are left free to admit their children into the covenant of Abraham and observe other God-given rites and ceremonies of Israel, if they so desire, when they accept . . . Messiah . . . provided that it is distinctly understood that neither Jew nor Gentile can be saved by works of the Law, but only through the merits and mediations of our compassionate Messiah.[67]

This resolution—which proposed only the liberty and not the obligation of Jewish Yeshua-believers to observe certain traditional Jewish practices—was overwhelmingly defeated. One participant in the conference aptly captured the prevailing sentiment among Hebrew Christians of the time:

By this overwhelming decision the HCAA has closed the doors once and for all to all Judaizing propaganda, and the organization stands squarely on the pure evangelical platform, with the avowed aim, purpose, and object to preach the Gospel . . . to our Jewish people everywhere.[68]

Commenting on the rejection of Levy's proposal, Ariel writes:

It was one thing to establish an organization that came to offer a meeting ground for converts to discuss mutual problems and concerns and to promote the cause

66. Ibid., 209.
67. Cohn-Sherbok, *Messianic Judaism,* 34.
68. Ibid., 34.

of Jewish evangelism in the Protestant camp. It was another thing altogether to create a "Jewish church" or to observe the Law.[69]

Two decades later Levertoff and Gillet offered their far more radical proposal. In response to Gillet, Jocz voiced what was certainly the majority view in the Hebrew Christian world of the time.

> The nature of Judaism and Christianity is such that they exclude each other. . . . Church and Synagogue can only exist in eternal challenge to each other. Martin Buber has grasped this significant fact. Lev Gillet has not.[70]

Several Hebrew Christian churches developed in the 1930s, 1940s, and 1950s, but they were often linked to denominations and normally functioned as missionary centers rather than self-conscious embodiments of an autonomous, indigenous Jewish Christianity.[71] The example of Rabinowitz was never forgotten, and some church leaders were more receptive to the Rabinowitz model than were the majority of Hebrew Christians.[72] Nevertheless, the example of Rabinowitz would not be followed until the Hebrew Christian movement was transformed in the 1970s.

Jews for Jesus and Messianic Judaism

Hebrew Christianity and the 1960s

The cultural ferment of the 1960s threw Hebrew Christians in America and their institutions into the same turmoil that characterized the rest of American society. Three factors played an especially important part in turning their world upside down: a social movement (i.e., the youth counterculture), a cultural trend (i.e., ethnic self-assertion and pride), and a political-military event (i.e., the Six-Day War).

69. Ariel, *Evangelizing the Chosen People,* 49.

70. Jocz, *Jesus Christ,* 96.

71. "Within these Hebrew Christian churches, the background of Jewish believers was accepted. Yet there was little attempt to encourage loyalty to Jewish tradition. Many of these Jewish Christians married Gentile Christians, and their children generally lost any connection with Judaism. Among those who married other Jewish believers, their children frequently retained some connection with their Jewish background, but such sensitivities gradually faded with the next generation." Cohn-Sherbok, *Messianic Judaism,* 54. See Ariel, *Evangelizing the Chosen People,* 131, 221.

72. While the Hebrew Christian Alliance of America voted down the resolution proposed by Mark Levy, the Episcopal Church approved a similar resolution proposed by Levy. Ariel, *Evangelizing the Chosen People,* 49; Cohn-Sherbok, *Messianic Judaism,* 24. See also the words of Canon G. H. Box and the Rev. Th. Lindhagen cited in Cohn-Sherbok, *Messianic Judaism,* 25.

The countercultural youth of the 1960s called into question the comfortable middle-class values of their parents' generation. In the religious sphere, this upheaval among America's young people took the form of the Jesus movement. Those involved in this subset of the youth counterculture rejected the institutional forms of American Christianity (e.g., church buildings, music, liturgy, dress, clerical structure) and sought a simpler, more immediate religious experience and way of life. This caused special tensions for the Hebrew Christians, as Ariel notes:

> The missions had worked for decades to build a solid, respectable reputation as a means to secure their position in evangelical eyes. They identified themselves with and promoted evangelical middle-class propriety. They had, for the most part, a very difficult time relating to the counterculture and rejected it vehemently.[73]

What Ariel says about the missions was true for the Hebrew Christian world as a whole. At the same time, the Jesus movement opened new opportunities for the growth of Hebrew Christianity, since many of the young people involved in it were Jewish.[74]

The second factor that would reshape Hebrew Christianity in America was the rise of ethnic self-assertion and pride during the late 1960s. In the African American community, the civil rights movement of the late 1950s and early 1960s, with its goals of racial integration and a color-blind society, had given way to the more militant quest for "black power." A parallel phenomenon was evident among Mexican Americans (Chicanos) and Native Americans. In general the ideal of the American melting pot, in which diverse ethnic groups blended together and adopted the patterns of the dominant culture, was giving way to a new pluralistic ideal, in which ethnic minorities sought to preserve their distinctive identities.

In the Jewish world, this led to a celebration of Jewish ethnicity. This trend was intensified among Jews by the third factor: the Six-Day War of 1967, in which the Israeli army won a spectacular victory over its foes. Ariel comments on the significance of this event for the Jewish community, the evangelical community, and the Hebrew Christians:

> A watershed event that . . . played a role in initiating the ideology and rhetoric of the new missionary era was the Six-Day War. The war in June 1967 between Israel and its Arab neighbors had a profound impact on the image of Israel and

73. Ariel, *Evangelizing the Chosen People,* 197.
74. I have personally observed that the vast majority of current leaders in the Messianic Jewish movement became Yeshua-believers through the Jesus movement between 1967 and 1973.

Jews in America, with a particularly strong effect on both the Jewish and evangelical communities.[75]

The positive image of Israel in America at the time deepened Jewish pride and national feeling. The reunification of Jerusalem also reinforced the eschatological Zionism of dispensationalist evangelicals and elicited fresh support for Christian missionaries to the Jews.

These three new developments of the late 1960s set the stage for a major reordering of the Christian missions to the Jews and of the Hebrew Christian movement. The trajectory established in the early 1800s with a more positive attitude toward the Jewish people and Judaism would continue, and the model championed by Rabinowitz would finally carry the day.

Jews for Jesus

In 1970 Moishe Rosen, a missionary for the American Board of Missions to the Jews (ABMJ), moved to San Francisco, the center of the counterculture, to launch an ABMJ branch oriented to the new generation of inquiring youth. That branch became known as "Jews for Jesus." Like Kleenex in relation to facial tissue, the name of Rosen's missionary organization would become synonymous in popular discourse with the wider movement of which it was a small but significant part.[76]

Rosen gathered a talented, creative group of young Jewish Yeshua-believers. Drawing upon his experience as a political activist and the forms of street protest current on college campuses at the time, Rosen and his youthful band of unconventional missionaries rewrote the textbook on missionary methodology. They composed new music and short theater pieces drawing upon traditional Jewish themes, and they performed them on the streets of San Francisco. They distributed humorous handwritten tracts employing Yiddish expressions and references to Jewish food and symbols. They wore T-shirts with "Jews for Jesus" printed boldly on the front or back and, with their blue jeans and longish hair, looked more like Berkeley activists than like the traditional stereotype of a missionary. The appearance was that of the counterculture, the feel was that of resurgent Jewish ethnic pride, and the message emphasized Yeshua's identity as a Jew and the claim that belief in Yeshua made a person more rather than less Jewish.

75. Ariel, *Evangelizing the Chosen People*, 198.
76. Jews for Jesus became independent of ABMJ in 1973.

Ariel recognizes Rosen's strategic and tactical innovations but rightly stresses that the essential message proclaimed by Jews for Jesus is identical to that announced by previous generations of missionaries.

> Jews for Jesus should be viewed as a revitalized form of the old evangelical quest to evangelize the Jews. Its novelty and uniqueness were not in its message, which missionaries had been preaching to American Jews for several generations, but in the fact that its leader was the first to realize that there was a new generation of American Jews with new interests and values and that he was willing to use new forms to approach them. . . . In an attempt to evangelize more effectively, Jews for Jesus promoted symbols and rites that came from what had been traditionally viewed as a different religious community, yet its goal remained to Christianize Jews and persuade them to join the evangelical community and share its values. In the final analysis, Jews for Jesus should be viewed as an avant-garde arm of the movement to evangelize the Jews and of evangelical Christianity in one of its more adaptable, expansive modes.[77]

Jews for Jesus staff are usually trained in evangelical seminaries and ordained in evangelical churches. The theology promoted by the organization is of a conservative evangelical variety, emphasizing the need for explicit faith in Yeshua in order to qualify for the life of the world to come:

> Put bluntly, is Jesus the One in whom all people, Jews and Gentiles, need to have faith in order to be saved? The primary saving message of the Bible, Old and New Testaments, is: "Repent and turn to God on His terms." That is the message the prophets brought to Israel, and that is the message the body of believers today must bring to both Israel and the nations. . . . None of us . . . is called in any event to make determinations as to "exactly who goes where" [i.e., to "heaven" or "hell"]. . . . But we *are* called to say that humanity is steeped in sin, that there are eternal consequences in life, and that we must repent and turn to God on His terms—that is, through faith in Y'shua.[78]

The official Jews for Jesus stance regarding Jewish practice is couched in traditional evangelical language and, while permitting such practice, underlines its nonobligatory nature:

77. Ariel, *Evangelizing the Chosen People*, 219.

78. Rich Robinson and Ruth Rosen, "The Challenge of Our Messianic Movement—Part 2," *Havurah* 6, no. 3 (Fall 2003): 4–5. *Havurah* is a Jews for Jesus publication directed to a Messianic Jewish audience, and Robinson and Rosen are Jews for Jesus staff workers. Rosen is the daughter of the organization's founder.

> Jews for Jesus affirms Jewish believers who, for the sake of honoring our heritage
> and developing a Jewish testimony, choose to give up some of what grace allows
> to conform to dietary standards and various other Jewish practices. As long as
> such practices are not presented as incumbent upon others in the body of Mes-
> siah—Jewish or Gentile—we hope to be an encouragement to those who desire
> to uphold their Jewish identity in this way.[79]

While encouraging the continued ethnic identity of Jewish Yeshua-believers,
Jews for Jesus is cautious about connecting that identity to traditional Jewish
religious practice.

Thus Jews for Jesus is much less radical in vision than Rabinowitz. In relation
to our five ecclesiological principles, Jews for Jesus, like the dominant forms of
Hebrew Christianity that preceded it, affirms only the first—Israel's irrevocable
election and covenant. Jews for Jesus has effectively and self-consciously carried
the torch as the heirs of the nineteenth-century evangelical missionary outreach
to the Jewish people, and on substantive matters it has not moved beyond the
Hebrew Christian consensus of the 1950s. Looking at Jews for Jesus in sociological terms, Ariel is justified in his claim that "Jews for Jesus was an agent of
evangelical Protestantism acting to Christianize Jews and bring them into the
evangelical community."[80]

Messianic Judaism

As Rosen was shaking up the missionary establishment by tapping into the
energies and talents of the youth counterculture, something similar was occurring in the Hebrew Christian Alliance of America. In the case of the Alliance, the
youth themselves seized the initiative. In the spirit of the late 1960s, they were
looking for a more spontaneous, informal, and ethnically authentic expression
of their faith. Between 1967 and 1970, the Young Hebrew Christian Alliance
(YHCA) was established under the leadership of Manny Brotman. Dan Cohn-
Sherbok describes their first conference:

> In 1970 the YHCA held its first conference at Messiah College in Grantham,
> Pennsylvania. Approximately 45 young people attended, staging a gathering
> very different from conferences held by the HCAA. For the first time free-form
> prayer took place, and the name Yeshua was used instead of Jesus. One of the
> pressing concerns was the relationship of the Hebrew Christian community to
> the Jewish people.[81]

79. *Havurah* 6, no. 3 (Fall 2003): 3.
80. Ariel, *Evangelizing the Chosen People*, 211.
81. Cohn-Sherbok, *Messianic Judaism*, 58.

While the initiative came from the youth, its advance and eventual ascendancy in the Alliance as a whole depended upon the sponsorship of a veteran of the Hebrew Christian movement, Martin Chernoff. A contemporary of Rosen, Chernoff was elected president of the Hebrew Christian Alliance in 1971. Cohn-Sherbok notes the important changes that occurred during the initial years of his tenure:

> Under Chernoff's influence a major shift took place within the movement: in the 1970s a growing number of young people were committed to maintaining a culturally Jewish lifestyle, in the mode advocated by Rabinowitz in the nineteenth century, and Levy and Zacker in the early half of the twentieth century. Such determination led these young people to press for the movement to change its name from the Hebrew Christian Alliance of America to the Messianic Jewish Alliance of America. . . . At the 1975 Biennial Conference, a similar motion was proposed and passed.[82]

The change in name was of great significance. It signaled a shift in the movement's sense of identity. The youth wanted more independence from the Christian churches and greater integration with the Jewish world.

Along with the change in name came a new focus on the development of distinct congregations of Jewish Yeshua-believers. In the tradition of Rabinowitz, Lichtenstein, and Lucky, the legitimacy of Jews participating in denominational churches was now called into question. The Messianic Jewish congregations that emerged in the 1970s put aside the Protestant hymns and customs that prevailed in the Hebrew Christian churches of the previous decades and created new worship forms that synthesized charismatic praise, Israeli dance, and fragments of traditional Jewish liturgy. The day of worship shifted from Sunday to Saturday. Many congregations encouraged the observance of the biblical dietary laws and the wearing of traditional head coverings and prayer shawls. Soon congregational associations were formed: the Union of Messianic Jewish Congregations (UMJC) in 1979 and the International Alliance of Messianic Congregations and Synagogues (IAMCS) in 1986.

In its view of Messianic Jewish congregational life and of biblically based Jewish practice as normative rather than optional for Messianic Jews, the Messianic Jewish congregational movement went far beyond Jews for Jesus in institutionalizing the tradition of Rabinowitz, Lichtenstein, and Lucky. As Ariel states, "The novelty of the Messianic Jewish movement that came about in the 1970s and its Jewish Christian ideology was that a set of notions and aspirations that had previously been expressed only sporadically, partially, and hesitantly found a stronger

82. Ibid., 65.

and more assertive voice and became a more acceptable option."[83] Citing Hugh
Schonfeld's statement of 1936, Kjaer-Hansen calls Rabinowitz "the Herzl of Jewish
Christianity."[84] In light of the developments of the last three decades, Rabinowitz
could now be called "the Herzl of the Messianic Jewish movement."

At the same time, Ariel concludes that this movement, like Jews for Jesus,
still operates within the Christian rather than the Jewish sphere. This is evident in the relationships forged by Messianic Jewish leaders with the Christian
world, but even more importantly in the movement's theology, which remains
recognizably evangelical Protestant:

> Though Messianic Judaism strove for recognition by both Christians and Jews,
> it did not attempt to become a Jewish denomination alongside Orthodox and
> Conservative Judaism. . . . They did not try to join the synagogue but rather at-
> tempted to become a new subdivision within evangelical Christianity with its own
> distinctive characteristics and set of congregations, but not beyond the accepted
> theological norms of the evangelical world.[85]

Ariel notes that Christian missionaries initially attacked the new movement.
However, in doing so they misjudged its nature, which was in fact as evangelical
as its Hebrew Christian antecedent:

> The new trend was, in actuality, much less radical than the missionaries thought
> it to be. It did not deviate in essence doctrinally from what the older movement
> stood for. It was, after all, a child of that movement.[86]

In particular, the missionary emphases on "accepting Jesus as Savior" and evangelizing the Jewish people were carried over into Messianic Judaism. Speaking
of one leading congregation, Ariel writes:

> Loyalty to the Christian evangelical theology and agenda is manifested in its
> insistence that all people need to accept Jesus as their Savior in order to ensure
> their salvation, become better human beings, and join the body of Christ, the
> community of true believers.[87]

Ariel examines the writings of three key theological voices within the Messianic
Jewish world (Daniel Juster, David Stern, Arnold Fruchtenbaum) and finds that

83. Ariel, *Evangelizing the Chosen People*, 221.
84. Kjaer-Hansen, *Joseph Rabinowitz*, ix.
85. Ariel, *Evangelizing the Chosen People*, 233.
86. Ibid., 235.
87. Ibid., 226.

they all agree on "the high priority Messianic Jews should give to evangelism and the duty of non-Jews to support them in their efforts."[88] This is why Ariel asserts that "Messianic Judaism has been the logical outcome of the rhetoric and activity of the missionary movement and its dispensationalist theology."[89]

Ariel's assessment of the Messianic Jewish movement is largely correct. It is still for the most part a missionary movement moored in evangelical Protestantism. As we will see, segments of the movement—not yet prominent when Ariel's book was published in 2000—show signs of taking on a different character. However, the movement as a whole originated as an evangelical missionary phenomenon and maintains that status.

Where does missionary Messianic Judaism stand in relation to our five ecclesiological principles? First, it affirms Israel's irrevocable election and covenant. Second, it acknowledges the normative force of basic Jewish practice. Third, it has no consensus on the validity of rabbinic tradition, though many share the critical posture of Rabinowitz. Fourth, some form of bilateral ecclesiology (though not under that name) would be assumed by most within this congregational movement. Fifth, while national solidarity with Israel is emphasized, the movement is primarily evangelistic rather than ecumenical. As with Rabinowitz (but not Levertoff and Gillet), many if not most in the Messianic Jewish movement see the Jewish people throughout the last two millennia as alienated from the saving life of God because of lack of explicit Yeshua-faith.

Hebrew Catholicism

Before turning to the early signs of an emerging postmissionary Messianic Judaism, we should look at a surprising movement that has received too little attention: Hebrew Catholicism. Though far less developed than Protestant Hebrew Christianity and independent Messianic Judaism, Hebrew Catholicism has traveled on a parallel track. Its distinctive ecclesiological setting has facilitated a set of penetrating insights regarding the Jewish people and the church. That setting has also inhibited the ready acceptance of other important insights, but the inhibition may be temporary.

While the fervent eschatological and missionary concern for the Jewish people characteristic of the nineteenth-century Protestant world was not replicated in Catholicism with the same force, one can find similar sentiments voiced and actions undertaken. The most striking example is that of the Ratisbonne broth-

88. Ibid., 250.
89. Ibid.

ers, Theodor and Alphonse, sons of a wealthy Alsatian Jewish banker. Theodor became a Catholic in 1827 and was ordained a priest three years later. In 1842 Alphonse followed the pattern set by his older brother and became a Catholic. Unlike previous Jewish converts to Catholicism, this pair did not leave their Jewish identity at the baptismal font. They shared the conviction that God's promises to the Jewish people were soon to be accomplished. Therefore they moved to Jerusalem and founded there the Sisterhood of our Lady of Zion and the Congregation of the Fathers of Zion, which were focused in part on the conversion of the Jewish people.[90] The words and actions of the Ratisbonne brothers show that the currents flowing in the Protestant world were also affecting Catholicism.

While many Jews became Roman Catholics during the twentieth century, the first to champion a self-conscious "Hebrew Catholicism" was Fr. Elias Friedman. If Rabinowitz is the Herzl of (Protestant) Jewish Christianity, then Friedman deserves the same designation for its Catholic correlate. Born John Friedman in South Africa, the young medical doctor entered the Catholic Church in 1943, becoming a Carmelite monk in 1947, a priest in 1953, and a member of the Stella Maris Monastery in Haifa, Israel, in 1954—just six years after the birth of the Jewish state. A dedicated Zionist, he saw in the restoration of a Jewish homeland and the reunification of the city of Jerusalem under Jewish authority signs that the "times of the Gentiles" referred to by Yeshua in Luke 21:24 were coming to an end.[91] The monk unequivocally proclaimed Israel's irrevocable election and celebrated Vatican II's official legitimization of this doctrine and the Council's advocacy for a more positive attitude toward the Jewish people.

However, Friedman wanted his church to go further. In 1965, while the Vatican Council was still in session, and several years before the birth of the Messianic Jewish movement in America, Fr. Elias proposed the establishment of a distinct Hebrew Catholic community. He presented his idea to the Catholic bishops of South Africa, who showed genuine interest in the novel proposal. The Catholic Liturgical Commission of Southern Africa subsequently recommended to the pope that such a community be founded. However, the Vatican took no official action. Undeterred, in 1979 (the same year in which the Union of Messianic Jewish Congregations was established), Fr. Friedman launched a grass-roots organization, the Association of Hebrew Catholics. The long-term goal of the Association was the formation of a Hebrew Catholic community, to be formally recognized by the pope. In 1987 Friedman published *Jewish Identity*, a book explaining and defending the Hebrew Catholic agenda. The indomitable Jewish monk passed away in

---

90. Elias Friedman, O.C.D., *Jewish Identity* (Mt. Upton, NY: Miriam, 1987), 133–37; Gillet, *Communion*, 176.

91. Ibid., 114.

1999, but the Association he founded remains. In 2003 his movement took a major step toward achieving its goal with the ordination of Jean-Baptiste Gourion, an Algerian Jew, as bishop serving "non-Arab Catholics" in the land of Israel.[92]

At the heart of Friedman's case is a simple yet profound argument based on the principle of Israel's election. Friedman's argument deserves to be heard outside the realm of the Roman Catholic Church as well as within it. The initial premise of the argument consists of an assertion of Israel's irrevocable corporate election and of the corporate mediation of that election to its individual members:

> A person is born an Israelite in the sense of possessing at birth an innate quality which we call the "election factor." The quality is not hereditary. It is personal. It results from a transcendental relation between the person and the divine will, mediated by the community of the elect. It is because one is born into the elect people that one is born an Israelite. The "election factor" is irrevocable for the person so born, since the gifts of God are without repentance. It is revocable for his descendants, not by an act of will but where the descendants have ceased to belong to a community, mediator of the "election factor."[93]

Friedman states here a truth that is self-evident to most committed Jews, but that tends to elude individualistic evangelical Protestants (and Jewish Yeshua-believers shaped by the evangelical environment): the Jewish community mediates Jewish identity and election. To be a Jew (or, in Friedman's preferred terminology, an Israelite) is to be a member of the Jewish (or Israelite) community. If one leaves the Jewish/Israelite community, one remains a Jew/Israelite, but one's descendants do not.

The second premise of Friedman's argument consists of the observation of what happens to Jews/Israelites who enter the (Catholic) church. He formulates this observation by citing a decision by the Israeli Supreme Court in 1962 regarding the citizenship status of Fr. Daniel Rufeisen, a fellow Jewish member of Friedman's Carmelite monastery in Haifa. We would expect Friedman to object to the decision and reasoning of the Supreme Court in this case, since it denied Fr. Daniel's right to be considered a Jew under Israel's law of return.[94] Instead, Friedman finds the reasoning of Moshe Silberg, the Judge President of the Israeli Supreme Court, to be incontrovertible:

> "The Jewish converts, as experience teaches us, have cut themselves off completely from their people, for the simple reason that their sons and daughters marry into

---

92. "Jewish Bishop Aims To Reconcile Two Religions," *Forward*, February 27, 2004, 2.
93. Friedman, *Jewish Identity*, 72.
94. The Law of Return grants the rights of Israeli citizenship to all Jews who seek that status.

other peoples." In consequence, guided by a healthy instinct for survival, the
Jewish people was convinced that conversion was destructive of Jewish identity
and closed its doors on the convert.

. . . It was a weighty argument, based on irrefutable observations. Some Christian
missionaries tendentiously advance the claim that a Jew who embraces Christianity
is a "completed Jew". True or not, . . . the claim has no bearing on the argument from
historical rupture, which concerns not the convert himself, but his descendants,
as Justice Silberg declared with extreme precision. These are lost to their people.
They cease to play any role in the molding of its future. Sadly enough, the profound
remarks of the Court fell on deaf ears, where most Christians were concerned.[95]

Of course Protestant Hebrew Christians have noted the same fact. In 1940 Jocz
wrote:

Baptism has proved the greatest danger to continued Jewish existence. It is the first
step towards assimilation. This is borne out by the fact that in spite of the steady flow
of Jewish converts to the Christian Church, there has been so far no Hebrew-Christian
tradition possible. Prof. Dalman once remarked: "If all the Jews who have embraced
Christianity had remained a distinct people instead of being absorbed by the nations
among whom they dwelt, their descendants would now be counted by millions." But
Jewish Christians, so far, have not been able to retain their identity.[96]

Jocz makes the observation but draws no conclusion from it. This is where
Friedman differs from his Protestant kinsman.

In his 1979 manifesto written for the launching of the Association, Friedman
finds fault with this "regime of assimilation" not only because of its effect on the
individual convert and his or her descendants, but also because of the message
it conveys to the Jewish people as a whole:

The effects of the regime of assimilation on the convert's fellow Israelites are no less
destructive. Quite apart from the justifiable criticism that the convert has betrayed
his people, they perceive the regime of assimilation as an expression of Gentile

95. Friedman, *Jewish Identity,* 19. The 1979 manifesto adopted at the founding of the Association of Hebrew Catholics states this point as follows: "At present, the admission of the Jewish
convert to the Church is governed by a regime of assimilation, which systematically ignores the
specific elements of his identity, recognized nevertheless by Vatican Council II *(Lumen Gentium*
para. 16). The ultimate effect of the regime is to alienate the convert from his people of origin and
prepare the way for the total absorption of his descendants into the Gentile community. Between
themselves, converts may have a past in common, but they have no present and no future in common. Whatever be the sentiments, virtues or attainments of the individual convert, he has no way
of transmitting his historical identity, as an Israelite, to his descendants. These, in consequence,
cease eventually to be Israelites, as daily experience shows to be the case."

96. Jocz, *Jesus Christ,* 226.

contempt for Jewish identity and a real menace to their historical survival—for if all Jews were to be converted, only to be assimilated, the Jewish People would cease to exist: hence, their total opposition to the Christian Mission.

However, the main issue is not the offense caused to Jewish sensibilities by the church's forced "regime of assimilation," but the fact that this regime nullifies the divine election! As a result, Friedman rejects all missionary efforts directed to the Jewish people that will end in the destruction of Jewish/Israelite identity:

> The irrevocability of the Election authorizes one to reject the policy of active proselytizing of Israelites in circumstances which expose their specific identity and that of their descendants to deterioration and loss. For being a violation of the divine order it has never succeeded on any but a very limited scale.[97]

In line with Paul's teaching in Romans 11, Friedman sees Jewish resistance to Yeshua-faith as an element in the divine plan that will be reversed only at the end of the age, when the Jewish people will accept Yeshua collectively (i.e., as an ordered community). In the meantime, Christian missions threaten the integrity of Jewish life. Friedman thus portrays the Christian missionary to the Jews in vivid and unflattering terms:

> Where the Jews are concerned, God, in fact, had drawn a veil over their eyes, until the time should arrive for them to accede, collectively, to the faith. During that period, only a remnant would believe. Never has the Christian mission to the Jews succeeded in overcoming what was a divine decree. The Christian missionary willfully blinded himself to the fact that he was menacing the survival of the Jewish people and exciting the enmity of an intelligent, vocal and outraged world community. The relentless obstinacy of the Christian missionary in pursuing his policy of proselytizing Jews, is a glaring example of religious fanaticism.[98]

In an ironic twist, Friedman describes the missionaries as "blinded" and as displaying "relentless obstinacy"—terms traditionally reserved for those Jews they target! God had "drawn a veil" over the eyes of the Jewish people, but the missionary "willfully blinded himself"!

Friedman thus opposes active missionary work among the Jewish people. What positive action does he urge the church to take? He describes his program as "the eschatological approach":

97. Friedman, *Jewish Identity*, 84.
98. Ibid., 167.

> The eschatological approach takes its point of departure in a reading of the signs of the times. It is oriented to the collectivity, not to individuals. It focuses attention on the status of the Jewish convert, who is envisaged as that part of Jewry which has accepted the Law of Christ. . . . It is conscious of the overpowering influence of divine providence in the process of the admission of Jewry to the faith. It limits the human role to collaborating with the intentions of providence. . . . It is, finally, sensitive to Jewish objections against the Christian mission, but also to the extent to which the Jew is responding to the pressure of a loving providence.[99]

While the church should not initiate missionary programs directed at the Jewish people, Friedman acknowledges that there will always be individual Jews (like himself) who become Yeshua-believers and enter the church. In preparation for God's dealings with the Jewish people at the end of the age, and as an expression of respect for Israel's irrevocable election, the church should urge all such Jews to associate with one another and to do their best to maintain their identity as Jews/Israelites.

> A beginning must be made by changing the regime of assimilation with its cruel effects on the identity of the convert. Every Jewish convert needs to be registered as an Israelite at the moment of baptism and his descendants likewise. During his catechism he should be taught the doctrine of the Church concerning the identity of the Jewish people. After all, the existence of the "election factor" places an obligation on the Church to act in consequence by encouraging converts to associate in order to build their new identity in continuity with their past.[100]

Ultimately, this can only be accomplished through "a Hebrew community, juridically approved by the Holy See."[101] Such a community will itself then become a "sign of the times":

> The community, when it comes into being one day, will be seen for what it is: an eschatological sign of the times, raised up before a Church in crisis and for the encouragement of a jaded world.[102]

Friedman displays the same eschatological consciousness that inspired the missionaries he castigates. However, the program of action he proposes leads beyond the missionaries to a postmissionary Christian approach to the Jewish people.

99. Ibid., 169.
100. Ibid., 172.
101. Ibid., 171.
102. Ibid., 173.

In other matters, Friedman's views resemble those of the Hebrew Christians. While he resoundingly affirms Israel's irrevocable election and the need for Jews/Israelites to maintain a distinctive national existence, he nevertheless accepts the view that the law of Moses has been annulled by the death and resurrection of the Messiah. Therefore he opposes traditional Jewish practice and sees rabbinic Judaism as an invalid religion.[103] Furthermore, he argues that the designation "Jew" should be applied only to one who accepts the authority of the Torah. This is why he uses the terms "Hebrew" rather than "Jewish" and "Israelite" rather than "Jew." Such idiosyncratic usage detracts from the force of his overall presentation. This is unfortunate, since his core argument deserves to be taken seriously.

In relation to our five ecclesiological principles, we find that Friedman (1) affirms Israel's irrevocable covenant, (2) rejects the validity of Jewish practice and (3) rabbinic tradition, (4) upholds the bilateral structure of the ekklesia, and (5) partially supports solidarity with Israel and an ecumenical rather than missionary role for the Jewish ekklesia. His support for (5) is only partial because of his rejection of (2) and (3) and his consequent inability to discern Israel's mission to the church. Practically, it is also limited because Hebrew Catholicism will be constrained by its ecclesial environment from ever entering fully into the mainstream of Jewish life.

While Friedman's vision of Hebrew Catholicism suffers from major deficiencies, it also offers essential insights that can further the development of a postmissionary Messianic Judaism.

Postmissionary Messianic Judaism?

Over the past decade, numerous changes have occurred within the Messianic Jewish movement. One of the most significant developments has been the emergence of voices explicitly advocating a *bilateral ecclesiology in solidarity with Israel that affirms Israel's covenant, Torah, and religious tradition.* In doing so, these voices follow the course first articulated by Levertoff and Gillet.

In 1999 the Union of Messianic Jewish Congregations (UMJC) began a multi-year process of arriving at its own definition of Messianic Judaism. Major papers on this topic were delivered at the UMJC national conferences of 2000 and 2001. In July of 2002, the delegates of the UMJC approved a statement that derived from these papers.[104] It consists of two parts—an initial basic statement,

103. Ibid., 66–81. These positions are not shared by all Hebrew Catholics.

104. The substance of this statement is recognized by UMJC leadership as authoritative and is unlikely to change in the near future. The precise wording of the statement, on the other hand, will likely be refined over the coming years.

and then an expanded version of the basic statement that elaborates on its key components. The basic statement is as follows:

> Messianic Judaism is a movement of Jewish congregations and congregation-like groupings committed to Yeshua the Messiah that embrace the covenantal responsibility of Jewish life and identity rooted in Torah, expressed in tradition, and renewed and applied in the context of the New Covenant.[105]

From the beginning Messianic Judaism is presented in corporate terms. The focus is on the shaping of a community life rather than on individual identity. Moreover, the communities at issue are Jewish in nature. They do not merely contain Jews; they are themselves Jewish. However, they are Jewish communities of a particular sort: they are "committed to Yeshua the Messiah." Furthermore, they honor the Torah and Jewish tradition. Already we see the rudiments of a *bilateral ecclesiology in solidarity with Israel that affirms Israel's covenant, Torah, and religious tradition.*

What is implicit in the basic statement becomes explicit in the expanded statement. The first paragraph of the expanded statement is as follows:

> Jewish life is life in a concrete, historical community. Thus, Messianic Jewish group-ings must be fully part of the Jewish people, sharing its history and its covenantal responsibility as a people chosen by God. At the same time, faith in Yeshua also has a crucial communal dimension. This faith unites Messianic Judaism and the Gentile Christian Church, which is the assembly of the faithful from the nations who are joined to Israel through the Messiah. Together Messianic Judaism and the Gentile Church constitute the one Body of Messiah, a community of Jews and Gentiles who in their ongoing distinction and mutual blessing anticipate the shalom of the world to come.[106]

Messianic Jewish groups must be properly related to both the Jewish people and the Christian church. The relationship with the Jewish people is addressed first. Subsequently, the relationship with the Christian church is affirmed. That church is defined as the ekklesia of the Gentiles, and the statement sees this church as "joined to Israel through the Messiah." In this way Israel is given primacy. However, the relationship between the Jewish and Gentile ekklesia*i* is given great prominence, as it foreshadows the peace and reconciliation of the age to come.

---

105. *Defining Messianic Judaism* (Albuquerque, NM: Union of Messianic Jewish Congrega-tions, 2002), 3. The definition is printed on the back of *Kesher* (a journal published by the Union of Messianic Jewish Congregations) beginning with no. 16 (Fall 2003) and is also available at the UMJC Web site (www.umjc.org).

106. *Defining Messianic Judaism*, 3.

The second paragraph emphasizes the practical priority of Messianic Jewish groups seeking adequate integration with the wider Jewish world:

> For a Messianic Jewish grouping (1) to fulfill the covenantal responsibility incumbent upon all Jews, (2) to bear witness to Yeshua within the people of Israel, and (3) to serve as an authentic and effective representative of the Jewish people within the body of Messiah, it must place a priority on integration with the wider Jewish world. Such integration must then be followed by a vital corporate relationship with the Gentile Christian Church.[107]

One of the three reasons given for this priority is the need "to bear witness to Yeshua within the people of Israel." This reason could be interpreted in a traditional missionary sense, as the conveying of a saving message—derived from an external source—that is discontinuous with the religious tradition of postbiblical Judaism. However, it could also be interpreted in a postmissionary sense, as the unveiling of the messianic mystery underlying Jewish historical existence and religious tradition. The notion of bearing witness also does not necessarily imply a programmatic initiative, but could be expressed through a congregation's entire way of life. Regardless, this second reason should not distract us from the point of the paragraph as a whole. It is not portraying the Jewish community as an external mission field, but as "home." And while the Jewish ekklesia represents Yeshua (but not the Gentile ekklesia) within the Jewish world, it also represents "the Jewish people within the body of Messiah."

The third and fourth paragraphs stress the importance of Jewish practice, expressed in the context of Jewish tradition, for Messianic Jewish groups:

> The Messianic Jewish way of life involves an attempt to fulfill Israel's covenantal responsibility embodied in the Torah within a New Covenant context. Messianic Jewish halakhah is rooted in Scripture (Tanakh and the New Covenant writings), which is of unique sanctity and authority. However, it also draws upon Jewish tradition, especially those practices and concepts that have won near-universal acceptance by devout Jews through the centuries. Furthermore, like most other branches of Judaism, Messianic Judaism recognizes that halakhah must be dynamic as well as faithful, for it involves the application of the Torah to a wide variety of changing situations and circumstances.

> Messianic Judaism embraces the fullness of New Covenant realities available through Yeshua, and seeks to express them in forms drawn from Jewish experience and accessible to Jewish people.[108]

107. Ibid.
108. Ibid.

The fourth paragraph acknowledges that there are aspects of Messianic Jewish life that will distinguish it from the rest of the Jewish world. However, it underlines the importance of finding authentic Jewish ways of expressing these distinctives. In the context of the whole statement, it is clear that the reason for doing so is not primarily missionary. Instead, it is a way of fulfilling the "covenantal responsibility" of wholehearted participation in Jewish life.

This statement is significant, since it presents Messianic Judaism as a branch of Judaism and emphasizes the importance of practical integration with the wider Jewish world. Combined with the statement's positive approach to Jewish practice and Jewish tradition, it comes close to affirming the vision presented in this volume—a *bilateral ecclesiology in solidarity with Israel that affirms Israel's covenant, Torah, and religious tradition.*[109]

The UMJC statement defining Messianic Judaism provides a snapshot of an organization grappling with its Jewish identity, its Hebrew Christian antecedents, and its own evangelical past. As we have seen, that evangelical past was also a thoroughly missionary past. However, it involved an unusual type of missionary orientation—one that assigned a unique role in the divine purpose to the group being targeted and a unique value to that group's religious heritage. Over time, that missionary orientation developed into a new form of life seeking a measure of continuity with Judaism but still maintaining a missionary posture. It is possible that a new phase of this movement may now be under way, one in which ecclesiological concerns take precedence over evangelistic concerns and integration with the Jewish world is given precedence over integration with the church world—for the church's as well as Israel's sake. If this is the case, then the nineteenth-century missionary movement contained within it the potential for a dramatic internal transformation—a gift of enormous value to the church and to the Jewish people.

---

109. The response to this statement offered by Jews for Jesus demonstrates their position as representatives of the traditional Hebrew Christian position: "According to these statements, messianic Judaism is the Jewish wing of the Body of Christ. . . . At any rate, the above quotes define messianic Judaism as a congregational movement in which Torah and tradition are kept. It seems to exclude Jewish believers in Jesus who are part of the First Lutheran or First Baptist Church, who value their Jewish identity and heritage but do not feel compelled to 1. consider themselves apart from their Gentile brothers and sisters, or 2. keep the Torah, aside from the basic moral commandments or 3. regard extra-biblical traditions and rabbinical interpretations of Scripture as a necessary part of their lives." Rich Robinson with Ruth Rosen, "The Challenge of our Messianic Movement, Part One," *Havurah* 6, no. 2 (May 2003): 2–3.

9

HEALING THE SCHISM

A Restored Jewish *Ekklesia*

In this volume I have argued for the truth of three interrelated propositions. First, the New Testament—read canonically and theologically in the light of history—teaches that Israel's covenant, way of life, and religious tradition have enduring validity and importance, even when Israel proves unwilling or unable to explicitly recognize its Messiah. Second, the failure of the Gentile ekklesia to receive and confirm this truth contributed decisively to the rupture between the ekklesia and the Jewish people—a rupture that constitutes a debilitating schism in the heart of the people of God. Third, this schism was manifested first in the rejection of the validity and importance of the Jewish ekklesia and of its integration within the wider Jewish world, and the healing of this schism requires the restoration of such an ekklesia. The restoration of the Jewish ekklesia would link the Gentile ekklesia to Israel and enable it to legitimately identify with Israel's history and destiny without succumbing to supersessionism. The restoration of the Jewish ekklesia would also enable the Jewish people to appreciate Yeshua-faith as an indigenous Jewish reality, extending the reign of Israel's God among the nations.

What would such a restored Jewish ekklesia look like? In the previous chapter we assessed Hebrew Christianity and Messianic Judaism according to five basic ecclesiological principles: upholding God's election of the Jewish people, affirming Jewish practice, honoring Jewish tradition, taking its place as part of a bilateral ekklesia, and maintaining an ecumenical vision for the relationship between the Jewish people as a whole and the twofold ekklesia. These principles provide markers for identifying the sort of Jewish ekklesia whose presence can facilitate the healing of the schism.

As a postmissionary reality, the restored Jewish ekklesia will take its stand as part of the Jewish people. In the words of the UMJC definition statement, it "must place a priority on integration with the wider Jewish world." This has far-reaching implications. The traditional Hebrew Christian model, which, as seen in the last chapter, is essentially missionary in orientation, involves ranking one's social identities so that one's core identity as part of the missionary body defines one's attitude toward the other groups one also identifies with. Employing the nineteenth-century distinction between religion and nationality, the Hebrew Christian's core identity is religious (i.e., the Christian faith, held in common with other Christians), whereas his or her secondary identity is national (i.e., membership in the Jewish people). The Hebrew Christian attitude toward the Jewish people (the secondary grouping) is thus defined by its Christian convictions. For the restored Jewish ekklesia, on the other hand, Jewish identity will be both religious and national. Furthermore, it will find Yeshua himself *within* Judaism and the Jewish people. Therefore its Judaism and its loyalty to the Jewish people will not compete with its Yeshua-faith and its loyalty to the Gentile ekklesia. The radical, unqualified identification of Jewish Yeshua-believers with the Jewish people and its religious tradition may trouble some Christians when they first encounter it. However, if they truly renounce supersessionism and recognize the ecclesiological implications of claiming a part in Israel's heritage, they will embrace the new relationship with the Jewish people made possible for them by the reconstituted Jewish ekklesia, and rejoice in it.

At the same time, the Jewish ekklesia will, as the UMJC definition states, "bear witness to Yeshua within the people of Israel." The Jewish ekklesia will not hide its light under a bushel. Its Yeshua-faith and its Judaism are not two separate realities but one integrated whole. Its Yeshua-faith will affect every dimension of its life, including its participation in the wider Jewish world. However, its witness to Yeshua will be rendered in a postmissionary mode. Its postmissionary mode of bearing witness has three crucial features. First, the Jewish ekklesia will realize that it must first receive the testimony borne by the wider Jewish community to the God of Israel before it is fit to bear its own witness. It must hear before it can speak. It must learn before it can teach. What it receives, hears, and learns will affect the substance—and not just the form—of what it gives, says, and teaches. Second, the Jewish ekklesia bears witness to the One already present in Israel's midst. It does not need to make him present; it only needs to point other Jews to his intimate proximity. The Jewish ekklesia bears witness to the One who sums up Israel's true identity and destiny, who lives within Israel and directs its way, who constitutes the hidden center of its tradition and way of life. In the words of Joseph Rabinowitz, it bears witness to "*Yeshua Achinu*"—Yeshua our Brother, who, like Joseph, rules over the Gentiles while providing for the welfare of his own family who do not recognize him. For the Jewish ekklesia, all Judaism is Messianic Judaism, because all Judaism is Messiah's Judaism. Third, the Jewish ekklesia bears witness discreetly, sensitively, and with restraint. It is always aware of the painful wounds of the past and seeks to bear witness to Yeshua in a way that brings him honor from among his own.

As a postmissionary body, the Jewish ekklesia will also stretch out its hands to the Gentile ekklesia and bring it into a structured ecclesial relationship to the Jewish people. It brings the church to Israel rather than bringing Israel to the church. Yet by bringing the church to Israel, it also brings Israel to the church. It represents Israel to the church, i.e., the church of the nations. In doing so, it bears witness to the church and the world of the reconciling power of Yeshua's atoning sacrifice and becomes a present sign of the future redemption. As the UMJC definition states, the Jewish and Gentile ekklesiai together constitute "a community of Jews and Gentiles who in their ongoing distinction and mutual blessing anticipate the shalom of the world to come."

The restoration of the Jewish ekklesia, and a progressive healing of the schism between the church and the Jewish people, would have enormous consequences for the life of the ekklesia. The letter to the Ephesians speaks of the relationship between Jews and Gentiles in Messiah as the archetype of the reconciliation that Yeshua brings to the world. Tragically, the Christian era brought intensified hostility rather than peace to Jewish-Gentile relations. This called into question from the outset the Christian claim to a mission of universal reconciliation. The restoration of the Jewish ekklesia would provide the Christian church with an opportunity for repentance and a renewal of its vocation in the world.

The restoration of the Jewish ekklesia would contribute to the healing of other schisms that have wounded the Christian church over the centuries. George Lindbeck has summoned the church to view itself in an Israel-like way—as a people rather than as a voluntary organization ordered around a set of common beliefs.[1] Lindbeck contends that such an identity would better enable the church to maintain a differentiated unity. In the world of American Protestantism, such an identity would also counter the rampant individualism that undermines

---

1. George A. Lindbeck, *The Church in a Postliberal Age* (Grand Rapids: Eerdmans, 2002), 1–10; "The Church as Israel," in Braaten and Jenson, *Jews and Christians*, ed. Carl E. Braaten and Robert W. Jenson (Grand Rapids: Eerdmans, 2003), 78–94.

ecclesial community and prevents Christians from even recognizing schism as
an evil. But how can the Christian church develop an Israel-like identity without
falling into supersessionism? I have argued here that this can occur only through
the restoration of the Jewish ekklesia.

The restoration of the Jewish ekklesia would provide the church with an essential resource for combating the dualism that has been its continual temptation
through the centuries. Irving Greenberg sees this dualism as a consequence of
Christian alienation from Judaism:

> Each religion paid a price in dismissing the other. Christianity skewed toward
> dualism, minimizing the religious significance of carnal matters, the law, and
> the body. . . .
>   . . . To the constant Jewish critique that the world was manifestly unredeemed
> (therefore, Jesus could be no true redeemer), Christianity responded by spiritual-
> izing redemption (and dismissing Judaism as a "carnal" religion). The conjunction
> of anti-halakhic thinking and the dismissal of biology (Christians are children of
> Abraham in the spirit) encouraged an otherworldly focus and reinforced a dual-
> ism that often pitted the soul against the body and the flesh against the spirit.
> Rootedness in the land also was spiritualized away; no land was sacred, and only
> the heavenly Jerusalem really mattered.[2]

While its core message of the incarnation militates against such dualism, the
Christian church has struggled to work out the implications of this message. Too
often the spirit, the abstract ideal, and the universal have overwhelmed the body,
concrete reality, and ethnocultural particularity. The fleshly presence of a Jewish ekklesia would serve as a constant reminder that God's redemptive purpose
entails the consummation and not the destruction of the created order.

That the Christian church needs the Jewish ekklesia to work out the nondualistic implications of the Incarnation supports a point made earlier in
this volume: the church cannot adequately understand the meaning of the
Incarnation without grasping the ongoing significance of Yeshua's Jewish
identity.[3] To grasp the ongoing significance of Yeshua's Jewish identity, the
church must realize the ongoing significance of the Jewish people. To realize the ongoing significance of the Jewish people, the church needs to have
a living covenantal bond to the Jewish people—a bond established by the

---

2. Irving Greenberg, *For the Sake of Heaven and Earth* (Philadelphia: Jewish Publication Society,
2004), 44, 223. Greenberg also describes the price Judaism paid for dismissing Christianity—but
that is material for another book. I am writing this volume for Christians and am therefore focus-
ing only on the Christian side of the schism.

3. See chapter 6.

restoration of the Jewish ekklesia. The church serves a resurrected Jew whose glorification perfected rather than annulled his Jewishness. To appreciate that Jewishness, the Gentile church needs an earthly and corporate Jewish companion.

The Gentile church likewise needs such an earthly and corporate Jewish companion in order adequately to hear, understand, and respond to the Word of God in scripture. Traditional Jewish and Christian teaching affirms the need for participation in the people of God in order to rightly receive the Word of God. If that people is twofold in nature, then Jews and Christians need to hear and study scripture together. This is already happening in academia—but too often such "interfaith" study presumes the perpetual separation of the two communities and entails the bracketing of religious convictions in order to meet on neutral turf. To hear the Word of God properly, Jews and Christians must study together as *one* differentiated community. This requires the restoration of the Jewish ekklesia.

In sum, the restoration of the Jewish ekklesia promises a renewal of the Christian church's reading of scripture, understanding of the Incarnation and its nondualistic implications, and actualization of the church's own identity and vocation. The ekklesia of the nations has much to gain from the restoration of the ekklesia of the circumcision.

The schism between the Jewish people and the ekklesia can be healed without coming to full agreement over Yeshua's messianic identity. The New Testament implies that disagreement over Yeshua's identity will continue till the end of the age, but it does not predict a schism with the same longevity. This is why John Howard Yoder can say of the schism, "It did not have to be."[4] "Schism" refers to the division of these two groups into separate religious communities. It also implies the enmity that has historically transpired between them—but the enmity can be overcome, as it has been in twenty-first century America, and the schism remain. The healing of the schism means the establishing of a structured ecclesial relationship. This can occur if the church adopts a *bilateral ecclesiology in solidarity with Israel that affirms Israel's covenant, Torah, and religious tradition.* While this is a necessary condition of the healing, it is not sufficient. Full healing of the schism will occur only when the wider Jewish community accepts the Jewish ekklesia as a legitimate participant in Jewish communal life.

---

4. John Howard Yoder, *The Jewish-Christian Schism Revisited,* ed. Michael G. Cartwright and Peter Ochs (Grand Rapids: Eerdmans, 2003), 43–66.

Practical Steps Forward

The establishment of a postmissionary Jewish ekklesia should be a long-term goal for the Christian churches. It is a goal that the churches should pray for and encourage, though they cannot achieve it on their own. Jewish Yeshua-believers must first grasp this vision and labor to make it a reality. However, the Christian churches can act in a way that will make this more likely. There are three steps that can be taken immediately. First, the churches should revitalize their efforts to foster respect for Judaism and the Jewish people among Christians. Though much has been accomplished in the past generation, more remains to be done. In particular, Christians need to see Judaism and the Jewish people in the christological perspective presented in chapter 6. Once they do so, dedicated Christians—including evangelicals—will see the preservation and strengthening of the Jewish people and the Jewish religious tradition as part of their own ecclesial mandate as a Yeshua-believing community in solidarity with Israel.

Second, the Christian churches should heed the words of Michael Wyschogrod and recognize that the rejection of supersessionism requires a dramatic change in the way they treat Jews who become Yeshua-believers within the context of the Gentile ekklesia.[5] If the covenant with Israel remains in effect, if Jewish practice rooted in the Torah constitutes the proper means of expressing that covenant, and if Jewish religious tradition determines the overall shape of that Jewish practice, then the Gentile ekklesia should urge Jews in its midst to fulfill their covenantal responsibilities and live as observant Jews. As a beginning, the churches should publicly and explicitly renounce their traditional teaching that prohibited such practice. Many have done so privately and implicitly, but this error has been so damaging that it requires a more formal retraction. Such a retraction would at least return the churches to the position enunciated by Justin Martyr. However, to return to the assumptions prevailing at the Jerusalem Council of Acts 15, the churches must go further and assert that Jewish Yeshua-believers are not only free to live as Jews, but obligated to do so.[6]

As Lev Gillet argues, the participation of Jewish Yeshua-believers in the Gentile ekklesia is not an ideal arrangement. It will be very difficult for Jews in

5. Wyschogrod has made this point time and again. The following is typical: "Had the Church believed that it was God's will that the seed of Abraham not disappear from the world, she would have insisted on Jews retaining their separateness, even in the Church. . . . Since the Church did not assign to the Jew who became a Christian such special status, it can be inferred that—quotations from Paul (Romans 11:28–29) to the effect that God does not repent of the gifts he makes notwithstanding—the Church seriously holds that its election superseded that of the old Israel." *Abraham's Promise* (Grand Rapids: Eerdmans, 2004), 183–84.

6. As Fr. Elias Friedman proposes, all Jews who are baptized should receive instruction that reinforces their Jewish identity and their commitment to the Jewish people.

such circumstances to fulfill their obligations as Jews. However, there are tens of thousands of Jews who are currently involved in the Christian churches, and more will become involved in the future. What pastoral approach should the churches adopt in dealing with people in this situation? If there is a healthy Messianic Jewish congregation in the vicinity, the church should recommend that Jews in their midst become involved with that congregation. In a Roman Catholic context, pastoral authorities could recommend that Jewish Catholics participate in the Association of Hebrew Catholics or a similar group. The church could also recommend that Jews in their midst attend events occurring in the wider Jewish world. However, in many cases no reasonable way will be found for these people to fulfill their obligations as Jews. What then? In such circumstances many Jewish Yeshua-believers will likely conclude that they are unable to practice their Judaism. In particular cases this may be the only feasible result, given the conflicting obligations they face and the limited opportunities available. Nevertheless, the churches should not treat such cases as normal, even if they are common, and they should not deny the objective existence of an obligation, even if circumstances in given cases make it inadvisable to fulfill that obligation.

Third, the churches should initiate dialogue on local, national, and international levels with the Messianic Jewish movement as it currently exists. As seen in the previous chapter, this movement tends to have a missionary rather than an ecclesiological focus. Nevertheless, the movement is dynamic and ever changing. The churches should engage the Messianic Jewish movement in serious conversation and encourage development in a postmissionary direction.

A New Stage in Ecclesial History

As seen in the previous chapter, a renewed eschatological sense in the Christian world contributed substantially to the emergence of Hebrew Christianity and Messianic Judaism. After nearly twenty centuries, two phenomena arose simultaneously, each claiming to be the resurrected form of a long-buried Jewish way of life—the Jewish state in the land of Israel, and the Jewish Yeshua-movement. The first great wave of Jewish immigration to the land began in the same year that Rabinowitz stood on the Mount of Olives and concluded that Yeshua was Israel's Messiah. Messianic Judaism originated in the years immediately following the reunification of the city of David. Many today see these events as "signs of the times" that point to a new and decisive stage in God's dealings with Israel, the church, and the world. The restoration of a *bilateral ekklesia in solidarity with Israel that affirms Israel's covenant, Torah, and religious tradition* would certainly confirm such a perspective.

Even for those reluctant to adopt such an eschatological perspective, the restoration of a bilateral ecclesiology in solidarity with Israel should still be a compelling goal. We have argued that the Christian church and the Jewish people together constitute the one people of God and, in a sense, the one Body of Messiah. The schism in the heart of this people has damaged each side and resulted, among Christians, in a truncated vision of the church's own identity and the identity of its Messiah. To rediscover its own catholicity, the church must rediscover Israel and its relationship to Israel.

In speaking of the schism between the Western and Eastern churches, John Paul II has stated that each church now breathes with only one lung. This is an apt metaphor, especially if we extend it by seeing the air breathed by the church as the Spirit of God. With only one functioning lung, the church's capacity to receive and impart the Spirit is restricted. This metaphor is even more applicable to the primal schism that wounded the ekklesia in its infancy. The church must come home to Israel, if it would again breathe freely and deeply.

Name Index

SCRIPTURE INDEX

315